AUSTERITY

The Lived Experience

In *Austerity: The Lived Experience*, Bryan M. Evans, Stephen McBride, and their contributors examine the practical, ground-level side of the austerity equation.

Economically, austerity policies cannot be seen to work in the way elite interests claim that they do. Rather than softening the blow of the economic and financial crisis of 2008 for ordinary citizens, policies of austerity slow growth and lead to increased inequality. While political consent for such policies may have been achieved, it was reached amid significant levels of disaffection and strong opposition to the extremes of austerity. The authors build their analysis in three sections, looking alternatively at the theoretical and ideological dimensions of the lived experience of austerity, how austerity plays out in various public sector occupations and policy domains, and the class dimensions of austerity. The result is a ground-breaking contribution to the study of austerity politics and policies.

BRYAN M. EVANS is a professor in the Department of Politics and Public Administration at Ryerson University.

STEPHEN MCBRIDE is a professor and Canada Research Chair in Public Policy and Globalization in the Department of Political Science at McMaster University.

Austerity

The Lived Experience

EDITED BY
BRYAN M. EVANS AND
STEPHEN MCBRIDE

UNIVERSITY OF TORONTO PRESS
Toronto Buffalo London

© University of Toronto Press 2017
Toronto Buffalo London
www.utppublishing.com
Printed in Canada

ISBN 978-1-4875-0257-7 (cloth)   ISBN 978-1-4875-2203-2 (paper)

∞ Printed on acid-free, 100% post-consumer recycled paper with vegetable-based inks.

Library and Archives Canada Cataloguing in Publication

Austerity : the lived experience / edited by Bryan M. Evans and Stephen McBride.

Includes bibliographical references.
ISBN 978-1-4875-0257-7 (cloth). – ISBN 978-1-4875-2203-2 (paper)

1. Economic policy. 2. Financial crises. 3. Equality. I. Evans, Bryan M., 1960–, editor II. McBride, Stephen, editor

HD87.A97 2017   338.9   C2017-904305-6

This book has been published with the help of a grant from the Federation for the Humanities and Social Sciences, through the Awards to Scholarly Publications Program, using funds provided by the Social Sciences and Humanities Research Council of Canada.

University of Toronto Press acknowledges the financial assistance to its publishing program of the Canada Council for the Arts and the Ontario Arts Council, an agency of the Government of Ontario.

Contents

Acknowledgments   ix

1 Austerity as Lived Experience: An Introduction   3
BRYAN M. EVANS AND STEPHEN MCBRIDE

PART ONE: THEORY AND IDEOLOGY

Introduction: Manufacturing the Common Sense of Austerity   17
BRYAN M. EVANS AND STEPHEN MCBRIDE

2 Articulating Austerity and Authoritarianism: Re-imagining Moral Economies?   20
JOHN CLARKE

3 Speaking Austerity: Policy Rhetoric and Design beyond Fiscal Consolidation   40
SORIN MITREA

4 No Deal Capitalism: Austerity and the Unmaking of the North American Middle Class   63
ERIC PINEAULT

5 Framing the Economic Case for Austerity: The Expansionary Fiscal Contraction Hypothesis   97
ELLEN D. RUSSELL

PART TWO: IMPACT AND CONSEQUENCES

Introduction: Austerity on the Ground   121
BRYAN M. EVANS AND STEPHEN MCBRIDE

6 Care and Control in Long-term Care Work   125
DONNA BAINES

7 "Negotiate Your Way Back to Zero": Teacher Bargaining and Austerity in Ontario, Canada   145
BRENDAN A. SWEENEY AND ROBERT S. HICKEY

8 Austerity and the Low-Wage Economy: Living and Other Wages   164
BRYAN M. EVANS, STEPHEN MCBRIDE, AND JACOB MUIRHEAD

9 Immigration in an Age of Austerity: Morality, the Welfare State, and the Shaping of the Ideal Migrant   195
SUSAN BARRASS AND JOHN SHIELDS

10 Pension Reforms in the Context of the Global Financial Crisis: A Reincarnation of Pension Privatization through Austerity?   222
YANQIU RACHEL ZHOU AND SHIH-JIUNN SHI

PART THREE: CLASS, RESISTANCE, ALTERNATIVES

Introduction: The Old Strategies Don't Work, so What's Possible?   249
BRYAN M. EVANS AND STEPHEN MCBRIDE

11 From Austerity to Structural Reform: The Erosion of the European Social Model(s)   251
CHRISTOPH HERMANN

12 Austerity of Imagination: Quebec's Struggles in Translating Resistance into Alternatives   272
PETER GRAEFE AND X.H. RIOUX

13 Social Democracy and Social Pacts: Austerity Alliances and Their Consequences   293
BRYAN M. EVANS

14 Austerity and Political Crisis: The Radical Left, the Far Right, and Europe's New Authoritarian Order 317
   NEIL A. BURRON

15 Conclusion 344
   STEPHEN MCBRIDE AND BRYAN M. EVANS

Contributors 355

Acknowledgments

The editors gratefully acknowledge funding from the SSHRC Connections Grants program, and the McMaster University Institute for Globalization and the Human Condition (Austerity Research Group), which made it possible to hold a workshop at McMaster University in October 2014. At the workshop, draft versions of these chapters were presented and intensively discussed by workshop participants. Sorin Mitrea and Jacob Muirhead provided invaluable assistance in organizing the workshop. We would like to thank the anonymous reviewers who provided very detailed and helpful comments on the manuscript. We also wish to sincerely thank Daniel Quinlan of the University of Toronto Press for his wise counsel and leadership in guiding this manuscript to publication.

Bryan M. Evans and Stephen McBride

AUSTERITY

The Lived Experience

1 Austerity as Lived Experience: An Introduction

BRYAN M. EVANS AND STEPHEN MCBRIDE

The title of this volume, *Austerity: The Lived Experience*, is intended to convey that the objective of the contributions presented here is to illuminate austerity in experiential terms. Austerity is presented as a composite of policies, including fiscal consolidation, structural reforms of the public sector, and flexibilization of labour markets. Austerity policies have been informed by neoclassical economics and New Public Management theories that served as a transmission belt bringing neoliberal ideas and practices into state administration. They provided the intellectual basis for the restructuring of the state and public services. The array of targets and objectives was, and remains, broad. These include implementation of privatization and marketization of public services, flexibilized labour markets, including that of the public and non-profit sectors, reduced public subsidies, constrained access to and benefit levels for disability and health compensation, elimination of early retirement schemes, reduced unemployment benefits, and ending policies that shortened working time. With *Austerity: The Lived Experience* we explore the articulation of the austerity message and the lived consequences of its ideological triumph and policy implementation, but also we explore the possibility of resistance, leading to alternatives.

Although fiscal consolidation is an important component of our broader view of austerity, we do not confine ourselves or our contributors to it. In the first place, the fiscal consolidation component is often explicitly linked, by those proposing it, to structural reform of both the public sector and the labour market. Even if the link were not explicitly made, the implementation of fiscal consolidation on the public sector is quite direct, as expenditures are cut or constrained, and the impact of pro-cyclical budget balancing on labour markets is equally apparent.

4   Austerity: The Lived Experience

In both cases, the lived experience of austerity is filtered through a restructured and diminished public sector, and the flexible, precarious, and insecure labour market associated with these policies. To the extent that public discourse focuses on the fiscal aspects of austerity, it ignores the links identified in our broader definition that are fundamental to experiencing its impact.

Perhaps the most dramatic political response to the policy of fiscal consolidation, a euphemism for austerity, was the ascent and ultimate electoral victory of the radical Left Syriza party in Greece. A particularly poignant election poster used by Syriza during the January 2015 election campaign, which resulted in its forming government, simply read "Hope Is Coming." Riding high on the expectation that the "fiscal waterboarding" would end, the Greek people placed their collective hope in the once diminutive Syriza and elected the first expressly anti-austerity, anti-neoliberal party to government. Greece became the first country to elect such a party in the European Union. Yanis Varoufakis, radical economist and soon to be finance minister, said of that night, "Greek democracy today chose to stop going gently into the night. Greek democracy resolved to rage against the dying of the light" (Queally 2015). However, as subsequent history tells us, the politics was much more complex than the act of simply electing a government that did not accept what other powers had subjected them to. Instead, like a smaller version of the reanimation of the zombie economics shortly after the crisis was stabilized, severe austerity not only remained the norm for Greece but indeed deepened. The plight of Greece was by every measure as ugly as, or worse than, that of the United States in the Great Depression of the 1930s (Alderman et al. 2015). But there was to be no Greek version of the New Deal, and Tsipras was no Franklin Delano Roosevelt. In less than six months, the dream, and struggle, to shake off the chains of the global Minotaur of neoliberal capitalism was in tatters. Consequently, for Greece, the lived experience of a particularly nightmarish regime of austerity wears on. And, in certain contrast, there is the case of Canada. Rarely does the outcome of a Canadian national election become international news, but in 2015 that is precisely what happened. Paul Krugman, writing in the *New York Times*, declared, "Keynes Comes to Canada," stating, "What strikes me most is its [the outcome of the election] clear rejection of the deficit-obsessed austerity orthodoxy that has dominated political discourse across the Western world. The Liberals ran on a frankly, openly Keynesian vision, and won big" (Krugman 2015). The headline of an article in the

Guardian published the day following the 19 October election similarly declared, "The Liberals' victory in Canada signals people's desire for anti-austerity politics" (O'Toole 2015). The Liberal Party, led by Justin Trudeau, presented the Canadian electorate with a platform designed to reflect the concerns of the 99 per cent. The platform's title – *A New Plan for a Strong Middle Class* – effectively summed up the political strategy. At the heart of the platform was an unorthodox commitment to deficit financing. After a decade of tax cutting and balanced budget orthodoxy, which characterized Conservative fiscal policy (and one should not forget that the decade prior, that of the Chrétien-Martin Liberals, was also a period where fiscal conservatism was the prevailing orthodoxy), Trudeau's Liberals promised to run $10 billion deficits for their first two years in power, a decrease in this figure in the third year, with a return to a balanced budget in the fourth year (Liberal Party of Canada 2015, 12). Indeed, as prime minister, Trudeau said, "A lot of people are on the austerity side, thinking they have to control government spending. Canada is positioning itself on the investment side" (Flavelle 2016). However, while simply stating that a deficit was not a horrible thing may well have been an unconventional proposition, the promise was still modest. With the 2016 Budget, the platform promises were rolled out as policy. Total program expenses for 2016–17 were projected to be 14.6 per cent, according to 2016 Budget Report (Department of Finance 2016b, 234). In comparison, the previous year's Conservative equivalent expenditures equalled 13.6 per cent of GDP. The first Trudeau budget brought in an annual deficit larger than expected, at $29.4 billion, pushing total program expenditures to $291.4 (ibid.). A different party in government may well have made different choices. So the Trudeau Liberals represent a cautious break with the previous two decades of retrenchment. Anti-austerity perhaps, but in a measured and moderate form.

Contemporary reality, in stark contrast to the optimism and hope that punched through the cracks in the edifice of austerian hegemony in the early months of the 2008 crisis, is now itself cracked and stumbling. Even the advances of the Far Right, as illustrated by the success of Trump in the US presidential election, Brexit, and impressive polling results for such parties in Germany, France, the Netherlands, Austria, and Sweden, to mention several, are fuelled partly by the angst and anger fomented by inequality, globalization, and the perceived threat of immigration, as well as the indifference of an elite that has exacerbated the declining conditions of daily life through the implementation of austerity. Indeed, in the early months of the crisis, Keynesian tools and policy interventions reminded us that the state could act, and be activist, in the cause of common good. Some hoped this was a harbinger of the potential for a more fundamental and even radical break with the ideology, politics, and praxis of "There Is No Alternative." It was all so much more complex than that. With the capitulation of Syriza, the ongoing hollowing of social democracy, and the very limited challenges to neoliberalism, Colin Crouch's very apt question deserves repeating: "What remains of neoliberalism after the financial crisis?" As does his still more apt response: "Virtually everything" (Crouch 2011, 179). Austerity is back as a seemingly intractable reality.

We should emphasize that this book is not built on national case studies. All the chapters are exploring some aspect of the lived experience of austerity and aim to do so in a theoretical way, drawing empirical substance from examples chosen by the authors (the examples are often comparative, but sometimes national or subnational). The chapters composing *Austerity: The Lived Experience* are organized in three thematic sections. In the first section, we examine the theory and ideology informing austerity's articulation and the social and cultural mechanisms working to construct an accepting and internalizing "common sense" in populations who are subject to this policy roll-out. Contributions primarily addressing this theme focus on framing austerity in ways that draw upon deeper moral economies and concepts (e.g., how individualized, "common sense" responses to problems of the person are generalized to society; or older concepts like *fairness* are transformed to new meanings). The role of (even discredited) academic arguments such as "expansionary fiscal contraction/consolidation" are deployed by governments seeking to justify austerity measures that, in reality, are flanking mechanisms designed to diminish the prospects of alternatives to austerity. The overall effect is that consent (even if disaffected consent) is obtained. That said, there are residuals on which resistance could conceivably be built as a result of the actual lived experience with austerity that stand in direct contradiction to the discourses of justification and obfuscation.

John Clarke (chapter 2: "Articulating Austerity and Authoritarianism: Re-imagining Moral Economies?") explores austerity as a transnational and national political project. He suggests the austerity project reworks established political-cultural tropes in an attempt to manage a conjuncture full of economic, political, and social contradictions. In doing so, it draws on and reassembles anti-statism and moral authoritarianism to construct an imagined moral economy. Drawing on examples from the UK/British/English formation, the chapter explores how a distinctively imagined moral economy of "shared sacrifice," denigration of the public realm, and a discourse of "earned fairness" attempts to mobilize popular anxiety and anger while redirecting such sentiments away from the sites of political and economic power responsible for the crisis.

Sorin Mitrea (chapter 3: "Speaking Austerity: Policy Rhetoric and Design beyond Fiscal Consolidation") undertakes a comparative study of Canada and the United Kingdom, which demonstrates how austerity shapes subjects in more nuanced ways than simply through imposed material hardship or ideological internalization of neoliberal logics. Instead, it is proposed that austerity operates dialectically through political discourses and policy implementation to inure subjects to the devolution of social policy and the expansion of precarity. The lack of sustained resistance to austerity is explained by material obstacles to mobilization and the partial internalization to neoliberal discourses working in tandem. In essence, there is a certain substance to TINA. Eric Pineault (chapter 4: "No Deal Capitalism: Austerity and the Unmaking of the North American Middle Class") takes on the ubiquitous and seemingly nearly meaningless narrative of the "middle class" and unpacks this term theoretically and ideologically in an examination of the politics that is at its foundation. Here the pro-cyclical policies of austerity that contribute to stagnation should not be interpreted as misguided policy but rather as an attribute of neoliberal class politics. In this interpretation, the elite wage a class struggle from above, resulting in a disappearing "middle class." Moving beyond the account that depicts the middle class as an ideological veil covering up more fundamental class relations, this chapter develops an understanding of the meaning of "middle class" and its seeming incapacity to resist the attacks on its living standards.

Ellen Russell (chapter 5: "Framing the Economic Case for Austerity: The Expansionary Fiscal Contraction Hypothesis") completes this section with a contribution that explores the astonishingly broad, mainstream, cross-party embrace of austerity as orthodoxy, despite continuing global economic fragility following the 2008 financial crisis. To persuade their national publics to accept further painful restructuring, austerity was showcased as the appropriate policy response to initiate economic recovery. The economic argument for this course of action was expressed through the expansionary fiscal contraction hypothesis, which contends that austerity would encourage economic growth. This chapter considers the proposition that the remarkable influence of the hypothesis can be attributed in large part to other ways that it served the neoliberal agenda. The core argument advanced is that it helped to shield neoliberal capitalism from the possibility that democratic forces might successfully mobilize in pursuit of economic alternatives.

Our second section delves directly into austerity at the intersections of policy roll-out and lived experience at the individual and community scale. Our contributors seek to answer the question, what are austerity's consequences? A number of specific occupational groups and/or public/social services are profiled. These include the aged and disabled in long-term care facilities, along with the feminized and racialized workforce that provides care to them; those retired from the workforce who depend on pension for income; immigrants whose experience is increasingly conditional on whether they fall into desired or undesirable categories. Beyond these particular groups is the experience of the broad and, some would argue, disappearing middle class whose relative prosperity and stability was the cornerstone of broadly prosperous Western liberal democracy in the Keynesian era. Underlying these discussions are issues of legitimacy and legitimation, a key concept in earlier state theories, and the way it may have been partially displaced by coercive practices experienced in the everyday lives of those living with austerity policies. Here we observe the authoritarian turn in neoliberalism in its most granular expression. Workers in the long-term care sector are controlled, and "clients" are marginalized and neglected. Pensioners have experienced decades of retrenchment, and future generations will experience a deepening of the same as a result of today's austerity. Only some immigrants are now considered desirable. All are now subject to limited access to welfare services and to diminished rights. Workers in the education and health sectors are targeted, as budgets are severely constrained and quality of the service is undermined, except for the growing numbers who can afford and opt for private provision. Growing economic inequality rests upon a large low-waged sector of precarious workers with diminished rights and benefits, compared to the stressed core workers. Established social models, and the protections they afforded, have been diminished.

Donna Baines (chapter 6: "Care and Control in Long-term Care Work") situates the role of state services, and that of those who provide such services, within an important debate. The coercive role of the police and military is obvious, but what is contentious is how coercion and state control are extended through the human care programs expressed in health and social services. This chapter applies a more nuanced approach to this debate by contending that the practices associated with New Public Management in the context of fiscal restraint and the resulting scarcity of resources shrink the role for caring in the labour process while extending that of control.

Brendan Sweeney and Robert Hickey's contribution (chapter 7: "'Negotiate Your Way Back to Zero': Teacher Bargaining and Austerity in Ontario, Canada") is centred on understanding why public school teachers and their unions across North America became targets for government austerity measures. Despite the common goal to reduce or constrain costs of publicly funded elementary and secondary education, the nature and impact of government-imposed austerity varied significantly across jurisdictions. Unsurprisingly, in many US states, austerity policies targeted teachers' unions specifically, often vilifying them as impediments to necessary education reform. In other jurisdictions, such as Ontario, austerity policies did not question the legitimacy of teachers' unions, but instead aimed to modify the political-institutional structures that govern education sector collective bargaining and employment relations. This chapter draws upon a case study of the lived experiences of Ontario teachers and their unions. Teacher union responses to austerity in Ontario were pragmatic both in workplace militancy and political activism. The current study contributes to the literature on union responses to austerity by analysing the complex nature of union-government relations.

Bryan Evans, Stephen McBride, and Jacob Muirhead (chapter 8: "Austerity and the Low-Wage Economy: Living and Other Wages") start from the premise that a capitalist labour market always included a variety of differentially rewarded strata within the working class. The existence of a low-wage sector therefore is nothing new, nor are efforts to resist or challenge the conditions experienced by people whose incomes typically fall far below the poverty line. In recent decades, under the rubric of neoliberalism, structural and political factors in many Western states have combined to expand the low-wage sector in a context of austerity measures and increased inequality. In policy terms, this is represented by intensified efforts to flexibilize the labour market and to impose conditionality (often predicated on entering or re-entering the low end of the labour market) for the receipt of social benefits. Using a comparative lens, this chapter examines how, in the era of austerity, various social and political forces have nevertheless pushed for policies to address low wages and associated poverty, particularly living-wage campaigns, and seeks to identify the extent to which and the conditions in which they can succeed.

Susan Barrass and John Shields (chapter 9: "Immigration in an Age of Austerity: Morality, the Welfare State, and the Shaping of the Ideal Migrant") explain and critique the moral economy of neoliberal immigration policy in the post-crisis period. State deficits and debt, it is contended here, have not only been used to shrink public expenditures on social programs but have also become the basis for reframing Canadian immigration policy. Morality looms large in both instances, where self-sufficiency is privileged to mitigate "freeloading." Reformed immigration policy in this context results in curtailed access to social benefits in addition to a redefinition of what the "ideal immigrant" should possess in skills and capital. This chapter examines the transformation of immigration policy and how this contributes to the construction of a new ideal immigrant.

Yanqiu Rachel Zhou and Shih-Jiunn Shi (chapter 10: "Pension Reforms in the Context of the Global Financial Crisis: A Reincarnation of Pension Privatization through Austerity?") explore the impact of the 2007–8 financial crisis through the prism of pensions. Specifically, the wave of pension reforms that followed in the wake of the crisis are the subject of analysis. What is contended here is that the pension reforms carried out under the umbrella of austerity during and since the onset of the crisis are essentially a continuation of welfare retrenchments since the 1980s and pension privatization since the 1990s. To some extent, the paradigm of pension privatization that was once at risk of extinction has now de facto revived as a consequence of the crisis.

The third and final section is concerned with class, resistance, and alternatives to austerity. We are conscious that there has been resistance to austerity and some assessment of the nature and prospects for this ongoing and future resistance is also attempted. Its limits are emphasized in the face of class assault by capital on workers and social rights. For some, material realities that result from austerity (flexibilization, outsourcing, privatization, concentration of wealth, inequality) create the necessary conditions for acceptance of those very policies. However, political and social disengagement results alongside signs of resistance. Disengagement is partly the consequence of the apparent exhaustion of traditional oppositional forces like social democracy. Other authors acknowledge this but seek to locate possibilities for resistance and to draw the theoretical links between it and the development of alternative political economies and the chance of embedding them in political vehicles that can implement them. Finally, the scale of resistance, both Right and Left, is surveyed and expanded. Here the chief threat identified is elite attachment to liberalism at the expense of democracy. The possibilities of political alternatives remain alive, but in the context of a crumbling liberal democratic "centre," what precise form these alternatives will take is an open question. Certainly, if persuasion fails to produce sufficient consent, however disaffected, then coercion is already evident and might, as Burron's chapter notes, become more pronounced.

Christoph Hermann (chapter 11: "From Austerity to Structural Reform: The Erosion of the European Social Model[s]") analyses the shift from austerity to structural adjustment in Europe, as well as the consequences of crisis policies for the European social model. In doing so, the crisis is traced from its origins in the American housing market to its arrival in Europe as a banking crisis, and then as a crisis of public households, triggering a wave of austerity. At the same time the European Commission and member states used the crisis to enforce major reforms, seeking to reduce the rights of workers. The same policies were further promoted as structural adjustment outside the crisis countries. In this regard the chapter establishes the trajectory for establishing a new normal of class relations in Europe.

Peter Graefe and Hubert Rioux (chapter 12: "Austerity of Imagination: Quebec's Struggles in Translating Resistance into Alternatives") consider Quebec's experience with austerity in historical perspective by examining the political responses to such measures from the 1990s to the present. An enduring question has been the translation of alternatives into policies through partisan politics, and recent developments suggest a narrowing of possibility. The authors undertake to develop a better understanding of the limitations of resistance by employing Dufour's (2009) "Political Action Diamond," a heuristic tool for mapping the strategies of movements. In considering the various attempts to counter austerity at each point of the political action diamond, some elements of alternatives come to the fore. However, the analysis concludes with the observation that, in Quebec, the politics have grown more defensive.

Bryan M. Evans (chapter 13: "Social Democracy and Social Pacts: Austerity Alliances and Their Consequences") explores the participation of social democracy in forging austerity in the post-crisis period and assesses the emergence of a new radical Left in response. The politics and political role of social democracy has transformed profoundly through the period following the 2008 crisis. Post-crisis social democracy has been a key force in forging multi-class austerity alliances. Participation in "grand coalitions" with conservative parties and resort to neo-corporatist social dialogue to negotiate the terms of austerity are all hallmarks of this practice. The result in many cases has been a "Pasokification" – a term coined to capture the implosion of social democratic parties, the most spectacular of which has been the demise of Greece's PASOK (Pan-Hellenic Socialist Movement), which could count on the support of more than 40 per cent of Greek voters in most elections since 1981 but has now been reduced to no more than 6 per cent. An important development emerging from this is the growth and persistence of parties of the radical Left in response, in part, to the neoliberalization of social democracy.

And finally, the volume concludes with Neil Burron (chapter 14: "Austerity and Political Crisis: The Radical Left, the Far Right, and Europe's New Authoritarian Order"). Drawing from the radical political economy literature on austerity and political crisis, Burron addresses the political dimensions of the crisis resulting from growing contradictions between liberal democracy and neoliberal capitalism. Manifestations of the political crisis include the resurgence of street politics, the collapse of governments, the suspension of liberal-democratic procedural norms, and polarization between the Far Right and radical Left. Despite growing popular discontent, however, both the radical Left and the Far Right have largely failed to provide alternatives of widespread popular appeal. In these circumstances, the outcome of this re-politicization remains to be determined.

The goal of this volume is to develop greater insight and understanding of the impact of state policies on populations by concentrating on the lived experience of austerity. Theories and case studies of how austerity is articulated and becomes accepted/internalized in subject populations, as presented here, serve to weave together intersections of ideational policy and lived experience of those policies. This necessarily involves discussion of the ways austerity is framed to draw upon deeper moral economies and concepts, with the effect that consent (even if disaffected consent) is obtained.

The imposition and maintenance of austerity on populations who had no part in creating the economic crisis is contradictory. This is true at the economic, political, and social levels. Economically, the policies don't work in the way that elites claim they work. Slow growth and increased inequality seem characteristic of permanent austerity. Politically, consent may have been created but amidst much disaffection. Yet governments are defeated, only to be replaced by ones that are indistinguishable or are coerced into capitulation, heightening frustration and malaise. Meanwhile, opposition to the extremes of austerity is itself depicted as extremism. Socially, inequality and precarious work give rise to well-founded diminished expectations.

The lived experience of austerity involves a great deal of blame transfer. The private sector that caused the crisis managed to transfer the blame for it to the public sector, which, in turn, is heavily engaged in transferring the blame to the populace. Rather than identifying the sites of power responsible for the current situation, there is a tendency for citizens to assume individual blame, either on their own behalf, or through other "unworthy" individuals against whom resentment is mobilized. Blame, too, is avoided by diversions such as the expansionary fiscal consolidation theory, which depicts present pain as necessary for long-term improvement and suggests that, in any case, there is no alternative, thus disempowering those who seek alternatives. Victims abound in this tale of the lived experience of austerity. They are not passive, as the chapters on long-term care recipients, pensioners, the low-waged, the declining middle class, and those who work in these fields and the educational and health sectors make clear. But they face a context in which traditional forces of opposition such as social democratic parties have been found wanting. And if discourse doesn't produce compliance, coercion is practised as through what are effectively structural adjustment processes, long practised against developing countries but now applied to advanced countries, as can be seen in the machinations of the Troika in imposing austerity on recalcitrant governments such as that of Syriza in Greece. In some locales, minority nationalist movements, combining class and national aspirations to a non-austerian future, may offer a promising political vehicle, but the general picture is one of sporadic resistance and significant political disengagement.

REFERENCES

Alderman, Liz, Larry Buchanan, Eduardo Porter, and Karl Russell. 2015. "Is Greece Worse Off than the U.S. during the Great Depression?" *New York Times*, 9 July. https://www.nytimes.com/interactive/2015/07/09/business/international/is-greece-worse-off-than-the-us-during-the-great-depression.html.

Crouch, Colin. 2011. *The Strange Non-Death of Neoliberalism*. Cambridge, UK: Policy.

Department of Finance. 2016a. "Fiscal Reference Tables 2016." https://www.fin.gc.ca/frt-trf/2016/frt-trf-16-eng.asp.

– 2016b. *Growing the Middle Class: 2016 Federal Budget*. Ottawa: Government of Canada. http://www.budget.gc.ca/2016/docs/plan/toc-tdm-en.html.

Dufour, Pascale. 2009. "From Protest to Partisan Politics: When and How Do Collective Actors Cross the Line: Sociological Perspective on Québec Solidaire." *Canadian Journal of Sociology* 34 (1): 55–81.

Flavelle, Dana. 2016. "Liberals Set to Spend Billions in Investment with Its Upcoming Federal Budget." *Toronto Star*, 18 March. https://www.thestar.com/business/2016/03/18/a-budget-that-chooses-investment-over-austerity.html.

Krugman, Paul. 2015. "Keynes Comes to Canada." *New York Times*, 23 October. https://www.nytimes.com/2015/10/23/opinion/keynes-comes-to-canada.html?_r=0.

Liberal Party of Canada. 2015. *A New Plan for a Strong Middle Class*. Ottawa: Liberal Party.

O'Toole, Emer. 2015. "The Liberals' Victory in Canada Signals People's Desire for Anti-Austerity Politics." *Guardian*, 20 October. https://www.theguardian.com/commentisfree/2015/oct/20/canada-voted-politics-anti-austerity-justin-trudeau-liberals.

Queally, Jon. 2015. "Yanis Varoufakis – Who Called Austerity 'Fiscal Waterboarding' – Appointed Greek Finance Minister." Common Dreams, 17 January. http://www.commondreams.org/news/2015/01/27/yanis-varoufakis-who-called-austerity-fiscal-waterboarding-appointed-greek-finance.

Statistics Canada. 2016. Cansim Table 380-0064: Current Prices, Unadjusted, Annual Sums, GDP at Market Prices.

PART ONE

Theory and Ideology

Introduction: Manufacturing the Common Sense of Austerity

BRYAN M. EVANS AND STEPHEN MCBRIDE

The overarching objective of this volume is to come to some greater understanding of how austerity invades and shapes our everyday lives as individuals and collectivities of individuals. The four chapters composing Part One of this book address the ideational dimensions, theory, and ideology, which ultimately provide the connective tissue linking ideas, values, and morality to the material political and public policy manifestations of austerity. The internalization of the idea of austerity, both by individuals and the state, provides the foundation for its acceptance as the prevailing common sense and, consequently, the intellectual and moral architecture for a specific policy framing of the economic problems through and after the 2008 crisis. At a variety of levels, austerity builds on what makes sense at the individual or household level. Faced with hard times, individuals or households may have little alternative but to practise some "belt tightening." The extension of this "common sense" to the governmental level and the resulting proposition that government finances should be managed like those of a household does not logically follow. Collective restraint and restructuring may be the last thing an economy needs to recover from a crisis. As a result, such an approach needs to be framed in ways that build on individual sensibilities and received rationality, and exclude other possible alternatives.

Austerity is a dangerous idea with a long history, as Mark Blyth (2013) has made clear. Yet its resiliency takes some effort to understand. The four contributions in this section provide insights into the longevity of austerity and its ability to generate at least disaffected consent from populations whose interests are harmed by the policies it entails. Austerity is variously analysed as a "failure," which is animated through authoritarian populism (John Clarke); as a moral economy of individual responsibilization informing austerian "common sense" (Sorin Mitrea); in terms of the political and ideological meaning of the discourse of the 99 per cent and the 1 per cent (Eric Pineault); and, finally, as a thorough examination of the enduring ideological power of the theoretical and policy anchor of austerity – the concept of expansionary fiscal consolidation/contraction (Ellen Russell).

Central to Clarke's chapter is Stuart Hall's concept of authoritarian populism, which he applies as a way of thinking about the political strategy of the UK's Liberal-Conservative Coalition government of 2010–15. Clarke's interest is in the failure (or at least stalling) of the neoliberal project and on elite efforts to rescue it. Incomplete projects require continuous renewal in order to press on and avoid imploding as a consequence of their own contradictions. Similarly, Mitrea's account of the lack of sustained resistance to austerity – caused by a combination of material obstacles to mobilization and the partial internalization of neoliberal discourses as applied to the behaviour and outlook of individuals – dovetails nicely with Clarke's chapter. Both emphasize the processes and considerable efforts that go into constituting and reconstituting passivity in those at the receiving end of austerity policies. The difficulties of mobilizing effective resistance to austerity underpins Eric Pineault's argument about the condition of the middle class, forty years into neoliberalism, and is accentuated by almost a decade of post-crisis austerity. Admittedly it is difficult to generalize, given the broad range of the term *middle class*, but there is a sense that its material conditions and future prospects are in decline. Yet it remains largely de-politicized in the sense that no viable alternatives have attracted its support. To some extent this is the result of the factors presented by Clarke and Mitrea, but it also depends on the mobilization of "expertise" to present a rational case for austerity. Ellen Russell, in analysing one ingredient of the expert argument for austerity policies, points out that the importance of such arguments lies less in their ultimate validity (since many, including expansionary fiscal contraction that she deals with, are ultimately discredited and fall into disuse) than in their ability to justify the policies, at least for a time, and to deflect attention from alternatives by creating an aura of scientific legitimation for the orthodoxy being pursued.

It may be that all these devices are approaching their limits. We cannot point to the development of a counter-hegemonic alternative, backed by an array of social and political forces capable of displacing the austerian approach. However, there are isolated and often intense manifestations of opposition to the status quo. In the United Kingdom, for example, the "Brexit" referendum on membership in the European Union seems to threaten the British party system and indeed the very existence of the British state. The Brexit referendum in particular looks like an expression of rage by those who voted to leave the EU, not only rage at the faceless technocrats in Brussels but also at the smug cosmopolitan elites of all political parties who have ruled the United Kingdom for decades. The elite response was similarly one of rage at those who had dared to vote against the consensus view. Many currents of political dissatisfaction can be discerned in the campaigns surrounding these referenda, but arguably an important aspect is a rejection of the moral economy of "shared sacrifice," manufactured by the elites, and its replacement by sometimes incoherent subaltern hostility to all that looks and sounds like the consensus of the last forty years. It remains to be seen how widespread this dissatisfaction is (there is plenty of evidence that it is not confined to the United Kingdom), and whether it is capable of overcoming the factors, identified in these chapters, that sustain some sort of consent to the prevailing orthodoxy.

2 Articulating Austerity and Authoritarianism: Re-imagining Moral Economies?

JOHN CLARKE

Prologue: The Where, When, and What of Austerity

One challenge of writing about austerity is to locate or specify the thing itself. It multiplies across time and space, while serving to name several different projects, practices, meanings, and what Raymond Williams called "structures of feeling" (1977, 129–35). Austerity has a long history: Florian Schui traces it as one recurring pole in debates about consumption that stretch back to classical philosophy. He argues that it works as a form of "consumption critique" (2014, 3). The accumulated inheritance of such debates infuses ideas of austerity with a distinctive moral weight or significance: "The persuasive power of austerity arguments lies in part in the way in which they allude to familiar moral and cultural categories of moderation, selflessness and cathartic cleansing. Even where we do not understand the economic logic associated with austerity arguments – or where they are presented without a compelling economic rationale – their emotional appeal is strong" (9). More recent histories borrow from, and add to, this cultural valorization of austerity. For example, historians of Britain have pointed to the years of the Second World War and afterwards as marked by a political and moral commitment to austerity as a form of collective self-sacrifice (Kynaston 2007; Zweiniger-Bargielowska 2000). This history appears to lend more recent political deployments of austerity added weight, in the form of a stock of (more or less) common knowledge on which appeals to sacrifice, self-restraint, and suffering can draw (although see Kynaston's careful distinction of the differences between the two eras: Kynaston 2010). In contrast, Mark Blyth's recent "history of a dangerous idea" locates austerity as a twentieth-century phenomenon, arguing that it is "not until you get states that are big enough to cut that you really get debates about cutting the state down" (2013, 170) before focusing on early experiments with austerity in the 1930s – and their painful consequences.

Although "austerity" has emerged as the dominant global wisdom for addressing the "problem of public debt" and has circulated widely, particularly across the European Union and North America, we need to remember that the global North is a relative latecomer to the regime of fiscal austerity. The South has had a rather longer (and harsher) exposure to its rigours (see, for example, Adepoju 1993, and Ferguson 2006 on Africa; Canak 1989, and Lustig 1995 on Latin America; and Yeldan 2001 on Turkey and the International Monetary Fund). That history is a reminder about the controversial economics and politics associated with austerity. The currently dominant consensus about fiscal austerity continues an approach established in the IMF's "structural adjustment" policies in which public debt, public spending, and public services are all viewed as problems to be overcome (to liberate enterprise, growth, and development).

More banally, the term has also been used extensively in the field of welfare state studies as a proxy for fiscal constraint and retrenchment in Northern welfare state systems after the mid-1970s. In this context, austerity does not seem to carry the symbolic political charge of its current deployments (see, for example, Pierson 1998, 2002; Kittel and Obinger 2003; and Korpi and Palme 2003). However, the long-running accumulation of pressures on public spending – and their anti-welfarist and anti-statist rationales – forms a critical part of the conditions of possibility for the current formations of austerity (an issue to which I will return in the next section).

These different appearances of austerity across time and space contribute to the problem of identifying what sort of thing austerity is or, perhaps more accurately, points to the multiplicity of forms that austerity might take. Is austerity, then, an idea (dangerous or otherwise) or a philosophical principle? Is it, rather, an ideology or political discourse? Each of these keeps austerity primarily in the realm of the symbolic, while other approaches have treated it primarily as a policy, a program, or a political project (ranging from structural adjustment to what Peck 2012 has called "austerity governance"). But here, too, there are significant differences. Is austerity to be treated primarily as a governmental economic policy – and therefore subject to debates about economic analysis, outcomes, and performance? This question raises issues about how to evaluate austerity – on its own terms (have budgets been balanced, or economic growth encouraged?) or in more heterodox economic framings (see the critiques of both theory and practice of austerity in work by Boyer 2012; Krugman 2013; Guajardo, Leigh, and Pescatori 2014; Wren-Lewis 2015; and some of the discussions on VOXEU in Corsetti 2012).

Meanwhile, scholars working in the fields of health, public, and social policy have argued that austerity needs to be evaluated for its effects on populations, rather than economies (e.g., Ortiz, Chai, and Cummins 2011; McKee et al. 2012; Clark and Heath 2014; O'Hara, 2014). Stuckler and Basu argue explicitly for the need to reframe economic policy in such terms, trying to shift the focus from the "body politic":

> Suppose we reframe the debate to focus on "body economics": the health effects of our economic policies. Since our economic policies have a huge impact on health, they ought to pass the same rigorous tests that we apply to other things that affect our health, like pharmaceuticals. If economic policies had to be proven "safe" and "effective," just like any drug being approved for our patients, we might have an opportunity to make our societies safer and healthier. Instead, at the moment, in those countries where austerity is ascendant, we're undergoing a massive and untested experiment on human health, and left to count the dead. (Stuckler and Basu 2013, xx–xxi)

The shift in focus to "body economics" is dramatic and illuminating (see also Mitrea, this volume on bodies and politics). Like others working in this genre, Stuckler and Basu find depressing amounts of evidence about the social and health impacts of austerity programs, particularly those that undermine, shrink, or remove forms of the social "safety net" in times of the most urgent need: "counting the dead" is not a metaphorical point.

Finally, austerity is also framed as a political economic program or project, located within the relations, forces, and contradictions of capitalism and decisively connected to the financialised crisis of 2007–9 and its consequences. Even here, there are significant differences between those who foreground the unfolding dynamic of class interests and the exploration of political-ideological strategies and formations at both global and national levels. At times these are bridged (not always stably) by analyses of political rationalities and modes of governing (e.g., Peck 2010, 2012; Brown 2015). As I will argue in the following section, these approaches also have to confront questions of time, space and form: austerity risks being both universal and elusive.

Crises and Contradictions: The Conjuncture of Austerity

The preceding section is not just a trainspotter's guide to different appearances of austerity. Rather, it provides a way of posing problems of time, space, and form that seem central to its discussion. So how might some of the questions of time, space, and form be resolved, at least provisionally? I will suggest three conditions for what follows as my versions of empirical analysis. The first concerns time: recognizing that austerity has a long history is not the same as treating it as either continuous or recurrent in any simple sense. Instead I think austerity is assembled anew in specific times and places, but in ways that draw on – or at least try to mobilize – older stocks of knowledge and sentiments. This more disjointed sense of austerity's history invites us to pay more attention to the political and ideological/discursive work that is being done to make *this* austerity, rather than treating it as already known and recognizable. At any one point, then, austerity condenses different times (or temporalities) in more or less stable bundles.

Second, the same arguments might also apply to questions of space and place. Austerity is not universal (hence a certain fascination with Iceland, for example), nor is it everywhere the same when it does appear. For instance, Peck's dissection of austerity urbanism (2012) addresses a specific political and governmental combination of space and scale that is the United States: "Neoliberal austerity measures operate downwards in both social and scalar terms: they offload social and environmental externalities on cities and communities, while at the same time enforcing unflinching fiscal restraint by way of extralocal disciplines; they further incapacitate the state and the public sphere through the outsourcing, marketization and privatization of governmental services and social supports; and they concentrate both costs and burdens on those at the bottom of the social hierarchy, compounding economic marginalization with state abandonment" (650). Although such "urbanising" processes are visible in other governmental spaces, they do not necessarily take the same form as that of the United States. There is a risk here of oscillating between a return to methodological nationalism (producing comparisons of differently nationalized austerities) or being overwhelmed by a methodological globalism in which distinctions are submerged by universalising accounts of change. So political spaces, governmental formations, and even constitutional forms (federal versus highly centralized state systems, for example) continue to play a role as animating contexts, mediating forces, and sites of translation – but always relationally (this view is developed more fully in Clarke et al. 2015). Specific places and formations are always engaged by relations with forces, institutions, and apparatuses that are transnational, establishing the conditions of possibility that frame national, regional, and local articulations of austerity (and other programs and policies). Of course, in the process, the emerging dynamics of austerity programs rework the given formations of space and scale – not least by the relentless competitive framing of places and the downward or decentralizing character of austerity policies that Peck identifies. At the same time, spatial relations – or perhaps spatial imaginaries – are themselves deployed in the making of austerity governance and in resistance to it: for example, in representations of the European Union and member states in different national politics. For example, the emerging political opposition in Spain and Greece identified the EU and, more particularly, Germany, as the perpetrators of austerity during elections in 2014.[1] In a rather different way, the UK Coalition government has always distinguished itself from the members of the eurozone by its capacity to establish its own austerity.

Third, there are questions about how to identify the forms in which austerity appears: is the focus of analysis primarily on policies (of different kinds), political-economic projects, political-ideological discourses, or even cultural forms and genres in which austerity is promoted, questioned or displayed? The present contains all of these (and more?), but each poses particular problems of analysis, evaluation, and critique. In what follows, I will take up some specific aspects of political-ideological discursive work of austerity as practised by the Conservative-led UK Coalition government (2010–15), with an emphasis on the *work* that dominant discourse does – and the political outcomes that it seeks to achieve. But that does mean addressing how austerity is being deployed and enacted in one very specific (time and space) setting.

I want to suggest that this understanding of time and space (as multiple and interconnected) points to a version of "conjunctural analysis" in which the present or the "here and now" – is a condensation of different temporal and spatial relationships. The present in this view is also a condensation of multiple social forces – not just a singular dynamic – and an accumulation of tensions, antagonisms, and contradictions. In *Marxism*

---

[1] Pablo Iglesias MEP for Podemos: "We will now work with other parties from the south of Europe to make it clear that we don't want to be a German colony" (Gómez 2014).

and Literature (1977), Raymond Williams insisted on the importance of distinguishing between "epochal analysis" and "authentic historical analysis":

> In what I have called epochal analysis, a cultural process is seized as a cultural system, with determinate dominant features: feudal culture or bourgeois culture or a transition from one to the other. This emphasis on dominant and definitive lineaments is important and often, in practice, effective. But it then happens that its methodology is preserved for the very different function of historical analysis, in which a sense of movement within what is ordinarily abstracted as a system is crucially necessary, especially if it is connected with the future as well as the past. In authentic historical analysis it is necessary at every point to recognize the complex interrelationships between movements and tendencies both within and beyond a specific effective dominance. It is necessary to examine how these relate to the whole cultural process rather than only to the selected and abstracted dominant system. (121)

Williams goes on to name those elements "beyond a specific effective dominance" as the residual and emergent: the residual marks the persistence of issues and questions that cannot be addressed from within the dominant; the emergent names the issues, questions, and answers that emerge in opposition to the dominant – and that the dominant always attempts to exclude or incorporate (reviving itself in the process). I find myself regularly going back to Williams's distinctions, because they give a sort of methodological template for analysing the present, which stops the temptation to simply focus on the dominant – as though neoliberalism or austerity occupies a world uncluttered by anything else. Conjunctures are, in these senses, heterogeneous – made up of multiple temporalities, spatial relationships, social forces, antagonisms, and contradictions. In what follows, I will try to tease out elements of the "dominant" in the context of UK austerity politics, but also give some attention to its limits – especially its capacity to mobilize forms of consent in the light of residual and emergent currents. In doing so, I will return to a concept of political rule elaborated by Stuart Hall in the 1980s – authoritarian populism – as a way of thinking about the political strategy of the Coalition government of 2010–15.

Elsewhere (Clarke 2010), I suggested that crisis, contradiction, and conjuncture might be interlaced concepts that enable us to think about the present as the accumulation of failure: failed, stalled, or incomplete hegemonic projects that try to combine economic, social, and political restructuring with the securing of popular consent to that project. Such projects have failed to resolve many of the contradictions they set out to overcome, and have needed constant renewal to stave off political antagonisms and social disaffection. I am, in that sense, interested in failure. Rather than celebrating the achievements of capital, neoliberal rule, or austerity governance, there may be analytical and political mileage in thinking about them as failures, or at least as innovations demanded by previous failures – failures to resolve "blockages to progress," failures to construct new settlements that stabilize the conditions of capital accumulation, failures to construct the "neoliberal subject" in all its glory, and more. I do not mean to deny their successes, but I think the intensity of innovation, the weight of insistence, and the anxiety with which even vaguely glimpsed alternatives are denied and repressed suggest that much remains at stake. For these reasons, Peck's way of reframing austerity offers a way of emphasizing the contradictory and unfinished character of the conjuncture that I find remarkably helpful:

> Austerity has become a strategic space for the contradictory reproduction of market rule, calling attention to the ways in which neoliberal rationalities have been resuscitated, reanimated and to some degree rehabilitated in the wake of the Wall Street crash of 2008–2009. By definition, however, this does not define a sustainable course. Beyond its internal contradictions, austerity urbanism has already become a site of struggle in its own right, though it remains to be seen whether the latest wave of occupations, protests and resistance efforts will mutate into a politics of transformation. To be sure, the multiple pathways of resistance politics cannot be simply "read off" from these newly formed maps of urban austerity, but resistance politics will nevertheless have to be prosecuted across fiscal and institutional terrains (re)shaped by austerity urbanism. What can be said, for now, is that if austerity defines a new normal, it is a state of normalcy at the very cusp of crisis. (2012, 651)

Peck's elegant counterposing of the "new normal" and the "cusp of crisis" is immensely suggestive – and reminiscent of Gramsci's description of the life of the state as a "series of unstable equilibria" (1971, 182). In the following sections, I will look in more detail at how austerity has been mobilized in the United Kingdom (itself an unstable geopolitical formation, where discursive challenges to austerity have increasingly emerged in Scotland and Wales). The financial crisis of 2007–9 threatened British banks, among others, and was a focus for a massive program of public spending to support at-risk banks, provide market guarantees, and pump money into the economy in the form of "quantitative easing" funds designed to create liquidity. The overall cost of these measures is still debated (though the support for at-risk banks is estimated to have been around £123 billion (*Guardian* n.d.). Such subsidies, guarantees, and financial injunctions were central to the transformation of a crisis of private sector institutions into a problem of public debt. The 2010 general election was fought on the terrain created by the financial crisis – and proved inconclusive. However, a coalition of Conservative and Liberal Democratic parties took office, committed to tackling the problem of public finances ("getting the deficit under control"). In the process, *austerity* became a political keyword.

Imagining a Moral Economy of Inequality

The Conservative-led coalition in the United Kingdom made a concerted effort to imagine the economy as a moral economy, in which society is held together by social/moral bonds, rather than the individualist/transactional model held to be at the heart of neoliberalism (the term is borrowed from E.P. Thompson, 1971, albeit somewhat bent in the process). This is a complex challenge, given the contradictions that must be managed, or magically resolved, in this imaginary, not least the celebration of waged work (often in the figure of "hard-working families") in the face of the degradation of waged work and frozen or falling wages (see, inter alia, Standing 2011; Weeks 2012). This imagined moral economy has been articulated around three key themes identified by the Conservative political leadership of the Coalition but more widely disseminated in public and political discourse – each element, and the ensemble, aspiring to become established as the hegemonized "common sense" of the conjuncture. These three elements are the conception of the "Big Society" (articulated by David Cameron, the Conservative leader, while in opposition); the second is austerity itself, represented as a politics of "virtuous necessity" (Clarke and Newman 2012); and the third is the central role occupied by a discourse of morality. These three, I suggest, are woven together in the trope of "fairness," which has functioned as a discursive device that legitimates an authoritarian populist approach to the economy, and to welfare reform in particular.

The first "big idea" in Cameron's Conservatism was the concept of the "Big Society," articulated as a counterpoint to the "Big State."

Through counter-posing state and society in this way, Cameronian conservatism hoped to reclaim the field of the social for economic liberalism while legitimizing the reduction of public spending. In the Hugo Young Lecture in 2009, David Cameron argued,

> The size, scope and role of government in Britain has reached a point where it is now inhibiting, not advancing the progressive aims of reducing poverty, fighting inequality, and increasing general well-being. Indeed there is a worrying paradox that because of its effect on personal and social responsibility, the recent growth of the state has promoted not social solidarity, but selfishness and individualism ...
>
> The first step must be a new focus on empowering and enabling individuals, families and communities to take control of their lives so we create the avenues through which responsibility and opportunity can develop. This is especially vital in what is today the front line of the fight against poverty and inequality: education. (Cameron 2009a, 1)

The imagery and the project of the "Big Society" have proved unstable and uncertain, and have, in significant ways, mutated into a more persistent concern with "personal responsibility" alongside the commitment to "rolling back the state" (or at least carefully selected parts of it). The profound anti-statism of the Coalition has been underpinned by the rise of "austerity" in the aftermath of the financial crisis of 2007–9, and its careful reconstruction into a fiscal crisis of the state (and the question of public debts and deficits, Clarke and Newman 2012).

> The age of austerity demands responsible politics.
> Over the next few years, we will have to take some incredibly tough decisions on taxation, spending, borrowing – things that really affect people's lives.
> Getting through those difficult decisions will mean sticking together as a country – government and people.
> That relationship, just as any other, is strengthened by honesty; undermined by dishonesty. (Cameron, 2009b)

The anti-statism of the Big Society combined with austerity in ways that connected with the third focus of Conservative policy and politics in this period: the revival of ideas of morality – with attacks on the risks of "moral collapse" (following the English riots of 2011; Cameron 2011) and claims of a "moral mission" to cut dependency (Cameron 2012).

In the program of welfare reform undertaken after the 2010 election, the idea of a moral economy was articulated through the key trope of "fairness" (see also Clarke 2014). The articulation is captured in this view of the "economic plan": "First, our long-term economic plan for Britain is not just about doing what we can afford, it is also about doing what is right. Nowhere is that more true than in welfare. For me the moral case for welfare reform is every bit as important as making the numbers add up: building a country where people aren't trapped in a cycle of dependency but are able to get on, stand on their own two feet and build a better life for themselves and their family" (Cameron 2014).

In an earlier speech, Cameron took William Beveridge's imagery of the "five giants" (Want, Disease, Ignorance, Squalor, and Idleness), which had demanded a "cradle to grave" system of social security in 1942, and substituted new giants – the first of which was "unfairness":

> Our reforms are just as profound as those of Beveridge 60 years ago. He had his great evils to slay. Squalor. Ignorance. Want. Idleness. And Disease.
> Here are mine.
> First, unfairness.
> What are hard-working people who travel long distances to get into work and pay their taxes meant to think when they see families – individual families – getting 40, 50, 60 thousand pounds of housing benefit to live in homes that these hard working people could never afford themselves?
> It is an outrage. And we are ending it by capping housing benefit.
> The second evil: injustice.
> Here's the choice we give our young people today.
> Choice one: Work hard. Go to college. Get a job. Live at home. Save up for a flat. And as I've just said, that can feel like forever.
> Or: Don't get a job. Sign on. Don't even need to produce a CV when you do sign on. Get housing benefit. Get a flat. And then don't ever get a job or you'll lose a load of housing benefit.
> We must be crazy.
> So this is what we've done.
> Now you have to have to sign a contract that says: you do your bit and we'll do ours.
> It requires you to have a real CV and it makes clear: you have to seek work and take work – or you will lose your benefit. And we're going to look at ending automatic access to housing benefit for people under 25 too.
> If hard-working young people have to live at home while they work and save, why should it be any different for those who don't? ...

So let's be clear: in British politics today it is this party saying no-one is a write-off, no-one is hopeless … and with Iain Duncan Smith leading this revolution let this be the party that shows there is ability and promise in everyone. (Cameron 2012)

At stake here are familiar, if revised and reanimated, distinctions between the deserving and undeserving – articulated by the Chancellor of the Exchequer in 2012 as the divide between the "strivers" and the "shirkers": "Where's the fairness for the shift-worker, leaving home in the dark hours of the early morning, who looks up at the closed blinds of their next door neighbour sleeping off a life on benefits … We speak for all those who want to work hard and get on … They strive for a better life. We strive to help them" (Osborne 2012; see also Hasan 2012).

It was this same spirit of fairness that was deployed by the then Work and Pensions Secretary Iain Duncan Smith to justify the cap on benefits (available to a single household) when he argued, "For too many people, benefits have become a way of life. That is why we are introducing the benefit cap, at £500 a week, so someone cannot earn more money than a family on an average income" (Sheldrick 2013).

The Centre for Social Justice, founded by former Conservative leader Iain Duncan Smith, has provided a focal point for this moralization of welfare reform, producing reports on "Breakdown Britain" and "Breakthrough Britain" (e.g., Social Justice Policy Group, 2006, 2007). Duncan Smith was the Secretary of State for Work and Pensions throughout the 2010 government and continued in the first year of the subsequent Conservative government. In this role, he was responsible for the intensifying program of welfare reform that has included the project to create an integrated benefit system (Universal Credit); the revision and outsourcing of disability benefits (in the form of "Personal Independence Payments"; see Ryan 2015); the "bedroom tax" (intended to limit the number of rooms a person/household on housing benefit is entitled to; and the enforcement of "work experience" as a condition of receiving benefits. He resigned his position in 2016 over further cuts to disabled people's benefits being proposed in the March budget.

The justifications for this consistent and intensifying program of welfare reform have been varied, but have always circled around moral questions about dependency and fairness. The idea of fairness has been re-articulated from a thinly egalitarian notion about forms of entitlement and justice (less than equality, more than inequality) to one that aims to legitimate attacks on the poor and welfare users

(Clarke 2014).[2] At stake in all these discussions of fairness and the principle of "making work pay" is a sustained effort to obscure the growing degradation of waged work and the stalling of average wages during the last decade. Osborne's "strivers" have not, in fact, been rewarded, while the distributions of both income and wealth have become more unequal. The numbers of the "working poor" have grown, with an increasing number of those in work having wages supplemented by public support (in the form of "working tax credits"). In 2015, the campaigning group Citizens UK argued that supermarket workers' wages were subsidized by around £11 billion per annum (Sabin 2015).

The "unfairness" of benefits has provided a vocabulary that draws on what are perceived to be established British virtues (the "sense of fair play," etc.) to manage the contradictions and potential antagonisms resulting from deepening inequalities (and the experiences of economic failure) by displacing the focus of attention from the rich to the poor, misrepresenting the nature of poverty in the process. The framing around "fairness" enables an imagined moral economy to be elaborated, in which shared sacrifice and mutual obligation are represented as governing social and economic relations. It has also underpinned an increasingly brutal assault on welfare provision, in which austerity was interwoven with fairness as the twin logics of "welfare reform."

The Attractions of Authoritarian Populism?

In the final section, I want to return to the ways in which austerity – not least as entangled with fairness – has continued and contributed to the political formation that Stuart Hall named as "authoritarian populism" (Hall et al. 1978; Hall 1979, 1988). Hall coined the phrase to denote a complex mixture of tendencies: towards a populist mode of political articulation (drawing on the work of Ernesto Laclau (2002) on Latin American politics in particular) in combination with the expansion or deepening of the coercive repertoire of state apparatuses and the weakening of democratic controls in the name of "defending society."

---

2 Fairness was given an earlier "modernizing" inflection by the Labour Party, as exemplified in a speech from Gordon Brown on his way to becoming leader of the party and prime minister in 2007: "Everything we have done … is driven by one thing: our united commitment to fair rules, fair chances, and a fair say for all … These are for me the best of British values: responsibilities required in return for rights; fairness not just for some but all who earn it."

In his 1979 article, he argued for this understanding of the complex formation rather than the designation "fascism" to describe moves in the British state: "What we have to explain is a move toward 'authoritarian populism' – an exceptional form of the capitalist state – which, unlike classical fascism, has retained most (though not all) of the formal representative institution in place, and which at the same time has been able to construct around itself an active popular consent. This undoubtedly represents a decisive shift in the balance of hegemony ... It has entailed a striking weakening of democratic forms and initiatives, but not their suspension" (15).

This argument raises two issues for me. First, are we still in a conjuncture dominated by "authoritarian populism"? Certainly, successive UK governments (and some of those elsewhere) have normalized the "exceptional state," not just changing the balance between different types of state apparatus (investing in the coercive, penal, and security elements) but also conforming the welfare agencies to the disciplinary spirit of authoritarian reforms. Most recently, the Coalition government of 2010–15 and its Conservative successor have seemed intent on driving out of the last traces of the post-war social democratic or labourist settlement through further reconstructions of the forms, conditions, and agencies of welfare. This has been accompanied by the denigration and degradation of democratic processes and possibilities, despite a constant rhetoric of promoting participation and bewailing declining political involvement (Brown 2015; in neoliberal and austerity framings, democracy is neither economic nor efficient).

This normalization of authoritarianism is by no means the only political/governmental trend, but it has been a striking one, both in the agencies of the state (however decentralized, privatized, and entrepreneurial they may have become) and in the political culture of hostility and antagonism towards those defined as marginal: the shifting cast of enemies within and outwith the nation. More speculatively, this authoritarian populism also seems to underpin and enable a culture of "rage" towards despised others: a rage that flows on grimly predictable lines towards women, sexual minorities, ethnic and religious minorities, and the "poor" (fuelled by the rise of what has been termed "poverty porn": see, for example, Mooney and Hancock 2012).

This leads me to the second issue arising from "authoritarian populism" – to what extent has this proved stable and successful political formation? Here, I fear, my answers get more tangled. The emergent combination of authoritarianism, populism, and neoliberal individualism has been the consistently dominant political formation during the last forty years in the United Kingdom (or at least in parts of the United Kingdom), as it has elsewhere, particularly in anglophone contexts. However, following Raymond Williams, this dominant needs to be analysed in its coexistence with residual and emergent formations. The dominant assault on statism and welfarism has undoubtedly reduced public support for some forms of welfare provision (particularly for the unemployed and lone parents) to new lows (see YouGov polls and the annual British Social Attitudes Survey: Park et al. 2014). Nevertheless, what we might call "residual" orientations to collectivism and welfarism persist – not least in the continuingly high support for a publicly provided and funded National Health Service, which remained at over 95 per cent between 1985 and 2012. Meanwhile across the same period, in response to a question offering choices of different tax-reduction/increase and spending reduction/increase levels, less than 10 per cent have opted for the "reduce taxes/reduce spending" combination (Appleby and Roberts 2013). The attitudes study also reveals little support for abandoning universalism and targeting public services of the poorest/most in need. Such residual orientations to public welfare and well-being have also been embodied in a variety of initiatives by civil society organizations (from alternative welfare provision, such as food banks, to wider critiques and legal challenges to welfare regulations).

These orientations and actions mark a distinctive "hold-out" in the face of liberal/neoliberal/austerity-dominated public and political discourse. In particular, they may account for the continuing crab-like "reforms" on the financial, organizational, and professional structures of the NHS, since frontal assaults appear to risk political unpopularity. The persistence of such public sentiments should interrupt triumphalist (or depressive) accounts of how we are all neoliberal now. However, it does not necessarily provide a very strong foundation for a wider front of politics to counter the austerity project, since its lessons do not appear readily transferable. It does, however, suggest that scanning the political-cultural landscape more carefully to identify the forms of residual and emergent orientations that sit alongside and in tension with the dominant might be worthwhile. The emergent forms are, I suspect, always more difficult to identify, appearing in small-scale, experimental innovations in the interstitial spaces (e.g., current experiments with the commons or alternative forms of democracy). Often they are difficult to identify because they do not necessarily look like "politics" as currently institutionalized or anticipated (Dean 2014).

There are unstable political affiliations and alignments that indicate growing dissent and dissatisfaction with the dominant parties of austerity, which range from populist, nationalist, xenophobic responses (the Front National in France and UKIP in England) to alternative "Lefts" (e.g., Syriza, L'altra Europa, Podemos in Europe; see Horvat 2014). In late 2014, the *Independent* ran an editorial about newly released data from the research organization Income Data Services, revealing the still-widening gap between highest and lowest earners (i.e., income, not wealth, differences). It suggested growing detachment from established politics might be an effect of this dynamic (in the United Kingdom meaning highest earners now earn 120 times the lowest, an "advance" on the 47 times that prevailed in 2000). The editorial suggested,

> The perception and reality of this unfairness, and the perception that globalisation is to blame, accounts for a good deal of the disaffection from politics that has pervaded Western societies, with "insurgent" parties, often nationalistic or worse, gaining ground steadily …
>
> We should not be dismayed if voters refuse to accept this new Edwardian-style "Upstairs, Downstairs" society and protest as they have across the eurozone in recent years and in England in 2011, as well as voting for ever more maverick parties. (*Independent* 2014)

There are instances of disaffection in different registers: withdrawal from politics; cynical compliance with the performance of politics; insurgent attempts to regain forms of privilege by those who feel threatened by social movements and social change; and many forms of nostalgia that imagine communities lost to modernity, globalization, and the market.

This is not the place to explore this issue fully (much less to resolve it). Instead, I will end by marking out two of the orientations that continue to act as guides to conducting such an analysis. First, I have argued for the importance of doing conjunctural analysis (in the spirit of Hall and Williams). For me, this insistence on attending to the heterogeneous forces, relations, contradictions, and possibilities that constitute a conjuncture is an indispensable way of doing critical analysis. Second, I want to argue for the importance of treating subjects (collective and individual) as plural or multiple. The search for pure subjects (revolutionary, conservative, neoliberal) seems increasingly futile (and mistaken). Instead we might consider the states of paradox, ambivalence, uncertainty, and contradiction in which people might "live their imaginary relations to the real relations of existence" (to misquote Althusser). In this respect, Gramsci's understanding that common sense is plural, constituted by many common senses, seems to me a crucial insight. For Gramsci, we are always "the product of the historical process to date which has deposited in you an infinity of traces without leaving an inventory ... Moreover, commonsense is a collective noun, like religion: there is not just one common sense, for that too is a product of history and a part of the historical process" (1973, 324–5). This conception of the fragmentary and heterogeneous formation of common sense is vital, because it marks the site of the work of political articulation that is involved in attempts to "hegemonize" particular elements or fragments of common sense in order to create the illusion of a shared, unitary, and coherent conception of the world.

From such a starting point, we might think of subjects (individual and collective) who carry, inhabit, and mobilize different aspects of common sense, and these need not be coherent or consistent. Together, they provide tools to map the conjuncture and the forms of consent and dissent and the peculiar and unstable combinations in which these are lived (see, for example, the discussion of citizenship in Kirwan, McDermont, and Clarke (2016). Here I turn (not for the first time) to the productive ways in which Jeremy Gilbert has posed the question of consent, especially the idea of "disaffected consent," against the over-reading of the dominant. Such over-reading has, he suggests, two problems.

First, it ignores the possibility that, as Gramsci points out, subaltern groups may at times consent only "passively." Second, it ignores the variety of ways in which different groups can be mobilized, recruited, pacified, neutralized, or marginalized by a hegemonic project: for example, in the case of neoliberalism, it is clear from the foregoing analysis that only the core neoliberal elite and key strategic sectors of its periphery (notably corporate management) have to be recruited to any kind of active belief in neoliberal norms, as long as no singular alternative wins widespread popular support, in order for the rest of a population to remain convinced of the unviability of any political challenge to those norms. The result may well be a broadly shared culture of "disaffected consent," wherein a general dissatisfaction with neoliberalism and its social consequences is very widespread, but no popular alternative is able to crystalize or cohere with sufficient potency to develop the necessary critical mass to challenge neoliberal hegemony (Gilbert 2013, 18).

There is, then, "unfinished business" in the question of consent. We have a frustrating gap between the grand narratives of domination and rule and the more small-scale studies of how people live and think about their subordination – the gap is precisely the space in which varieties of "consent" (and dissent) might be discovered and mapped. This is not a proposal for an academic exercise (though it would be good if someone got the funds for it), but a matter of urgent political concern: a way of establishing the conditions of possibility for changing affiliations, attachments, and articulations towards doing things "otherwise."

REFERENCES

Adepoju, A., ed. 1993. *The Impact of Structural Adjustment on the Population of Africa*. London: United Nations Population Fund and James Currey.

Appleby, J., and C. Roberts. 2013. "Health: How Have the Public's Views of the NHS Changed over the Last 30 Years?" In *Social Attitudes 30*, ed. A. Park, C. Bryson, E. Clery, J. Curtice, and M. Phillips, 87–114. London: National Centre for Social Research.

Blyth, M. 2013. *Austerity: The History of a Dangerous Idea*. Oxford: Oxford University Press.

Boyer, R. 2012. "The Four Fallacies of Contemporary Austerity Policies: The Lost Keynesian Legacy." *Cambridge Journal of Economics* 36 (1): 283–312. https://doi.org/10.1093/cje/ber037.

Brown, G. 2007. "Gordon Brown Speech in Full." BBC, 11 May. https://www.theguardian.com/news/datablog/2011/nov/12/bank-bailouts-uk-credit-crunch.

Brown, W. 2015. *Undoing the Demos*. New York: Zone Books.

Cameron, D. 2009a. "The Big Society" (The Hugo Young Lecture). http://conservative-speeches.sayit.mysociety.org/speech/601246.

– 2009b. "The Age of Austerity," 26 April. http://conservative-speeches.sayit.mysociety.org/speech/601367.

– 2011. "PM's Speech on the 'Fightback after the Riots." https://www.gov.uk/government/speeches/pms-speech-on-the-fightback-after-the-riots.

– 2012. "David Cameron's Conservative Party Conference Speech: In Full." *Telegraph*, 10 October. http://www.telegraph.co.uk/news/politics/conservative/9598534/David-Camerons-Conservative-Party-Conference-speech-in-full.html.

– 2014. "David Cameron: Why the Archbishop of Westminster Is Wrong about Welfare." *Telegraph*, 18 February. http://www.telegraph.co.uk/news/politics/david-cameron/10646421/David-Cameron-Why-the-Archbishop-of-Westminster-is-wrong-about-welfare.html.

Canak, W.L., ed. 1989. *Lost Promises: Debt, Austerity, and Development in Latin America*. Boulder, CO: Westview.
Clark, T., and A. Heath. 2014. *Hard Times: The Divisive Toll of the Economic Slump*. New Haven, CT: Yale University Press.
Clarke, J. 2010. "Of Crises and Conjunctures: The Problem of the Present." *Journal of Communication Inquiry* 34 (4): 337–54. https://doi.org/10.1177/0196859910382451.
Clarke, J., D. Bainton, N. Lendvai, and P. Stubbs. 2015. *Making Policy Move: Towards a Politics of Assemblage and Translation*. Bristol: Policy. https://doi.org/10.1332/policypress/9781447313366.001.0001.
Clarke, J., and J. Newman. 2012. "The Alchemy of Austerity." *Critical Social Policy* 32 (3): 299–319. https://doi.org/10.1177/0261018312444405.
Corsetti, G. 2012. "Has Austerity Gone Too Far?" VOX, 2 April. http://www.voxeu.org/article/has-austerity-gone-too-far-new-vox-debate.
Dean, J. 2014. "Tales of the Apolitical." *Political Studies* 62 (2): 452–67. https://doi.org/10.1111/1467-9248.12035.
Ferguson, J. 2006. *Global Shadows: Africa in the Neo-liberal World Order*. Durham, NC: Duke University Press. https://doi.org/10.1215/9780822387640.
Gilbert, J. 2013. "What Kind of Thing Is 'Neoliberalism'?" *New Formations* 80–1: 7–22. https://doi.org/10.3898/nEWF.80/81.IntroductIon.2013.
Gómez, L. 2014. "The Untamed Ambition of Podemos, the Surprise Victor in Sunday's Poll." *El País in English*, 26 May. http://elpais.com/elpais/2014/05/26/inenglish/1401117195_606542.html.
Gramsci, A. 1971. *Selections from the Prison Notebooks*, edited by Geoffrey Nowell Smith and Quintin Hoare. London: Lawrence and Wishart.
Guajardo, Jaime, Daniel Leigh, and Andrea Pescatori. 2014. "Expansionary Austerity? International Evidence." *Journal of the European Economic Association* 12 (4): 949–68. https://doi.org/10.1111/jeea.12083.
Guardian. n.d. "Bank Reforms: How Much Did We Bail Them Out and How Much Do They Still Owe?" https://www.theguardian.com/news/datablog/2011/nov/12/bank-bailouts-uk-credit-crunch.
Hall, S. 1979. "The Great Moving Right Show." *Marxism Today*, 14–20 January.
– 1988. *The Hard Road to Renewal*. London: Lawrence and Wishart.
Hall, S., C. Critcher, T. Jefferson, J. Clarke, and B. Roberts. 1978. *Policing the Crisis: Mugging, the State and Law and Order*. Basingstoke, UK: Macmillan.
Hasan, M. 2012. "Strivers v Shirkers? Ten Things They Don't Tell You about the Welfare Budget." *Huffington Post*, 17 December. http://www.huffingtonpost.co.uk/mehdi-hasan/welfare-budget-10-things-they-dont-tell-you_b_2314578.html.

Horvat, S. 2014. "The Return of the Left in Europe." Aljazeera, 31 May. http://www.aljazeera.com/indepth/opinion/2014/05/leftist-parties-eu-elections-2014531151436907842.html.
Independent. 2014. "The Death of Equality." 13 October.
Kirwan, S., M. McDermont, and J. Clarke. 2016. "Imagining and Practising Citizenship in Austere Times." *Citizenship Studies* 20 (6–7): 764–78.
Kittel, B., and H. Obinger. 2003. "Political Parties, Institutions, and the Dynamics of Social Expenditure in Times of Austerity." *Journal of European Public Policy* 10 (1): 20–35.
Korpi, W., and J. Palme. 2003. "New Politics and Class Politics in the Context of Austerity and Globalization: Welfare State Regress in 18 Countries, 1975–95." *American Political Science Review* 97 (3): 425–46. https://doi.org/10.1017/S0003055403000789.
Krugman, P. 2013. "How the Case for Austerity Has Crumbled." *New York Review of Books*, 6 June.
Kynaston, D. 2007. *Austerity Britain 1945–51*. London: Bloomsbury.
– 2010. "Austerity Was a Hard Sell in the 40s. Today It's Harder Still." *Guardian*, 21 June. http://www.theguardian.com/commentisfree/2010/jun/21/austerity-hard-sell-budget-2010.
Laclau, E. 2002. *On Populist Reason*. London: Verso Books.
Lustig, N., ed. 1995. *Coping with Austerity: Poverty and Inequality in Latin America*. Washington, DC: Brookings Institution.
McKee, M., M. Karanikolos, P. Belcher, and D. Stuckler. 2012. "Austerity: A Failed Experiment on the People of Europe." *Clinical Medicine* 12 (4): 346–50. https://doi.org/10.7861/clinmedicine.12-4-346.
Mooney, G., and L. Hancock. 2012. "Poverty Porn and the Broken Society." *Variant* 39/40. http://www.variant.org.uk/39_40texts/povertp39_40.html.
O'Hara, M. 2014. *Austerity Bites: A Journey to the Sharp End of the Cuts in the UK*. Bristol: Policy.
Ortiz, I., J. Chai, and M. Cummins. 2011. "Austerity Measures Threaten Children and Poor Households: Recent Evidence in Public Expenditures from 128 Developing Countries." Social Science Research Network. https://papers.ssrn.com/sol3/papers.cfm?abstract_id=1934510.
Osborne, G. 2012 "George Osborne's Speech to the Conservative Conference." *NewStatesman*, 8 October. http://www.newstatesman.com/blogs/politics/2012/10/george-osbornes-speech-conservative-conference-full-text.
Park, A., J. Curtice, and C. Bryson, eds. 2014 *British Social Attitudes 31*. London: National Centre for Social Research.
Peck, J. 2010. *Constructions of Neoliberal Reason*. Oxford: Oxford University Press. https://doi.org/10.1093/acprof:oso/9780199580576.001.0001.

– 2012. "Austerity Urbanism." *City: Analysis of Urban Trends, Culture, Theory, Policy, Action* 16 (6): 626–55. https://doi.org/10.1080/13604813.2012.734071.
Pierson, P. 1998. "Irresistible Forces, Immovable Objects: Post-Industrial Welfare States Confront Permanent Austerity." *Journal of European Public Policy* 5 (4): 539–60. https://doi.org/10.1080/13501769880000011.
– 2002. "Coping with Permanent Austerity: Welfare State Restructuring in Affluent Democracies." *Revue française de sociologie* 43 (2): 369–406. https://doi.org/10.2307/3322510.
Ryan, F. 2015. "Why This Personal Independence Payment Anniversary Is No Celebration." *Guardian*, 8 April. https://www.theguardian.com/society/2015/apr/08/personal-independence-payment-anniversary-pip-disabled-coalition-benefit.
Sabin, Lamiat. 2015. "Supermarket Workers' Minimum Wage Pay Topped Up by £11bn in Benefits, Says Citizens UK." *Independent*, 12 April. http://www.independent.co.uk/news/uk/home-news/supermarket-workers-minimum-wage-pay-topped-up-by-11bn-in-benefits-says-charity-10170426.html.
Schui, F. 2014. *Austerity: The Great Failure*. New Haven, CT: Yale University Press.
Sheldrick, G. 2013. "'Working Is Not Worth It': Benefits Mum Rakes in £70,000 in Welfare." *Express*, 27 March. http://www.express.co.uk/news/uk/387308/Working-is-not-worth-it-Benefits-mum-rakes-in-70-000-in-welfare.
Social Justice Policy Group. 2006. *Breakdown Britain*. London: Centre for Social Justice.
– 2007. *Breakthrough Britain*, vol. 2. London: Centre for Social Justice.
Standing, G. 2011. *The Precariat: The New Dangerous Class*. London: Bloomsbury Academic.
Stuckler, D., and S. Basu. 2013. *The Body Economic: Why Austerity Kills*. New York: Basic Books.
Taylor-Gooby, P. 2013. *The Double Crisis of the Welfare State and What We Can Do about It*. Basingstoke, UK: Palgrave. https://doi.org/10.1057/9781137328113.
Thompson, E.P. 1971. "The Moral Economy of the English Crowd in the Eighteenth Century." *Past & Present* 50 (1): 76–136. https://doi.org/10.1093/past/50.1.76.
Weeks, K. 2012. *The Problem with Work: Feminism, Marxism, Antiwork Politics and Postwork Imaginaries*. Durham, NC: Duke University Press.
Williams, R. 1977. *Marxism and Literature*. Oxford: Oxford University Press.
Wren-Lewis, J. 2015. "The Austerity Con." *London Review of Books* 37 (4): 9–11.
Yeldan, A.E. 2001. "On the IMF-Directed Disinflation Program in Turkey: A Program for Stabilization and Austerity or a Recipe for Impoverishment and Financial Chaos?" https://papers.ssrn.com/sol3/papers.cfm?abstract_id=290539.
Zweiniger-Bargielowska, I. 2000. *Austerity in Britain: Rationing, Controls and Consumption, 1939–1955*. Oxford: Oxford University Press.

3 Speaking Austerity: Policy Rhetoric and Design beyond Fiscal Consolidation

SORIN MITREA

This chapter was originally entitled "We're Austerians Now." However, that was too colloquial and inaccurate: we have been austerians for quite some time. Which is to say, the underlying discourses of austerity (in parallel with rather than resulting from contemporary fiscal consolidation) have been historically and contemporarily celebrated and diffused to the level of "common sense."[1] Specifically, discourses on individual responsibility, sacrifice, discipline, the future, and reduced consumption form the basis of "moral austerity" as a discursive regime that transcends fiscal policy. The legibility of these discourses makes policy proscriptions and realities based on them more understandable and salient to individuals, and may explain why people have not "rallied against" austerity.[2] This chapter will explore the "common sense" of austerity in Canada by exploring the similar, austere ways we discuss obesity, consumer debt, and government debt. While the economic, ideological, material, political, and rhetorical elements of austerity have been analysed, the discursive message of austerity, its genealogy, and its legibility have not been sufficiently examined. At its most basic level, austerity is about disciplined and reduced consumption (Levitas 2012, 335). However, austerity is more than a material condition and policy orientation, it is a moral economy[3]

---

1 As "a way of thinking that is itself rarely thought about" (Knight 1998, 106; Hall and O'Shea 2013, 8).
2 Understanding austerity as a set of moral discourses diffused through common sense may help to explain disaffected (conditional, grudging) consent for its policies (Clarke and Newman 2012, 316; Borges et al. 2013).
3 The set of shared understandings and expectations of how an economy should work, how obligations and entitlements in addition to explicit rules of exchange should function (Clarke and Newman 2012, 315).

in which the politics of consumption are negotiated through material, temporal, and moral logics. "Moral austerity" inculcates and shapes a common sense around individual responsibility for reduced consumption as a virtuous necessity (Clarke, this volume). Failure to heed this call is framed as a threat to the future of the self and the community.

Crisis and Austere Trajectories

The contemporary political and policy interest in austerity is informed by the 2007–8 global financial crisis (GFC), which was the result of a private credit-led boom that was linked to the aggregation of complex and dangerous financial innovations (occurring in the United Kingdom and United States) (Boyer 2012, 284). Although neoliberal ideology may have failed, its practices continue by "presenting existing socio-economic conditions as failing and neoliberalism as the best solution" (Aalbers 2013, 1053). Thus, while the initial response to the crisis was widespread agreement on the need for stimulus – endorsed and supported by the G20 in November 2008 and in April 2009 – this quickly shifted to a "need to address growing deficits" (Levinson 2013, 92). It was at this point that a "bait and switch" occurred, wherein the debt of the global banking system (between $3 trillion and $13 trillion) was transitioned to government balance sheets, transmuting a banking crisis into a sovereign debt crisis generated by "out of control" public spending (93).

Austerity proponents claim that exorbitant public indebtedness is ruining the major economies and that neoliberal measures such as cutting spending (wages, prices, general spending, while cutting taxes) to eliminate deficits and debts would result in economic growth (Levinson 2013, 93; Blyth 2013, 2). Although this view was empirically and conceptually flawed,[4] it still gained traction with international policy experts (Levinson 2013, 94). Austerity policies also have "lock-in effects," wherein cuts to public expenditures, revenue, and less economic stimulus leave governments with fewer options for addressing economic downturns (91).

---

4 For example, the "seminal" work of Reinhart and Rogoff on the "causal" relationship between debt to GDP ratios and economic stagnation used incorrect data and excluded other data. Ultimately, the relationship was a simple correlation – slow growth was more likely to cause public debt than vice versa (Levinson 2013, 94).

Studying austerity is important for several reasons: (1) it is a response to an endogenous crisis in neoliberalism, which has *not* resulted in consistent articulations of alternatives, let alone their pursuit (Clarke and Newman 2012, 300); (2) it asymmetrically increases precarity, hurting the most vulnerable (Blyth 2013, 13; Ortiz and Cummins 2013, 55; MacGregor 1999, 108; Marks and Little 2010, 196); (3) the idea that austerity promotes growth ("expansionary austerity") has been conceptually and empirically disproven (Levinson 2013, 93; Russell, this volume). Indeed, countries that implemented austerity experienced declines in their GDP proportional to the intensity of austerity (Levinson 2013, 94; Krugman 2014); (4) it has public salience via disaffected consent (Borges et al. 2013; Clarke and Newman 2012, 316) – it was, after all, the 2010 "Word of the Year" according to Merriam-Webster (Walters 2013); (5) while austerity has been disproven to aid growth and has been demonstrated to cause suffering, it is still a politically salient idea (Boyer 2012, 283; McBride 2014; Krugman 2014) and framed as a shared responsibility and "virtuous necessity" (Clarke and Newman 2012, 316; Clarke, this volume).

The literature evinces several possibilities for explaining austerity's sustained salience and use, ranging from instrumental and ideological commitments to neoclassical economics (Levinson 2013), psychological lock-in effects on policy elites and politicians (McBride 2014), the obfuscation of neoliberal outcomes (Forkert 2014; Nicholson 2013; Levitas 2012), and the compounding effects of austerity policies (i.e., reduced revenues undermine the possibility of future spending) (Pierre 1995). However, these explanations do not address how austerity is *constructed* at its most basic discursive level as moralized individual responsibility for reduced consumption.

Austerity is more than a policy orientation, it is a moral economy built around practices of consumption that frame individual responsibility for reduced consumption as a practice of "good citizenship" (Wright and Roberts 2013, 572).[5] Failure to make the virtuously necessary shared sacrifices compelled by crisis threatens the future of the subject and the community (Clarke and Newman 2012, 316). I propose examining austerity as a moral discourse, analysing how the individualization, moralization, and responsibilization of consumption and the future may contribute to disaffected consent by constructing austerity as common sense.

---

5 Other valences include "fairness" (Clarke and Newman 2012).

This chapter is concerned[6] with how obesity, consumer debt, and government debt are framed by individuals and the state in Canada since the GFC so as to unpack the moral economy of austerity. Although moral austerity is tutelary insofar as it works to shape the behaviour of subjects through broad social relations or the state, it is reinforced by coercive mechanisms that work upon physical bodies and their material contexts,[7] constituting a "material base" of austerity in addition to the retrenchment of the social state (MacGregor 1999, 108; Marks and Little 2010). Moral austerity narratives are mobilized for subjects who are read by the state and social discourses as capable of self-responsibilizing (the alternative, for those "unwilling or unable," is abnegation, surveillance, and criminalization). The uncertainty inherent and constructed in moments of crisis results in the reassertion of moralized discourses *through* the state and other actors, evincing a growing interest in the character of the other (Hay 1999, 317; Wardhaugh 2007, 41). Parsing the historical roots of the concept of austerity (as reduced consumption), its moral valences, and the diffuse areas in which it operates in society may shed light on its resilience as a policy orientation.

Scope and Morality

Morality is important because public interest in politics increases when there are "moral issues" at stake, both in voter turnout (Schecter 2009, 89) and in discourses on social provision, such as questions of moral character levelled at welfare recipients (Clarke and Newman 2012, 311; Marks and Little 2010, 195). Concurrently, states are increasingly

---

6 This chapter will not explicitly address the instrumentality of this moral economy: (1) its function as a social structure of accumulation (Keil 2002; Levinson 2013); (2) its obfuscation of neoliberal outcomes, morally and discursively facilitating the devolution of social policy provision (Hall and O'Shea 2013; Pathak 2013); (3) exempting wealthy subjects by focusing on indebtedness (Keil 2002; Nicholson 2013; Levitas 2012). Rather, the focus is on how morality and consumption operate across contexts to demonstrate the legibility of austerity. Finally, the material influences (flexibilization, outsourcing, privatization, concentration of wealth, etc.) on the legibility of moral austerity (increasing and devolving responsibility for precarity to the individual while pushing a narrative of individual responsibility) deserve more time and attention than can be afforded in this chapter (Hall and O'Shea 2013; Whitworth and Carter 2014).
7 For example, workfare policies, the criminalization of poverty, and the growing conditionalities attached to and surveillance of social support for the vulnerable.

displaying paternalistic concern with everyday morality and self-regulation (Pathak 2014, 90; Forkert 2014, 41). Finally, the moralization of consumption (and work) is a historically legible discourse, ranging from Roman political commentary to the Judeo-Christian tradition to Puritanism and contemporary neoliberalism: reduced consumption, individual responsibility, self-reliance, sacrifice, and discipline are framed as virtues and tied to "good citizenship" (Walters 2013; Hudson and Coukos 2005, 9). Moral austerity, then, is a contemporary affirmation of these historical discourses focused on inculcating a sense of individual responsibility around reduced consumption so as to secure the future of the subject and community.

Moral austerity is particularly conducive to "common sense legibility" because it constructs *a shared discursive regime* of consumption that ties bodily discourses ("bloat," "tightening the belt"), moralism ("shared sacrifice and the future of the community"), and individual responsibility applied to the individual and the state. For example, obesity and (consumer/government) debt are both signs of immoral and irresponsible consumption that threaten the future of the Canadian health-care system or economy, the solution being individual or state "belt tightening" to contain this consumption (Elliott 2007, 139; Pinto 2013, 106; Knight 1998, 109). Moral austerity's discursive regime continues a tradition of anthropomorphizing the state through metaphors ("the body politic"), tying the state, the body, and the subject together to create a unified level of analysis while obfuscating neoliberal outcomes and retaining meaning across different contexts.

Methods and Common Sense

This chapter utilizes narrative policy analysis (NPA) to highlight how ideas and narratives (at times in place of "evidence") shape broad social discourses as well as policy conceptualization, choices, and implementation (e.g., framing welfarism as immoral dependence may be more likely to result in welfare-to-work programs instead of demand-side labour market policy) (Pinto 2013, 96).

In this way, moral austerity evokes the "common sense" of self-disciplined consumption as a moral, responsible, and individual act for the future of the self and the community. As former prime minister Stephen Harper remarked, "We have to govern ourselves responsibly, we have to live within our means ... to grab that [competitive] future" (Harper 2013).

Futurity, Consumption, and Responsibilization

Moral austerity is contingent on framing individual responsibility for reduced consumption as a "virtuous necessity" *because excess consumption threatens the future* of the self and the community (Clarke and Newman 2012, 306, 312). Externalizing legitimacy and realization to the future creates a temporal structure in which progress or even survival becomes contingent on a narrative of (at times "shared") sacrifice, subsequently foreclosing alternatives (Latimer 2013, 22). With moral austerity, government social support, "bailing out individuals," or demand-side labour market policies are foreclosed possibilities for individuals while increased taxation and regulation are discursively foreclosed for the state. Historically, austerity as a religious discourse was deeply interwoven with the futurity of sacrifice wherein present asceticism was to be rewarded in the afterlife (Walters 2013). Although shared sacrifice acknowledges the inherent interdependence of human society, it often elides (but is contingent on) the subject or object *for which sacrifice is undertaken* (Nail 2013). In the case of contemporary austerity, the contingent element is the future self *but also the future of the polis*[8] (Nail 2013).

"Virtuous necessity" frames austerity (as reduced consumption) as "necessary," and its adoption illustrates an act of virtue through moral framings of the irresponsibility of "excess consumption" (Clarke and Newman 2012, 306, 312). The necessity of reduced consumption in Canada is framed via "shared sacrifice": government "cannot afford" the cost of excessive benefits for public sector workers (and the cost of welfare programs), and so must "tighten the belt like families do" (Brennan 2013). Here moral austerity frames the state as irresponsibly consuming public finances *because* it undermines the future of the polity.

Part of the behavioural goals of moral austerity are to inculcate self-containment via responsibilizing reduced consumption. In "crises" in which resources are framed as scarce, reduced consumption becomes a moral imperative so that the subject is contained and does not become a burden on the community (Evans 2011, 552). The ethic of material and economic restraint was a defining element of the Protestant ethic, common to all Judeo-Christian traditions and virtually all

---

8 Obfuscating the structural dispossession and concentration of wealth, power, and opportunity in neoliberal societies (Nicholson 2013; Levitas 2012; Keil 2002).

major religions, found in early American moralism, economic theories, self-help books, discourses on the body, and relatively recent trends of neoliberal devolution (552). Reduced consumption is also defined by futurity in moral austerity, wherein government and individuals must manage their "excess" (debt and/or obesity) for "their own future" as well as for the community's. However, moral austerity's narrative of individual responsibility for reduced consumption illustrates a contradiction (which will be explored later) insofar as late capitalism is driven tremendously by private (individual) consumption.

Moral austerity utilizes responsibilization to construct a common sense of individual responsibility based on the assumption that rises in inequality and poverty are a result of individual failings rather than structural design (MacGregor 1999, 108). Responsibilization through state policies morally equates self-care, discipline, responsibility, and self-containment ("you are responsible for yourself, but also for your effect on others") with good citizenship and the realization of future security (Whitworth and Carter 2014, 110). Prominent in the Protestant ethic, responsibility today is bound with notions of responsiveness, answerability, and agency (Trnka and Trundle 2014, 137). In the case of moral austerity, the individual is called upon to *answer* the moral weight of improper consumption (as a personal choice for which each is responsible – intersecting with rational choice theory) and its future consequences (for the subject and society) through discipline, sacrifice, and reduced consumption (138). Thus, while responsibility can operate in non-individualizing discursive regimes, it is framed through autonomy (individualization) and personal choice by austerity as "common sense" (137; Knight 1998, 125; Whitworth and Carter 2014, 110). The common sense legibility of individual responsibility for reduced consumption (as will be demonstrated below) circumscribes political possibilities and may contribute to disaffected consent.

Austere Histories

"The newest ideologies are a mere reprise of the oldest, which long antedate those hitherto known." (Adorno and Horkheimer 2002, 42)

The history of austerity's discursive foundations – moral and individual responsibility for reduced consumption to secure the future of the self and community – are historically far reaching. What follows are brief forays into interconnected moments that illustrate the historical legibility of austerity's discourses and a social and political interest in the character of the other. Moral austerity is present in pre- and non-Judeo-Christian traditions, including Sufi texts such as Al-Ghazali's writings on the austerity of the Prophet Muhammed and the argument of non-Christian Roman historian Ammianus Marcellinus (typical in the fourth century) that Rome fell to the Visigoths because it was "infected by the effeminacy of a laxer way of life" (Walters 2013).

The Latin root of the word *austerity* is *austerus*, which translates as "severe" and combines two strands of meaning: rectitude, strictness, and self-control combined with asceticism (Nicholson 2013, 26). Indeed, the language of sacrifice is inextricably bound with austerity (Nail 2013). In the Judeo-Christian tradition, austerity features prominently and transitions from explicit connotations of severity (towards others) to asceticism (a way of life *to which people submit themselves*): the rigorous religious practice of self-discipline, hard work, and abstinence (sacrificed consumption) as a testament to God, Jesus Christ, and the community exemplified by the "monastic way of life" (Walters 2013; Knight 1998). The balance between work and prayer was dissolved by Puritanism and the Protestant ethic, which focused on austerity (and work) as a core virtue *in and of itself* (Walters 2013).

The increasing "loss of faith" in the nineteenth century saw religious austerity shift towards secular moral austerity through the shifts of the Protestant ethic, inspiring a renewed and heightened moral zeal[9] (Hudson and Coukos 2005, 9). The Protestant ethic moralized "bourgeois virtues" of thrift (reduced consumption), self-reliance (self-containment), industry (activation), and self-discipline by framing their alternatives as the source of suffering: those who worked hard and had *personal fortitude to save* rather than spend (consume) *irresponsibly* would not only be most *socio-economically well off*, but also receive God's highest grace of *everlasting* salvation (futurity) (Kolozi 2013, 49). In this way, the Protestant ethic bound morality, individualism, and self-responsibility regarding consumption with sacrifice and discipline as necessary values for the future of the subject and community.

The history of moral austerity, from (pre-)Judeo-Christian notions, to the Protestant ethic, to Margaret Thatcher in England and Mike Harris[10]

---

9 Seen today in obsessions with the moral character of welfare recipients (Clarke and Newman 2012, 311).
10 Ontario's premier from 1995 to 2002 who campaigned on a populist and austere platform.

in Canada were marked by these beliefs (Hudson and Coukos 2005, 9). In this way, austerity fuses righteousness and morality with reduced consumption and physical deprivation *contingent on self-discipline* (Nicholson 2013, 26). Tying moral worth (and later, "good citizenship") with individual austerity is instrumentally useful for inculcating responsibilization. Indeed, the erosion of social rights through austerity is often framed through the language of sacrifice as a necessary factor for economic recovery (Nail 2013). However, whether altruistic (e.g., parents sacrificing consumption for their children) or instrumental (e.g., the religious logic that renunciation will be rewarded), sacrifice is a moral and virtuous act undertaken *by the self for the future*.

Liberalism, Rational Choice Theory, and Neoliberal Common Sense

Austerity's policy (and economic) history is woven through liberal political thought, rational choice theory, and neoliberal common sense. In response to the concentrated power of the absolutist state, Liberalism constructed the individual as a unitary, self-interested actor whose autonomy (individual rights privileged over group rights or concerns) was paramount (Held 2006, 262–8). Liberal economics shared this anxiety of the state, particularly its far-reaching powers of arbitrary dispossession and arguing that its debts were deeply problematic (Smith and Hume in the eighteenth and nineteenth centuries) (Blyth 2013, 116). Consequently, the state was something to be distrusted, curtailed, bypassed, *and therefore* minimized (116). Although austerity policies do not apply to the pre-twentieth century because there were no large spending states to target, there was in its place a common sense as to the role and scope of the state in life (116).

These principles are evident contemporarily in neoliberalism and rational choice theory, the latter providing ostensibly "scientific" (via behavioural psychology) legitimation for individual self-interest and self-constitution,[11] thereby informing responsibilization (Stewart 1993, 317–18). The rise of neoliberalism is marked by the increasing legibility of several ideas in policy, politics, economics, and culture: (1) the individual is the normative centre of society and should be as unencumbered as possible by rules and collective responsibilities; (2) the market

---

11 The idea that life experiences are a result of individual choices and abilities, eliding context and social structures.

is the most effective means through which individuals can maximize their own utility; (3) state actions that interfere with individual autonomy or market relations lead to an autocratic society, regardless of intentions (Pierre 1995, 55–6; Hackworth and Moriah 2006, 511).

While the public sector became increasingly involved in the market in the immediate post–Second World War period (so as to sustain redistribution and gain access to private sector growth), the 1970s–1980s saw the reverse as a result of decreasing private sector growth and political shifts towards neoliberalism (Pierre 1995, 55–6). The contemporary moment, in contrast, is characterized by a convergence of politics and economics "because economic theory and a general market based philosophy[12] are penetrating areas that used to be reserved for political control" (56). The marketization of the state has been met with social diffusion or "neoliberal common sense" characterized by competitive, individualistic market-driven, entrepreneurial, and profit-oriented outlooks (Hall and O'Shea 2013, 11). Although it is likely that few have read Adam Smith, David Hume, or John Locke in detail or in passing, many do not question the foundational logic and rationality of free markets, competition, and individual responsibility (and self-interest) espoused by neoclassical economics (10). Neoliberalism offers strong moral judgments of dependence (and "laziness") and government size/scope (criticizing "tax and spend" parties) (15). Neoliberal common sense, particularly in an age of austerity marked by the scarcity of support, employment, and growth, cultivates an obsession with questions of morality, moral character, and possibilities of moral rescue or reformation around work and debt (Clarke and Newman 2012, 311; Marks and Little 2010, 195).

Indeed, responsibilizing discourses in state policies were the result of neoconservative critiques (rooted in the Protestant ethic) of the "self-absorbed materialism" of consumer capitalism and evince a tension with an economy driven by private consumption (Kolozi 2013, 45). However, this tension may be key to maintaining private accumulation by situating the subject as individually responsible for bearing the precarity wrought by neoliberalism and austerity (in declining social supports, stagnating wages, employment, and working conditions, and

---

12 Including market criteria for allocating public resources, an emphasis on efficiency and results, limited regulation, expenditure cuts, privatization, and a general shift away from public solutions to social problems.

deteriorating democratic freedoms) (Levitas 2012, 331). Moral austerity's emphasis on individual responsibility for reduced consumption *is necessary* to legitimate and morally enforce the retrenchment of the state, while for capital it locates responsibility for weathering financial instability in the individual. In this way, the subject still consumes, but is utterly responsible for the consequences *and maintenance* (e.g., avoiding bankruptcy and the inability to consume via credit) of consumption (Forkert 2014, 44; Levinson 2013, 90).

Body as a Site and Spectacle

The human body is an important site for understanding the intersection of morality, consumption, the individual, and the state, because it has been a "persistent metaphor for social and political relations throughout human history" (Turner 2003, 2006; Clarke, this volume). The state and society are understood as a body via the "body politic" (e.g., the "head of state"), a metaphor for understanding the state, community, and consumption (Turner 2006, 224). For example, the depiction of the state in Hobbes's *Leviathan* is a man composed of a multitude of smaller men, while political science students in Canada understood municipalities and the federal government as a body (Laponce 1984, 988). Obesity connotes melancholy, excess, and lack of control and has been typically regarded as an *individual moral failure* and sign of social corruption, while diet and exercise (sacrifice and discipline) imply responsible regulation of the body, consequently benefiting society (Turner 2003, 2). Rationing (reduced consumption), as a form of self-containment, thus becomes a fundamental part of the management of the body *and* society (2).

A central theme in neoliberal critiques of the welfare state has been that a "bloated" public sector and welfare system have produced "bloated" subjects who consume (by collecting welfare) but do not produce (Pathak 2013, 64). The bodily metaphors of obesity politicize bodies and anthropomorphize politics in a way that allows the metaphors *and the meanings they contain* to travel across the state and subject (Wright and Roberts 2013, 580). The framing of reduced consumption as a moral virtue operates in a context of individual responsibility for self-sacrifice, discipline, and containment so as to protect the future of the self and society. Consequently, moral austerity's criticism of government "bloat" and responsibilization of consumer debt tie the state, the body, and the subject across a single individual level of analysis in order to facilitate a cohesive meaning, and thus common sense.

The Austere Body

Our first case study of moral austerity is bodily consumption: obesity, like individual debt and government debt, is framed nearly ubiquitously as a moral failure of the individual (Harrison 2012, 329; McPhail, Chapman, and Beagan 2011, 302). The media and government policies expound individual responsibility through self-disciplined consumption (and thus, sacrifice) as a way to contain the self, because "fat people" are "bad citizens" who put *the future* of themselves and the community at risk through their *irresponsibility* (Harrison 2012, 329). Good citizenship and good bodies are defined by *virtues* of self-control, discipline, reduced consumption, and containment (329). Obesity, like other areas of "dangerous consumption," engenders a social and political interest in the self-regulation of the other: discussions of Stephen Harper's 2006 visit to Kandahar and his views on seal hunting frequently focused on whether he was a good moral example for Canadians because he appeared overweight (Elliott 2007, 135). The body of a politician, therefore, is of interest to the body politic (135). In Canada, good citizenship is framed through bodily metaphors of leanness, while fatness is a moral failure and an example of bad citizenship (Elliott 2007; Harrison 2012; McPhail, Chapman, and Beagan 2011).

The individual's choice in moral austerity is consistently framed in the context of the effect on the community – how the citizen affects the polis – so as to maintain the primacy of the individual while providing a mechanism for responsibilization (Elliott 2007, 138). The socialized risk health-care system is of particular concern, with former Ontario minister of health promotion Jim Watson arguing, "As a taxpayer, I don't want to fund this person's quadruple bypass because they haven't taken care of themselves," while former health minister Anne McLellan began a "war on fat," stating that "fat Canadians imperil health care," as "the system could become unaffordable unless citizens take more responsibility for their health" (139). We cannot sustain our health-care system – representing a threat to the polis – if people are not individually responsible for their health by disciplining their consumption (139). Good citizenship is equated with answering the virtuous and common sense necessity of self-responsible containment and disciplined consumption; i.e., people who are "in control of their own bodies" (143).

The responsiblization of moral austerity is also illustrated in the Ontario Government's Health Plan for Battling Childhood Obesity, which focuses on educating parents (for children) and adolescents on how to make *"healthy choices"* to avoid obesity, because "it hurts all of us" by adding a burden to the health-care system (costing the Canadian "economy up to $7 billion a year") (Healthy Kids Panel 2013, 7; emphasis mine). Although stress, precarity, and the cost of healthy food are acknowledged as factors affecting obesity, the focus is overwhelmingly on individual responsibility to "make healthy food choices" and "cope with stresses"[13] (21, 24). Similarly, Health Canada's web portal on "healthy living" is titled "It's Your Health" and provides Canadians "with information [they] need to make *informed decisions* about [their] health and safety" (Health Canada 2013; emphasis mine). The "obesity" section states that *"poor eating habits* (excessive consumption; emphasis mine) [and their] contribution to obesity are critical public health challenges," focusing on individual behavioural failures as threats to the future of the community. According to Health Canada, obesity is addressed by "moderating the amount of food that you eat and by building physical activity in your daily life" (Health Canada 2013). Just as with the Plan for Battling Childhood Obesity, corporate interests and complicities are elided, as are social responses to structural problems such as stress, inequality, and cost of living. "Making good choices" evokes discipline and sacrifice: varieties of food and portion sizes contribute to improper consumption *if individuals choose to consume,* if they succumb to improper consumption. The common sense of these suggestions – better choices, exercise – sustains the legibility of moral austerity as an individual responsibility for reduced consumption.

The moralization of bodily consumption is increasingly commonsensical: regardless of social class, teenagers in Ontario discursively constructed themselves and others as healthy/unhealthy on the basis of fast food consumption (McPhail, Chapman, and Beagan 2011, 306). One girl said that watching her overweight sister eat "kind of disgusts [her]," while a teen boy said, "People eat really horribly. The obesity rates around here [are] out of control" (304). Teens frequently contrasted themselves with those who were perceived to irresponsibly consume fast food: "[*Other people*] have reckless abandon for their health," while participants called fast food "super greasy," "disgusting," "gross," and

---

[13] This is not to say that individual responsibility is not an important element in good health/debt outcomes, but moral austerity's responsibilization utilizes the concept to devolve risk to individuals, abnegating them.

"nasty" (305, 304). "Good and bad" citizenship, in this case, is morally constructed through improper and excessive consumption: the most idealized citizen was the one who never consumed fast food, followed by those who did rarely *and felt guilty* (and are therefore saveable!), while those who consumed the most *and felt no guilt* were the worst, as they were the least responsible and the most deviant (306). This is crucial, because it demonstrates how moral austerity's responsibilization of consumption has common sense legibility (306).

A Responsible Government Is an Austere Government

Moral austerity's concern with bodies in terms of consumption, discipline, sacrifice, and obesity extends to contemporary discourses of the state and organizations. In neoliberalism, central government is seen as an excess, a sort of "political obesity," while "lean government" will result from a regimentation of society and responsible self-discipline of the body: a "lean and mean state (via decentralized and localized provision) can provide better social services" (Turner 2006, 224; Turner 2003, 2). Austerity is directly informed by these moral ideas of government size and consumption, demanding a smaller and less intrusive state *for the good of the community* (Knight 1998). Government debt (consumption) is also stigmatized as amoral spending that "we can't afford" (Turner 2003, 3; Knight 1998, 109). If obesity is framed as a loss of sovereignty over the body, than governmental obesity via debt is a loss of control in the body politic.

In Canada, the rise of neoliberal common sense is exemplified in Ontario's "Common Sense Revolution" promulgated by Mike Harris, wherein what was framed as a "crisis" of exorbitant public indebtedness (resulting from "irresponsible fiscal management," as opposed to trade deficits and shifts in the regional political economy) sought to shape common sense around right-wing populism, a strong "us vs them" rhetoric, and the moralization of consumption (Knight 1998, 106). The legacy of the Protestant ethic is evident in Harris's goal of creating a system that "rewards ... values such as hard work, personal responsibility, self-reliance, [and] individual initiative" (Knight 1998, 127). There was a moral resonance around budgetary deficits and their "sources" (e.g., "bloated" bureaucracy, public sector benefits, and lazy and dependent welfare recipients) as costs that Ontario "couldn't afford," with governmental and personal austerity as the only solution (125; Kolozi 2013, 49). In this way, debt was framed as *morally suspect* and a *burden on future generations.* Both individual bodies (welfare recipients) and the body politic (state debt and expenditures) must internalize self-discipline and reduce their consumption in order to contain themselves and secure the future of the community (Clarke, this volume).

Austerity returned to Canada after the GFC, with 2010 marking a new round of fiscal austerity featuring social service retrenchment, devolution, and privatization, with spending cuts to federal departments and freezes to some public sector operating budgets intended to save $17.6 billion over five years[14] (Whiteside 2014, 175). Austerity policies are framed as responses to "crisis" in Canada so as to construct a "climate of fear" around economic insecurity, its "decadent" causes, and the promise of continued precarity (Russell 2014, 55). This framing evokes moralizing responses targeting those (including the state) who "consume irresponsibly" as threats to the future of the community (Hay 1999, 317; Wardhaugh 2007, 41). Even in late 2014 in Canada when the budget was all but balanced, former prime minister Harper called "alternatives" to austerity (not cutting spending, increasing taxes, and "ignoring" deficits) "basket cases" (Canadian Press 2014b).

While the virtuous necessity of "shared sacrifice" often means abnegating the most vulnerable, it is also used to discipline government spending (MacGregor 1999, 108; Marks and Little 2010, 196). One opinion piece before the Ontario 2014 election stated, "If you make five bucks a day, you can't spend ... eight ... It's time to tighten some public belts," while an editorial argued that government must be forced "to live within its means as families across this province do every day in tough times" (Simpson 2014; Editorial 2014). Progressive Conservative candidate Tim Hudak said directly, "We are asking government to tighten its belt, the way everyday Ontarians have," in order to "bring back jobs" (Hudak 2014). However, moral austerity has engulfed the political spectrum, shifting questions to how austerity should be implemented rather than whether it should be. For example, the (ostensibly) social democrat New Democratic Party's Andrea Horwath stated, "If citizens are expected to tighten their belts ... it's only right that government does the same," while the centrist Liberal Party's Kathleen Wynne tasked Finance Minister Charles Sousa with "tightening the province's belt" and said, "Government could be leaner" (Canadian Press 2014a; Babbage 2014;

---

14 Budget 2012 introduced cuts totalling $5.2 billion; Budget 2013 reduced transfers to persons (particularly the elderly), a freeze in operational funding, and an asset fire sale; Budget 2014 saw $14 billion in cuts (Macdonald 2014).

Brennan 2013). Shared sacrifice intersects with expansionary austerity as a form of futurity while identifying the "sources of excess consumption" (debt): Tim Hudak stated, "There is going to be so much debt in the province to pay for unaffordable increases for government workers" that investment will be driven away (Brennan 2013). Government consumption (expenditure and debt) is framed in the same way that individual obesity and consumer debt are: bodily discourses ("belt tightening" as shared sacrifice) evoking moral laxity, individual irresponsibility, and over-consumption. The virtuous necessity of austerity (reduced consumption) is anchored in the futurity of economic performance and job growth, sustaining moral austerity's common sense.

Austere Citizenship

In the post-GFC period, moral austerity was increasingly deployed in discourses on consumer and government debt (Mahmud 2012, 482). After the crisis, bodily discourses were evoked: "Fat consumer debt biggest risk in Canada" and "similar with any diet ... we advise Canadians to take a hard look at discretionary spending [improper consumption] and be prepared to make some *tough choices* on where to *trim the fat*" (Mudry et al. 2014, 55, emphasis mine; Babad 2012; Remiorz 2013). These discourses build on the moralization of obesity as a sign of *individual* moral laxity, irresponsible consumption, and lack of control marked by "bad choices" (resulting from ignorance, incompetence, or sheer irresponsibility) (Mudry et al. 2014, 65). This lack of control, then, is framed as a threat to the polis, which can be remedied only by taking responsibility, disciplining the self, and making sacrifices ("tough choices") to reduce improper consumption and its build-up ("debt-fat").

The shift from a concern over general consumption to a specific concern with debt builds upon the Protestant ethic's fear and stigmatization of debt (as feckless, greedy, decadent), constructing saving as its positive moral opposite (thrift, frugality, discipline) (Kolozi 2013, 50; Livingstonel and Lunt 1993, 966). What emerges is a kind of "debt morality" in which "over-consumption" threatens the future of the subject and polity, necessitating self-disciplined sacrifice (Forkert 2014, 47).

The common sense of moral austerity is evident in opinions on consumer debt. A Royal Bank of Canada (RBC) poll conducted in October 2013 stated, "38 per cent [of] Canadians are anxious about their debt levels, up from 34 per cent in 2012" (RBC 2013). However, moral austerity was on the horizon, as "there is a noticeable trend to *responsible debt behaviour* over the past year," with Canadians "reining in spending" (RBC 2013; emphasis mine). Of course, the ratio of Canadian household debt to disposable income reached a record 163.3 per cent in March 2015 (Canadian Press 2015a). Although responsibilization utilizes moral discourses to inculcate reduced consumption, it cannot account for the material effects of austerity in lower growth, which results in precarious employment and low compensatory interest rates, all driving consumers to spend and survive on credit. However, increasing debt may be due to survival, rather than "irresponsible," consumption, as Canadian retail sales dropped by 2.3 per cent in February 2015 (despite plummeting gas prices) (Canadian Press 2015b).

Similar to the children who delineated moral and non-moral behaviour through fast food consumption, non-debtors subscribe to a "common sense" notion that debt is morally wrong: one man was "strongly against debt and considers that debts are a source of shame, indicating a failure to manage one's money," while another woman was "strongly opposed to debt [and] believes strongly that people's lives are under their own control and that how things turn out is their responsibility" (Livingstonel and Lunt 1993, 977–83).

Moral austerity's concern with individual responsibility for reduced consumption is on display in the post-GFC financial literacy narratives in Canada, defined as the "knowledge and skills needed to make *responsible* economic and financial *decisions*" (Pinto 2013; emphasis mine; Ministry of Education 2010, 7). The "virtuous necessity" of individual responsibility to reduce consumption is underscored by the effect that failure would have on the future of the community: as former finance minister Jim Flaherty said, "Our economy is built on millions of everyday financial decisions by Canadians" who "cannot effectively manage their personal finances" (Task Force on Financial Literacy 2010; Pinto 2013, 105). MPP Leeanna Pendergast, co-chair of the task force stated, "Students today are ... *future* consumers and investors. We have to *change habits and nurture ... a culture of responsibility*" (Pinto 2013, 106; emphasis mine). The task force constructed "good citizens" by evoking a moral responsibility to discipline consumption for the future of the nation, wherein financial literacy helps people responsibilize into "*caring citizens who can contribute to a strong economy and cohesive society*" (Ministry of Education 2010, 21; emphasis mine; Pinto 2013, 111). Financial education also teaches individuals "the discipline to save" and budgeting in order to keep debt "under control" (Ministry of Education 2010, 21). These quotes highlight the state's deepening interest in individual morality, compelling responsibilization through appeals to the future of Canada's economy.

Moral austerity's responsibilization in consumer debt makes the future of the Canadian economy contingent on the reduced consumption and containment of individual debt as a virtuous necessity. This "common sense" policy narrative obfuscates the devolution of responsibility to the individual, while industry is insulated from further regulation, because, as Jim Flaherty stated, "Consumer protection is only one side of this 'two-sided coin,' where the other side is personal responsibility" (Pinto 2013, 106). This illustrates Joseph Stiglitz's (2011) argument that neoclassical economics has long proceeded on the assumption that macroeconomic policy is contingent on the execution of microeconomics, ultimately eliding the former in favour of micro-regulation: an ideal site for the responsibilization of moral austerity and financial citizenship (167)!

Austere Conclusions?

Austerity is more than a policy orientation or material condition, it is a moral discourse in which consumption is politicized and anthropomorphized to facilitate responsibilization. The future becomes the temporal site for which virtuously necessary shared sacrifice is undertaken. This shared discursive regime has been applied to obesity, government debt, and consumer debt in Canada since the GFC. Indeed, austerity as an adjective is a powerful idea, conjuring images of effort, discipline, and moral superiority: an austere person is self-controlling, disciplined, and responsible, one who is able to put "higher things" first, unlike "lesser, impulsive" people (Nicholson 2013, 27). Individual austerity is framed as being just as virtuous, essential, and beneficial as that undertaken by the state (26; Levinson 2013, 93; Blyth 2013, 2). This analysis speaks to and complicates the dichotomy between imposed and self-inflicted austerity insofar as the common sense of individual responsibility for reduced consumption is diffused and widely legible.

The common sense legibility of moral austerity is likely due in no small part to the fact that individual responsibility is a necessary virtue in social relations – neoliberal or otherwise. The common sense of moral austerity delineates the range of acceptable understandings and responses to consumption, leading us to question what these discursive dynamics say about the relationship between the state and citizens. Perhaps we can read moral austerity and responsibilization as forms of securitization, of locating risk in individuals and containing them. Moral austerity works to create self-reliant (contained), self-disciplining, and flexible (overall, docile) bodies that can bear more and more risks so that wealth and power can be perpetually concentrated (Mahmud 2012, 483).

REFERENCES

Aalbers, M.B. 2013. "Debate on Neoliberalism in and after the Neoliberal Crisis." *International Journal of Urban and Regional Research* 37 (3): 1053–7. https://doi.org/10.1111/1468-2427.12061.

Adorno, T., and M. Horkheimer. 2002. *The Dialectic of Enlightenment*, ed. G.S. Noerr, trans. E. Jephcott. Stanford: Stanford University Press.

Babad, M. 2012. "Fat Consumer Debt Biggest Risk in Canada, Mark Carney Says." *Globe and Mail*, 8 March. http://www.theglobeandmail.com/report-on-business/top-business-stories/fat-consumer-debt-biggest-risk-in-canada-mark-carney-says/article552230/.

Babbage, M. 2014. "Wynne Warns of 'Difficult Choices' Ahead." CTV News, 24 June. http://toronto.ctvnews.ca/wynne-warns-of-difficult-choices-ahead-1.1883866.

Blyth, M. 2013. *Austerity: The History of a Dangerous Idea*. Oxford: Oxford University Press.

Borges, W., H.D. Clarke, M.C. Stewart, D. Sanders, and P. Whiteley. 2013. "The Emerging Political Economy of Austerity in Britain." *Electoral Studies* 32 (3): 396–403. https://doi.org/10.1016/j.electstud.2013.05.020.

Boyer, R. 2012. "The Four Fallacies of Contemporary Austerity Policies: The Lost Keynesian Legacy." *Cambridge Journal of Economics* 36 (1): 283–312. https://doi.org/10.1093/cje/ber037.

Brennan, R.J. 2013. "Tim Hudak Targets 'Giveaways to Government Workers.'" *Toronto Star*, 4 December. https://www.thestar.com/news/queenspark/2013/12/04/tim_hudak_targets_giveaways_to_government_workers.html.

Canadian Press. 2014a. "Andrea Horwath Promises 'Accountability' Minister." CBC News, 14 May. http://www.cbc.ca/news/canada/toronto/ontario-votes-2014/andrea-horwath-promises-accountability-minister-1.2642953.

– 2014b. "Stephen Harper Targets Justin Trudeau in Speech to Supporters in Calgary." CBC News, 7 July. http://www.cbc.ca/news/politics/stephen-harper-targets-justin-trudeau-in-speech-to-supporters-in-calgary-1.2698447.

– 2015a. "Canadian Household Debt Hits Record High of 163.3% of Disposable Income." HuffPost Business, 12 March. http://www.huffingtonpost.ca/2015/03/12/household-debt-canada-2015_n_6854406.html.

- 2015b. "Canadian Retail Sales Post Biggest Drop since April, 2010." HuffPost Business, 20 February. 20http://www.huffingtonpost.ca/2015/02/20/statistics-canada-says-re_n_6720404.html.
Clarke, J., and J. Newman. 2012. "The Alchemy of Austerity." *Critical Social Policy* 32 (3): 299–319. https://doi.org/10.1177/0261018312444405.
Editorial. 2014. "We Endorse Tim Hudak, for Ontario." *Toronto Sun*, 8 June. http://www.torontosun.com/2014/06/08/we-endorse-tim-hudak-for-ontario.
Elliott, C.D. 2007. "Big Persons, Small Voices: On Governance, Obesity, and the Narrative of the Failed Citizen." *Journal of Canadian Studies / Revue d'études canadiennes* 41 (3): 134–49. https://doi.org/10.3138/jcs.41.3.134.
Evans, D. 2011. "Thrifty, Green or Frugal: Reflections on Sustainable Consumption in a Changing Economic Climate." *Geoforum* 42 (5): 550–7. https://doi.org/10.1016/j.geoforum.2011.03.008.
Forkert, K. 2014. "The New Moralism: Austerity, Silencing, and Debt Morality." *Soundings: A Journal of Politics and Culture* 56 (56): 41–53. https://doi.org/10.3898/136266214811788808.
Hackworth, J., and A. Moriah. 2006. "Neoliberalism, Contingency and Urban Policy: The Case of Social Housing in Ontario." *International Journal of Urban and Regional Research* 30 (3): 510–27. https://doi.org/10.1111/j.1468-2427.2006.00675.x.
Hall, S., and A. O'Shea. 2013. "Common-Sense Neoliberalism." *Soundings: A Journal of Politics and Culture* 55:8–24. https://doi.org/10.3898/136266213809450194.
Harper, Stephen. 2013. "A Conversation with Stephen Harper." Council on Foreign Relations, 16 May. http://cfr.org/canada/conversation-stephen-harper-prime-minister-canada/p35473.
Harrison, E. 2012. "The Body Economic: The Case of 'Childhood Obesity.'" *Feminism & Psychology* 22 (3): 324–43. https://doi.org/10.1177/0959353512445357.
Hay, C. 1999. "Crisis and the Structural Transformation of the State: Interrogating the Process of Change." *British Journal of Politics and International Relations* 1 (3): 317–44. https://doi.org/10.1111/1467-856X.00018.
Health Canada. 2013. "It's Your Health." http://www.hc-sc.gc.ca/hl-vs/iyh-vsv/life-vie/index-eng.php.
Healthy Kids Panel. 2013. *No Time to Wait: The Healthy Kids Strategy*. Toronto: Queen's Printer for Ontario.
Held, D. 2006. *Models of Democracy*. 3rd ed. Stanford: Stanford University Press.
Hudak, T. 2014. "Tim Hudak, Candidate for Niagara West–Glanbrook in Ontario Provincial Election 2014." Raise the Hammer. http://elections.raisethehammer.org/candidate/252/4.

Hudson, K., and A. Coukos. 2005. "The Dark Side of the Protestant Ethic: A Comparative Analysis of Welfare Reform." *Sociological Theory* 23 (1): 1–24. https://doi.org/10.1111/j.0735-2751.2005.00240.x.

Keil, R. 2002. "'Common-Sense' Neoliberalism: Progressive Conservative Urbanism in Toronto, Canada." *Antipode* 34 (3): 578–601. https://doi.org/10.1111/1467-8330.00255.

Knight, G. 1998. "Hegemony, the Media, and New Right Politics: Ontario in the Late 1990s." *Critical Sociology* 24 (1/2): 105–29. https://doi.org/10.1177/089692059802400106.

Kolozi, P. 2013. "The Neoconservative Critiques of and Reconciliation with Capitalism." *New Political Science* 35 (1): 44–64. https://doi.org/10.1080/07393148.2012.754668.

Krugman, P. 2014. "The Return of Expansionary Austerity." *New York Times*, 11 April. https://krugman.blogs.nytimes.com/2014/04/11/the-return-of-expansionary-austerity/?_php=_php=true&_type=blogs&_php=true&_type=blogs&_r=1.

Laponce, J. 1984. "Nation-Building as Body-Building: A Comparative Study of the Personalization of City, Province and State by Anglophone and Francophone Canadians." *Theory and Methods* 23 (6): 977–91.

Latimer, H. 2013. "The Straight Line: Sexuality, Futurity, and the Politics of Austerity." *English Studies in Canada* 39 (4): 21–4. https://doi.org/10.1353/esc.2013.0046.

Levinson, M. 2013. "Austerity Agonistes." *Dissent* 60 (3): 91–5. https://doi.org/10.1353/dss.2013.0071.

Levitas, R. 2012. "The Just's Umbrella: Austerity and the Big Society in Coalition Policy and Beyond." *Critical Social Policy* 32 (3): 320–42. https://doi.org/10.1177/0261018312444408.

Livingstonel, S., and P. Lunt. 1993. "Savers and Borrowers: Strategies of Personal Financial Management." *Human Relations* 46 (8): 963–85. https://doi.org/10.1177/001872679304600804.

– 2014. "Budget 2014: Let Stagnation Reign." *Behind the Numbers: A Blog from the CCPA*, 11 February. http://behindthenumbers.ca/2014/02/11/budget-2014-let-stagnation-reign/.

MacGregor, S. 1999. "Welfare, Neo-Liberalism and New Paternalism: Three Ways for Social Policy in Late Capitalist Societies." *Capital and Class* 23 (1): 91–118. https://doi.org/10.1177/030981689906700104.

Mahmud, T. 2012. "Debt and Discipline." *American Quarterly* 64 (3): 469–94. https://doi.org/10.1353/aq.2012.0027.

Marks, L., and M. Little. 2010. "Ontario and British Columbia Welfare Policy: Variants on a Neoliberal Theme." *Comparative Studies of South Asia, Africa and the Middle East* 33 (2): 192–203.

- 2014. "In Austerity We Trust." In *Orchestrating Austerity*, ed. D. Baines and S. McBride, 20–8. Black Point, NS: Fernwood Publishing.
McPhail, D., G.E. Chapman, and B.L. Beagan. 2011. "'Too Much of That Stuff Can't Be Good': Canadian Teens, Morality, and Fast Food Consumption." *Social Science & Medicine* 73 (2): 301–7. https://doi.org/10.1016/j.socscimed.2011.05.022.
Ministry of Education. 2010. *A Sound Investment: Financial Literacy Education in Ontario School*. Toronto: Government of Ontario.
Mudry, T.E., I. Sametband, T. Strong, D. Wulff, J. Michel., and S. St George. 2014. "'Where I'm Coming From': A Discourse Analysis of Financial Advice Media." *Journal of Financial Therapy* 5 (1): 55–79. https://doi.org/10.4148/1944-9771.1055.
Nail, B.W. 2013. "Austerity and the Language of Sacrifice." Critical Religion Association, 15 October. https://criticalreligion.org/2013/10/15/austerity-and-the-language-of-sacrifice/.
Nicholson, M. 2013. "Fuck Austerity." *English Studies in Canada* 39 (4): 25–8. https://doi.org/10.1353/esc.2013.0053.
Ortiz, Isabel, and Matthew Cummins. 2013. "Austerity Measures in Developing Countries: Public Expenditure Trends and the Risks to Children and Women." *Feminist Economics* 19 (3): 55–81.
Pathak, P. 2013. "From New Labour to New Conservatism: The Changing Dynamics of Citizenship as Self-Government." *Citizenship Studies* 17 (1): 61–75. https://doi.org/10.1080/13621025.2012.716215.
- 2014. "Ethopolitics and the Financial Citizen." *Sociological Review* 62 (1): 90–116. https://doi.org/10.1111/1467-954X.12119.
Pierre, J. 1995. "The Marketization of the State: Citizens, Consumers, and the Emergence of the Public Market." In *Governance in a Changing Environment*, ed. G. Peters and D. Savoie, 55–81. Montreal and Kingston: McGill-Queen's University Press.
Pinto, L.E. 2013. "When Politics Trump Evidence: Financial Literacy Education Narratives Following the Global Financial Crisis." *Journal of Education Policy* 28 (1): 95–120. https://doi.org/10.1080/02680939.2012.690163.
RBC. 2013. "Canadians Paying Off Their Debt the Good Old-Fashioned Way – Spending Less: RBC Poll." 29 October. http://www.rbc.com/newsroom/news/2013/20131029-debt-poll.html
Remiorz, R. 2013. "Canadians Not Following Through on Debt Paydown Resolutions." CBC News, 30 April. http://www.cbc.ca/news/business/canadians-not-following-through-on-debt-paydown-resolutions-1.1336021.
Russell, E. 2014. "The Strategic Use of Budget Crises." In *Orchestrating Austerity*, ed. D. Baines and S. McBride, 44–55. Blackpoint, NS: Fernwood Publishing.

Schecter, D.L. 2009. "Legislating Morality outside of the Legislature: Direct Democracy, Voter Participation and Morality Politics." *Social Science Journal* 46 (1): 89–110. https://doi.org/10.1016/j.soscij.2008.12.002.

Simpson, P. 2014. "Tighten Public Belt and Stop Whining." *Hamilton Spectator*, 5 June. http://www.thespec.com/opinion-story/4557555-tighten-public-belt-and-stop-whining/.

Stewart, J. 1993. "Rational Choice Theory, Public Policy and the Liberal State." *Policy Sciences* 26 (4): 317–30. https://doi.org/10.1007/BF00999475.

Stiglitz, J. 2011. "Rethinking Macroeconomics: What Went Wrong and How to Fix It." *Global Policy* 2 (2): 165–75. https://doi.org/10.1111/j.1758-5899.2011.00095.x.

Task Force on Financial Literacy. 2010. *Canadians and Their Money: Building a Brighter Financial Future*. Ottawa: Government of Canada.

Trnka, S., and C. Trundle. 2014. "Competing Responsibilities: Moving beyond Neoliberal Responsibilization." *Anthropological Forum* 24 (2): 136–53. https://doi.org/10.1080/00664677.2013.879051.

Turner, B.S. 2003. "Social Fluids: Metaphors and Meanings of Society." *Body & Society* 9 (1): 1–10. https://doi.org/10.1177/1357034X03009100⁚.

– 2006. "Body." *Theory, Culture & Society* 23 (2–3): 223–29. https://doi.org/10.1177/0263276406062576.

Walters, J. 2013. "The Meaning of Austerity: Theological Perspectives." St Paul's Institute, 5 March. http://www.stpaulsinstitute.org.uk/dialogue/james-walters/article/2013/mar/05/the-meaning-of-austerity-theological-perspectives.

Wardhaugh, R. 2007. "Productivity and Popular Attitudes toward Welfare Recipients in Saskatchewan, 1970–1990." In *Redefining Productivity for Social Development and Well-being*, ed. F. Douglas and G. Geller, 41–74. Regina: University of Regina Press.

Whiteside, H. 2014. "P3s and the Value for Money Illusion." In *Orchestrating Austerity*, ed. D. Baines and S. McBride, 172–80. Blackpoint, NS: Fernwood Publishing.

Whitworth, A., and E. Carter. 2014. "Welfare-to-Work Reform, Power and Inequality: From Goveranance to Governmentalities." *Journal of Contemporary European Studies* 22 (2): 104–17. https://doi.org/10.1080/14782804.2014.907132.

Wright, B., and M. Roberts. 2013. "Reproducing 'Really Useful' Workers: Children's Television as an Ideological State Apparatus." *Rethinking Marxism* 25 (4): 566–91. https://doi.org/10.1080/08935696.2013.842700.

4 No Deal Capitalism: Austerity and the Unmaking of the North American Middle Class

ERIC PINEAULT

He is not aware of having any history, his past being brief as it is unheroic; he has lived through no golden age he can recall in time of trouble.

– Mills (1951, xvi)

To put it bluntly, classes do not exist as separate entities, look around, find an enemy class and then start to struggle. On the contrary, people find themselves in a society structured in determined ways (crucially but not exclusively, in production relations) they identify points of antagonistic interest, they commence to struggle around these issues and in the process of struggling they discover themselves as classes.

– Thompson (1978, 149)

The 2008 crisis and the austerity policies that followed have seen the emergence of new markers of class conflict: on the one hand the widespread adoption of the 99 per cent vs 1 per cent polarity, and on the other the omnipresence of discourses on the crisis, decline, and end of the North American middle class. From a Thompsonian perspective, one can say that the political economy of late neoliberalism is eventuating a new class polarity, a new process of class formation through polarization. It is an ongoing and emerging process, still frail and uncertain. But process it is, at least if we apply the great Thompsonian methodological principle that if it looks like class struggle, acts like class struggle, then it just might be class struggle.

In this chapter I will explore three interlinked issues. I will first examine in what way the emergence of the 1 per cent versus 99 per cent polarity express the social experience of ordinary North Americans of capitalist dynamics – dynamics that don't fit in a political economy where the "middle class" would be the hegemonic figure. I will then highlight how the debate on the unmaking of the middle class reflects an experience of the emerging contradictions of a "no deal" form of capitalism. Finally, I will sketch a theoretical model of class polarization that can make sense of the emerging polar figures of the 1 per cent as representing the power of capital and the 99 per cent as the experience of a wage-earning majority of new class relations to accumulation and conflict.

What's in a Name?

As ever-deepening social inequality becomes a core feature of advanced capitalist societies, the division between a proverbial 99 per cent and the 1 per cent has become a defining way to measure, illustrate, and denounce this growing rift in public discourse, in the policy community in North America, and among social movements on both sides of the Atlantic. One can go back to the original work by Edward N. Wolff, which culminated in *Top Heavy* to find the initial research on income and wealth, using percentiles such as the 1 per cent as a way to illustrate and analyse inequality. Looking back at Wolff's work in the 1990s and early 2000s such as Wolff (2010), these percentiles have a strictly descriptive function but no social substance. Furthermore, though the 1 per cent do figure prominently in the analysis of inequality that Wolff proposes, this stratum has no polar opposite. It designates a class called "the rich," whereas the rest of society is sliced up into wealth strata. There is no 99 per cent. Finally, the middle class, which is at the centre of Wolff's analysis, is loosely defined using median wealth ownership or through the more classical definition of those households found in the second, third, and fourth quintiles in a social stratification system based on a hierarchy of five strata. These comments do not in any way aim to diminish the quality of Wolff's pioneering work on the empirics of wealth inequality. On the contrary, it is methodologically and analytically sound, as it was scientifically relevant in the early 2000s. But it does highlight the qualitative change in the social representation of inequality brought on by the work of Thomas Piketty and Emmanuel Saez during this same period.[1]

---

1 For an overview of the "Picketty moment," see Foster and Yates (2014), on which much of what is developed in this section is based.

The first systematic work with a polarized representation of percentiles was a group of obscure working papers at the National Bureau of Economic Research published by Piketty and Saez on long-term top income trends for advanced capitalist countries (Piketty and Saez 2001). These papers where originally noticeable for the method of income and wealth measurement developed by both researchers, which consisted of the use of income tax micro data to produce long-term series on wealth and income distribution. The enquiry was widened through a collaboration involving economists and social scientists from a wide range of countries and culminating in the World Top Incomes Data Base. It was also in this work that the polarity between the 1 per cent and 99 per cent, in terms of wealth and income, was first expressed in dramatic forms through what became iconic statistical charts. It was through the migration of these charts from the geeky world of inequality research into the boisterous world of business media[2] and then mass media after the crisis of 2008 that the polarity entered the public sphere and gained social substance. Rather boring "variables" were gradually transfigured into markers of class polarity. By the time Piketty published his monumental *Capital in the Twentieth Century*, in French in 2013 and then in English a year later, the polarity had taken on a life of its own in public discourse and in the more discreet sphere of social research.[3] It had become standard fare for a growing number of empirical studies

---

2 A decisive event in this process was the publication by Citigroup of two infamous research notes on "Plutonomy" in the mid-2000s, which proposed a Marxian and one could even add Gramscian interpretation of Piketty and Saez's data as proof of the existence of a distinctive class and accumulation regime called Plutonomies in three large advanced capitalist countries: Canada, the United States, and the United Kingdom. The so-called Plutonomy memos have been deleted from Citigroup's website, but they can still be found in some corners of the web. They offer a sobering read.

3 As argued by many critics of Piketty, the main limitation of this work is the theoretical confusion surrounding the concept of capital. The reader can find an excellent review in Foster and Yates (2014). James Galbraith's review of *Capital* is by far the most decisive critique of Piketty on this topic. One can also find an excellent criticism in Lance Taylor (2014), as well as the responses by Harcourt and Nell in the same journal. For the purposes of this chapter, the main limit of Piketty is that he conflates various forms of wealth – financial and non-financial – with the more basic category of capital, and he supposes that an aggregate rate of return on this disparate assemblage of assets somehow is an objective economic reality instead of simply an awkward analytical construct. Moreover, Piketty does not propose a theory of class formation in advanced capitalism. This becomes particularly blatant when he examines the growth of business executive incomes.

on inequality by such agencies as the OECD and national agencies such as Statistics Canada. The latter's 2006 report entitled "Earnings and Incomes of Canadians over the Past Quarter Century" constructed around the 1 per cent and 99 per cent polarity was actually accused by right-wing pundits in the Canadian mainstream media of stirring up "class war."

For all its methodological limitations, the comparison captured public imagination, even though as a statistical tool it fails to define central features of contemporary inequalities. As shown early on by Piketty and Saez themselves (2001), the figure of the 1 per cent hides the fact that the real statistical group that is driving up its income and wealth share in many OECD societies is the 0.1 per cent or even the narrower 0.01 per cent. It also conflates very different forms of accumulation: finance-based, patrimonial, and corporate capitalist. The 99 per cent veils the very important differences in outcomes in the neoliberal era between the poor and excluded, the working poor and the upper-middle-class stratum of salaried professionals (Posca and Tremblay-Pepin 2013). Neither measure can express inequalities in race or gender. The figure of the "oppressed ninety-nine" in particular implies that well-paid professionals such as white male engineers, middling managers, or university professors become comrades in struggle with black and mostly female underpaid and precarious Walmart "associates" or young over-educated and racialized hamburger flippers. And neither number, in itself, expresses the forces or causes of the growing political economic rift in advanced societies.

That being acknowledged, the polarity remains an inescapable lens through which North Americans, in particular, continue – six years after Occupy, nine years after the great financial crisis – to refer, in order to come to terms with the inequalities engendered by decades of neoliberalism and advanced capitalist development. Beyond its usefulness and validity in social science, this numerical polarity of 1 per cent versus 99 per cent has imposed itself as a symbolic marker of a reflexive contradiction working the political economy and culture of our societies. Quantitative difference has acquired a disquieting qualitative reality: gradation has morphed into polarization. This in itself is important. In the North American hegemonic imaginary that came out of the New Deal and structured debate on inequalities during the second half of the twentieth century, social divisions were understood through the prism of a stratified continuum of social positions (Wright 2009; Schor 1985). Though there was no consensus concerning the stratifying principle, and social research did uncover barriers and mechanisms that entrapped certain categories of people inside a limited space of the continuum, the ladder of privilege was the dominant framework in which debate on inequality could take place. Even Marxists such as Erik Olin Wright or Nicos Poulantzas worked inside this framework, while searching for the exact lieu of a fundamental separation between capitalists and non-capitalists. The 1 per cent versus the 99 per cent expresses a system of class inequality outside of this framework. We have been forced to move on in popular discourse and among the economic policy community, from measures and expressions of stratification to one of polarization.

In this sense the 1 per cent and the 99 per cent, as well as their polarity, have become potent *signifiers* (Freitag 2011) in our political economy above and beyond the particular, variable, contradictory, and limited significations they have carried. It is my opinion that a critique of the political economy of advanced capitalism must neither dismiss these signifiers as ideological veils devoid of value, nor lionize or fetishize them. As signifiers they are able to structure expressions, both popular and scientific, personal and public, as well as give voice to policies and protests, because they carry and mediate significance: they make sense where other categories such as bourgeois, proletarian, petty bourgeois, and white collar don't. Our task is thus to analyse how these signifiers have come to mediate the social understandings of inequality and what their ascendance teaches us about the nature and presence of class division and struggle and ultimately contradiction in contemporary capitalism. Finally, by taking these words seriously – as categories of practice and praxis – we can contribute to the experiential process described by Thompson of class formation in a context where class struggle seems, for the moment, a top-down affair, as the critical analysis of neoliberalism as a political economy regime has shown.

What then is in a name such as the 1 per cent or the 99 per cent? Certainly not a statistical truth, an exact measure that distributes individuals or households precisely into discrete groups. Rather, we are confronted with a principle of partition or division of society based on polarization between groups whose contours are difficult to measure precisely because of the dynamic nature of this form of social division. Both groups are being driven apart from one another, economic development is pulling them on distinct trajectories, inequality is a result, as is the moral/political problem that emerges from this disjoined trajectory. Both groups are formed in the process of polarization; neither pre-exists this dynamic. In fact, each signifier of the polar structure functions as a powerful metonym; each number "stands for" a social category in construction. The 99 per cent as opposed to the 1 per cent means "everybody" and anybody; the metonym designates not the majority but stands for normalcy. The metonym 1 per cent does not designate a minority, but the abnormal, the exception, the statistical aberration, what should not be but has become.[4] This temporal element between the 1 per cent and the 99 per cent is crucial; it designates a form of historicity. The 1 per cent[5] through their economic and political trajectory in the last decades have differentiated themselves from the rest of society and *thus have produced the unity of the 99 per cent*. And it is because the 1 per cent is "what should not be, but is becoming" that the 99 per cent has become the "oppressed" 99 per cent of Occupy. The appearance of these signifiers in public discourse implies the recognition, not only of a processual principle of partition based on opposition but of a space for the development of a normative principle of social justice that reflexively engages polarization.

The development of the 1 per cent is thus experienced as a historical force that has fundamentally changed North American societies; in producing the 99 per cent something has been broken. What has this polarity grown out of and left in its wake? It is precisely the class formation whose decline, death, and crisis has been lamented in North American public discourse since the great financial crisis and is now cast as the primary victim of austerity policies: the extended and stratified middle class – represented as retrospectively hegemonic during the "golden age" of capitalism (Schor 1985). Be it Occupy, the economists of the IMF or of the OECD, trade union leaders here in Canada and in the United States, all agree that the polarity of the 1 per cent versus the 99 per cent signifies somehow the end of the hegemonic status of the middle class in North America (Sharpe, Arsenault, and Harrison 2008). And thus our polarity implies this third figure that it has grown out of: the

---

4 And thus if the 99 per cent can be conceived as the mass, it is difficult to attribute to the 1 per cent as it appears in social discourse the attributes of an elite, knowing that elites are able to legitimize their social positions by appealing to tradition, education, merit or effort, forms of legitimacy that the 1 per cent does not appear to enjoy in the current context.
5 From here on, the terms *1 per cent* and *99 per cent* are used not as statistical realities but as metonyms, as argued above.

extended and stratified middle class,[6] considered to be the product of the capital/labour compromise that inaugurated and drove that golden age of advanced capitalism, from the late 1940s into the 1970s (Marglin and Schor 1985). As a social category, the idea of an extended, non-oppositional, inclusive middle class captures the experience of several generations of wage labourers in North America as producers, consumers, and political actors.[7] It is fascinating to note that the reference to the "extended middle class" is predominant today, during its "unmaking," rather than during class struggle by labour, which resulted in the so-called fordist social compromise. I argue that the narrative of the declining "middle class" points to a complex of social relations that cannot be anymore. It is a figure of the receding past: the middle class has become a signifier of our relation to a bygone golden age of advanced capitalism. On the other hand, the polarity of the 1 per cent and 99 per cent – and each metonymic figure in and of itself – stands in the place previously occupied by each side of the capital/labour relation in this golden age, but this relation is now emancipated from the constraints of "compromise" in what one could call a new "no-deal" capitalism built around a new political economy of polarization. In the conceptual language of Raymond Williams (1980), the extended middle class is a residual social category, whereas the polarity of the 99 per cent vs 1 per cent as emergent and still fragile social categories of class are caught up in the movement of austerity, and each can help us understand the trajectory of late neoliberalism (Pineault 2014).

I will explore this triad by first returning to the notion of the extended middle class – a category I explored in a previous volume on austerity (Baines and McBride). Its formation – non-oppositional and based on the principle of extension – will be used to highlight those processes of

---

6 The notion of an extended middle class that includes white collar and blue collar workers, professionals and unqualified labour in a vast continuum will be studied extensively further on.

7 One can find canonical exposés of this idea of the middle class in the writings of Stiglitz (2012) and Atkinson (2015). It is also central to the discourse among the established trade union movement in Canada and in the United States, and of course most political parties right and left of centre pretend to uphold the interests of the "working" middle class. This actually led senior officials of Employment and Social Development Canada to produce an internal study, "What We Know about the Middle Class in Canada" (2013) whose conclusions are framed largely in terms of crisis and decline. Finally, since Occupy, there has been a great number of major reports in the press on the decline and crisis of the North American middle class, such as in the *New York Times* (2015).

polarization that are now "unmaking" the hegemonic position of this class. The attempt to theorize the middle class as a social class is thus not pursued in and of itself, but is rather a tool to model current class processes tied to polarization. An important aspect of this analysis will be to examine if and how this polarization ties itself to the fundamental opposition between wage labour and capital that "middle-class-ness" muddles and obscures. I will then turn to the two other figures of our triad and examine whether I can offer an interpretation of the 1 per cent as capital and of the 99 per cent as labour, taking into account the metonymic characteristics delineated above and in what way the polar relation between these figures expresses contradictions inherent in advanced capitalism.

The Class That Does Not Struggle

Our discussion of middle-class-ness starts in the murky waters of class self-identification. Surveys show that a significant proportion of North American labourers and wage earners have tended to identify themselves as "middle class," and this marker of class identity competes directly with another marker: working class (Hout 2007). In the surveys reviewed by Hout as well as by Curtis (2013), middle-class-ness has slightly grown at the expense of working-class-ness over the last fifty years in North America. Since the great crisis, however, according to some surveys, this tendency has reversed. Ekos pollster Frank Graves has shown that self-identification as middle-class has shrunk from the 60–70 per cent bracket in the pre-crisis years to a 45–50 per cent bracket in the United States and in Canada for years 2013 and 2014 (Graves 2014). When it is not altogether dismissed as marred by false consciousness and capitalist alienation, class self-identification data are often considered to be skewed by "middle-class identity bias" that is explained by group reference theory. This theory holds that polled individuals identify as middle class by transforming their immediate social environment into a reference that is used as a comparative. They also tend to measure class through a comparison of consumption relations instead of through the lens of production relations. As shown by Curtis, this is increasingly so in societies and economies where inequality is low and real income is growing for the majority, whereas in societies characterized by polarization and income stagnation or depression, middle-class identity bias is less prevalent. This leads Curtis to argue that middle-class-ness is tied to socio-political conjunctures where rigid "us" versus "them" ideologies are not determining and individuals do not feel compelled to distinguish their position within class structure (Curtis 2013, 220), in particular because of faith in strong institutions of social solidarity. If we weave these elements together, we have some basic elements to define middle-class-ness as an objective experience that refers to the trajectory of a significant mass of labourers and wage-earners during the latter half of the twentieth century in North America.

Middle-class-ness thus understood is not a fixed state; it does not refer positively to a group defined in terms of income, occupation, or property, nor does it identify an ambiguous social position such as the "professional and managerial class" sandwiched between powerful and opposed poles such as the working class and a modern incarnation of the capitalist class (Ehrenreich and Ehrenreich 2013). Middle-class-ness is (or was) a process, both subjective and objective, of social integration where middle-ness acts as a principle of reference for a system of stratification and inclusion that mobilizes the institutions of struggle of the working class while emptying them of the oppositional principle that created them. The institutions at the heart of the post-war fordist compact – the trade unions and the labour movement more widely, collective agreements, labour law, the redistributive social state – were the product of working-class struggles during the first half of the twentieth century in North America, as elsewhere in the advanced capitalist world (Friot 2012; Therborn 2012). They permitted the de-proletarianization of vast segments of the working class, and as newer working-class strata were formed among the burgeoning white- and pink-collar labour forces they permitted these workers to avoid proletarianization and struggle for a range of entitlements won over by the stronger industrial unions in the manufacturing sector (Castel 2003). But these very same institutions were profoundly ambivalent, the fruit of a compromise. The empowerment of workers was tied to their functional integration in advanced capitalist economies both as mass producers and mass consumers through the wage relation (Aglietta 1979). Put another way, the institutions rest on a tension between workers as material producers and workers as wage-earners. It was as material producers that workers struggled for these institutions, but if they were empowered as wage-earners they were disempowered as producers as managerial control over the labour process was institutionalized (Coriat 1994). The very institutions of working-class empowerment limited the exercise of their social power – their praxis – to the betterment and extension of their status as economically functional wage-earners (Dudzick and Reed 2015).

This contradictory process – a dialectic of disempowerment and empowerment –led to the formation of the extended middle class as a hegemonic complex in a Williamsian sense (Williams 1980). Betterment meant increasing employment security, growth of average income, and an expanding horizon of mass consumption as the "American way of life"; and this became a central objective of the labour movement and of progressive public policy during the post-war era in Canada and in the United States. Extension meant the absorption of other segments of the labour force into a stabilized wage relation whose productive identity was estranged from traditional working-class references and culture, such as the growing white-collar and service segments[8] (Castel 2003). This was an especially important process in the rapidly growing public sector labour force, whose unionization became a priority for the labour movement during this period. Antithetical to an oppositional working-class identity built on the imaginary of the material producer, as noted by C.W. Mills in the early 1950s, these segments on the other hand could readily identify with a class identity built around a social wage relation and its mass consumption norm (Mills 1951). The emphasis on the consumption norm as a marker of class identity and its group reference effect was thus a central subjective dimension of the sentiment of middle-ness that displaced social identities based on materially productive identity (Baudrillard 2014). This was reinforced by the objective force of what Baran and Sweezy in their seminal *Monopoly Capital* (1966) analysed as the "sales effort": an immense investment of social energy in the production of a hegemonic culture of mass consumption.

Of course workers in general and specific segments of the labour movement have episodically returned to oppositional practice as material producers, and the sixties and seventies even saw a cumulative development of working-class radicalism (Friot 2012), but overall middle-class-ness imposed itself as the determining class formation process in North America. In any hegemonic complex, Williams reminds us, reside side by side dominant, emergent, and residual cultures. In postwar North America, the traditional working-class oppositional culture subsisted as a residual, and various emergent oppositional cultures appeared – and the New Left, including Williams himself, invested hope in the social movements that shaped them – but none were able to

---

8 This process of extension was also a process of exclusion in particular, through mechanisms of racialization.

successfully challenge middle-class-ness as an objective and subjective force. Full employment, income growth, rising consumption, and economic security became the objectives of labour mobilization and progressive state intervention. This was feasible because of the post-war accumulation regime in North America, where production locked in with consumption through rising wage income that captured a significant part of productivity gains, and generated three decades of strong macroeconomic growth and prosperity (Marglin and Schor 1985). The subjective sentiment of middle-class-ness was the objective experience of this process, and it was built upon the centrality of the wage relation of advanced capitalism – wage relation that, in the language of Baran and Sweezy (1966) was defined by the constraint of surplus absorption.[9]

Hegemony in the tradition of Raymond Williams is not a static structure of domination, rather it is an open process of incorporation constantly remade through social practices. Middle-class-ness as a non-oppositional class process was thus perpetually in the making during the post-war era re-baptised today as the golden age of advanced capitalism. As a hegemonic class relation, middle-class-ness was made of a "whole body of practices and expectations; our assignments of energy; our ordinary understanding of the nature of man and of his world. It is a set of meanings and values, which as they are experienced as practices appear as reciprocally confirming" (Williams 1980, 413).

The foundation of this process was the institutionalized wage relation best described by the regulation school (Aglietta 1979; Coriat 1994). It was irreducible to one fixed characteristic such as relative income level, occupation or cultural status; it cut across these differences, all the while combining them as dimensions in a system of stratification skewed towards middle-ness that both included and excluded. Inclusion was the norm, while exclusion was the marginal, the oddity. The farther one was positioned from the middle, the more one was in a position of anomaly, subject to mechanisms of inclusion (such as social programs or aggressively progressive income tax) or exclusion (such as permanent underemployment). Inclusion and exclusion as well as stratification created a system of legitimate "inequalities" based on

---

9 All class societies are built around the structures through which a dominant class extracts a surplus from the dominated. Advanced capitalism is probably the first class society where class domination is based on the capacity to make a significant segment of the dominated absorb the surplus they produce. The extended middle class is the outcome of this new form of class domination.

three core values of middle-class-ness: meritocracy, social mobility, and social stability through economic and social security. These values where incorporated in the collective agreements signed by trade unions; they presided over the functioning of pension schemes and social insurance programs; they conditioned the reforms of the education system that led to mass post-secondary education programs; they were the organizing principles of the two great structures of wage-based solidarity, unemployment insurance, and progressive income tax; they were the values that presided over the development of the welfare state in North America and eventually would be transfigured by American pragmatists such as John Rawls (a progressive interpretation was given by Michael Walzer) and economists as far apart as Kenneth Arrow and John K. Galbraith into a general philosophy of justice and social welfare. These values and the systems of social stratification they organized also challenged the legitimacy of other modes of inequalities based on inheritance, property, or race and gender, and thus became systems of social incorporation. Middle-class-ness was thus also a process of continued extension, the absorption of social strata into what became a vast continuum of social positions around a stratified wage relation. Extension, as inclusion coupled with growth and prosperity measured as the capacity to consume, was the principle of historicity as progress and development of this post-war advanced capitalist order.[10]

The contemporary angst concerning middle-class decline is in great part attributable to the collapse of this principle of historicity and the incapacity to imagine a reactivation of an economic and political order able to sustain a renewed middle-class extension tied dynamically to capitalist accumulation. Quite to the contrary, the contemporary conjuncture is characterized by accumulation dynamics that undermine what's left of the institutions that reproduced the wage relations of middle-class-ness as argued by a great number of economists (Atkinson 2015) all the while engendering new forms of economic and political inequality that fall outside its system of legitimization as it was constructed during the capitalist golden age. Neoliberalism has been only partly successful in redefining middle-class-ness and its core values. The principle of "middle-ness" remains antithetical to neoliberalism's basic premises as a political economy regime, and thus merit, social mobility, and security in a neoliberal regime tend to become values of

---

10 On this, see Easterly's notion of "middle-class consensus" (2001).

exclusion from the mass instead of inclusion. The individual entrepreneur replaces the collective of wage-earners as the paragon of middle-class-ness (Foucault 2004).

This is the conjuncture that explains, I think, the rise and pervasiveness in public debate of the 1 per cent vs 99 per cent polarity. It has grown inside a horizon delineated by the wage relation, but captures a novel and impossible situation, from the perspective of middle-classness. In this new polarity, the middle is not in a position of dominance over the ends, which are marginalized and must be "normalized" through systems of inclusion. Instead, the situation is inverted. The 1 per cent have excluded themselves from the mechanisms and determinants of the wage relation in which everyone else is included and depends on. This exclusion from the top has produced a position of dominance not only over those who are still captured in the structures of the wage relation, but also over the structures themselves. As argued by many in this volume and its predecessor, austerity then is the concrete class struggle from above to (1) finalize the disempowerment of the working class by liquidating what is left of the institutions of labour in the name of middle-class autonomy, (2) reconfigure the wage relation to enhance the social power of this new social elite by mobilizing the same core values of middle-class-ness but giving them new meaning, and (3) protect and sustain the accumulation regime on which the power of this capitalist elite rests by fostering new forms of economic growth based on finance, globalization, and dispossession.

The first process outlined above, aiming to finalize the disempowerment of the working class by liquidating what is left of the institutions of labour in the name of middle-class autonomy, thus casts the rigidities of the unionized wage-earner status as a limit to the autonomy of the flexibilized entrepreneurial wage-earner. It sees the fiscal solidarity of a progressive tax system as a barrier to individually produced social mobility. It considers social programs such as education systems as mechanisms that should select and sustain the excellent while managing the excluded. It entails state intervention that should favour private initiatives of protection from social risks, such as individual retirement savings schemes. What were seen as pillars of a middle-class social compact – collective agreements and a unionized workforce, progressive fiscal and budgetary policies, public education and pension systems – are now cast as those very barriers to middle-class autonomy and self-realization. This brings us to a second process aimed at reconfiguring the wage relation to enhance the social power of this new social elite by mobilizing the same core values of middle-class-ness but giving them new meaning. *Meritocracy* loses all foundation in the collective agency of workers and is exclusively defined in terms of the individual acquisition and skilful use of "human capital." *Social mobility* is not the outcome of a wage relation able to leverage a claim on productivity gains (either directly at the firm level, or indirectly through a redistributive fiscal system) but is the product of individual entrepreneurial action in an economic field understood as a competitive marketplace. *Economic security*, traditionally understood as the protection of individual wage-earners from forms of social risks as well as inclusion of the excluded, inverts itself into new forms of social protection against individuals seen as risk vectors and the managed exclusion of the risky included. Paradoxically, even in this context of a neoliberal political economy regime, and of austerity as class struggle from above, advanced capitalism as an economic system still rests on accumulation through the coupling of mass production, mass labour, and mass consumption (Stockhammer 2011). The wage-earner's labour and consumption are still needed to produce and absorb the surplus inherent to the economy's dynamics, even though the accumulation regime is now marked by financialization, globalization, and dispossession (Baragar and Seccareccia 2008). Betterment can then take the form of facilitated access to consumer credit instead of average wage growth (Montgomerie 2009), extension and inclusion can take place at a global scale instead of a national or continental scale (Pezzini 2012). This last development could lead to middle-class-ness shedding its extended and inclusive form and returning to its traditional narrow form as an intermediary class sandwiched between opposed poles (Therborn 2012).[11] The extended middle class, non-oppositional in nature, cannot become an agent of struggle in this conjuncture. Its decline can be lamented, or the globalization of its

---

11 Much of the contemporary development economics literature concerning a supposed "global middle class" does define middle-class-ness in this narrow way, as those above the mass of the merely subsisting and below the oligarchy of third world elites. Their political function is to act as buffer between these two poles and form the eventual foundation for the development of Western-like liberal democracies (Easterly 2001). They are defined by their capacity to consume in patterns that are recognizable from a North American world view, by the accumulation of "human capital" meritocratically transformed into economic status, by upward social mobility and finally by a combination of collective and individual claims on savings and insurance schemes (Banerjee and Duflo 2008; Kharas 2010). For an example, see Pezzini (2012).

neoliberalized narrow form can be celebrated. This brings us to a last question: Does the new polarity of the 1 per cent vs 99 per cent point to the emergence of a new oppositional class that can struggle against the capitalist elite in this new context?

Class as Polarization: The 1 Per Cent against the 99

Thompson reminds us that "class eventuates as men and women live their productive relations, and as they experience their determinate situations, within the inherited culture and expectations, and as they handle these experiences in cultural ways" (Thompson 1978, 150). Polarization is not only subjective experience, it is a fundamental class formation process driven by – and shapes and determines – a capitalist accumulation regime. Our understanding of the dialectic between the structure of accumulation and the class formation process draws on Wood's interpretation and extension of Thompson's theoretical argument (Wood 1995, chapter 3) against structuralist and overly deterministic approaches to class formation. If one cannot deduce a class structure and practice from a theoretical "stage" of capitalist production relations, neither Wood nor Thompson argue that there is no relation between class and accumulation. On the contrary, Wood argues, class formation is an outcome of the dialectic between the "production of social relations of production," their institutionalization and development as an empirically and historically contingent accumulation regime, and the experience of this process in class ways, which orient and determine this production through culture and struggle.

I have argued that austerity consists of a class struggle from above, that it is part of a much wider process linked to the development of neoliberalism as a political economy regime, articulated to an accumulation regime characterized by financialization and a tendency towards stagnation (Foster 2008; Pineault 2014). This struggle has undermined the system of stratification typical of middle-class-ness, all the while building the foundations for a narrow neoliberalized middle class that excludes most wage-earners in North America. This has come across in various class self-identification surveys, as the working-class marker has crept up at the expense of the middle-class marker since the great financial crisis. Though I don't think that resistance to class struggle from above can renew with the imaginary and culture of the oppositional working-class identity of the nineteenth and early twentieth century, that of the material producer of the industrial world,[12] I do think that, as wage-earners, the 99 per cent could develop a new oppositional class culture able to struggle in the current conjuncture – the 99 per cent understood not as the statistical category, but as a metonym of that class of producers that has been institutionalized by the wage relation of advanced capitalism. It has been as wage-earners that they have been struggling to defend and even expand the power of the institutions of labour in this process as polarization (Aglietta 1979). Finally, as wage-earners they could give themselves a renewed identity as producers that could have a potentially revolutionary character (Friot 2012).

The task here is to explore – in very preliminary fashion – how such a process could come about. Have the rapidly changed accumulation dynamics and forms that mark our times uncovered and laid bare, in a new form, the basic rift between capital and labour? A rift between those whose relationship to accumulation and expanded reproduction of capital is one of command and mastery, what the 1 per cent designates, whereas the mass – the 99 per cent – is being pushed into a relation of service to these processes of accumulation and expanded reproduction, of financial capital in particular, and constrained to the simple reproduction of this dominated condition? To further explore this process of polarization I propose a return to the basic theory of class opposition that Marx developed in *Capital*, particularly in his chapters on simple and expanded reproduction.[13] I will draw the contours of a

---

12 We are also wary of the various avatars of this industrial working class that have been touted by some Marxist schools as representing the new productive class, such as knowledge workers. The main limit of these approaches is that they carry over from classical political economy a distinction between "productive" and "non-productive" labourers and thus between value-creating and non-value-creating labour. This then implies a hierarchy among producers between essential and non-essential segments of the working class, or between those who's labour is deemed to prefigure the future post capitalist society and those whose labour is tied to the past. In agreement with Baran and Sweezy, I believe that in advanced capitalism the economic distinctions between productive and non-productive labour do not hold, and with Friot, that they are politically counter-productive.

13 I do not wish to argue that all was said, done, and written sometime in the 1860s, and that all we need to know are the eternal truths contained in the Marxian corpus, *Capital* in particular. I am interested in recovering the form that Marx develops to analyse accumulation and reproduction as polarization. I will thus draw a simple and basic but powerful model of class polarization from Marx's work. Finally, it is also important to note that since this is not an exercise in "Marxian studies," I will not devote significant space to citations from Marx's *Capital*, nor will I discuss the interpretations that chapters 23 and 24 have received through time.

structural model of class polarization whose properties and characteristics will then be mobilized to propose an analysis of the class oppositions that we think stand behind what is currently being lamented in public discourse as "growing inequality" and "decline of the middle class" as well as experienced in the everyday lives of the mass of North Americans as the rift between the 1 per cent and the 99 per cent.

Some Ontological Foundations of Class Polarity in Modern Societies

Marx opens his *Communist Manifesto* with the structural oppositions that he deemed shaped history as class struggle. From the standpoint of the manifesto, class opposition is not simply a question of diverging interests or of the relative well-being of the minority leaving a majority in poverty or misery. Marx, inspired here, as elsewhere, by Hegel's model of the master and servant dialectic in the *Phenomenology* (Dufour and Pineault 2009) developed a dramatic and agonistic conception of class opposition, rich in dialectical possibilities, as class struggle that rent the whole of society into two structurally linked poles. Across his writings Marx used a plurality of models of class struggle and class structure. Polarization was specific to periods of class formation where the subtleties of social stratification or differentiation melted into frank opposition. This dialectical approach to class formation is at the heart of volume 1 of *Capital*. It appears in key moments of Marx's argument, such as in the initial analysis of the process by which money can be transformed into capital, the analysis of the struggle over the working day, or the analysis of simple and expanded reproduction. It is from these last chapters that I will draw the theoretical elements needed to construct our model of class polarization. A presentation of the dialectical moments of polarization will serve as a basis for the construction of a theory of class formation, while dialectical moments will be reworked into specific dimensions of class polarity.

Before examining this dialectic, a prior question must be answered: if polarization implies a rift, a rendering of a whole that then forms two opposed poles, what is the nature of the whole prior to the rift? The question brings us to the terrain of Marx's ontology, the way his materialism informed his conception of the essence of human beings,[14] of society as an ensemble of social relations as well his conception of historicity. Franck Fischbach has shown that activity and expressivity are central concepts of

---

14 Discussed in Thesis 6 of the *Theses on Feuerbach*.

Marx's ontology of production. These concepts, uncovered in the philosophical explorations in the 1844 manuscripts, are also central to Marx's mature writings such as *Capital*[15] (Fischbach 2015). This ontology can be formulated in the following proposition: we are all the direct and indirect producers of the social and to some extent natural world in which we live. It is through the daily activities of direct and indirect labour, consumption, and leisure that we produce this world as our world, though this can take an alienated or inverted form. That brings us to this definition of society's "material base" as a mode of production: "This mode of production must not be considered simply as being the reproduction of the physical existence of the individuals. Rather it is a definite form of activity of these individuals, a definite form of expressing their life, a definite *mode of life* on their part. As individuals express their life, so they are. What they are, therefore, coincides with their production, both *what* they produce and *how* they produce" (Marx 1998, 37). In Marx's words, whether it be in the 1844 manuscripts, *The German Ideology* or in the study of the labour process in *Capital*, producing defines our capacity to express ourselves as objective beings. The capacity was conceptualized by Marx as self-activation (*Selbstbestätigung*). Reflexive (*Verdopplung*) self-activation defines us as human beings, as producers, but Marx also insists that the aim of production as our activity – as human activity – is not constrained by the question of subsistence, but is rather oriented expressively. Later in *Capital*, Marx will insist that this specifically sets apart humans from other living beings constrained by subsistence. We produce in order to express a determined mode of life.

These two ontological dimensions of human production are determining aspects of the class formation process as polarity: self-activation and expression of mode of life will help us define the most basic and primary means through which the producer, either as single human being, or as the totality called society, will be cleft in two poles through an ensemble of social relations. Class polarization in a capitalist society initially is an asymmetrical relation that each pole has to these two ontological aspects of production. Capitalism can be defined by the social relations of property it implies, by the pervasiveness of the commodity form, its corrosive effect on social unity, or the omnipresence of an oppressed and exploited industrial proletariat. It begins to define itself as social formation and

---

15 Fischbach is among a new generation of French philosophical interpreters of Marx's thought as social philosophy. Author of many books on Marx's thought, a condensed synthesis of his work has recently been published as *Philosophies de Marx* (2015).

historic force, when the expanded reproduction of its constitutive social relations as a social system and economy become the end and point of departure of production relations turned entirely towards accumulation (Meszaros 1995). Accumulation is not just the individual pursuit of a singular capitalist – whether merchant, manufacturer, or money lender – it forms the very historicity of a capitalist society, and thus appears to each and every one and is experienced as a whole in the guise of economic growth, or in a wider and more ambiguous form as "development" and even "progress" (Meszaros 2010). The economic process in capitalism, by which a society produces its social world, is immanently a process of accumulation, and class polarity expresses itself as an asymmetrical relation to this accumulation (Kalecki 1943).

Modern capitalism is a monetary production economy, and thus the *economic* form of this accumulation process will imply the reproduction of capital as monetary relations. When Marx begins to enquire on the origin of surplus value in *Capital*, he begins by asking how and in what social conditions money is transformed capital. This becoming is the point of departure of class polarization. In chapter 4, the formally equal producers of commodities in the market transform themselves into the unequal polarity of capitalist and labourer, which appear through their skewed relation to money and the capacity to spend it as capital, that is as a surplus beyond and above what is needed for subsistence.

According to the perspective developed in *Capital*, it is not the wealth of the capitalist, nor the relative poverty of the worker that defines the relation of each class to accumulation. Neither does the direct ownership or non-ownership of means production quite define class asymmetry, given not only in advanced capitalism the prevalence of incorporated forms of capitalist property but also in classical capitalism the possibility of an "entrepreneurial" capitalist to purchase these in the market. In capitalism, as a monetary production economy in the Kaleckian sense, asymmetry is defined as the difference between one group that can spend money as capital and thus accumulate by actively initiating accumulation, and a second group that must obtain money to subsist and thus hires out its productive capacity to others.[16]

---

16 In contemporary "neo-Kaleckian" models this is known as the capacity for autonomous expenditure, which is distinguished from "induced expenditures." The state as well and large capitalist corporations have the capacity to initiate the latter. Erstwhile wage-earners as well as small business are constrained to the latter. On this see Lavoie (2014, chapter 6).

Simply put, capitalists can put their money to work, whereas workers must work for their money. Class asymmetry is thus not just something that appears during the labour process when one gets to boss/coordinate/control the activity of another. This can happen in various social contexts that might have nothing to do with capitalism. Asymmetry has to do with an inverse relation to the process that marks the reproduction of a monetary production economy from investment, to labour, to consumption.

It is at this point that the surface "economic relations" tie in to the more profound ontological relations outlined above. If, in Marx's words, producing defines our capacity to express ourselves as objective beings, in capitalism the social relation most of us have to this defining capacity of humanity is inherently skewed. In capitalism, only a marginal minority have effectively the social capacity to sustain such a creative and autonomous relation to objective activity. Most have lost part or all of this capacity. They have been reduced to a purely subjective force: the capacity to labour for others. Marx called this a loss of the capacity of self-activation. It is typical of the capitalist labour process. With it comes the loss of self-expression and ultimately alienation when I relate to my own activity as something estranged. We have all felt this at some point in our working lives, and we all strive to develop meaningful, creative, and expressive labour, sometimes with the mitigated success of self-employment, sometimes by resisting inside our workplaces the tendency towards uncreativity and monotony, sometimes by managing spaces and moments of meaningful work. But globally this is done in social context where self-activation is – at least in the formal monetary economy – largely a power lost to another.

The other here is defined by his capacity to "activate us," that is to set in motion our labour as creative, productive, expressive (and often not so expressive) social activity, and thus as objective reality.[17] That is precisely how his money is ultimately put to work, through our bodies, minds, and souls. What we see as the basic economic process of our society (our daily activities of direct and indirect labour, consumption and leisure that produce this world), the other relates to as an accumulation that he has the social capacity to initiate, that he actively

---

17 This process of subjectivation that creates on the one hand the capitalist who must spend money to capture another's activity as labour thus degraded all other social activities as private "non-labour" along gendered lines; see Federici (2004), specifically chapter 2, "The Accumulation of Labor and the Degradation of Women."

organizes, and from which he can appropriate the fruits of this process in the form of a surplus. Now the fruits of this process, the surplus, at the level of abstraction with which we are examining the problem, is essentially the expanded means to initiate a new cycle of accumulation, which from the perspective of the wage-earning labourer appears as a new autonomous spur of economic activity, as "growth." For the major part of the history of advanced capitalism, this cycle of accumulation was materialized in the continued growth and expansion of corporate power and organizational capacity in our economy, both of which appeared to labourers as full employment. It is only recently that this cycle has taken the form of a growth of financial circulation and of the organizational capacity to expand this circulation's grasp of the economic process.

Concretely class asymmetry is thus a differential relationship towards investment, labour, and consumption. Capitalists have the a priori power to invest and to give direction to investment (Kalecki 1943). Obviously market constraints and the search for productivity orient and guide these investment decisions, but in the end their aim is accumulation. Wage-earners must passively await the moment when this investment becomes reality as expenses in the economic process, which translates into employment for their class. This is considerable power, since today's investment decisions by private corporations largely determine the contours of tomorrow's daily life and labour, the forms and mechanics of our future productive apparatus, and the nature of the commodities that will engender our future wants, needs, and desires. The same differential structure applies to labour and consumption. One class dominates these moments of the economic process, while the other is dominated by these processes but nonetheless depends on them. One class is given a priori the capacity to act on these processes, while the other must passively wait to be employed in these same processes. One class uses the expansive nature of these processes as they are instituted in capitalism to accumulate power over the economic process, while the other class, as Marx often remarks, enters the economic process as it left it the day before, with neither more nor less.

But asymmetry is just the initial logical moment of a wider dialectical process of polarization, which implies both relations of interdependence and latent or overt conflictuality (Dufour and Pineault 2009). The tragic and agonistic nature of class polarity is grounded in the fact that this asymmetry rests on the real dependence of both classes on each other, as one mediates the reproduction of the other's class position to accumulation. To put it in Marxian-Hegelian terms, class polarity implies that the capitalist's social practice produces the labourer, and that the labourer's social practice produces the capitalist. This is not simply a question of constructing an identity against that of the other, nor is it a divisional logic, where the separation of one extremity engenders duality. It is a sociological truism that class expresses itself as distinction and difference in the social spaces of politics and culture. But in the economic sphere, capitalist and wage-earner cannot exist without the other, because one's practice is the other's reproduction. Capitalists produce employment and plan the production of and investment in society's means of expression and subsistence; workers, over and above the production of their means of subsistence, reproduce money as capital through surplus labour and validate production and investment through consumption. Their acceptance (or resistance) to revolutionize the way they work and live in their daily lives validates (or invalidates) capitalist investment and thus the system's self-expansion.

Asymmetrical interdependence is inherently conflictual, because it is contradictory. It is contradictory because the social power of the dominant class, in a situation of polarization, grows through the intensification of the exploitation of the dominated class. Exploitation implies that the economic process is structured to ensure the accumulation of economic power in the hands of the dominant class. In concrete terms, this can mean encroachment of real wages so that the profit rate grows, or it can mean an acceleration of change in productive and consumption norms that tightens the gears between production and consumption – in both cases, the capacity to invest more capital, to further dominate the economic process. And social activity in general expands, as do new mechanisms of class domination. While there are no formal limits to the intensification of exploitation, a point can be reached where this relation becomes unsustainable as an economic process, demand falls to low (2000s), accelerated change in the labour process leads to disefficiencies (1970s) or to higher unemployment rates (1930s) (Lavoie 2014). No inherent social mechanism in the class relation as described above exists to stop the dominant class from pushing the system to such limits, and during these limit periods, polarization can actually deepen and speed up as a social process, at least in Marx's view. Interdependence implies that the dominated are in a position to resist and subvert the mechanisms wielded by the dominant, in the terms set by the system of constraints of the class relation by encroaching on profits, by limiting capitalist power over investment, production, or capitalist initiative, by reappropriating the social surplus as state power through the fiscal system. Or they can actually act to break free of this relation. This depends on the legitimacy of the system as a whole and the reflexivity of the dominated as a class, just as the dominant can act to break free of the system constraints that might have been instituted to limit their power. Latent class conflict can then explode into "class war" or active struggle when legitimacy completely breaks down, and a radicalized form of class reflexivity saturates society. Be it through latent or overt conflictuality, the dominated reclaim their historicity in the sense that they activate themselves as producers of their world.

Modelling a New Class Polarity

What light does this structural model shed on the emergent 1 per cent versus 99 per cent polarity? The results presented here are, of course, very preliminary, but can be proposed as a useful working hypothesis when tied to well documented features of capitalist development in the current neoliberal conjuncture (Baines and McBride 2014).

If we are the direct and indirect producers of our world, a world characterized by advanced capitalism, then in what context is this world produced? Mainly through social relations that cohere in the form of the large corporations that dominate production and consumption relations in advanced capitalist societies (Lavoie 2014). Alongside these private capitalist organizations there exist public and state institutions that are also dominant structures of production, and they are organized along similar bureaucratic and organizational lines, though their institutional finalities are distinct (Hibou 2013). It is my hypothesis that the new polarity expresses a deep and profound change in both these structures and thus a new rift in the relations of production of society, relations that include obviously labour but also wider conditions of social existence.

Drawing on previous work on neoliberalism as class struggle (Pineault 2014), the emergence of the 1 per cent as a metonymic figure of the capitalist class designates a new rift actively produced by this group as an agent of change through active struggle. This class offensive is more than a simple reaction or restoration. It is the deployment of new forms of capitalist asymmetry, interdependencies, and conflictuality that have blown away previous class positions between capital and labour, the so-called capital-labour compromise of the golden age discussed above. In the absence of an effective countervailing power, such as unions and a progressive welfare state (Evans 2014; Peters 2014), the 1 per cent have embarked upon a seemingly revolutionary program of social change that is now blamed for having dissolved the very pillar of North American advanced capitalism that was the extended middle class. It has thus produced the 99 per cent as its passive counterpart.

What is the actual composition of this active 1 per cent? Again, I am pinpointing the "metonymic" 1 per cent, not the actual percentile. This group would include the corporate and financial elites that dominate and control corporate forms of capital as well as those who, as rentiers, own and control significant financial capital (including rights on land and/or real estate) with which they can exercise allocative, strategic, or speculative economic power, which means that they can "act" on material reality through autonomous monetary expenses (Lavoie 2014; Carroll 2004). Therein lies the material base of their class power: the dependence of society for its material reproduction, on an ensemble of large corporate organizations embedded in a monetary production economy. Corporate executives, directors, board members, senior partners, and traders in financial organizations all share a common power over society as those that will direct and control the reproduction of these organizations according to a capitalist finality of growth and accumulation (Carroll 2004). They have become the 1 per cent because they have given a specific direction to this accumulation process. In previous work on austerity I had drawn on Harvey (2005) and had identified three main tiers to the accumulation process particular to the neoliberal era: accumulation through flexibilized production, accumulation by financialization, and accumulation by dispossession.

Drawn together, these three tiers mark the fault lines where asymmetries, interdependencies, and conflictualities will be produced that are inherent to the new direction of the accumulation. It is beyond the scope of this chapter to discuss the details of this new accumulation regime and the interpretations it has given rise to among political economists. Here I will insist only on the coherence and articulation of the three tiers into an organic whole governed by the overall process of financialization. Flexibilized production relations combined with wage repression and permanent organizational restructuring are not only compatible with the growth of financial forms of capital. They actually provide the fodder for the development of financial mediations of the industrial sphere. The same can be said for permanent public sector restructuring and the permanent fiscal crisis engendered by regressive changes in the tax system.[18] Both these processes of permanent restructuring imply strengthened executive power inside private and public organizations, centralization of decisional capacity, and liquidation of sites of resistance to change, loose employment ties being favoured over tight employment conventions (Lapointe and D'Amours 2014; Standing 2011). New asymmetries arise on either side of these developments. The centrality of financial accumulation[19] in this new regime divides the 1 per cent and the 99 per cent between those who in this sphere wield allocative, strategic, and speculative power and those who are excluded from this potentiality. This partitions society between a 1 per cent remunerated in financial instruments directly (stock options) or indirectly (restricted share units), able to buy into hedge funds, able to acquire loans for financial speculation, and those who must passively allow their wage-earned savings to be transformed into financial capital by fund managers (members of the 1 per cent) who then wield the power of the fund. This partition is also between forms of remuneration that are tied to the profit norm of corporations (those of the 1 per cent) and those that are tied to the "cost norm," the 99 per cent, the latter in constant adjustment to guarantee the stability of the former. This has led to the long stagnation of the wage rate since the onset of the neoliberal political economy regime, and is seen by many political economists as a main driver of the low investment and growth rates that have characterized neoliberalism (Baragar and Chernomas 2012).

The constraint of permanent organizational restructuring, combined with centralized strategic and allocative power, introduces a new asymmetry between capital and labour, the latter being the "object" of the restructuring process and the former being the active subject, initiator, and author

---

18 The austerity stagnation cycle that has permitted the 1 per cent to significantly restructure the state's structures and fiscal policies, creating on the one hand occasions for investment (Whiteside 2015) and on the other hand isolating capital-based incomes from fiscal circuits.

19 Financialization of the overall accumulation process implies that the 1 per cent defines itself first and foremost through its capacity to initiate cycles of valorization that take on a financial form and then accumulate capital in a financial form. Autonomous expenditures are thus first directed towards financial circuits. But more profoundly the 1 per cent is that class of individuals who control the financial innovation that drives "financialization" in all sectors of the advanced capitalist economy. They not only personally accumulate assets in a financial form, but they have transformed capitalist valorization in general so that it takes a financial form, while the 99 per cent have been enclosed in a real economy subsumed by this process (Crotty 2010).

of change (Froud et al. 2006; and Hibou 2012).[20] Out of this arises a paradox of positions. Never have executive churn rates been as high among North American corporations, as star CEOs, CFOs, and others move from one organization to another, and yet never has executive power been so entrenched. On the other hand, the flexibilized labour force, from middle management downwards, is locked into the process of permanent change by executives who have the capacity to opt out.[21] The same paradox, of being locked in and confronted by agents of change who can opt out, confronts wage-earners as citizens entitled to social services but obliged to pay taxes, as austerity measures profoundly restructure the state (Baines and McBride 2014) and open fronts of valorization through privatization and 3Ps (Whiteside 2015).[22] In terms of sociopolitical identity this also engenders a paradox: while the 1 per cent can present itself as an agent of progressive reform and even revolutionary change, groups such as unions trying to preserve some form of countervailing power in the private corporate sector, or struggling to maintain entitlements in the social sphere are caught up in a defensive/conservative stance.

New interdependencies arise from these new asymmetries. I will dwell on two important and well-documented interdependencies

---

20 The profound changes that stem from flexibilized production relations have been blamed on technological change and on globalization both of which have imposed a harsher competitive environment on large corporations forcing them to engage in more intensive innovation and cost control. Both have implied wage moderation, labour force reduction and delocalization of production towards low cost pools of labour, and this has been blamed for stagnating wages and weakened demand in advanced capitalist economies. Paradoxically the dual process of globalization and technological innovation is precisely what large multinational corporations have invested in, and they are central dimensions of the restructuring process outlined above (Lapointe and D'Amours 2014).
21 This paradox is revealed in full force when large corporations enter into bankruptcy procedures not so much because they are unviable as businesses, but because this opens an opportunity for radical organizational change, including in particular collective agreements and pension obligations that have immense impacts on the cost versus profit norm arbitrage.
22 Asymmetry is also produced through the institutionalization of economic globalization in the form global free trade deals that constitutionalize corporate power. Whether it be NAFTA, TPP, or the various European free trade deals being negotiated, these all have in common the recognition of transnational corporate rights that limit the exercise of democratic power by sovereign states.

between the 1 per cent and the 99 per cent that concern financial accumulation primarily, but tie in to the other tiers. In advanced capitalism, even in a low-wage, low-investment, and low-growth accumulation regime, value locked into mass production must be realized through mass and sustained consumption. While the consumption norm of flexibilized and precarized wage earners has become dependent on various forms of credit (Montgomerie 2009; Passarella 2014), the access on a mass and systematic scale to this credit rests on the capacity of financial elites to produce more or less stable innovations so that these debts can be absorbed in financial circuits. The same relation of interdependence applies to the control and valorization of mass savings through pension and mutual funds: the financial power of investment banks and fund managers rests on their capacity to capture, mobilize, and control wage-earner savings (Pineault 2013).[23] The result is a constant pressure on the 99 per cent for deeper integration into financial relations controlled by the 1 per cent, which means a further paradox: households will accumulate debt and passive financial investments in a parallel fashion. This ties into a deeper asymmetry inherent to the contemporary mass structure of financial circulation. The exercise of speculative and allocative power by the 1 per cent is entirely dependent on the financial relations in which the 99 per cent are locked in. Debt will feed financial circulation with needed asset and income streams (Lapavitsas 2009), savings with demand for financial assets, can be mobilized as leverage or speculated against by the 1 per cent; put another way, an agile hedge fund or high-frequency trading shop has an organic need for the slow and massive investment patterns of pension funds and mutual funds, and they will profit from the repackaging of securitized debt.

Finally, new conflictualities arise from this class structure. Their overall characteristic is determined by the historic role of the 1 per cent as bearer of class conflict from above. This has led to the curious and distressing reversal, in areas where organized labour still has some form of

---

23 Capitalists will furthermore favour forms of retirement savings that have the following characteristics: the fund must not be attached to any form of collective countervailing power, it must be an individualized scheme, and the savings must be directed towards structures that can transform them into financial capital under elite control. This explains the current capitalist offensive in Canada against defined benefit pension funds inherited from the fordist era, and in favour of "voluntary" retirement accounts offered by private financial institutions, all while corporate directors continue to be granted defined benefit pension schemes.

countervailing power, between the progressive and conservative positions; in a strict sense the 1 per cent tends to act according to a principle of constant and radical change, while labour tends to act according to a principle of resistance and conservation of social entitlements. This bring us back to Raymond Williams's distinction between residual and emergent class positions, which we will explore in the conclusive part of this chapter. Before doing so, I want to underline the fact that this is but an exploratory venture into what the 1 per cent vs 99 per cent polarity could imply if examined in the theory of class division that I have outlined based on new French interpretations of Marx's "practical materialism." The picture remains sketchy and incomplete, but I hope that it can bring us beyond the current cul-de-sac of class theory outlined by Eric Olin Wright in 2009.

Conclusion: Residual and Emergent Class Resistance to Neoliberalism and Austerity

The above delineated dimension of class as polarization must be understood not as static traits but processually as dynamic social relations of change. How can this theoretical model of class polarization help us answer our initial questions concerning the 1 per cent versus 99 per cent as well as discourses on the decline of the middle class? To speak again with the categories of Raymond Williams, wage-earner resistance can take two forms in the current conjuncture: residual or emergent. We can lament the decline of the extended middle-class and blame the capitalist elite for the under-performance of advanced capitalist economies in growth and investment. Or we can mobilize what is left of the institutional power of the labour movement and struggle for a return to a high-growth, high-investment cycle of accumulation, where once again wage-earner-based demand is the key macroeconomic variable[24] – an accumulation regime where the surplus is absorbed by articulating production to consumption, through full employment. Such a cycle of growth and accumulation is possible only if the chains of wage moderation are broken, if value added is functionally shared between wages and profits, if investment is not directed towards financial circulation, if austerity does not undermine the state's own role as an

---

24 Such a vision has been outlined by the International Labour Organization as "wage-led growth." See Lavoie and Stockhammer (2014).

economic stabilizer and producer of goods and services. This project of what could be called the "post-Keynesian Left" is for the moment the dominant alternative inside the labour movement in North America and Europe. It does imply at some point that the 1 per cent be forced into a deal with the 99 per cent, recognizing the essential role of wage-earners as consumers, not only as value-creating producers. I think that this perspective has two serious limitations.

The first concerns the analysis of the contradictions of the current accumulation regime by the "post-Keynesian Left." To put it bluntly, it is not at all obvious that the capitalist elite can be forced into a deal with the 99 per cent precisely because the capitalist elite's specific class relation to accumulation does not necessarily imply mass consumption by a homogeneous middle-class stratum of wage-earners to realize its capital. Globalization and financialization have changed the dynamics of accumulation, and the 1 per cent has been able to flourish during the post-crisis period of slow growth and weak demand. The contemporary capitalist elite do not seem to need the high growth rates and high real investment rates in the centre that were the norm in the golden age (Crotty 2010; Foster 2008). And thus though austerity means hard times for wage-earners, it also – in a very anti-Keynesian way – can mean good times for capitalists (Taylor 2014).

The second limit is of a totally different nature. It can be argued that the return to a high-growth, high-investment accumulation regime with appropriately shared value added would be ecologically unfeasible, if not all-out disastrous – at least in the given form of our current metabolic relations based on fossil fuels and the wasteful use of natural resources. Put another way, the production and consumption norms of advanced capitalism are not ecologically viable. Their content must be questioned and revolutionized (Sorman and Giampietro 2013). This second limit opens the door to a different paradigm of wage-earner resistance to austerity and neoliberalism as class struggle from above. While wage labourers can engage in class struggle over the nature of the wage relation itself, the institutions of labour could be used to engage in a struggle for a socialization of the production and consumption norms that define the wage relation, an ecological socialization. This would imply breaking away from two defining objectives of the labour movement: growth for growth's sake and full employment. It would imply re-empowering wage-earners as producers, not as producers of industrial goods, but as producers of the wage relation itself. Such struggle would be radical in its implications, since it would take aim at the initial asymmetry between capital and labour, an asymmetry that the post-Keynesian Left leaves intact and actually even mobilizes. Such a struggle is also radical in the sense that its outcome does not rest on the need to strike a deal with the 1 per cent. On the contrary, an ecological socialization of the wage relation – as argued by Friot – does away altogether with the figure of the capitalist. It is in its very essence revolutionary, since interdependence would be socialized and asymmetry abolished.

This emergent culture of opposition is at the heart of the nebulae of social movements struggling for the ecological transition of our societies and economies, from anti-fracking movements to those for climate justice or for de-growth. The missing link in this chain of struggle has traditionally been the labour movement. It would seem that this is beginning to change, as organized labour joins ecological groups in the struggle against climate change and for the de-carbonification of developed economies. The next step would be to resist as the producers of the materiality of society against a mode of production that is not only exploitative and wasteful, but ecologically destructive. It is my hope that the class struggle in the current conjuncture can become a struggle led by wage-earners to redefine production itself.

REFERENCES

Aglietta, Michel. 1979. *A Theory of Capitalist Regulation: The US Experience*. London: Verso.
Atkinson, A. 2015. *Inequality: What Can Be Done*. Cambridge, MA: Harvard University Press. https://doi.org/10.4159/9780674287013.
Baines, Donna, and Stephen McBride, eds. 2014. *Orchestrating Austerity*. Winnipeg: Fernwood.
Banerjee, Abhijit V., and Esther Duflo. 2008. "What Is Middle Class about the Middle Classes around the World?" *Journal of Economic Perspectives: A Journal of the American Economic Association* 22 (2): 3–28. https://doi.org/10.1257/jep.22.2.3.
Baragar, F., and R. Chernomas. 2012. "Profit without Accumulation." *International Journal of Political Economy* 41 (3): 24–40. http://doi.org/10.2753/IJP0891-1916410302.

Baragar, F., and M. Seccareccia. 2008. "Financial Restructuring : Implications of Recent Canadian Macroeconomic Developments." *Studies in Political Economy* 82 (1): 61–83. https://doi.org/10.1080/19187033.2008.11675064.

Baran, Paul A., and Paul M. Sweezy. 1966. *Monopoly Capital*. New York: Monthly Review.

Baudrillard, Jean. 2014. *The Consumer Society: Myths & Structures*. Atlanta: Sage

Carroll, William. 2004. *Corporate Power in a Globalizing World*. Oxford: Oxford University Press.

Castel, Robert. 2003. *From Manual Workers to Wage Laborers: Transformation of the Social Question*. New Brunswick, NJ: Transaction Publishers.

Coriat, Benjamin. 1994. *L'Atelier et le chronomètre*. Paris: Christian Bourgois.

Crotty, J. 2010. "The Bonus-Driven 'Rainmaker' Financial Firm: How These Firms Enrich Top Employees, Destroy Shareholder Value and Create Systemic Financial Instability" (rev.). PERI Working Paper 209. https://ideas.repec.org/p/uma/periwp/wp209_revised3.html.

Curtis, J. 2013. "Middle Class Identity in the Modern World: How Politics and Economics Matter." *Canadian Review of Sociology/Revue canadienne de sociologie* 50 (2): 203–26. https://doi.org/10.1111/cars.12012.

Dudzick, Mark, and Adolph Reed, Jr. 2015. "The Crisis of Labour and the Left in the United States." *Socialist Register* 51:351–75.

Dufour, Frédéric Guillaume, and Éric Pineault. 2009. "Quelle théorie du capitalisme pour quelle théorie de la reconnaissance? " *Politique et Sociétés* 28 (3): 75–99. https://doi.org/10.7202/039005ar.

Easterly, W. 2001. "The Middle Class Consensus and Economic Development." *Journal of Economic Growth* 6 (4): 317–35. https://doi.org/10.1023/A:1012786330095.

Ehrenreich, Barbara, and John Ehrenreich. 2013. *Death of a Yuppie Dream: The Rise and Fall of the Professional-Managerial Class*. New York: Rosa Luxemburg Foundation.

Employment and Social Development Canada. 2013. "What We Know about the Middle Class in Canada." Memorandum to the deputy minister of employment and social development. 2013 HR-NHQ 027637.

Evans, Bryan. 2014. "Social Democracy in the New Age of Austerity." In *Orchestrating Austerity*, ed. Donna Baines and Stephen McBride, 79–90. Halifax: Fernwood.

Federici, Silvia. 2004. *Caliban and the Witch*. London: Autonomedia.

Fischbach, Franck. 2015. *Philosophies de Marx*. Paris: Vrin.

Foster, J.B. 2008. "The Financialization of Capital and the Crisis." *Monthly Review* 59 (11). https://monthlyreview.org/2008/04/01/the-financialization-of-capital-and-the-crisis/.

Foster, John Bellamy, and William Yates. 2014. "Piketty and the Crisis of Neoclassical Economics." *Monthly Review* 66 (6). https://monthlyreview.org/2014/11/01/piketty-and-the-crisis-of-neoclassical-economics/.

Foucault, Michel. 2004. *La Naissance de la biopolitique, Cours au Collège de France (1978-1979)*. Paris: Seuil.

Freitag, Michel. 2011. *Introduction à une théorie générale du symbolique*. Vol. 2, *Dialectique et Société*. Montreal: Liber.

Friot, Bernard. 2012. *Puissances du Salariat*. Paris: La Dispute.

Froud, Julie, Johal Sukhdev, Adam Leaver, and Karel Williams. 2005. *Financialization and Strategy, Narrative and Numbers*. London: Routledge.

Graves, Frank. 2014. "The Ekos Poll: Middle-Class Misery and the New Age of Stagnation." iPolitics, 19 September. http://ipolitics.ca/2014/09/19/the-ekos-poll-middle-class-misery-and-the-new-age-of-stagnation/.

Harvey, David. 2005. *A Short History of Neoliberalism*. London: Verso.

Hibou, Béatrice. 2012. *La Bureaucratisation du monde à l'ère néolibérale*. Paris: La Découverte.

– 2013. *La bureaucratisation néolibérale*. Paris: La découverte.

Hout, M. 2007. "How Class Works in Popular Conception: Most Americans Identify with the Class Their Income, Occupation, and Education Implies for Them." Working paper, Survey Research Center, University of California, Berkeley. http://ucdata.berkeley.edu/rsfcensus/papers/Hout-ClassIDJan07.pdf.

Kalecki, M. 1943. "Political Aspects of Full Employment." *Political Quarterly* 14 (4): 322–30. https://doi.org/10.1111/j.1467-923X.1943.tb01016.x.

Kharas, Homi. 2010. "The Emerging Middle Class in Developing Countries." OCED Development Centre Working Paper No. 285. http://www.oecd-ilibrary.org/development/the-emerging-middle-class-in-developing-countries_5kmmp8lncrns-en.

Lapavitsas, Costas. 2009. "Financialised Capitalism: Crisis and Financial Expropriation." *Historical Materialism* 17 (2): 114–48. https://doi.org/10.1163/156920609X436153.

Lapointe, Paul-André, and Marie-Ève D'Amours. 2014. *Nouveau régime de relations du travail. Cahier de transfert CT-2014-010, ARUC – Innovations, travail et emploi, Département des relations industrielles*. Quebec City: Université Laval.

Lavoie, Marc. 2014. *Post-Keynsian Economics: New Foundations*. Cheltenham, UK: Edward Elgar.

Lavoie, Marc, and Engelbert Stockhammer, eds. 2014. *Wage-Led Growth: An Equitable Strategy for Economic Recovery*. London: Palgrave Macmillan.

Marglin, Stephen, and Juliet Schor, eds. 1985. *The Golden Age of Capitalism: Reinterpreting the Postwar Experience*. Oxford: Clarendon.

Marx, Karl. 1998. *The German Ideology*. New York: Prometheus Books.
Meszaros, Istvan. 1995. *Beyond Capital*. London: Merlin.
– 2010. *The Structural Crisis of Capital*. New York: Monthly Review.
Mills, C.W. 1951. *White Collar: The American Middle Classes*. Oxford: Oxford University Press.
Montgomerie, J. 2009. "The Pursuit of (Past) Happiness? Middle-Class Indebtedness and American Financialisation." *New Political Economy* 14 (1): 1–24. https://doi.org/10.1080/13563460802671196.
New York Times. 2015. "Middle Class Shrinks Further as More Fall Out Instead of Climbing Up." 25 January.
Passarella, M.V. 2014. "Financialization and the Monetary Circuit: A Macro-Accounting Approach." *Review of Political Economy* 26 (1): 128–48. https://doi.org/10.1080/09538259.2013.874195.
Peters, John. 2014. "Neoliberalism, Inequality and Austerity in the Rich World Democracies." In *Orchestrating Austerity*, ed. Donna Baines and Stephen McBride, 50–64. Winnipeg: Fernwood.
Pezzini, Mario. 2012. "An Emerging Middle Class." OECD Observer. http://oecdobserver.org/news/fullstory.php/aid/3681/An_emerging_middle_class.html.
Piketty, Thomas. 2014. *Capital in the Twenty-First Century*. Cambridge, MA: Harvard University Press. https://doi.org/10.4159/9780674369542.
Piketty, Thomas, and Emmanuel Saez. 2001. "Income Inequality in the United States, 1913–1998," NBER Working Papers 8467, National Bureau of Economic Research.
Pineault, Éric. 2013. "Réification et massification du capital financier: une contribution à la théorie critique de la financiarisation à partir de l'analyse de la titrisation." *Cahiers de recherche sociologique* 55:117–54.
Pineault, Eric. 2014. "Neoliberalism and Austerity as Class Struggle." In *Orchestrating Austerity*, ed. Donna Baines and Stephen McBride, 91–104. Winnipeg: Fernwood.
Posca Julia, and Simon Tremblay-Pepin. 2013. "Les inégalités: le 1% au Québec." Montreal: IRIS. http://iris-recherche.qc.ca/publications/1pourcent.
Schor, J.B. 1985. "Changes in the Cyclical Pattern of Real Wages: Evidence from Nine Countries, 1955–80." *Economic Journal (London)* 95 (378): 452–68. https://doi.org/10.2307/2233220.
Sharpe, S.H.A., Jean-François Arsenault, and Peter Harrison. 2008. *The Relationship between Labour Productivity and Real Wage Growth in Canada and OEDC Countries*. CSLS Research Report no. 2008-8. Ottawa: Centre for the Study of Living Standards. http://www.csls.ca/reports/csls2008-8.pdf.

Sorman, A.H., and M. Giampietro. 2013. "The Energetic Metabolism of Societies and the Degrowth Paradigm: Analyzing Biophysical Constraints and Realities." *Journal of Cleaner Production* 38:80–93. https://doi.org/10.1016/j.jclepro.2011.11.059.

Standing, Guy. 2011. *The Precariat: The New Dangerous Class*. London: Bloomsberry.

Stiglitz, J. 2012. *The Price of Inequality: How Today's Divided Society Endangers Our Future*. New York: W.W. Norton.

Stockhammer, E. 2011. "Wage Norms, Capital Accumulation and Unemployment: A Post-Keynesian View." *Oxford Review of Economic Policy* 27 (2): 295–311. http://doi.org/10.1093/oxrep/grr013.

Taylor, L. 2014. "The Triumph of the Rentier? Thomas Piketty vs Luigi Pasinetti and John Maynard Keynes." *International Journal of Political Economy* 43 (3): 4–19. https://doi.org/10.1080/08911916.2014.1002296.

Therborn, Göran. 2012. "Class in the Twentieth Century." *New Left Review* 78 (2): 5–29.

Thompson, E.P. 1978. "Eighteenth-Century English Society: Class Struggle without Class?" *Social History* 3 (2): 133–65. https://doi.org/10.1080/03071027808567424.

Whiteside, Heather. 2015. *Purchase for Profit: Public-Private Partnerships and Canada's Public Health Care System*. Toronto: University of Toronto Press.

Williams, Raymond. 1980. *Culture and Materialism*. London: Verso.

Wolff, E.N. 1996. *Top Heavy: A Study of Increasing Inequality of Wealth in America*. Updated and exp. ed. New York: New. http://thenewpress.com/books/top-heavy.

– 2010. "Recent Trends in Household Wealth in the United States: Rising Debt and the Middle-Class Squeeze – an Update to 2007." *Levy Economics Institute Working Paper* 589, 1–58. http://doi.org/10.2139/ssrn.1585409.

Wood, Ellen Meiksins. 1995. *Democracy against Capitalism*. Cambridge: Cambridge University Press. https://doi.org/10.1017/CBO9780511558344.

Wright, E.O. 2009. Towards an Integrated Analytical Approach. *New Left Review* November (60): 101–16.

5 Framing the Economic Case for Austerity: The Expansionary Fiscal Contraction Hypothesis

ELLEN D. RUSSELL

Despite the grave and persistent global repercussions of the 2008 financial and economic crisis, by the early 2010s austerity was making comeback. Governments initiated a rapid "exit strategy" from the moderate economic stimulus measures implemented to mitigate the global economic downturn and abruptly began to embrace dramatic government spending cuts. The legitimation of this public policy U-turn faced considerable obstacles in the immediate aftermath of the most profound crisis of neoliberal capitalism thus far. Critics of neoliberalism, including social movements such as Occupy Wall Street, were quick to argue that deregulation, the rising influence of corporations, financialization, and growing inequality and other neoliberal hallmarks contributed to the crisis (Crotty 2012; Kotz 2009; Wisman 2013; Wade 2009; Stockhammer 2011). To the extent that the public viewed the 2008 financial and economic crisis as an indictment of neoliberal capitalism itself, additional austerity measures were vulnerable to the critique that further neoliberalism could not solve the problems created by neoliberalism.

In light of these challenges to the legitimacy of neoliberal capitalism in the immediate aftermath of the financial and economic crisis, the familiar neoliberal arguments on behalf of austerity faced considerable obstacles. Typically austerity is justified via such recurrent themes as the demonization of social programs, the portrayal of any (real or imagined)[1]

---

[1] Politicians have many incentives to overstate fiscal pressures. In addition to using fiscal pressures as political cover to allow them to implement unpopular spending cuts, the exaggeration of fiscal pressures has the added advantage that the fiscal squeeze is likely to pass relatively quickly. Once the fiscal monster is slain, presiding politicians have the opportunity to paint themselves as heroic saviours of the public purse. For example, this ploy has been finely honed in Canadian politics (Russell 2014).

government fiscal pressures as tantamount to an impeding sovereign debt crisis, and the denunciation of "big" government. While these motifs were again invoked to legitimate austerity in the early 2000s, they were made more problematic in the prevailing context. For example, the neoliberal vilification of "big" government was less credible since the public had just witnessed widespread government economic stabilization measures to mitigate the crisis emanating from the neoliberalized financial sector. In this context, government intervention was not likely to be regarded as a burden on society. Nor was it a straightforward matter to legitimate austerity measures by inflaming public fears about government finances. Abruptly increasing budget deficits were largely thanks to government expenses to stabilize and stimulate the economy (including systemic supports and bailouts to private sector firms).[2] Thus deteriorating public finances could be viewed as a burden inflicted on the public by the necessity of stabilizing neoliberal capitalism rather than evidence of a profligate public sector. Since government social programs had not provoked the crisis, and it was readily apparent that the most vulnerable were continuing to suffer immensely, why should cuts to social programs be the logical and necessary focus of government action?

Since economic recovery was far from certain in the late 2000s and critiques of neoliberal capitalism abounded, the legitimation of austerity required a reframing of the usual neoliberal arguments. To justify austerity while economic crisis was still fresh and the "green shoots" of recovery were difficult to discern, neoliberal themes were recalibrated to reflect a pressing public preoccupation: what should the government do to reverse the economic downturn and stimulate economic growth and employment? If austerity could be framed as the credible response to the urgent need for employment, prosperity, and stability, then the public might be persuaded to overlook critiques of neoliberalism and tolerate further painful austerity measures. Thus the economic case for austerity relied heavily on convincing the public that austerity constituted a necessary step towards economic recovery.

The economic case for austerity has long relied on neoliberal capitalism's enormously influential justificatory economic theory, neoclassical economics (Chang 2002; Grabel 2000; Finlayson et al. 2005;

---

2 As is the case in any economic downturn, government budget deficits were also exacerbated by the downward pressure on tax revenues that accompanies declining economic activity.

Weintraub 1999). Depending on the particular contextual requirements, various elements of neoclassical logic have often been marshalled to persuade the public of the legitimacy of particular neoliberal initiatives. For example, the neoliberal argument on behalf of the economic benefits of tax cuts was famously promoted by the "Laffer curve," which argued that tax cuts would allow economic growth and generalized prosperity to "trickle down." Despite debates concerning its validity,[3] the Laffer curve exerted enormous influence promoting the purported economic rationale for neoliberal political agendas in public debate.

Creating an economic rationale for austerity faced a particularly challenging theoretical hurdle in the early 2010s. As hegemonic as neoclassical economic theory had become in the neoliberal era, Keynesian economic theory remained influential on the question of how governments should promote economic recovery during a profound economic crisis. Relying heavily on the lessons from the Great Depression, Keynesians contend that economic recovery in times of crisis requires substantial and sustained government economic stimulus. Even decidedly neoliberal national governments had resorted to stimulus measures at the peak of the financial and economic crisis, thereby reinforcing the credibility of the Keynesian rationale.

To both counter Keynesian influence and legitimate austerity while economic recovery was tenuous (at best), advocates of austerity sought to present a theoretical rationale for the proposition that austerity would promote economic growth. The most prominent theoretical intervention on behalf of pro-growth austerity was the (ironically named) "expansionary fiscal contraction" (EFC) hypothesis (also referred to as "expansionary fiscal consolidation," among other terms).[4] The most outstanding spokesperson for the EFC was Alberto Alesina. Alesina worked with several co-authors to dispute the Keynesian case for prolonged government economic stimulus, and to advance the argument that austerity could contribute to economic expansion.[5]

---

3 Mirowski (1982) set out several criticisms of the Laffer curve at the height of its influence.
4 Below we will use these terms, as well as "expansionary fiscal adjustments" and "pro-growth austerity" interchangeably.
5 Prominent contributions to the expansionary fiscal contraction literature include Alesina and Perotti (1995); Alesina, Perotti, and Tavares (1998); Giavazzi and Pagano (1990); Alesina and Ardagna (1998); Alesina and Ardagna (2009); Alesina, Favero, and Giavazzi (2015); Alesina et al. (2015); Alesina (2012).

In its strongest version, the EFC hypothesis argued that austerity measures (also known as fiscal contraction or fiscal consolidation) could stimulate economic growth during an economic downturn. Moreover, the EFC hypothesis implied that typical Keynesian economic stimulus measures would sabotage economic recovery. Because they argued that austerity could promote economic growth, advocates of the EFC hypothesis reassured governments that following austere fiscal policies need not be punished by voters, since the public would be inclined to forgive the suffering imposed by austerity in return for austerity's capacity to deliver economic growth (Alesina, Perotti, and Tavares 1998; Alesina 2010). This pro-austerity theory was immensely influential among policy architects.[6] By 2010, Alesina had become the "new favorite of fiscal hawks" by providing the "theoretical ammunition that fiscal conservatives want" (Coy 2010).

This chapter considers the case advanced for austerity by proponents of the EFC hypothesis. Our concern is the not primarily with the methodological technicalities or empirical validity of pro-austerity economic theory, although the EFC hypothesis was subjected to many serious methodological critiques, and it appears (at this early stage in empirical examination) that austerity measures implemented in accordance with the EFC hypothesis fell short in their purported objective of encouraging economic growth.[7] Whatever the weaknesses of the case advanced on behalf of austerity, it was dramatically successful in giving policy architects and public opinion–makers the theoretical justification to pursue austerity measures. This provokes the question, Why would policymakers enthusiastically embrace austerity in this precarious economic context, given that the economic evidence that austerity would promote economic recovery was (to be generous) controversial?

Regardless of the validity of the purported connection between austerity and the promotion of economic growth, this chapter argues that austerity measures implemented in the aftermath of the global

---

6 For example, Alesina appeared before the meeting of the European Union's economic and finance ministers in Madrid in April 2010 to present the case for austerity, thus paving the way for the agreement to shrink budget deficits at the Group of 20 Summit.
7 Important articles critiquing the expansionary fiscal contraction literature include Jayadev and Konczal (2010); Guajardo, Leigh, and Pescatori (2011); Perotti (2013); Gros and Maurer (2012). As Krugman concludes, "Alesina and Ardagna ... [have] been more thoroughly refuted by both academic criticism and real-world experience than any other popular doctrine I can think of" (Krugman 2013c).

economic and financial crisis served the neoliberal agenda in other ways. The EFC hypothesis helped to shield neoliberal capitalism from the possibility that democratic forces might seize on the opportunity presented by periodic economic crises to legitimate the pursuit of economic alternatives. Indeed, calls for a "global new deal" with an explicitly redistributive design rapidly followed the crisis of 2008 (Hein 2011; Ortiz 2009; Barbier 2010; Ortiz, Chai, and Cummins 2010; Zhang, Thelen, and Rao 2012). If Keynesian approaches to promoting economic recovery were left unchallenged, the neoliberal project might be vulnerable to popular forces' demands that economic stimulus be designed to pursue redistributive goals. The post-2010 austerity measures were immensely successful in foreclosing the opportunity for stimulatory policies with redistributive attributes. On the contrary, this austerity initiative facilitated attacks on progressive social programs that might have been resistant to neoliberal incursions under more sanguine economic circumstances.

This chapter begins with a brief presentation of the Keynesian argument for government stimulus to promote economic recovery, and considers the opportunity for debate about redistribution that the Keynesian theoretical framework facilitates. The next section presents the EFC hypothesis, and its case on behalf of pro-growth austerity. The final section examines how the austerity agenda defended the neoliberal project from democratic demands for more progressive alternatives, while also providing grounds to extend elements of the neoliberal restructuring that had thus far been politically difficult to achieve.

The Keynesian Argument against Austerity

Keynesian economic theory arose in the Great Depression in response to the urgent need to rekindle economic growth in the midst of widespread and persistent economic crisis. Keynesianism highlighted one pathology of private sector capitalism: business investment behaviour can be destabilizing. From a Keynesian viewpoint, investment is highly sensitive to business confidence. Pessimistic expectations about the future state of the economy discourage investment, which prolongs economic downturns (Crotty 1992; Dow 2012). The vicissitudes of investor confidence create both the peril that the economy may stagnate indefinitely as pessimistic businesses refuse to invest, as well as the possibility that investors are prone to becoming "irrationally exuberant" during economic upswings, thus promoting the more dubious investment and financial activities that contribute to the next economic downturn. To moderate this erratic dimension of investment behaviour, Keynesianism argues that the state must step in to stabilize the economy.

The Keynesian analysis of the destabilizing implications of business confidence focuses on aggregate demand conditions.[8] Businesses invest only when they are confident they can sell their output to some combination of consumers, businesses, government, or purchasers abroad. During an economic downturn, the aggregate demand of these purchasers is weak. Because firms are pessimistic about the likelihood of finding purchasers for their output, they are reluctant to invest. Low business investment in turn limits employment and thus workers' capacity to consume, which further weakens aggregate demand conditions and intensifies low business confidence. A viscous cycle can ensue in which weak aggregate demand contributes to weak and unstable investment, while unstable or low investment exacerbates aggregate demand problems. So long as the investment decision remains in the hands of private capitalist firms, business are likely to subvert economic recovery by withholding investment at the very moment that the economy most urgently needs it.

Since advocates of Keynesianism overwhelmingly accepted the necessity of retaining the capitalist structure of industry,[9] they looked to government to create conditions conducive to vigorous investment spending via policies to stabilize aggregate demand. Government monetary policy can lower interest rates to encourage investment, although during economic downturns interest rates are likely low already, and in any case the lack of customers is a more pressing deterrence to investment than the cost of financing. Thus Keynesian economic theory embraced stimulative fiscal policy: the state should judiciously increase its spending (and/or lower its taxes) in an economic downturn, thereby enhancing aggregate demand conditions. This government economic stimulus would in turn buttress business confidence, as improved

---

8 This Keynesian attention to insufficient demand represents a rejection of "Say's law," which is an underpinning of neoclassical economic models.
9 While Keynes's thought can be interpreted in ways that support more activist industrial policies, the prominent appropriation of his thought has been in support of government aggregate demand management within an economy composed largely of private capitalist firms (see Crotty 1999).

aggregate demand conditions encourage businesses to invest. Government stimulus in combination with revived investment spending promotes economic recovery. By the standard precepts of Keynesianism, austerity measures in a weak economy will sabotage economic growth, since government fiscal restraint will make bad aggregate demand conditions worse, thereby further eroding business confidence.

For many decades following the Great Depression, consensus in economic theory largely endorsed the Keynesian proposition that economic stimulus was necessary to promote economic recovery. The prevailing view was that government stimulus ameliorated the Great Depression (and other economic downturns) and that the persistence of the Great Depression was attributed to the failure of policymakers to embrace more aggressively stimulatory policies.[10] The influence of Keynesianism in the post-war period was immense. Initial experiments in Keynesian economic stimulus, such as the iconic American "New Deal," became the template for an expanded state stewardship of capitalism as counter-cyclical government aggregate demand stabilization became a hallmark of Keynesian welfare state capitalism.

Neoclassical economic theory has made enormous inroads in discrediting many Keynesian ideas, as well as the New Deal–inspired government economic initiatives that were legitimated by Keynesian economic thought. One prominent aspect of the neoclassical repudiation of Keynes is its attack on the proposition that government fiscal stimulus can promote economic growth.[11] This reasoning has formed the basis of the resurgence of the so-called "Treasury View," which holds that government budgets should remain in balance, regardless of economic cyclicality. The balanced budget mantra gained considerable traction in the neoliberal era, often justifying the imposition of austerity

---

10 Brown famously concluded that New Deal fiscal policy was not sufficiently expansive to generate economic recovery: "Fiscal policy, then, seems to have been an unsuccessful recovery device in the 'thirties – not because it did not work, but because it was not tried" (Brown 1956). Friedman and Schwartz countered with *A Monetary History of the United States, 1867–1960* (1963), which argued that misguided government policies (notably Federal Reserve policy errors) transformed a relatively ordinary economic downturn into the Great Depression, and refuted the role of stimulative fiscal policy in ameliorating this situation.
11 Neoclassicals' adherence to Say's law and a renewed attention to the concept of Ricardian equivalence, as updated by Barro (1974) and others, have been foundations of this argument.

measures regardless of their economic consequences. Yet during the 2008 economic and financial crisis, the concerted international effort to engage in Keynesian-style economic stimulus measures suggests that the Keynesian argument on behalf of fiscal stimulus in a depressed and destabilized economy remained highly influential.

From the neoliberal point of view, one peril of government recourse to economic stimulus during an economic downturn was the possibility that stimulus measures might hinder larger neoliberal objectives. Since Keynesian economic thought and its tentative application in New Deal economic interventions inspired the creation of post-war welfare state capitalism, the embrace of Keynesianism in the late 2000s was fraught with possibilities that were inimical to the neoliberalized variant of capitalism. Democratic mobilization might successfully demand that stimulus measures be implemented that reinstate the welfare state era policies that neoliberals had successfully exiled from public policy debate.

Perhaps the most threating possibility for neoliberals was the potential that an economic crisis might provide the opportunity for social justice advocates to use Keynesian economic theory to promote fiscal stimulus measures designed to have redistributive implications. On the level of economic theory, the Keynesian case for government stimulus during an economic crisis does not dictate how governments should design their stimulatory measures.[12] Indeed, Keynesian logic is invoked to justify spending on all manner of things, most notably military expenditures (thus the moniker "the welfare/warfare state"). However, the larger "marginal propensity to consume" of low-income individuals suggests that government programs biased towards supporting the economically vulnerable have the most stimulative consequences. In the Keynesian welfare state era, social justice advocates had considerable success using Keynesian theory to legitimate the mildly redistributive government programs that moderated the harsher aspects of capitalism. Thus Keynesian welfare state capitalism became

---

12 Keynes famously observed, "If the Treasury were to fill old bottles with banknotes, bury them at suitable depths in disused coalmines which are then filled up to the surface with town rubbish, and leave it to private enterprise on well-tried principles of laissez-faire to dig the notes up again ... there need be no more unemployment and, with the help of the repercussions, the real income of the community, and its capital wealth also, would probably become a good deal greater than it actually is. It would, indeed, be more sensible to build houses and the like; but if there are political and practical difficulties in the way of this, the above would be better than nothing" (2008, 116).

characterized by political struggle concerning whether government spending should be redistributive and social justice-oriented or should focus on more overtly pro-business purposes.

Neoliberalism is threated by the possibility that democratic resistance to the neoliberal agenda may successfully appeal to Keynesian economic rationale to promote social justice and redistributive agendas. The neoliberal demonization of "big" government of the Keynesian welfare state era has largely been motivated to deter just such a possibility. Ostensibly neoliberals celebrate a small state that refrains from economic intervention, but despite the more inflamed anti-state rhetoric of advocates of neoliberalism, genuine laissez-faire capitalism has not been on the neoliberal agenda. State activities supporting business interests are encouraged (or at least accepted) by many neoliberals, as are social programs that, for example, create a steady supply of appropriately skilled labour. However, neoliberals unite in their condemnation of state redistributive activities. Neoliberals often seize on government budget pressures as an opportunity to foreclose democratic pressure to enhance government redistributive programs. Whatever their origin, budget difficulties have been a fortuitous pretext to depict redistributive social programs as causing unsustainable fiscal problems. Various rounds of austerity measures did much to dismantle the redistributive dimensions of state economic activities. Thus the neoliberal desideratum of a "small state" might be more adequately characterized as a state that eschews redistributive activities, despite its continued activism on behalf of capital.

An economic crisis presents a propitious opportunity for a revived Keynesianism to justify redistributive economic stimulus. To the extent that the economic crisis was attributed to the pathologies of neoliberal capitalism, such as the marked increase in economic inequality in the neoliberal era (Tridico 2012), this might amplify popular demands for redistributive economic alternatives. Should democratic forces parlay Keynesian arguments to legitimate demands for redistributive economic stimulus measures, this might open the door to the reinstatement of many of the more progressive aspects of the welfare state that neoliberals have so assiduously demolished.

Expansionary Fiscal Contraction: The Neoliberal Case against Keynesian Stimulus

The EFC hypothesis developed within neoclassical economic theory to provide an economic rationale linking austerity measures to the promotion of economic recovery and growth. At least in its more careful articulations, advocates of expansionary austerity acknowledge the validity of the Keynesian argument that government budget tightening undermines economic growth by putting downward pressure on aggregate demand (Hellwig and Neumann 1987). But the EFC literature argued that, *under certain conditions,* strict government fiscal discipline might also encourage economic growth. Austerity proponents argued that if the downward economic pressure of government fiscal pull-back (the Keynesian effect) is more than compensated for by the positive consequences of government fiscal discipline, then austerity measures are expansionary overall.

While Keynes's *General Theory* presented the case for aggregate demand stimulus by means of an extended treatise critical of many dimension of the prevailing neoclassical theory of his time, there is no single oeuvre that rebuts the Keynesian analysis from a neoclassical perspective. Alesina's successive publications became more bold in their endorsement of the pro-growth aspects of austerity, as the caveats and tentativeness of the once "weak" case on behalf of expansionary austerity were overlooked by the enthusiastic embrace of the EFC hypothesis in neoliberal circles.[13]

Like the Keynesian argument, the EFC hypothesis focuses on expectations. While the Keynesian analysis of expectations emphasizes future aggregate demand conditions and their impact on business confidence and thus investment, the EFC hypothesis focuses instead on expectations related to government finances. EFC proponents argue that economic stimulus measures weaken governments' finances, and thus provoke expectations of future tax increases to repair the damage that stimulus measures have inflicted on government budgets. According to the EFC hypothesis, expectations of future tax increases have the perverse result of weakening aggregate demand. As governments attempt to stimulate the economy by running counter-cyclical deficits, investors restrain their spending for fear of higher impending tax bills. Fears of future tax hikes also cause consumers to curb spending, although presumably the consumers in question are relatively high-income individuals who have discretion about whether and when to spend on non-essentials,

---

[13] Blyth (2013, 173–5) details how Alesina and Ardanga's initial admission that their case was "weak" had largely disappeared in the later articulations of expansionary austerity.

and who can readily borrow to spend. (Lower-income consumers have little choice but to use most of their income to meet their bills, regardless of their expectations about the future state of taxation.[14])

According to the EFC hypothesis, Keynesian economic stimulus may backfire because of expectations about future tax increases. If the contractionary implications of government economic stimulus (diminished private sector confidence for fear of future tax increases) outweigh the expansionary dimensions of economic stimulus (better aggregate demand conditions that boost private sector confidence), Keynesian economic stimulus produces the perverse result of undermining economic growth. By the same token, austerity measures implemented in a weak economy will stimulate growth so long as expansionary effects caused by increased consumer and investor confidence about their improved future tax liabilities outweigh the contractionary (Keynesian) effects that austerity measures have on aggregate demand.

As the EFC literature evolved, other claims were elaborated to buttress the case for the growth-enhancing potential of austerity. EFC proponents claimed that a credible commitment to austere fiscal policy would please international financial markets. Bondholders are likely to demand lower risk premiums on government bonds issued by countries demonstrating rigorous fiscal discipline. Consequently, these "credibility effects" encourage downward pressure on domestic interest rates. Expectations of lower interest rates reinforce the stimulatory properties of fiscal constriction. In addition, EFC advocates claimed that lower interest rates would enhance the appreciation of stocks and bonds, thus contributing to a "wealth effect" that stimulates domestic consumption and investment (Alesina and Ardagna 2009). Via these channels, governments that gain the favour of financial markets by demonstrating their austerity credentials could reinforce the expansionary dimensions of fiscal contraction.

The case made on behalf of expansionary austerity rested heavily on the empirical examination of countries purported to have experienced economic growth alongside periods of government fiscal contraction. As is the case in all such narrowly technical argumentation, methodological and other more technical concerns weigh heavily in

---

14 Eggertsson and Krugman (2012) rebutted that consumption may be more closely linked to current income, and investment to current profit, thus fiscal stimulus can be expansionary.

the legitimacy of the results. Critics have made a host of methodological and technical objections to the EFC hypothesis. For example, the IMF (Guajardo, Leigh, and Pescatori 2011) scrutinized the pro-austerity methodology and concluded that the EFC proponents identified episodes of fiscal contractions in a manner that tended to bias the results towards confirming the EFC hypothesis (95–6 and appendix 3.3). Given these and other concerns,[15] the IMF concluded that "fiscal consolidation typically reduces output and raises unemployment in the short term" (93).

Arguably the greatest weakness of the EFC hypothesis (and its greatest evidentiary challenge) lay in its applicability during an economic downturn. In order to both refute the Keynesian case for economic stimulus and legitimate the austerity measures implemented in the wake of the 2008 economic and financial crisis, the EFC hypothesis aspired to show not only that austerity could encourage growth under ideal conditions, but that austerity could be pro-growth during an acute economic downturn. Jayadev and Konczal (2010) examined Alesina and Ardagna's (2009) data to point out that their historical examples of "successful" fiscal consolidations did not include any country that restrained spending in an economic downturn. They found that countries that cut government budgets during an economic downturn often had lower growth and/or higher debt/GDP levels. This groundbreaking study provoked many re-examinations of Alesina's publications. Perotti, one of Alesina's earlier co-authors, conceded, "These results cast doubt on at least some versions of the 'expansionary fiscal consolidations' hypothesis and on its applicability to many countries in the present circumstances" (2013, 42).

Despite criticisms of the EFC scholarship, its advocates enjoyed immense influence following the 2008 economic and financial crisis. Consensus among the neoliberal policy elite converged around the proposition that the (relatively mild) stimulus measures implemented

---

15 For example, concerns were raised that fiscal contractions may be expansionary only when accompanied by other fortuitous contextual factors, such as favourable export conditions, currency devaluations, accommodative monetary policy, particular labour market institutions, and other circumstances (Guajardo, Leigh, and Pescatori 2011). These considerations raised doubts about possibility that a purportedly "successful" episodes of EFC could be replicated in other contexts, and imply a "fallacy of composition" problem (De Grauwe and Ji 2013), meaning that all countries cannot simultaneously succeed in a strategy that requires, for example, a devaluation of the domestic currency vis-à-vis its export partners.

in response to the crisis should be promptly rescinded. By 2010 it was "Alesina's hour" (Coy 2010), as the Economic and Financial Affairs Council of the European Council of Ministers embraced the EFC hypothesis and the pro-growth austerity message. As the president of the European Central Bank explained, "As regards the economy, the idea that austerity measures could trigger stagnation is incorrect ... In fact, in these circumstances, everything that helps to increase the confidence of households, firms and investors in the sustainability of public finances is good for the consolidation of growth and job creation. I firmly believe that in the current circumstances confidence-inspiring policies will foster and not hamper economic recovery, because confidence is the key factor today" (quoted in Polidori 2010).

Perhaps the most ignominious episode in the theoretical case advanced to advocate for austerity concerned the famous paper by Reinhart and Rogoff, "Growth in a Time of Debt" (2010). Reinhardt and Rogoff argued that high government debt reduced economic growth, and that governments whose debt level exceeded 90 per cent of GDP would suffer a growth rate cut by 50 per cent. "Growth in a Time of Debt" was widely cited to justify prompt and dramatic budget cuts, despite the fragility of the world economy, and in the estimation of Paul Krugman this paper had "more immediate influence on public debate than any previous paper in the history of economics" (Krugman 2013a). Although University of Massachusetts Amherst graduate student Thomas Herndon exposed the paper's rather rudimentary computational flaws that contradicted its dire predictions (Herndon, Ash, and Pollin 2014), Reinhart and Rogoff nevertheless were pivotal in legitimating a dramatic international turn towards austerity: "What the Reinhart-Rogoff affair shows is the extent to which austerity has been sold on false pretenses. For three years, the turn to austerity has been presented not as a choice but as a necessity. Economic research, austerity advocates insisted, showed that terrible things happen once debt exceeds 90 percent of G.D.P. But 'economic research' showed no such thing; a couple of economists made that assertion, while many others disagreed. Policy makers abandoned the unemployed and turned to austerity because they wanted to, not because they had to" (Krugman 2013a).

While the austerity was continuing to exert important international influence, initial empirical results were shedding doubt on the EFC hypothesis. The IMF's 2013 study found that "stronger planned fiscal consolidation has been associated with lower growth than expected," and this relationship was particularly strong early in the crisis (Blanchard and Leigh 2013). A second study confirms that fiscal consolidation motivated by a desire to reduce budget deficits had contractionary effects of GDP, and cast further doubt that the EFC literature tended to overstate the expansionary effects of fiscal contraction (Guajardo, Leigh, and Pescatori 2014). Thus early evidence suggests that the central justificatory discourse legitimating austerity – namely that austerity would promote economic growth – is in grave doubt.

The EFC hypothesis remains influential, despite its many critics. In the journalistic media, EFC arguments continue to be cited as evidence of the virtues of government spending restraint.[16] It appears that EFC proponents have made sufficient headway in legitimating austerity that the case for government fiscal contraction remains persuasive to many, despite the evidentiary weaknesses of the EFC hypothesis.

Austerity and the Neoliberal Project

What accounts for the remarkable influence of the EFC hypothesis' arguments promoting austerity, despite its theoretical weakness and dubious empirical validity? Regardless of the likelihood that government fiscal contraction would promote economic growth, the EFC hypothesis served the broader neoliberal agenda in other ways. In terms of its defensive value, the EFC hypothesis shielded neoliberalization from popular demands that might well have gained traction in the aftermath of an economic crisis. But the EFC hypothesis also made possible some aggressive neoliberal initiatives that might have been politically impossible without the legitimation conferred by the proponents of the EFC hypothesis.

In its most broad terms, the EFC hypothesis depicted governments' willingness to demonstrate their neoliberal credentials as the *sine qua non* of economic recovery. Because it elevated the confidence of financial markets, business investors, and higher-income consumers as the central requisite of economic recovery and growth, the EFC hypothesis encouraged governments to focus on securing the approval of these privileged groups. Since the EFC hypothesis argued that the confidence of these groups was derived from their expectations about future tax increases, any government actions that potentially exacerbate

---

16 For example, see Speer and Lammam (2014).

government budget problems (and thus increase the perceived likelihood of future tax increases) would subvert economic recovery.[17] Thus the EFC argument insisted upon the necessity of government accountability to the very groups who benefited the most from neoliberal capitalism: corporate investors and higher-income individuals. Because governments were urged by proponents of the EFC hypothesis to focus on securing the approval of the relatively privileged, politicians were insulated from popular demands of those suffering most from the economic crisis. Any response to democratic pressure that exacerbated government budget problems would subvert economic recovery if it offended the sensibilities of elites. Presumably governments that demonstrate rigorous fiscal discipline despite domestic political pressure have even more impeccable neoliberal credentials, thus enabling them to reap greater rewards conferred by the positive regard of high-income consumers and investors.

While it is possible to reduce government deficits and debt by both tax increases and spending reductions, advocates of the EFC hypothesis argued for spending reductions rather than tax increases (Alesina and Perotti 1995). This aversion to immediate tax increases is perhaps unsurprising, given the importance accorded expectations of future tax increases in the EFC hypothesis. However, the anti-tax message of the EFC hypothesis was particularly opportune in the wake of the financial and economic crisis. The crisis was widely seen as the having been caused by the inappropriate action of financial sector firms and their more highly remunerated employees who profited from dubious and systemically destabilizing activities. It was possible that the public might demand that those responsible for the crisis pay for the consequences of their actions in the form of higher taxes to defray the budgetary implications of government actions to mitigate the crisis. Even if they were not seen as causing or exacerbating the crisis, a further argument could be made for higher taxation of companies and high-income individuals. Since corporations and the "1 per cent" had benefited inordinately from the neoliberal era, it appeared reasonable for them to shoulder a greater

---

17 This logic was applied unevenly at best. Costly government expenses to support business interests in the financial crisis were apparently tolerable to high-income individuals and corporations, while government expenses to support the public were seen as much more ominous, perhaps because of the difficulty of scaling back these expenses when the crisis passed.

portion of the burden as neoliberal capitalism went into crisis. Thus by positioning anti-tax credentials as imperative for economic recovery, the EFC hypothesis sheltered the beneficiaries of neoliberalism from demands that this elite should be taxed more heavily to either atone for their culpability or restore greater equity.

According to the EFC hypothesis, government finances should be improved via spending cuts rather than tax increases because investors and high-income consumers view spending cuts as an indication that future tax increases would be less likely. The more aggressive the austerity measures, the more likely that these cuts will mollify the concerns of investors and high-income consumers. Thus to buttress governments' credentials for fiscal restraint, EFC proponents recommended that spending cuts be "large credible and decisive" (Alesina 2010). Moreover, this preference for large spending cuts meant that the EFC hypothesis could be employed to legitimate attacks on "entitlements" (Alesina and Ardagna 2009), particularly those with a redistributive dimension. As Alesina and Perotti conclude, "It is becoming increasingly apparent that cuts in the 'welfare state' will have to be a critical part of the necessary fiscal adjustments" (1995, 1). For example, the EFC hypothesis encouraged attacks on programs that supported the low-income aging citizens on the grounds that such entitlements were fiscally unsustainable. In response, some jurisdictions raised the age of retirement that triggers eligibility for publicly funded retirement income support, thus compelling low-income senior citizens to extend their work lives or face more impoverished circumstances.

Compelling low-income seniors to work later in life was not the only labour market consequence of the austerity programs implemented in accordance with the EFC hypothesis. Another sub-theme of the EFC that was popular among its neoliberal supporters is its celebration of "wage moderation" that can accompany fiscal contraction. Alesina and Ardagna explain that fiscal contractions focused on government spending cuts are likely to reduce government employment and put downward pressure on the wages of civil servants. Thus in conformity with the EFC hypothesis, government might take the opportunity to attack the wages and other working conditions of its own workforce, on the premise that any savings produced would make future tax increases less likely. "Wage moderation" may also be facilitated during the imposition of austerity by the direct intervention of the government in wage negotiations (Perotti 2013). These labour market conditions also put downward pressure on the wages of private sector workers (Alesina and Ardagna 1998, 2009). Either by explicit government design or by creating generally hostile labour market conditions, the EFC hypothesis offered the additional neoliberal "benefit" of wage moderation. This moderation was heralded as an important aspect of expansionary austerity, in that it encouraged increased profits, investment, and competitiveness (Alesina and Ardagna 2009, 38).

Conclusion

The EFC hypothesis does not command the prestige it enjoyed in the lead up to the austerity measures of the early 2010s. Of course this is not to say that its arguments may not regain prominence, particularly in the wake of future economic crises. The EFC hypothesis has been targeted by a number of empirical and theoretical rebuttals, and a flourishing scholarship speaks to the effectiveness of fiscal policy in promoting economic recovery.[18] Whatever the enduring stature of the EFC hypothesis in the retrospective analysis of economists, this chapter is concerned with the hegemonic influence of the EFC hypothesis for the length of time necessary to usher in the austerity policies that distinguished the early 2010s.

This chapter has argued that – regardless of its merits as an economic theory and its ability (or lack thereof) to promote economic recovery – the EFC hypothesis served neoliberalism as an opportune justificatory discourse to legitimate austerity policies. It was opportune in that it called for austerity measures that were designed to serve the wider neoliberal project both defensively and offensively. The EFC hypothesis defended neoliberalism from the possibility that a reinvigorated Keynesianism could serve as theoretical justification to respond to democratic pressures for more generous welfare state–style social programs, particularly those initiatives with a redistributive dimension. This protected the neoliberal project from the possibility that an economic crisis could serve as an opportunity to institute more egalitarian economic alternatives. The EFC also provided the discursive legitimation for an offensive neoliberal strategy. The EFC hypothesis supported aggressive attacks both on wages (particularly of civil servants) and on existing "entitlement" social programs. Thus the EFC hypothesis legitimated attacks on some of the remnants of welfare state–era social

---

18 See, for example, Delong and Summers (2012).

programs and employment relationships that had thus far resisted the pressures of neoliberalization. Thanks in part to the discursive legitimation conferred by EFC hypothesis, neoliberals were able to capitalize on a context of economic upheaval, uncertainty, and public anxiety to overcome democratic resistance to restructuring these holdouts to neoliberalization.

The austerity initiatives legitimated under the EFC banner have exacerbated some of neoliberal capitalism's most troubling features. For example, a case can be made that recent austerity measures contribute to rising income inequality that has characterized neoliberal capitalism. One important determinant of rising income inequality is real wage growth in the neoliberal era. Despite rising productivity, real wages of most workers have stagnated since the dawn of neoliberalism, while the incomes of the more affluent have increased dramatically. The austerity measures encouraged by the EFC hypothesis reinforce this downward pressure on wages of the less affluent workers. Certainly the "wage moderation" agenda of the EFC hypothesis directly seeks to lower the wages of public sector workers. But the wider ramifications of attacks on both social programs and labour market institutions include the buttressing of labour market conditions that contribute to wage stagnation. Mathieu Dufour and I have argued elsewhere that attacks on social programs intended to support the unemployed and other vulnerable workers have contributed to declining worker bargaining power, thus reinforcing the inability of workers to negotiate for wages that reflect their growing productivity (2015, 2016). For example, policy changes that compel lower-income workers to work further into old age reduce the bargaining power all workers, thus exerting downward pressure on the incomes of all low-wage workers.

To the extent that they have reinforced economic inequality, austerity initiatives have another pernicious effect. While claiming to promote economic recovery and growth, the measures implemented in conformity with the EFC hypothesis may have subverted these objectives. As the incomes of low- and moderate-wage workers are squeezed, they have less capacity to consume, thus detracting from the aggregate demand stimulus that promotes economic recovery. As a recent study published jointly by the World Bank Group has pointed out, "The shift of income away from labour (and, in particular, away from low-wage workers) towards capital (and top earners) might also have a negative impact on aggregate demand, to the extent that workers with below-average pay tend to have a higher consumption propensity ... which might result in a particularly adverse effect on the speed of recovery" (2014, 13).

If, indeed, the austerity measures implemented in the wake of the 2008 financial and economic crisis contributed to downward pressure on wages, economic inequality, and retarded economic recovery, how was it possible that a policy program with such perverse impacts could be successfully portrayed as a prescription for economic recovery? Although the profound economic crisis had in some ways discredited neoliberalism in the public eye, neoliberalism so dominated the discursive terrain that the public was persuaded that the solution to the crisis of neoliberal capitalism was the imposition of further neoliberalism. While this represents a lost opportunity to seize on the destabilization of economic crisis to promote economic alternatives, we have certainly not seen the last capitalist crisis. On the contrary, the exacerbation in inequality and the further reduction in the social safety net may well contribute to the next crisis. If so, opponents of neoliberal capitalism must be ready to counter the next incarnation of the EFC hypothesis and demand policy alternatives do not merely entrench the current neoliberal pathologies.

REFERENCES

Alesina, Alberto. 2010. "Fiscal Adjustments: Lessons from Recent History." Prepared for the Ecofin meeting, Madrid, 15 April. https://scholar.harvard.edu/alesina/publications/fiscal-adjustments-lessons-recent-history.
— 2012. "Fiscal Policy after the Great Recession." *Atlantic Economic Journal* 40 (4): 429–35. https://doi.org/10.1007/s11293-012-9337-z.
Alesina, Alberto, and Silvia Ardagna. 1998. "Tales of Fiscal Adjustment." *Economic Policy* 13 (27): 487–545. https://doi.org/10.1111/1468-0327.00039.
— 2009. "Large Changes in Fiscal Policy: Taxes versus Spending." NBER Working Paper no. 15438.
Alesina, Alberto, Carlo Favero, and Francesco Giavazzi. 2015. "The Output Effect of Fiscal Consolidation Plans." *Journal of International Economics* 96 (S1): S19–S42.
Alesina, Alberto, and Roberto Perotti. 1995. "Fiscal Expansions and Adjustments in OECD Countries." *Economic Policy* 21:207–47.
Alesina, Alberto, Roberto Perotti, and José Tavares. 1998. "The Political Economy of Fiscal Adjustments." *Brookings Papers on Economic Activity* 29 (1): 197–266.

Barbier, Edward B. 2010. *A Global Green New Deal: Rethinking the Economic Recovery*. Cambridge: Cambridge University Press. https://doi.org/10.1017/CBO9780511844607.

Barro, Robert. 1974. "Are Government Bonds Net Wealth?" *Journal of Political Economy* 82 (6): 1095–111.

Blanchard, Oliver, and Daniel Leigh. 2013. "Growth Forecast Errors and Fiscal Multipliers." NBER Working Paper no. 18779. https://doi.org/10.3386/w18779.

Blyth, Mark. 2013. *Austerity: The History of a Dangerous Idea*. Oxford: Oxford University Press.

Brown, E. Carey. 1956. "Fiscal Policies in the 1930s: A Reappraisal." *American Economic Review* 46:857–79.

Chang, Ha-Joon. 2002. "Breaking the Mould: An Institutionalist Political Economy Alternative to the Neo-liberal Theory of the Market and the State." *Cambridge Journal of Economics* 26 (5): 539–59. https://doi.org/10.1093/cje/26.5.539.

Coy, Peter. 2010. "Keynes vs Alesina: Alesina Who?" *Bloomberg Business*, 29 June.

Crotty, James. 1992. "Neoclassical and Keynesian Approaches to the Theory of Investment." *Journal of Post Keynesian Economics* 14 (4): 483–96. https://doi.org/10.1080/01603477.1992.11489912.

– 2012. "The Great Austerity War: What Caused the US Deficit Crisis and Who Should Pay to Fix it?" *Cambridge Journal of Economics* 36 (1): 79–104. https://doi.org/10.1093/cje/ber029.

De Grauwe, Paul, and Yuemei Ji. 2013. "The Legacy of Austerity in the Eurozone." Centre for European Studies.

Delong, J. Brandford, and Lawerence H. Summers. 2012. "Fiscal Policy in a Depressed Economy." *Brookings Papers on Economic Activity* 2012 (1): 233–97. https://doi.org/10.1353/eca.2012.0000.

Dow, Shelia. 2012. "Keynes on Knowledge, Expectations and Rationality." In *Rethinking Expectations: The Way Forward for Macroeconomics*, ed. R. Frydman and S. Phelps, 112–29. Princeton: Princeton University Press.

Dufour, Mathieu, and Ellen Russell. 2015. "Why Isn't Productivity More Popular?" *International Productivity Monitor* 28 (Spring): 47–62.

Eggertsson, Gauti B., and Paul Krugman. 2012. "Debt, Deleveraging, and the Liquidity Trap: A Minsky-Koo Approach." *Quarterly Journal of Economics* 127 (3): 1469–513. https://doi.org/10.1093/qje/qjs023.

Finlayson, Alan Christopher, Thomas A. Lyson, Andrew Pleasant, Kai A. Schafft, and Robert J. Torres. 2005. "The 'Invisible Hand': Neoclassical Economics and the Ordering of Society." *Critical Sociology* 31 (4): 515–36. https://doi.org/10.1163/156916305774482183.

Freidman, Milton, and Anna Schwartz. 1963. *A Monetary History of the United States, 1867–1960*. Princeton NJ: Princeton University Press.

Giavazzi, Francesco, and Marco Pagano. 1990. "Can Severe Fiscal Contractions Be Expansionary? Tales of Two Small European Countries." *National Bureau of Economic Research Macroeconomics Annual* 5:75–111.

Grabel, Ilene. 2000. "The Political Economy of 'Policy Credibility': The New-Classical Macroeconomics and the Remaking of Emerging Economies." *Cambridge Journal of Economics* 24 (1): 1–19. https://doi.org/10.1093/cje/24.1.1.

Gros, Daniel, and Rainer Maurer. 2012. "Can Austerity Be Self-Defeating?" *Intereconomics* 47 (3): 175–84.

Guajardo, Jaime, Daniel Leigh, and Andrea Pescatori. 2014. "Expansionary Austerity: International Evidence." *Journal of the European Economic Association* 12 (4): 949–68.

Hein, Eckhard. 2011. "Redistribution, Global Imbalances and the Financial and Economic Crisis: The Case for a Keynesian New Deal." *International Journal of Labour Research* 3 (1): 51–73.

Hellwig, Martin, and Manfred J.M. Neumann. 1987. "Economic Policy in Germany: Was There a Turnaround?" *Economic Policy* 2 (5): 103–45. https://doi.org/10.2307/1344622.

Herndon, Thomas, Michael Ash, and Robert Pollin. 2014. "Does High Public Debt Consistently Stifle Economic Growth? A Critique of Reinhart and Rogoff." *Cambridge Journal of Economics* 38 (2): 257–79. https://doi.org/10.1093/cje/bet075.

Jayadev, Arjun, and Mike Konczal. 2010. *The Boom Not the Slump: The Right Time for Austerity*. New York: Roosevelt Institute.

Keynes, John Maynard. 2008. *The General Theory of Employment, Interest and Money*. New Delhi: Atlantic Publishers.

Kotz, David. 2009. "The Financial and Economic Crisis of 2008: A Systemic Crisis of Neoliberal Capitalism." *Review of Radical Political Economics* 41 (3): 305–17. https://doi.org/10.1177/0486613409335093.

Krugman, Paul. 2013a. "The Excel Depression." *New York Times*, 18 April.

– 2013b. "How the Case for Austerity Has Crumbled." *New York Review of Books*, 6 June.

– 2013c. "Night of the Living Alesina, Continued." *New York Times*, 14 March.

Mirowski, Philip. 1982. "What's Wrong with the Laffer Curve?" *Journal of Economic Issues* 16 (3): 815–28. https://doi.org/10.1080/00213624.1982.11504034.

Ortiz, Isabel. 2009. "Fiscal Stimulus Plans: The Need for a New Global Deal." International Development Economics Associates, 1–6.

Ortiz, Isabel, Jingqing Chai, and Matthew Cummins. 2010. *Recovery for All: A Call for Collaborative Action*. UNICEF Social and Economic Policy Concept Note.

Perotti, Roberto. 2013. "The 'Austerity Myth': Gain without Pain?" In *Fiscal Policy after the Financial Crisis*, ed. Alberto Alesina and Francesco Giavazzi, 307–54. Chicago: University of Chicago Press.

Polidori, Elena. 2010. "Interview with Jean-Claude Trichet, President of the European Central Bank." *La Repubblica*, 16 June. https://www.ecb.europa.eu/press/key/date/2010/html/sp100624.en.html.

Reinhart, Carmen M., and Kenneth S. Rogoff. 2010. "Growth in a Time of Debt." NBER Working Paper no. 15639. https://doi.org/10.1257/aer.100.2.573.

Russell, Ellen. 2014. "The Strategic Uses of Budget Crisis." In *Orchestrating Austerity*, ed. D. Banes and S. McBride, 34–49. Halifax: Fernwood.

Russell, Ellen, and Mathieu Dufour. 2016. "Why the Rising Tide Doesn't Lift All Boats: Wages and Bargaining Power in Neoliberal Canada." *Studies in Political Economy* 97 (1): 37–55. http://dx.doi.org/10.1080/07078552.2016.1174462.

Speer, Sean, and Charles Lammam. 2014. "More Deficit Spending Not the Answer for Canada." *Financial Post*, 25 July.

Stockhammer, Engelbert. 2011. "Neoliberalism, Income Distribution and the Causes of the Crisis." In *The Financial Crisis: Origins and Implications*, ed. J.L. Oreiro, P. Arestis, and R. Sobreira, 234–58. New York: Palgrave Macmillan. https://doi.org/10.1057/9780230303942_11.

Tridico, Pasquale. 2012. "Financial Crisis and Global Imbalances: Its Labour Market Origins and the Aftermath." *Cambridge Journal of Economics* 36 (1): 17–42. https://doi.org/10.1093/cje/ber031.

Wade, Robert Hunter. 2009. "The Global Slump: Deeper Causes and Harder Lessons." *Challenge* 52 (5): 5–24. https://doi.org/10.2753/0577-5132520501.

Weintraub, E. Roy. 1999. "How Should We Write the History of Twentieth-Century Economics?" *Oxford Review of Economic Policy* 15 (4): 139–52. https://doi.org/10.1093/oxrep/15.4.139.

Wisman, Jon D. 2013. "Wage Stagnation, Rising Inequality and the Financial Crisis of 2008." *Cambridge Journal of Economics* 37 (4): 921–45. https://doi.org/10.1093/cje/bes085.

World Bank Group. 2014. "G20 Labour Markets: Outlook, Key Challenges and Policy Responses." Report prepared for the G20 Labour and Employment Ministerial Meeting, Melbourne, 10–11 September.

Zhang, Yanchun, Nina Thelen, and Aparna Rao. 2012. "Social Protection in Fiscal Stimulus Packages." In *Children in Crisis: Seeking Child-Sensitive Policy Responses*, ed. Caroline Harper, Nicola Jones, Ronald U. Mendoza, David Stewart, and Erika Strand, 226–46. London: Palgrave Macmillan. https://www.researchgate.net/publication/266672312_Social_Protection_in_Fiscal_Stimulus_Packages_Some_Evidence.

PART TWO

Impact and Consequences

Introduction: Austerity on the Ground

BRYAN M. EVANS AND STEPHEN MCBRIDE

The five chapters composing this section of the volume illustrate how austerity plays out in public sector occupations, social policy domains, and employment more generally. In other words, how austerity is experienced in daily life and what it means for individuals as workers and the working class as a collectivity. Specifically, these chapters traverse a range of experiences and sectors including the conditions of work in the long-term care sector (Baines), elementary and secondary teaching (Sweeney and Hickey), the expansion of the low-waged work labour market (Evans, McBride, and Muirhead), immigration (Barrass and Shields), and pensions policy (Zhou and Shi). Taken as a whole, these contributions do not simply and only paint a bleak picture of how work and workers have been deleteriously affected by austerity, but also importantly signal that if politics and policy have led to this moment, politics and policy can open up new counter-avenues leading to different outcomes.

In most of the countries composing the OECD, health and education are among the largest – if not the largest – spending envelopes of any government. In Canada, where both policy domains fall within the jurisdiction of the sub-national provinces, health and education taken as a whole take up two-thirds or more of the global budget. Throughout the OECD these are big budget items. Controlling or cutting costs necessarily involves restructuring service delivery and quality. Consequently, rolling out austerity in any meaningful way must cut into these politically sensitive areas of public policy.

Donna Baines presents her case study of long-term care through the frame of the "care-control duet"; that is, the paradox where social care, through the logic of Taylorization, becomes manifested not just as care but also as a means of control. Checklists, data gathering, and analytics not only provide the technical basis for individual worker performance management but also the management of resource inputs and their measurement against outcomes. Such means of Taylorized control contribute to the deskilling of front-line care workers and also serve as a conduit for austerity, allowing it to manifest in the most mundane daily interactions. But that is not the whole story. Controlled care works simultaneously with resistance as care workers find ways to provide more care, despite the machinery of control they work within. Similarly, and yet in a different context, Sweeney and Hickey's case study of collective bargaining strategies by elementary and secondary school teachers in Ontario illustrates the limits of resistance, which is based on an acceptance of the general rules of austerity but seeks to defend the sectional interests of one group of trade union members. In the case they study, pragmatism has become the prevailing ideological guide, not only in bargaining but in the realm of electoral politics. Rather than a blind loyalty to the Canadian social democratic party – the New Democratic Party (NDP) – Ontario's teachers' unions, in addition to unions outside of the education sector, have turned to strategic voting. That is a strategy of endorsing candidates of the party (in Ontario, the NDP, or the Liberals) most likely to defeat the aggressively anti-union Conservatives. This reflects not simply deeply held concerns about the Conservative policy agenda of austerity, but also derives from a long history of disappointment with social democrats in government who have adopted their own version of hard bargaining and public sector austerity. Thus support for the Liberal Party can emerge as the best or least-worst alternative.

In both cases, resistance is de-politicized but in rather different ways. Social care workers absorb personally the cost of austerity, while teachers take a sectional approach to bargaining that has no political program beyond winning some modest advances for their own members.

The limited forms of resistance noted above is obviously not a function of some ideological failing of public sector workers. The expressions of resistance observed flow from the real-life calculations of what is possible in a certain historical period. The political defeats inflicted upon workers over the past thirty years and more have yielded, with notable exceptions, a much more conservative approach to politics. Informing this retreat in no small way has been the remaking of the labour market after the "golden age" of the Keynesian welfare state era. Evans, McBride, and Muirhead, in their exploration of the new low-wage normal, note that low wages are endemic and derive from a politically constructed globalized international economy. The terms of the post-war settlement were restructured to facilitate a transfer of power from workers and their organizations to the market, a development that fuelled inequality, precarity, and the expansion of the low-waged sector. Still, such developments pose the question of whether a more positive restructuring could occur, leading to reversal of the imbalance of power. The publication of Piketty's *Capital in the Twenty-First Century* (2014) pushed income inequality into mainstream discourse and pointed to the vital role of political institutions in mitigating inequality. One expression of this reconsideration is a renewed interest in minimum wage policy as well as through living wage campaigns. This marks a return to the central questions first raised in political economy where income distribution was understood, even by neoclassicals, in class terms – where outcomes were a function of class power.

Immigration and pension policy, case studies presented by Barrass and Shields in the first instance, and Zhou and Shi in the second, provide concrete expressions of how the political narratives of austerity are used to divide workers across age or citizenship status. With respect to immigration policy, Canada, despite an image as a pro-immigration state, has re-conceptualized immigration as a tool for further labour market flexibilization concomitant with a reduced level of state support for immigrant settlement and integration.

Similarly, pension "reform," in the context of recovery from the Great Financial Crisis, is understood as part of a larger process or welfare state transformation. The market turmoil of the crisis eroded if not destroyed the investments that sustained defined benefit plans, a form of pension plan common in the public sector in particular. The result has been a shift in pension policy to encumber individual workers with risk and responsibility.

In sum, the contributions presented in this section demonstrate that austerity is not an abstraction but rather carries serious consequences, both immediate and in the longer term for workers. At the same time, permeating these vignettes are two truths – one, that austerity is constructed as inevitable because of market logics, but also, more positively, two, that political intervention to reverse or mitigate austerity is a viable option.

REFERENCE

Piketty, Thomas. 2014. *Capital in the Twenty-First Century*. Cambridge, MA: Harvard University Press. https://doi.org/10.4159/9780674369542.

6 Care and Control in Long-term Care Work

DONNA BAINES

Introduction

A lengthy debate has taken place across many literatures regarding the role of the state services as an extension of state control and coercion, and the role of public sector workers as political actors (Aronowitz and Bratis 2002; Block 2010; Chorney et al. 1997; Edwards 1978; Jessop 1990; Miliband and Miliband 1965; Miliband 1983; Panitch 2000; Smith 2000). This role is not limited to police and military, but extends into health and social services, where public sector care workers, often depicted as "angels of mercy," are seen as the long arm of the state, acting oppressively on behalf of dominant classes to ensure the smooth functioning of capitalism (Bailey and Brake 1980; Burman 2004; Galper 1975, 1980; Lavalette 2011; McLaughlin 2010). Rather than exclusively caring or controlling, Taylor-Gooby (2000) argues that the social care professionals, who grew in numbers and influence as part of the social welfare state, reflect the multiple ambiguities of that state in which social justice, equity, and care motives intertwined unevenly with motives of control, and at times, coercion (see also Bailey and Brake 1980; Lavalette 2011).

Drawing on data collected as part of a larger five-country research project on long-term residential care (LTC) for the frail elderly, this chapter argues that the care-control duet of social care took on a new, unstable homeostasis in the context of the scarce resources associated with austerity and New Public Management. Early theorizations from the larger study confirm that care work is increasingly technical and Taylorized, leaving little room for emotional or relationship-based care (Baines and Daly 2015) and interestingly, few opportunities for direct coercion of residents other than neglect (Hall 2004). These same dynamics have generated increased control of both workers and care recipients in order to meet the timelines and outcome targets stipulated in government contracts. In effect, workers act as conduits of state control, rushing their work with residents, providing thin, technical supports rather than holistic patient-centred care.

The objective of this chapter is twofold. First, drawing on the literature and qualitative data, it traces connections between the historical debates on state theory and control, and the current round of austerity. Second, the chapter uses the same qualitative data to highlight some of the dynamics of the changing terrain of LTC in the context of austerity, as an exemplar of care in this era of constraint. The first part of this chapter briefly summarizes the major, largely Marxist debates on welfare state control and coercion that flourished through the 1940s to the 1980s, and subsequent Foucauldian contributions. The second part of the chapter outlines the methods used to collect the data discussed in the balance of the chapter, and explores the experience of those providing and receiving long-term care.

The Welfare State, Care and Control

Though mainstream theories of the state tend to view it as an arbitrator of competing claims, Marxist, feminist, and other critical analyses view the state as (1) reflecting the interests of the ruling class in maintaining capitalist production and profit, and/or (2) an unequal equilibrium between the struggles and successes of subordinate groups versus dominant groups within the capitalist mode of production (O'Connor 1973; Orloff 2009; Poulantzas and Miliband 1972; Smith 2010; Showstack Sassoon 1987). Both sets of analyses see the state as undertaking two main sets of activities: legitimation and accumulation (O'Connor 1973; Chorney et al. 1977).

Social welfare, as an arm of the state, is argued to control and manage the unrest of the general population, including those who do not or no longer have a role in production, such as the very young, the elderly, those in frail health, people with disabilities, the criminalized, and so forth (O'Connor 1973; Poulantzas 1973). In Poulantzas's formulation (1973), human service workers are the indispensable "soft cops" of the capitalist state. In contrast, Galper (1980) argues that while the state represents the interests of the capitalist class, most social service workers work with oppressed populations and are well positioned to foster resistance and help build a new socialist society (see also Bailey and Brake 1980. Galper argues further that state services act (1) as a way to control populations outside of the labour force (frail elderly, other dependent adults, and by extension their family and friends), (2) through exclusion and isolation, (3) while providing governments a way to show concern for groups and interests other than those of corporations.[1]

The debate on state theory moved to a higher level of sophistication with the adoption of a conceptualization of the state as a dynamic and constantly changeable equilibrium of compromises between classes, dominant and subordinate groups, and their interests, as played out on the backdrop of capitalist production (Albo and Jenson 1989; Gulalp 1987; Panitch and Gindin 2000). Asserting the interests of subordinate groups, feminists, anti-racists, and others, argued likewise that the state reproduces conditions favourable to continued profit while simultaneously reflecting the successes and failures of struggles for equity (Evans and Wekerle 1997; Ng 1988; Walker 1990; Warskett 1993). Taylor-Gooby's (2000) argument embodied a similar dynamic of struggles and

---

1 Galper (1975, 1980) also delineated "functions" of the social welfare, including

  1 acting as a safety valve in periods of social stress and conflict, permitting reform groups to occasionally meet with success without fundamentally challenging the relations of production and inequity;
  2 bringing new populations more firmly into the electoral system to defend their gains;
  3 fostering divisiveness – individualized entitlement to benefits builds resentment from those who are excluded from benefits and, at the level of agencies, competition for funding means that some agencies win and some lose;
  4 legitimizing exclusion from the labour force by isolating and minimally maintaining people thought to not be useful to production (for example, people with disabilities, the aged, the very young);
  5 permitting governments (and corporations) to appear to show concern for people, not just corporations;
  6 undertaking day-to-day control of populations outside the workforce (for example, incarcerated people);
  7 re-socializing individuals to be productive, competitive, obedient, etc.;
  8 stigmatizing service users (such as those receiving public assistance), which deters people from applying for benefits or falling into situations that they may need services; and
  9 providing direct profit from provision of services (e.g., building social housing; providing private health care or LTC).

  Though all these aspects are active in all social welfare states, their relative power differs, depending on the successes and failures of subordinate groups and classes.

relative autonomy in that the multiply ambiguous mandate of the care professions associated with the rapid growth of the welfare state was not entirely social transformation (social justice), ameliorative, or social control, but in various circumstances one, the other, or a combination. As Wakefield (1998) observes, multiple motivators lie at the heart of care work – altruism among them, but also the need to control and at times coerce.

The social control debate took on a new dimension with Foucault's introduction of governing, not in a top-down manner, but horizontally through the internalization of dominant discourses, "professional knowledges" (including professional ethics and comportment), and the use of technologies of control such as digital assessment and case notes. These "expert" practices removed the need for direct, moment-to-moment supervision/control and permitted governance at great distances in dispersed settings (Cruikshank 1999; Rose 1990, 1996; Marston and McDonald 2006; McDonald and Marston 2002). The case of care work, the use of digital documentation transfers risk from funders (generally the government) to the management of funded agencies, and down to front-line workers. In effect, front-line workers become responsible for the documentation that provides continued funding for their employer. Though the IT permits close surveillance of worker output, this level of direct supervision is rarely warranted, as workers tend to internalize "the gaze" of supervisors and complete the documentation as part of their sense of themselves as ethical professionals (McDonald 2006; Smith 2007; Rossiter 2000). Though empirical research has establish that other kinds of publicly funded human services take on the state form and reproduce hierarchical, unequal, and controlling relations (Ng 1988; Walker 1990; Warskett 1993), LTC has not been explored as an exercise in state control, and it is to this that the balance of the chapter addresses itself.

Methods

The data analysed in this chapter are a subset of a larger five-country study of long-term care (in Canada, the United States, Sweden, Germany, and Norway). The data analysed here are drawn from two studies in one each of Canada (2012) and the United States (2013), using rapid ethnography (Baines and Cunningham 2013; Szebehely 2007; Handwerker 2001), a method of team research, taking place over a short period, in this case one to two weeks. The studies involved: interviews with players from all levels of the organization (forty-four in Canada and thirty-seven in the United States for a total of eighty-one, including residents, managers, clinical and front-line care and operations staff, volunteers, and family members; the sample was overwhelming female); participant observations; and a review of publicly available documents. Both aged-care facilities involved in these case studies were midsize (between 50 and 100 residents), non-profits, and viewed by the community as exemplary care providers. Data analysis involved multiple readings of the data until patterns and themes could be identified (Glesne 2005). Ethics approval was received from all the universities involved in the study. Limitations include the small number of case studies and the influence management may have exerted on the workers, as the study could proceed only with approval of management.

Nursing home care for older adults in Canada is among the most highly commercialized sector in health care, though it operates within the larger context of publicly funded systems (services are contracted out, while the government provides the funding for everything but a fee for board). In the United States, health care is largely private, though the public and non-profit sectors provide care to specific populations such as veterans, hard-to-serve populations, and, in the case of LTC, a range of elderly people at a range of prices and quality. Though there are differences between Canada and the United States, there are sufficient commonalities for broad sweep comparisons aimed at seeking similarities and differences (Patton 2002).

Findings

In this section of the chapter, the literature on control, care, and coercion is discussed ethnographically (Geertz 1994), intermixed with exemplar quotes from the data. The codes, which form the subsections of this larger findings section, include managerialism; new technologies; the reduction/removal of skills and autonomy; and resistance. The main participants in the study were front-line staff with few credentials (often called personal support workers – PSWs) and fully credentialled and college- or university-educated registered nurses (RNs). The balance of the article addresses (1) how care and control are experienced by those who provide on the front lines of long-term care provision, and (2) whether the data provide insight into LTC as part of the dynamics of the welfare state as noted above. Here I refer specifically to Taylor-Gooby's notion (2000) of the multiple ambiguities of the welfare state in which social justice, equity, and care intertwine unevenly with control, and Galper's (1980) observations that social welfare provision can provide much-needed support while simultaneously controlling populations outside of the workforce (the frail elderly and dependent adults) through exclusion and isolation, while providing governments a way to show concern for people, not just corporate profit, and ensure conditions for continued capitalist production.

Managerialism

The labour process and governmentality (Foucaudian) literatures discuss at length the impact of managerialism on care work (Carey 2009; Charlesworth 2010; Cunningham 2008; McDonald 2006; Rossiter 2000; Pollack and Rossiter 2010; Triantafillou 2012), and our data are largely confirmatory. Since the mid-eighties, Western governments shifted from more Keynesian, interventionist models to neoliberal approaches focused on reducing collective entitlements and public provision, concentrating instead on approaches that fostered individual self-reliance, individual responsibility for risk, and reduction of public expenditures (Clarke 2004; McBride 2014; McDonald 2006; for further discussions of neoliberal privatization strategies, see Zhou and Shi, and Barrass and Shields in this volume). Neoliberal notions of the need for cost and efficacy controls paved the way for the introduction of managerial models, such as New Public Management (NPM), which claimed to ensure that the remaining public services and contracted-out organizations were highly efficient and accountable, and that risk to the government and taxpayer was minimized.

In most Canadian and many American LTC facilities (including the ones reported on here) the government-required, NPM-compatible, computerized, measurement package is known as the Resident Assessment Instrument – Minimum Data Set, or RAI-MDS (designed to record outcomes for each service user). Our observation notes show that at various points in the day, the RAI-MDS computer program provides prompts to care workers to fill out various portions of the documentation and instantly relays this documentation to supervisors and upper administrators, who add their own metrics and provide the documentation to the government, in order to comply with contract requirements and ensure continued funding.

The documentation organizes the content, pace. and discipline of work as workers are prompted on screens that become "live" at certain points in the shift, to document particular activities (e.g., after meals, a screen becomes "live" for documenting how much each resident ate and drank and any difficulties encountered). Workers are given a certain amount of time to complete this documentation (and presumably the care tasks) before supervisors are informed that the worker is in arrears. As one supervisor joked, "If they don't do the documentation, I know it almost before they do" (Canada2 – RN). Activities that are not documentable on the live screens, such as open-ended, warm, and caring interactions of various lengths with patients and their families, tend to be eliminated from workers' busy shifts, which, of necessity, focus on thin, technical, measurable interventions. This contributes to deskilling, and the erosion of worker autonomy and reduced care for residents, which will be discussed in greater detail later in the chapter. Similarly, if activities do take place but are not documented, neither the worker nor the facility receives credit for them. A nurse manager agreed with me when I mentioned this to her, noting, "If it isn't recorded, it didn't happen" (Canada2 – RN).

At the Canadian study site, a nurse manager responsible for ensuring RAI-MDS reports are properly filed on time complained that documenting is "the most important thing staff does on a shift" but that "they let anything get in their way" (Canada2 – RAI coordinator). Unlike the front-line staff who spoke about the most important aspect of their job being that they "cared about the residents," care was invisible in the manager's discourse. This erasure of the labour involved in maintaining warmth and relationship is similar to the way that other kinds of care women perform is often largely invisible and taken for granted (e.g., in the home and larger community).

The observation note below highlights the tension between care work and documentation and how workers knew that the documentation was part of meeting government requirements rather than compelled by the care needs of the residents.

> Second afternoon shift: The care workers note, when I ask them directly, that the RAI-MDS form is all boxes and there is nowhere they can write a little story or a few lines about something interesting someone said or some little worry or concern people had, that everything is very, very constricted to the checkboxes. They seem annoyed by this but shrug it off as "what they [the government] want, so we gotta do it." (US1 – field notes)

Workers in the United States and Canada also commented on the fast pace and volume of work, as well as the ways they tried to make care

132 Austerity: The Lived Experience

less Taylorized and alienating: "We are always busy and there is almost never room for any extras, but I always try to do something extra for them [the residents] anyway" (US1 – PSW). The pace of this work took its toll: an experienced worker noted, "At the end of the day, I go home very tired. This is a very busy job" (Canada2 – PSW).

McLaughlin (2010) notes that managerialism has compelled agencies to become more controlling, in order to ensure continued government funding contracts, and this has compelled care workers to be more controlling with service users in order to complete their work and document it in a timely manner. A long-time front-line worker confirmed this: "Sometimes we have to rush people. We don't like it and they let us know that they don't like it – some of them complain all over the place – but the work has to get done when the work has to get done" (US1 – PSW). Similarly, though the Canadian facility told us that they are committed to patient-centred care and letting people sleep late if they want to, front-line staff repeatedly told us that they had to get everyone up, washed, dressed, and down for breakfast on time, even if "some of them don't like it some days" (Canada2 – PSW).

The Canadian data show that workers felt rushed, especially on particular shifts, such as the morning shift, as one worker said as she hurried to her duties, "Morning is our rush hour" (Canada2 – PSW). Despite the haste to complete and document front-line care, a division of duties was clear in both LTC facilities, with professional nursing staff (registered nurses) rarely undertaking hands-on care, instead spending most of their shift behind a desk, documenting care. For example, observation notes from a day shift stated,

> During this whole shift, the RN [who is known as the "nurse manager"] has been in her office. She seems rarely to leave it and I have not seen her do anything hands-on or care-related day-to-day tasks on the unit. She works almost exclusively on her computer though she did receive one phone call and hold a brief meeting with people I did not recognize. I would guess from their appearance and age that they are other RNs from the other floors. (Canada2 – field notes)

Hall (2004) argues that under neoliberalism, neglect is increasingly part of the experience of mental health patients during hospitalization. Though our study was not designed to capture evidence of neglect in LTC, our data show evidence of leaned-out care, stripped down to meet a minimum standard, with social and emotional needs set aside in the rush to meet technical care outcomes such as feeding, bathing, dressing, and toileting. Though both of the well-respected facilities we studied claimed to follow a model of patient-centred care (a model of care in which patients are encouraged to plan their daily activities and integrate into the community as much as possible), we saw no evidence of it, which raises questions as to what happens in facilities that are seen as average or suboptimal. Activities provided in the LTC facilities were staff led, rather than chosen by the residents. Staff rarely took people out of the facility, and we saw no evidence of individualized activities that integrated residents into a rich community social life. Instead, activities were low-skill, inexpensive, repetitive, in-house, group activities such as Bingo or chair exercise, which provided little socialization, normalization, or satisfaction, and, with the exception of Bingo, poorly attended.

Interestingly, despite this leaned-out environment, our observation notes also confirmed multiple instances of "care on the fly" where frontline staff were rushing up or down the hallways, stopped suddenly to have a short conversation with a resident or to ask if she needed something, and ducked off quickly to get it, before returning to their rush down the hall on the original task. When asked where on the form such interactions were documented, staff laughed and said, "That's just what we do. It don't go on no form" (US1 – field notes). The increased workload imposed on the front line by the RAI-MDS system seemed to remove possibilities for longer, opened-ended interactions with residents, leaving only these brief, relationship-building, care interactions. However, as noted above, the standardized, computerized forms did not contain a space to record these interactions, making some of the most important care undocumented and invisible.

New Technologies

Like our findings reported above, the literature comments extensively on the way that new technologies such as computerized assessment and documentation packages have increased the pace and volume of work and permitted governing at distance, enabling supervisors and managers at many levels of the facility to keep a close eye on the care that is being documented, and presumably, undertaken on any given unit and for any given service user (Marston and McDonald 2006; Pollack and Rossiter 2010). Our participant observations show that workers were often frustrated with the technologies they worked with and would tell us that completing computerized documentation took them away from the "real work on the floor." In a number of cases IT failed, making work even more challenging. For example, in one unit, a care worker who had never used a new computerized system threw up her hands in frustration and walked out of the nursing station saying, "That system is hopeless. It is totally wasting my time" (Canada2 – field notes). Other staff commiserated with her saying, "That thing never works" (ibid.).

Though supervisors claimed that all workers were well trained on all technologies, our observations suggested that workers received very little training on new systems and generally depended on other workers to teach them how to use systems. For example, the observation described above occurred after the worker had received exactly eight minutes training on a new system being piloted on the unit (the interaction was timed by the researcher, and the worker confirmed she had received no other training). When the worker new to the system ran into frustrations and asked a co-worker if she knew how to make the technology work, another worker laughed and said, "Don't ask me, that thing is always a headache." She added, "What do you expect, you only got five minutes training on it" (Canada2 – field notes).

Though our observations confirmed that front-line workers were frustrated with technologies, in interviews workers generally told us that the technology was "helpful" in order to "ensure quality care," that the computerized system was "fast," and that it "prevented copying from the day before" as the notes from earlier recording periods were blocked off (Canada2 – field notes; US1 – field notes). The RAI coordinator told us almost word-for-word the same thing. I asked how it was helpful to not know what had happened for residents on past shifts, as this record seemed important to informing current and future care. The RAI coordinator said that management could see the notes. but not the front-line, who provide the actual hands-on care. According to her, staff had a tendency "to copy" notes, a practice that she saw as negative, even though she conceded that often the residents' conditions did not change much from day to day, so notes tended to resemble those of the day before. However, through the new process of blocking out earlier notes, management maintained control over the processes of assessing how much care would be allotted to each resident. Keeping front-line workers in the dark about previous concerns and care was seen by the RAI coordinator as appropriate and constructive, as front-line staff could not be trusted with this kind of information. This suspicion of staff was surprising but can be seen as a hierarchical practice of professional power, with RNs asserting their assessment skills based on computerized data over the front-line staff's hands-on knowledge. This separation of front-line workers from planning care is a further example of Taylorization of work, restricting the autonomy and discretion of care workers to following instructions, and narrowing care to what can be measured and documented on the RAI-MDS forms. This will be discussed in greater detail below.

Removal/Reduction of Skills and Autonomy

Like the discussion above, the literature notes that although standardized metrics can increase productivity and provide greater control to managers and funders, resident information and care practices that do not fit standardized forms become invisible (Baines 2004; Carniol 2010; Safewright and McAuley 1997). Standardized forms also reduce staff's assessment and narrative case-note skills, as the forms restrict staff to answering a series of short answer questions and tick-box responses, thus removing their autonomy to omit questions that seem irrelevant or to add new data that seem pertinent. It also removes the need to think through questions and issues that may not be on the form. In short, standardized measures meet the needs of funders and employers, at the same time as they deskill workers and erase most of the lived realities and needs of care recipients and front-line staff (Baines, Charlesworth, and Cunningham 2013; O'Neill 2015; Ross 2011). As one worker told us, "Sometimes I got something to tell the girls on the next shift, just some little thing that I'm worried about someone, like a little feeling I got that somebody needs a little more checking on or something, but I got to tell them when I am rushing out the door, cause we got no place to write anything down anymore" (US1 – PSW).

Reduced autonomy and discretion also reduces personal or individualized responsibility to develop care relationships and care practices that extend beyond the documentation, as these activities are not recognized within managerial metrics or rewarded by managers. This may result in the eventual elimination of many of these skills over a period of time unless staff receive training and support to develop and maintain these skills. However, McLaughlin (2010) notes that under neoliberalism, most training for staff is market-driven, rather than professionally driven and responds to what employers see as priorities. Hence is unlikely to include skills that do not contribute to meeting outcome metrics. In short, employers' need for continued funding and staff who can document that they are meeting outcome measures will likely contribute further to skill loss and a narrow, more technical, and less academic focus on technical aspects of care and documentation, rather than educating workers to exercise critical thinking, professional autonomy, and discretionary decision-making. The observation note below underscores the way training for front-line care workers in the Canadian facility focused on the employer's requirements rather than meeting the interests or work-life challenges of the worker.

> A PSW says she was originally trained as a health aide but later had to take an intensive, workplace-based, PSW certification [two hours after work each day for eight weeks] which her employer contracted through a private provider. I said, "Oh, it's nice that you didn't have to go off-site for the course." She disagreed.
>
> Apparently, the teacher's instruction was very fast and not particularly clear. She was too tired after work to concentrate well, and the instructor would move through the material at a rapid pace, even if people said they needed him to slow down. She said that she never had time to do her readings or review notes and felt that she didn't get much out of the course. She laughed and said that she even "nodded off" in class a few times. She would have preferred a "real course" and that her college-based health aide course was much better. The course also disrupted home life, as she generally had time when she arrived home for a quick nap before taking care of her kids and family. She also reports that most of what she needs to know on the job she got from her original course and from co-workers.

Resistance

The literature on resistance in managerialized care suggests that resistance is usually motivated at a general level by workers' sense of themselves as caring people and moral actors, and at a specific level by care for and about the service users (Baines et al. 2012; Cunningham 2008; Ross 2011). Workers and managers simultaneously value and normalize this expression of and commitment to caring and equate it with being a good person and worker. As one nurse manager said, referring to how friendly and hard-working her staff seemed to be as we toured her unit, "There's no bad people in long-term care work. You won't find any bad people" (Canada2 – field notes). Given that it could not be recorded on the RAI-MDS, being a good and caring person did not seem to provide any direct rewards to staff, though it did smooth work relationships on the floor and seemed to add to the workers' sense of themselves as contributing to a greater good. Caring for service users beyond normal working hours and the dictates of the workplace was seen by workers as a way of resisting a larger uncaring system that did not give workers enough time to undertake care in ways that seemed right to them.

Many workers told us they would check in, by phone or in person, on residents: "Sometimes someone is doing so poorly and you aren't on for a few days, you can't help but worry, even though I know all the girls are doing the best they can. I worry. I just check in sometimes on my way by – I don't live too far from here – and maybe bring something little to cheer them up" (US1 – PSW). Workers in Canada also regularly came into work fifteen minutes early to ease shift change and shrugged it off as "good for everybody" (Canada1 – PSW).

Managers accepted unpaid overtime and extra initiative as part of the regular workday and did not regard worker's extra efforts as extraordinary. One nurse manager said that she tends to look for new staff who are willing to "do little extras" and that many of her staff "volunteer" on the unit after their shifts have ended. When I asked if this was considered unpaid overtime, the nurse laughed and said that she "couldn't make them go home if I tried" (Canada2 – field notes).

Though managers told us that workers are pleased to undertake extra, unpaid work, and workers largely agreed with this sentiment, workers also took what latitude they had to adjust working hours to those less heavily supervised and controlled. Our data show that some workers deliberately chose to work evenings or nights when fewer managers were on site. Two front-line workers reported with some humour, "Lots of the staff don't like working morning shift because all the bosses are around," whereas in the evening and the night shift "you're on your own and you can work how you want to without anyone looking over your shoulder all the time" (Canada2 – PSW). This general sentiment was confirmed, though sometimes more subtly, by those working evening and night shifts in Canada and the United States.

In the US case study, workers also used work-avoidance tactics to "get by and get back" (Friedman 1977), and fellow employees did not cooperate with management on curtailing these practices. For example, our field notes show that some workers were observed going on very long breaks during evening and night shifts. In one case the RN in charge repeatedly asked the other staff where a particular worker was. The workers just shrugged and said she "must be on break." The RN eventually told a worker to go find her and tell her to get back to work.

The worker said "OK," but after moving out of the RN's sight, she remained on the ward and continued to do her own work.

The deep saturation of privatization of care and NPM in the neoliberalized world meant there were fewer differences between the unionized (Canada) and non-union site (US) than one might expect. Wages and benefits were much higher in Canada, but in order to defend its members the union adopted low-conflict strategies. For example, the union had let the collective agreement expire without completing negotiations (expired contracts mean that the workers continue to work under the terms of the old contract). The union representative told us that, in the current climate of austerity, workplaces with lapsed agreement tended to eventually end up in arbitration, where the staff were likely to get a better deal than if they bargained with the employer. Thus, "foot dragging" on negotiations was a conscious resistance strategy for workers with little bargaining power and a management group that was restricted to the constrained funding that austerity-focused governments were willing to provide, leaving little or no room for improved wages and conditions. As one union activist quipped, "This is not the strategy of a powerful group."

Consistent with the social unionist strategies of most Canadian unionized LTC facilities, the union in this case study encouraged workers to be involved in larger social policy debates and to resist the austerity agenda of the government, though little activity was evident at the time of our study. This is not surprising, given that workers had heavy workloads, often held multiple jobs to make ends meet, and had multiple care responsibilities at home, leaving little time or energy for challenging inequities within and beyond the workplace. Despite these demands on their time and loyalties, workers in Canada and the United States sought dignity in their pressured and fast-paced work by extending additional care to their elderly clients, and thus resisting the parsimony of leaned-out, insensitive service provision. They also resisted by seeking shifts where supervision was lower (evenings and nights) and ignoring supervisors' directives to find workers taking lengthy breaks, as well as by taking long breaks.

Discussion and Conclusions

The data presented in this chapter confirm that in the current era of austerity and tight funding, LTC workers are tightly controlled by state practices of documentation of outcomes and the rapid and intense timelines for care work the outcome targets compel. Further, this control strips the work of much of its interactive, relationship-based content, contributing to the deskilling, particularly of workers on the front line of care. This compels LTC workers and their managers, who may desire to do otherwise, to exert increased downward control on residents in order to meet tight timelines, complete heavy workloads, and ensure that timely documentation is submitted at designated points in the day. In effect, workers and managers act as conduits of austerity-driven, pro-market state practices of cost cuts, efficiency, managerialism, and control, exerting pressure on service users, rushing their care, and losing much of the open-ended, relationship-based care content.

Our data also show that though technical "care" of people's bodies was generally provided, the elderly within tight time frames and dependent were maintained in quiet *social* neglect outside of the larger community, with few meaningful interactions or activities within leaned-out care. This confirms Galper's (1980) assertion that services of the welfare state often maintain populations, who are outside the workforce, in conditions of exclusion and isolation. Insufficient time and resources were made available in the facilities studied to provide patient-centred care (within which the patients are supported in setting priorities for their own care and activities and are integrated into the larger community) so residents remained isolated in the care facilities. This quiet social neglect could be remedied with increased funding and emphasis on the frail elderly as full, rights-bearing citizens who, in most cases, can, with adequate supports and resources, make decisions regarding their own activities and social integration.

In tandem with Galper's assertions that rather than exclusively promoting the interests of corporations and the wealthy, managerialized and contracted-out LTC permits governments to further legitimize themselves by displaying concern for the frail elderly and other frail adults. However, our data also showed difficulties and while current kinds and levels of care may be highly documentable, they rarely include the kinds of the relationship-based care interactions that are meaningful to residents, their families, and care workers. Hence, this tension may become a nodule of discontent around which resistance and change have potential to build.

The findings presented in this chapter suggest that everyday care in LTC does operate as a conduit of state control and passes on austerity in everyday interactions, lowering the expectations of LTC residents and their communities of support, fostering alienation among workers and some managers, and reproducing and normalizing a larger culture of parsimony and unmet needs. This extends the reach of austerity into even personal aspects of everyday life for vulnerable and frail people and contributes to feelings of helplessness in the face of its seeming omnipresence and hegemony. These dynamics highlight the resonance between earlier state theory debates and the current phase of neoliberal austerity. These dynamics also confirm that it continues to be important to understand care and other state workers as unintentionally controlling marginal and excluded populations through new mechanisms of micro-governing such as the RAI-MDS and the details of government funding contracts.

Also reflecting Taylor-Gooby's conceptualization of welfare state workers as mirrors of the ambivalent, social justice, social control missions of the welfare state, the data show that front-line workers and some managers comply with rushed, controlling care while simultaneously resisting by caring more during and beyond work hours. In these ways the workers and some managers both maintain and break the thread of neoliberal uncaring. They resist by stepping outside the control of dependent populations by treating people as deserving respect and holistic care. They simultaneously resist the way they are controlled though ITs and the metrics of government contracts to be automatons, providing alienating care to excluded and isolated residents. Repeatedly, in small and large ways, workers claim the right to have social connection and relationships that matter to them, not just to act as Taylorized machines operating in the interest of pro-market rationalization of resources and efficiency. These actions reflect John Clarke's observation in this volume that residual collectivism exists in various forms under the individualizing influence of neoliberalism and austerity. By participating in collectivist traditions and finding small ways to reinsert caring into their everyday work, these care workers are political actors, though most of their action takes place in the largely invisible and highly gendered realm of care for excluded populations.

Echoing the unstable equilibrium of the state, these forms of resistance are contradictory and highly unstable, in that while they meet some of the needs of residents, they simultaneously legitimize government social welfare practices unintentionally by making it look as if the system can work under austerity and that it is suitably caring. In short, care-worker resistance both enables and challenges neoliberalism. By adding additional hours of unpaid care and intensifying their work during paid hours of care, the workers are consciously self-exploiting and may eventually burn out or choose to resist in ways that more quickly and directly expose the unsustainability of the system. Not surprisingly, workers also undertake classic work avoidance, which may also expand rather than retract in a period of extended austerity and work intensification that seems to lie ahead.

REFERENCES

Albo, G., and J. Jenson. 1989. "A Contested Concept: The Relative Autonomy of the State." In *The New Canadian Political Economy*, ed. W. Clement and G. Williams, 180–211. Montreal and Kingston: McGill-Queen's University Press.

Aronowitz, S., and P. Bratis. 2002. *Paradigm Lost: State Theory Revisited*. Minneapolis: University of Minnesota Press.

Bailey, R., and M. Brake. 1980. "Contributions to a Radical Practice in Social Work." In *Radical Social Work and Practice*, ed. R. Bailey and M. Brake, 7–25. London: Edward Arnold.

Baines, D. 2004. "Caring for Nothing: Work Organization and Unwaged Labour in Social Services." *Work, Employment and Society* 18 (2): 267–95. https://doi.org/10.1177/09500172004042770.

Baines, D., S. Charlesworth, and I. Cunningham. 2013. "Fragmented Outcomes: International Comparisons of Gender, Managerialism and Union Strategies in the Nonprofit Sector." *Journal of Industrial Relations* 56 (1): 24–42. https://doi.org/10.1177/0022185613498664.

Baines, Donna, Sara Charlesworth, Ian Cunningham, and Janet Dassinger. 2012. "Self-Monitoring, Self-Blaming, Self-Sacrificing Workers: Gendered Managerialism in the Non-Profit Sector." *Women's Studies International Forum* 35 (5): 362–71. https://doi.org/10.1016/j.wsif.2012.07.002.

Baines, D., and Ian Cunningham. 2013. "Using Comparative Perspective Rapid Ethnography in International Case Studies: Strengths and Challenges." *Qualitative Social Work: Research and Practice* 12 (1): 73–88. https://doi.org/10.1177/1473325011419053.

Baines, D., and T. Daly. 2015. "Resisting Regulatory Rigidities: Lessons from Front-line Care Work." *Studies in Political Economy* 95 (1): 137–60. https://doi.org/10.1080/19187033.2015.11674949.

Block, F. 2010. *Revising State Theory: Essays in Politics and Postindustrialism*. Philadelphia: Temple University Press.

Burman, S. 2004. "Revisiting the Agent of Social Control Role: Implications for Substance Abuse Treatment." *Journal of Social Work Practice* 18 (2): 197–209. https://doi.org/10.1080/0265053042000231016.

Carey, M. 2009. "'It's a Bit Like Being a Robot or Working in a Factory': Does Braverman Help Explain the Experiences of State Social Workers in Britain since 1971?" *Organization* 16 (4): 505–27. https://doi.org/10.1177/1350508409104506.

Carniol, B. 2010. *Case Critical: Challenging Social Services in Canada*. Toronto: Between the Lines.

Charlesworth, S. 2010. "The Regulation of Paid Care Workers' Wages and Conditions in the Non-Profit Sector: A Toronto Case Study." *Relations industrielles/Industrial Relations* 65 (3): 380–99. https://doi.org/10.7202/044888ar.

Chorney, H., W. Clement, L. Panitch, and P. Phillips. 1997. "The State and Political Economy." *Canadian Journal of Political and Social Theory/Revue canadienne de théorie* 1 (3): 71–85.

Clarke, J. 2004. "Dissolving the Public Realm? The Logics and Limits of Neo-Liberalism." *Journal of Social Policy* 33 (1): 27–48. https://doi.org/10.1017/S0047279403007244.

Cruikshank, B. 1999. *The Will to Empower: Democratic Citizens and Other Subjects*. Ithaca, NY: Cornell University Press.

Cunningham, I. 2008. *Employment Relations in the Voluntary Sector*. London: Routledge.

Edwards, R. 1978. "Who Fares Well in the Welfare State?" In *The Capitalist System: A Radical Analysis of American Society*, ed. R. Edward, 244–51. New York: Prentice Hall.

Evans, P.M., and G.R. Wekerle, eds. 1997. *Women and the Canadian Welfare State: Challenges and Change*. Toronto: University of Toronto Press. https://doi.org/10.3138/9781442683549.

Friedman, A. 1977. *Industry and Labour: Class Struggle at Work and Monopoly Capitalism*. London: Macmillan. https://doi.org/10.1007/978-1-349-15845-4.

Galper, J.H. 1975. *The Politics of Social Services*. Englewood Cliffs, NJ: Prentice-Hall.

– 1980. *Social Work Practice: A Radical Perspective*. Englewood Cliffs, NJ: Prentice-Hall.

Geertz, C. 1994. "Thick Description: Toward an Interpretive Theory of Culture." In *Readings in the Philosophy of Social Science*, ed. M. Martin and L.C. McIntyre, 213–31. Cambridge, MA: MIT Press.

Glesne, C. 2005. *Becoming Qualitative Researchers*. White Plains, NY: Longman.

Gulalp, H. 1987. "Capital Accumulation, Classes and the Relative Autonomy of the State." *Science and Society* 51 (3): 287–313.

Hall, J. 2004. "Restriction and Control: The Perceptions of Mental Health Nurses in a UK Acute Inpatient Setting." *Issues in Mental Health Nursing* 25 (5): 539–52. https://doi.org/10.1080/01612840490443473.

Handwerker, W. 2001. *Quick Ethnography*. Walnut Creek, CA: Altamira.
Jessop, B. 1990. *State Theory: Putting the Capitalist State in Its Place*. University Park, PA: Penn State Press.
Lavalette, M., ed. 2011. *Radical Social Work Today: Social Work at the Crossroads*. London: Policy.
Marston, G., and C. McDonald, eds. 2006. *Analysing Social Policy: A Governmental Approach*. Cheltenham, UK: Edward Elgar Publishing.
McBride, S. 2014. "In Austerity We Trust." In *Orchestrating Austerity: Impacts and Resistance*, ed. D. Baines and S. McBride. Winnipeg: Fernwood Publishing.
McDonald, C. 2006. *Challenging Social Work: The Institutional Context of Practice*. Houndmills, UK: Palgrave Macmillan.
McDonald, C., and G. Marston. 2002. "Fixing the Niche? Rhetorics of the Community Sector in the Neo Liberal Welfare Regime." *Just Policy* 27 (August): 3–10.
McLaughlin, K. 2010. "The Social Worker versus the General Social Care Council: An Analysis of Care Standards Tribunal Hearings and Decisions." *British Journal of Social Work* 40 (1): 311–27. https://doi.org/10.1093/bjsw/bcn136.
Miliband, R. 1965. *Marx and the State in Democracy and the Capitalist State*. New York: Graeme Duncan.
– 1983. *Class Power and State Power*. London: Verso.
Miliband, R., and R. Miliband. 1965. *Marx and the State*. New York: International Publishers.
Ng, R. 1988. *The Politics of Community Services: Immigrant Women, Class and State*. Toronto: Garamond.
O'Connor, J. 1973. *The Fiscal Crisis of the State*. New York: St Martin's.
O'Neill, L. 2015. "Regulating Hospital Social Workers and Nurses: Propping Up an 'Efficient' Lean Health Care System." *Studies in Political Economy* 95 (1): 115–36. http://dx.doi.org/10.1080/19187033.2015.11674948.
Orloff, A.S. 2009. "Gendering the Comparative Analysis of Welfare States: An Unfinished Agenda." *Sociological Theory* 27 (3): 317–43. https://doi.org/10.1111/j.1467-9558.2009.01350.x.
Panitch, L. 2000. "The New Imperial State." *New Left Review* March–April, 1–20.
Panitch, L., and S. Gindin. 2000. "Rekindling Socialist Imagination: Utopian Vision and Working-Class Capacities." *Monthly Review: An Independent Socialist Magazine* 51 (10): 36–51. https://doi.org/10.14452/MR-051-10-2000-03_3.
Patton, M. 2002. *Qualitative Evaluation and Research Methods*. London: Sage Publications.
Pollack, S., and A. Rossiter. 2010. "Neoliberalism and the Entrepreneurial Subject: Implications for Feminism and Social Work." *Canadian Social Work Review/Revue canadienne de service social*, 155–69.

Poulantzas, N. 1973. *Political Power and Social Classes*. London: Verso.
Poulantzas, N., and R. Miliband. 1972. "The Problem of the Capitalist State." In *Ideology in Social Science: Readings in Critical Social Theory*, ed. R. Blackburn, 238–62. New York: Pantheon Books.
Rose, N. 1990. *Governing the Soul: The Shaping of the Private Self*. London: Taylor & Frances/Routledge.
– 1996. "Governing 'Advanced' Liberal Democracies." In *The Anthropology of the State: A Reader*, ed. Aradhana Sharma and Akhil Gupta, 144–62. Malden, MA: Taylor and Francis.
Ross, M. 2011. "Social Work Activism amidst Neoliberalism: A Big Broad Tent." In *Doing Anti-Oppressive Practice*, ed. Donna Baines, 251–64. Halifax: Fernwood.
Rossiter, A. 2000. "The Postmodern Feminist Condition: Practice and Research in Social Work." In *Postmodern Feminist Perspectives*, ed. Barbara Fawcett, Bridget Featherstone, Jan Fook, and Amy Rossitier, 24–38. Oxford: Psychology Press.
Safewright, M., and W. McAuley. 1997. "Control versus Consent in Long-term Care Case Management Programs: Implications for Public Policy." *International Journal of Public Administration* 20 (2): 267–93. https://doi.org/10.1080/01900699708525196.
Showstack Sassoon, A. 1987. *Women and the State*. London: Hutchinson.
Smith, K. 2007. "Social Work, Restructuring and Resistance: 'Best Practices' Gone Underground." In *Doing Anti-Oppressive Practice: Building Transformative, Politicized Social Work*, ed. D. Baines, 145–59. Halifax: Fernwood Books.
Smith, M.J. 2000. *Rethinking State Theory*. London: Routledge.
Smith, S. 2010. "Nonprofits and Public Administrations: Reconciling Performance Management and Citizen Engagement." *American Review of Public Administration* 40 (2): 129–52. https://doi.org/10.1177/0275074009358452.
Szebehely, M. 2007. *Carework in Scandinavia: Organisational Trends and Everyday Realities*. Paper presented to Fifth Annual ESPAnet Conference, Vienna, September.
Taylor-Gooby, P. 2000. "Risk and Welfare." In *Risk, Trust and Welfare*, ed. P. Taylor-Gooby, 1–18. London: Macmillan.
Triantafillou, P. 2012. *New Forms of Governing: A Foucauldian Inspired Analysis*. London: Palgrave Macmillan. https://doi.org/10.1057/9781137284594.
Wakefield, J.C. 1998. "Foucauldian Fallacies: An Essay Review of Leslie Margolin's *Under the Cover of Kindness*." *Social Service Review* 72 (4): 545–87. https://doi.org/10.1086/515778.
Walker, G.A. 1990. *Family Violence and the Women's Movement*. Toronto: University of Toronto Press.
Warskett, R. 1993. "Democratizing the State: Challenges from Public Sector Unions." *Studies in Political Economy* 42 (1): 129–40.

7 "Negotiate Your Way Back to Zero": Teacher Bargaining and Austerity in Ontario, Canada

BRENDAN A. SWEENEY AND ROBERT S. HICKEY

Introduction

Publicly funded elementary and secondary education constitutes one of the largest annual expenses of governments in affluent nations. In most Canadian provinces, funding for public education – the majority of which goes to teacher salaries – is second only to health care as their largest annual expense (Slinn and Sweetman 2012; Lysyk 2014). It is therefore no surprise that education budgets came under scrutiny following the economic crisis beginning in 2008 and during the implementation of austerity measures shortly after. However, the manner in which austerity measures were implemented and the narratives justifying its need varied. In some cases, austerity policies were packaged hand-in-hand with broader reforms that vilified teachers' unions and public school officials, characterizing them as impediments to student success and the meaningful and necessary restructuring of public education, sometimes through privatization. In other contexts, unions, school boards, and other governance actors engaged in collaborative partnerships in order to foster student success while managing budgets during trying economic times (Rubinstein and McCarthy 2012). And others emphasized the bottom line above all else.

This chapter draws upon a case study of collective bargaining and employment relations in the publicly funded education sector of the Canadian province of Ontario during the recent economic crisis and amid the implementation of cost-cutting measures generally associated with austerity. This case study demonstrates the fragility of union-party relations, the impacts of the use of legislation to achieve collective agreements in lieu of negotiated settlements, and the persistent pragmatism of contemporary public sector unions during a period of cost containment and budgetary restraint. In so doing, it engages with several bodies of literature, including those related to broader questions concerning the future of public sector unions in Canada (see Ross and Savage 2013) and the United States (see Lewin, Keefe, and Kochan 2012), as well as those that highlight challenges unique to the public sector, where the state concomitantly plays the role of legislator, financier, and employer (see Swimmer and Thompson 1995; Evans 2013). This permits a comparison of our case study with overarching trends and issues related to austerity, public sector collective bargaining and employment relations, and education reform. The case study also demonstrates a shift towards sustained pragmatism within certain Canadian public sector unions, thus engaging with recent research that examines the changing nature of union–party relationships in Canada (see Savage 2010; Savage and Smith 2013; Walchuk 2010; Evans and Smith 2015).

The chapter proceeds as follows. The first section summarizes literature related to contemporary union-party relations in Canada and the restructuring of public sector unions and collective bargaining in Canada and the United States. This section identifies key debates and themes in order to compare and contrast them with our case study. The second section provides an overview of the evolution of administration, policy, and collective bargaining in Ontario's publicly funded elementary and secondary education sector. The third section examines the relationships between education policy, austerity, and collective bargaining in Ontario's publicly funded elementary and secondary education sector immediately prior to, during, and since the economic crisis beginning in 2008, placing emphasis on the Government of Ontario's attempts to implement cost-cutting measures at the bargaining table and then through legislation in 2012. This is followed by a discussion of the case study in the context of current debates on union-party relations and the future of public sector collective bargaining.

Public Sector Collective Bargaining in an Age of Austerity

There has been renewed interest in public sector collective bargaining among social scientists and employment relations researchers amidst the economic crisis beginning in 2008 and the austerity measures that followed. Literature from the United States focuses on conceptual and policy debates regarding the function of public sector unions and collective bargaining and their purported role in the budgetary crises encountered by municipal and state governments. In this context, Lewin, Keefe, and Kochan (2012) evaluate arguments that US public sector workers are overpaid relative to private sector workers. They conclude that public sector workers were under-compensated when compared to their private sector counterparts, and that dispute resolution mechanisms and joint reform initiatives worked reasonably well. Keefe (2012) builds on the work of Lewin, Keefe, and Kochan, and found that the relative under-compensation of US public sector workers was balanced by better fringe benefits. He also engaged with debates on privatization and found little evidence that the privatization of public services led to cost savings. According to his study, this is the result of the high cost of monitoring and administering such contracts and the effectiveness of internal measures taken recently to manage budgets across US municipal and state governments. Finally, Katz (2013) poses broader questions and assesses whether or not a fundamental transformation is underway in US public sector employment relations. He concludes that despite widespread policy debates and some functional restructuring, such a transformation is not occurring. This, according to Katz, is due to sustained public sector union membership and positive attitudes among public sector workers regarding unions and collective bargaining.

In contrast to this stable view of public sector labour relations, Lafer (2013) contends that the specific attacks on public sector collective bargaining rights are part of a broader effort to constrain wages and roll back labour standards for workers, including the vast majority of US workers, who are not unionized. Lafer argues that the wave of legislation to restrict and dismantle public sector collective bargaining rights in Wisconsin, Ohio, Indiana, and elsewhere represented a coordinated strategy by national corporate lobbies and the American Legislative Exchange Council (ALEC). While proponents of the anti-union legislation, such as Wisconsin Governor Scott Walker, claimed that restricting public sector collective bargaining rights was needed to address the fiscal crisis facing state budgets, Lafer demonstrates that such changes had no impact on public finances. To him, the legislative initiatives against public sector unions and more broadly on basic employment standards represented structural changes to the institutions governing workplace standards and employment relations.

Lafer (2014) also argues that such anti-union legislation in the education sector is not primarily about changes to the institutions governing employment relations. According to him, the legislation directed at teacher unions reflects a broader corporate agenda to privatize the largest publicly funded segment of the US economy, public education. Referring to examples such as the fully privatized New Orleans Recovery School District and private educational services contractor Rocketship Education, Lafer argues that legislation against teacher collective bargaining is just the means to the broader end of privatizing public education. Given the size of public education budgets, private education contractors and affiliated vendors see tremendous revenue potential in a privatized elementary and secondary education sector. However, teachers' unions are not the only obstacles to the privatization agenda. Democratically elected local school boards – the employers of teachers – have also been targeted as impediments to education reform and market rule in elementary and secondary education (ibid.).

An equally robust body of literature on Canadian public sector collective bargaining and employment relations emerged over the same time. Ross and Savage (2013) make an important note pertaining to this literature, and distinguish between what is viewed through an employment relations lens and what examines the politics of public sector workers, unions, and collective bargaining. Research from both these approaches has proved important in sorting through conceptual and policy debates on the impacts of the recession and austerity on public unions and employment relations.

Several employment relations researchers draw upon empirical evidence that documents effective practices in building and sustaining productive labour–management relationships amid challenging budgetary environments (e.g., Chaykowski and Hickey 2013). Other scholars examine the potential impacts of policy reform on public sector collective bargaining practices, outcomes, and structure, dispute resolution mechanisms, and labour-management relations at the workplace or enterprise level (e.g., Chaykowski and Hickey 2014), several of whom focus specifically on the education sector (e.g., Rose 2012; Slinn 2012; Slinn and Sweetman 2012; Sweeney, McWilliams, and Hickey 2012; Williams-Whitt 2012). Writing in the context of austerity measures implemented post-2008, these authors argue that cost containment should not be the sole or guiding principle for reform to public sector employment relations, and that changes to practices, policies, and legislation are best achieved through consultations and that accord with the needs of both provincial- and workplace-level stakeholders.

Of particular interest to this case study is the emerging literature that examines the politics of public sector workers, unions, and collective bargaining in Canada (Savage 2010, Savage and Smith 2013; Walchuk 2010; Pilon, Ross, and Savage 2011; Evans and Smith 2015). As Savage and Smith (2013) note, the electoral politics of Canadian public sector unions is fragmented. This fragmentation is analogous to the paradoxical roles of the state in public sector employment relations (Evans 2013). While many Canadian public sector unions have some history of collaboration with the federal or provincial arms of the New Democratic Party (NDP), these relationships often proved tenuous, especially in instances when the NDP has been elected to lead provincial governments in British Columbia, Manitoba, Nova Scotia, Ontario, and Saskatchewan. This is related to the contradictory and dualistic role that the NDP has occupied during the transition from Left-leaning political ally of unions to the employer of public sector workers, manager of the public purse, and regulator of employment relations as they accede to government (Savage and Smith 2013).

The rise of neoliberal policies and the accompanying assault on union rights and freedoms since the 1980s profoundly influenced union-party relations in Canada. At the same time, the strategies adopted by both private and public sector unions in response to policy changes have not been uniform. Rather, they are influenced by several factors, including "a union's structural location vis-à-vis the government, its political culture and the political priorities of its leaders" (Pilon, Ross, and Savage 2011; in Savage and Smith, 2013, 51). However, there has been a trend towards electoral strategies to prevent militant anti-union right-wing parties (in Canada, the federal and provincial arms of the Conservative Party) from taking power. This has come in the form of strategic voting campaigns that attempt to consolidate support for the most viable non-Conservative candidate (usually NDP, Liberal, or Bloc Québécois) in a particular electoral riding. Savage (2010) argues that these campaigns represent a departure from social democratic principles within Canadian unions, that they constitute a defensive measure of a labour movement in retreat, and that they are symptomatic of the inability of Left-leaning parties to present a viable alternative to neoliberal political economic restructuring.

One prominent example of a strategic voting campaign is the Working Families Coalition. After a falling out between many of Ontario's unions and the provincial NDP in the mid-1990s, Mike Harris's vehemently anti-union Progressive Conservatives took control of the provincial legislature. In response to the widespread assault on labour rights and public sector spending, several unions – including the Canadian

Auto Workers (CAW), Ontario Secondary School Teachers' Federation (OSSTF), Ontario English Catholic Teachers' Association (OECTA), and several building and construction trade unions – created the Working Families Coalition, whose primary purpose was to divert support away from Conservative candidates through advertising campaigns (Walchuk 2010).

The support of the Working Families Coalition proved instrumental in 2003, when Dalton McGuinty's Liberal Party was elected to a majority provincial government. Within short order, the McGuinty Liberals committed hundreds of millions of dollars to the province's automotive industry, instituted card-check certification for building and construction trade unions, and concluded collective agreements with teachers that improved salaries and working conditions, and provided funding for hundreds of new teaching positions. Several other unions began supporting the Working Families Coalition, which helped defeat the provincial Conservatives and allowed the Liberals again a majority government in 2007 and a slight minority in 2011. However, the support of these unions and their strategic voting campaigns did not prevent unilateral government action when the McGuinty-led Liberals imposed austerity measures in 2012. These are explored in more detail below (in the context of publicly funded elementary and secondary education), and although they eroded the trust and goodwill between public sector unions and the Ontario Liberals (Evans and Smith 2015), they did not do so to the extent that the unions changed their tune come election time in 2014 when the Liberals led by Kathleen Wynne won a majority of seats in the provincial Parliament.

This case study is therefore understood in the context of broader questions about the legitimacy of public sector unions, the effectiveness of employment relations and collective bargaining practices and structures in the public sector during austerity, and debates surrounding contemporary union-party politics. In this context, one initial observation is that even during the most challenging periods in the history of Canadian public sector employment relations, the debates on the legitimacy of public sector unions did not take hold to the extent that they did in the United States. However, if we take Katz (2013) at face value, these debates – usually emerging from the Far Right – are at this point moot, as they did not lead to a fundamental transformation of public sector employment relations and collective bargaining in the United States and are therefore unlikely to do so in Canada. This, again, is related to the perceived value of unions to public sector workers and the effectiveness of cost-containment measures implemented – sometimes in collaboration with unions – during the aftermath of the recent economic crisis. Moreover, the coordinated efforts to promote the privatization of public education documented by Lafer (2014) do not appear as a major factor in the Canadian context. We are thus left to focus on the latter two questions, which pertain primarily to the structure, practices, and politics of public sector employment relations and collective bargaining during austerity.

Teacher Collective Bargaining in Ontario

The origins of teacher collective bargaining in the province can be traced to the 1944 Teaching Profession Act. This legislation required that all teachers be members in good standing of one of Ontario's five teachers' associations, which were organized according to gender, level of instruction (elementary or secondary), language of instruction (English or French), and denomination (non-denominational or Catholic). These associations did not wield collective bargaining rights akin to a union. Rather, they consulted with local school boards regarding teacher salaries, benefits, and working conditions.

Public sector workers across Canada won the right to unionize in the 1960s, and did so in record numbers (Heron 2013). Ontario's teachers, however, were granted this right several years after most Canadian public sector workers, including teachers in other provinces. In the absence of collective agreements and their requisite dispute resolution procedures, Ontario's teachers leveraged the requirement that they be members of their teachers' associations to improve salaries and working conditions through two innovative tactics: mass resignations and "pink lists" (Downie 1992). In the event of a dispute or impasse in consultations with a school board over salaries and working conditions, teachers at that particular school board were encouraged to resign en masse. Teachers were notified of this by a memorandum sent on pink paper that denied future support from the teachers' association to teachers who continued to work at the school board in dispute. Those who worked at "pink-listed" school boards were denied future membership in their respective teachers' association, and because membership was mandatory, they were thus unable to teach in the province's publicly funded elementary and secondary schools.

These tactics proved effective and disruptive, and prompted the provincial government to implement the School Boards and School

Teachers Collective Bargaining Act in 1975. This legislation granted collective bargaining rights to school boards (rather than the provincial Ministry of Education) and the five teachers' associations defined in the Teaching Profession Act. It also granted teachers the right to strike, provided for binding arbitration in the event of a dispute that jeopardized the school year, and made fact-finding and mediation requisites for work stoppages (Rose 2002). Moreover, it permitted provincial representatives of teachers' associations to assume control over local bargaining (although school boards had no equivalent provincial-level bargaining agent or signatory) and allowed multiple school boards to negotiate in concert if the teachers' association(s) involved agreed (Downie 1992). It is worthwhile to comment on the manner in which Ontario's teachers' associations were certified as bargaining agents; not by card-check certification or election, but by legislation enacted by the provincial Progressive Conservative government (my, how times have changed). This legislation stabilized employment relations and minimized disputes when compared to the rest of the public sector for nearly two decades (see Rose 2001).

Ontario teacher collective bargaining changed significantly during the 1990s. This began with legislated wage freezes and unpaid leave enacted by Bob Rae's NDP government in 1993, and culminated in sweeping reforms introduced by Mike Harris's Progressive Conservative government beginning in 1996. In addition to slashing hundreds of millions of dollars from education budgets, Harris amalgamated school boards, removed principals and vice-principals from teacher bargaining units, created the Ontario College of Teachers and gave them the responsibility for governing and regulating the teaching profession (formerly the responsibility of teachers' unions/associations), defined the terms of teacher collective agreements, and established common expiration dates. Importantly, the Harris government centralized funding for education within the Ministry of Education. This eliminated the authority of local school boards to control local budgets and to raise additional revenues for education through property tax levies. An unintended and eventual consequence of the centralization of education funding was the centralization of collective bargaining. Teachers reacted decisively, engaging in a two-week province-wide strike in 1997, as well as dozens of other work stoppages and work-to-rule campaigns over the next several years. For a more thorough review of teacher collective bargaining and employment relations under Mike Harris (and his successor, Ernie Eves), see Rose (2002) and Sweeney (2013).

Frustrated with the NDP and opposed to the Progressive Conservatives, Ontario's teachers engaged in strategic voting campaigns in the 1999 and 2003 provincial elections (Walchuk 2010). Their role in the Working Families Coalition was instrumental in helping to elect Dalton McGuinty's provincial Liberal Party to a majority government late in 2003. Styling himself as the "education premier," and with collective agreements between school boards and all four teachers' unions expiring in August 2004, McGuinty was tasked with repairing employment relations with those who had been so helpful on Election Day. He appointed high-ranking party member Gerard Kennedy as minister of education and helped conclude collective agreements between the smaller of the province's teachers' unions – the Ontario English Catholic Teachers' Association (OECTA) and the Association des enseignants et enseignantes franco-ontarien (AEFO) – and the Catholic and francophone school boards. These agreements provided modest improvements for teachers. However, negotiations between the larger and politically influential Ontario Secondary School Teachers' Federation (OSSTF) and Elementary Teachers' Federation of Ontario (ETFO) stalled.

Avoiding work stoppages by OSSTF and ETFO became a top priority. Beginning in November 2004, nearly three months after previous collective agreements expired, Kennedy convened a series of meetings with provincial teachers' union representatives (who were armed with strike mandates) and representatives of the Ontario Public School Boards' Association (OPSBA). The result was four-year collective agreements that included modest salary increases, significant improvements to teacher working conditions, and an agreement to hire hundreds of new full-time permanent teachers (thus reducing class sizes). Similar enhancements were then offered to Catholic and francophone school boards, OECTA, and AEFO, so long as they agreed to them within a fortnight. OECTA, AEFO, and their respective school boards were pleased with the enhancements, but frustrated with the timeline. This round of bargaining is considered by some (i.e., Kennedy) to be the first example of "provincial discussion table," or PDT, negotiations in Ontario's education sector. Others (i.e., OSSTF, ETFO), however, disagreed, and viewed the meetings as informational and consultative, and contended that any meaningful bargaining took place with school boards – the ultimate signatories to collective agreements (see Sweeney, forthcoming).

With the ongoing support of the Working Families Coalition, the McGuinty Liberals were re-elected to a majority government in 2007

(Walchuk 2010). Ontario's then-minister of education (and current premier) Kathleen Wynne engaged school boards and teachers' unions in a more formal version of the PDTs in advance of the expiration of collective agreements in August 2008 (and included several unions representing educational support staff). OECTA and the Ontario Catholic School Trustees' Association (OCSTA) concluded a four-year framework agreement in May 2008 that provided funding for 3 per cent wage increases annually and other improvements, so long as it was ratified locally by August. Claiming foresight regarding the impending economic turmoil (see Sweeney, forthcoming), OECTA negotiators accepted and ratified the framework agreement by the deadline. Similar framework agreements were accepted by AEFO and francophone school boards and by educational support workers' unions and ratified by the deadline.

Like the previous round of negotiations, OSSTF and ETFO did not conclude agreements by the August deadline. OSSTF sought to reorient collective bargaining away from the province and back to the school boards. This tactic proved unsuccessful, but, even during the onset of the recession, the Ministry of Education provided funding for enhancements similar to OECTA and AEFO when OSSTF and OPSBA concluded a framework agreement late in November. ETFO, which sought to redress funding gaps between elementary and secondary schools, held out until February 2009. However, and partly as the result of the mounting pressure of the economic crisis and from their membership, ETFO and OPSBA agreed to a framework. This framework was similar to that agreed to by the other unions, but the province provided annual salary increases of only 2 per cent in the first two years (and 3 per cent in the last two years), thus exacerbating the funding gap. ETFO saw this measure as punitive, while the provincial government claimed it was due to changing economic circumstances (Sweeney, McWilliams, and Hickey 2011). Whatever the case, trouble was on the horizon.

"Negotiate Your Way Back to Zero": Ontario Teacher Bargaining and Austerity

The Liberals sought to implement several changes in elementary and secondary education during the term of the 2008 collective agreements. The roll-out of full-day (rather than half-day) kindergarten across the province and the formalization of two-tier collective bargaining were perhaps the most important. Full-day kindergarten was lauded by education stakeholders, and two-tier collective bargaining had resulted in successive rounds of negotiations without work stoppages. However, maintaining this momentum during a period of budgetary restraint proved increasingly difficult.

Dalton McGuinty was re-elected in 2011, albeit with a minority government. The Liberals released a report on government spending and the delivery of public services early in 2012, the year in which teacher and educational support workers collective agreements were set to expire. Known the "Drummond Report," it included over 300 recommendations to curb public spending, 27 of which were targeted at elementary and secondary education (Ontario Ministry of Finance 2012). The provincial government sought to proceed with most, save for a recommendation to cancel full-day kindergarten.

Shortly after the release of the report, the Ministry of Education under Minister Laurel Broten convened PDTs with teachers' and educational support workers' unions. The ministry informed unions and school boards' associations that in light of the recommendations of the Drummond Report and their decision to proceed with full-day kindergarten, they would be seeking concessions. Because of the decision to proceed with full-day kindergarten, these concessions were more far-reaching than the unions – particularly OSSTF – originally anticipated. As one union representative quoted in Sweeney (forthcoming) noted,

> [The Liberals] put is in a box because they had committed to full-day Kindergarten, which is expensive but defensible. It is hard for us to say it is a bad idea. But they have spending cuts of $1.5 billion and are only putting $500 million into education. That extra billion has to come from somewhere ... They skillfully have found the pieces of our contracts that are hard to defend in public. They reversed the process and have taken the result of negotiation and did that first ... We start from minus $500 million and they are saying "negotiate your way back to zero."

These concessions included a two-year wage freeze (including a freeze in movement along seniority-based salary grids for teachers in their first ten years of service), reduced sick days, and a moratorium on gratuities for unused sick days payable upon retirement. ETFO withdrew immediately, AEFO withdrew soon after, and OSSTF withdrew after a counter-offer was rejected outright.

Perhaps in an effort to sustain the publicly funded Catholic school system, OECTA and OCSTA continued to negotiate at a PDT. They established a two-year framework agreement in early July that froze wages, halved teacher sick days, and eliminated gratuities for unused sick days, but maintained salary grid movement in exchange for three unpaid leave days. Also within the framework agreement was a commitment from the province to enshrine the two-tier bargaining system in legislation by August 2014. The parties were given until 31 December 2012 to ratify the framework locally; most did so well in advance of the deadline.

AEFO adopted a similar framework in August 2012. Yet despite the momentum associated with the framework agreements established with OECTA, AEFO, and their respective school boards, the Ministry of Education remained at impasse with OSSTF, ETFO, and OPSBA. Furthermore, a clause in the collective agreements negotiated in 2008 extended the current collective agreements for another year in the event that either signatory did not provided written notification of intent to bargain within 90 days prior to expiration. Because the Ministry of Education had convened PDTs – rather than school boards and teachers' unions convening formal bargaining – teachers would be due a wage increase of three per cent at the start of the school year in September barring a voluntarily negotiated settlement.

In response, the Ministry of Education implemented the Putting Students First Act in early September. This legislation authorized the provincial government to impose collective agreements on OSSTF and ETFO if they did not "negotiate" agreements within the parameters of OECTA's by 31 December. Both unions engaged in sporadic work-to-rule action, rotating strikes, and days of protest, and OSSTF achieved a small number of local agreements. However, neither endorsed the framework by the deadline. On 3 January 2013, Broter imposed a framework agreement similar to OECTA's on OSSTF-, ETFO-, and OPSBA-affiliated school boards. Both unions planned province-wide walkouts in protest, but cancelled them after the Ministry of Labour deemed them illegal. The Putting Students First Act, having served its purpose, was repealed later that month.

Dalton McGuinty resigned as Ontario's premier in February 2013. He was replaced by Kathleen Wynne, who, along with newly appointed minister of education, Liz Sandals, renegotiated the provincial framework agreements with OSSTF and ETFO. The renegotiated agreements included small enhancements to sick days and maternity benefits, and reduced the number of unpaid leave days (Lysyk 2014). ETFO also received a 2 per cent wage increase effective 1 September 2014 to reduce the salary gap between elementary and secondary school teachers.

The Wynne-led Liberals made good on their promise to develop legislation to guide teacher negotiations, and implemented the School Boards Collective Bargaining Act in April 2014. This act enshrined a process similar to the PDTs, whereby frameworks to address monetary items (e.g., salaries) are negotiated at the provincial level and others (e.g., scheduling) are negotiated at the school board level. They subsequently called a provincial election for June 2014. The teachers' unions continued to discourage the public to vote for the Conservatives, but did little to discourage votes for the Liberals, who, under Wynne's leadership, were re-elected to a majority government.

Teacher collective agreements with all four unions expired on 31 August 2014. School boards' associations, teachers' unions, and the Ministry of Education entered negotiations shortly after. Negotiations proceeded slowly as the result of a request by OSSTF that the Ontario Labour Relations Board (OLRB) clarify the issues that could be negotiated provincially and those that could be negotiated locally (Brown 2014). Negotiations continued throughout most of 2015, and OSSTF engaged in strikes at three school boards. Those same school boards challenged the legality of the strikes, ultimately winning a (rather convoluted) back-to-work order. School boards, teachers' unions, and the province eventually reached framework agreements in October and November 2015. Subsequently, many school boards and local teacher bargaining units did not conclude the local portion of their negotiations until several months after the framework agreements were reached.

Discussion: The Realities of Teacher Bargaining in an Age of Austerity

The case study of collective bargaining in Ontario's elementary and secondary education sector prior to and following the economic crisis beginning in 2008 provides several important insights into the impacts of austerity on public sector workers and unions. More specifically, it demonstrates how, unlike in the mid-1990s, public sector unions in Ontario pursued a sustained and persistent pragmatism in their relationships with the political party that introduced legislation that limited their right to strike in 2012 and subsequently imposed concessionary collective agreements early in 2013. Moreover, it demonstrates how periods of austerity (and change in general) serve as useful temporal junctures at which governments can increase their leverage at the bargaining table through the centralization of administration, financing, and labour relations. Rose (2004) initially discussed these trends over a decade ago, and a more recent study provides further evidence of governments consolidating their bargaining power over public sector workers and unions (Rose 2016).

The case study is, however, strikingly different from the debates concerning public sectors workers and education reform in the United States. The latter are replete with evidence of popular narratives that blame teachers' unions for the financial challenges facing US schools and school boards and for the lacklustre performance of students (see Rubinstein and McCarthy 2012; Lewin, Keefe, and Kochan 2012). Such narratives are almost inevitably accompanied by calls for a greater degree of privatization of elementary and secondary education. Yet these are almost completely absent in the case study of Ontario. Despite the far-reaching nature of the austerity measures implemented in Ontario, many of which came as a result of the Drummond Report, teachers' and other public sector unions representing educational support workers faced no serious threat to their right to exist. Indeed, the Drummond Commission was specifically forbidden to consider privatization initiatives in their mandate to recommend government reforms and austerity. Nor did the general model of education come under fire. Rather, and by some measures, there was actually an increase in the activities of school boards as the government continued to roll out full-day kindergarten across the province. This is readily interpreted by the authors as a general vote of confidence in Ontario's school system, which, according to the OECD, made significant progress under the McGuinty Liberals (OECD 2011). While the push for privatization has been significant in some segments of Canadian public administration (Hebdon and Jalette 2008), health and education retain overwhelming popular and political support as a public good. The austerity agenda in Ontario was therefore more about government control over collective bargaining outcomes and spending in the broader public sector than it was about a widespread reorganization of elementary and secondary education.

The recent rounds of teacher bargaining in Ontario also demonstrate several realities of public sector collective bargaining during an era of austerity. In Ontario's elementary and secondary education sector, four unions represent teachers, and each pursues different strategies to achieve specific goals according to its particular interests. Since the onset of the economic crises in 2008, there is little evidence of collaboration or broader solidarities among the four teachers' unions in opposition to government-imposed concessions and centralization. The idea that all four unions bargain together has never been seriously considered. Teachers' unions have even begun to pursue their election-time media campaigns independently, rather than under the umbrella of the Working Families Coalition, to which all four once belonged.

Perhaps the only evidence of collaboration is in a legal challenge of the Putting Students First Act. OSSTF, ETFO, and three unions representing educational support workers are challenging this legislation on the grounds that it violates the Canadian Charter of Rights and Freedoms. While each union initially brought forth an individual challenge, they have been deemed so similar that they will be considered together (Lysyk 2014). However, hearings did not begin until December 2015. These challenges are also testament to the increasingly legalistic nature of broader public sector collective bargaining, where, partly as the result of difficulties in achieving voluntarily negotiated collective agreements in an age of sustained austerity, unions and employers are increasingly reliant on the courts to determine the validity of the scope, structure, and outcomes of bargaining. In addition to the unions' challenge of the Putting Students First Act, this is evident in the delays in bargaining in 2014 and 2015 due to the need for OLRB clarification of the items that can be negotiated provincially and locally, and the OLRB challenge made by three school boards where OSSTF members were on strike. These school boards claimed that the strikes were illegal because they focused on provincial-level issues beyond the scope of local school boards.

At the same time, teachers' unions may not sense the same urgency to conclude an agreement as they once did. This is partly because voluntarily negotiated collective agreements are not likely to include significant enhancements to wages, benefits, and working conditions, but are likely to include some concessions. They have, however, introduced a new political calculus when it comes to job action. Teachers and other public sector workers have always had to consider how their job action might affect the delivery of public goods and services, and how, unlike in the private sector, their withdrawal of services through strikes often saves the government money. More recently, the threat that any job action deemed to be too disruptive – or even the threat of job action that may prove disruptive – will prompt back-to-work legislation almost immediately, or, as was evident in 2012, that pre-empts their ability to engage in meaningful job action. Teachers and their unions in Ontario are thus more careful and purposeful in their use of job action for fear that it could both tarnish their public image and prompt legislation that limits their ability to engage in job action or other tactics of resistance.

Conclusion

Austerity measures implemented by governments as a result of the recent economic crises have proven disruptive generally. They have also disturbed established and emerging relationships and practices in public sector collective bargaining that once appeared useful and promising. Consequently, the ability of public sector workers to perform their jobs delivering goods and services critical to the function of society has been compromised. The case of Ontario's elementary and secondary education sector demonstrates this. Furthermore, it shows how, in order to mitigate disruption, teachers' unions have pursued a persistent pragmatism in their relationships with political parties despite the imposition of concessions and limitations on their rights to bargain collectively and strike. They have also engaged in more litigious collective bargaining practices and limited their job action in order to avoid back-to-work legislation, or legislation that further limits their ability to engage in meaningful job action. These are, as we argue, increasingly common practices in public sector collective bargaining in an era of sustained austerity.

REFERENCES

Brown, Louise. 2014. "Ontario Teacher Talks Hit Quick Snag in New System." *Toronto Star*, 19 September.
Chaykowski, Rick, and Robert Hickey. 2013. *Building More Effective Labour-Management Relations*. Montreal and Kingston: McGill-Queen's University Press.
– 2014. "Principles for Labour Relations Reform in the Wake of the Drummond Report on Ontario's Public Services." *Canadian Labour & Employment Law* 17 (2): 379–91.
Downie, Bryan. 1992. *Strikes, Disputes, and Policymaking: Resolving Impasses in Ontario Education*. Kingston: IRC.
Evans, Bryan. 2013. "When Your Boss Is the State: The Paradoxes of Public Sector Work." In *Public Sector Unions in the Age of Austerity*, ed. S. Ross and L. Savage, 18–30. Winnipeg: Fernwood Publishing.
Evans, Bryan, and Charles Smith. 2015. "The Transformation of Ontario Politics: The Long Ascent of Neo-Liberalism." In *Transforming Provincial*

Politics: The Political Economy of Canada's Provinces and Territories in the Neo-Liberal Era, ed. B. Evans and C. Smith, 162–91. Toronto: University of Toronto Press.

Hebdon, Robert, and Patrice Jalette. 2008. "The Restructuring of Municipal Services: A Canada–United States Comparison." *Environment and Planning. C, Government & Policy* 26 (1): 144–58. https://doi.org/10.1068/c0634.

Heron, Craig. 2013. *The Canadian Labour Movement: A Short History*. 3rd ed. Toronto: James Lorimer.

Katz, Harry. 2013. "Is U.S. Public Sector Labor Relations in the Midst of a Transformation?" *Industrial & Labor Relations Review* 66 (5): 1031–46. https://doi.org/10.1177/001979391306600501.

Keefe, Jeffrey. 2012. "Public Employee Compensation and the Efficacy of Privatization Alternatives in US State and Local Governments." *British Journal of Industrial Relations* 50 (4): 782–809. https://doi.org/10.1111/bjir.12001.

Lafer, Gordon. 2013. *The Legislative Attack on American Wages and Labor Standards, 2011–2012*. Economic Policy Institute Briefing Paper #364. http://www.epi.org/publication/attack-on-american-labor-standards/.

– 2014. *Do Poor Kids Deserve Lower-Quality Education Than Rich Kids? Evaluating School Privatization Proposals in Milwaukee, Wisconsin*. Economic Policy Institute Briefing Paper #375. http://www.epi.org/publication/school-privatization-milwaukee/.

Lewin, David, Jeffrey Keefe, and Thomas Kochan. 2012. "The New Great Debate about Unionism and Collective Bargaining in the U.S. State and Local Governments." *Industrial & Labor Relations Review* 65 (4): 749–78. https://doi.org/10.1177/001979391206500401.

Lysyk, Bonnie. 2014. *Education Sector Collective Agreements: Special Report*. Toronto: Office of the Auditor General of Ontario.

OECD. 2011. "Ontario, Canada: Reform to Support High Achievement in a Diverse Context." In *Strong Performers and Successful Reformers in Education: Lessons from PISA for the United States*, 65–82. Paris: OECD. https://www.oecd.org/pisa/46623978.pdf.

Ontario Ministry of Finance. 2012. *Commission on the Reform of Ontario's Public Services*. Toronto: Queen's Printer for Ontario. http://www.fin.gov.on.ca/en/reformcommission/chapters/report.pdf.

Pilon, Dennis, Stephanie Ross, and Larry Savage. 2011. "Solidarity Revisited: Organized Labour and the New Democratic Party." *Canadian Political Science Review* 5 (1): 20–37.

Rose, Joseph. 2001. "From Softball to Hardball: The Transition in Labour-Management Relations in the Ontario Public Service." In *Conflict or*

Compromise: The Future of Public Sector Industrial Relations, ed. G. Swimmer, 66–95. Toronto: Oxford University Press.
– 2002. "The Assault on School Teacher Bargaining in Ontario." *Relations industrielle / Industrial Relations* 57 (1): 100–28. https://doi.org/10.7202/006712ar.
– 2004. "Public Sector Bargaining: From Retrenchment to Consolidation." *Relations industrielle/Industrial Relations* 59 (2): 271–94.
– 2012. "The Evolution of Teacher Bargaining in Ontario." In Slinn and Sweetman, *Dynamic Negotiations*, 199–220.
– 2016. "Constraints on Public Sector Bargaining in Canada." *Journal of Industrial Relations* 58 (1): 93–110.
Ross, Stephanie, and Larry Savage. 2013. "Introduction: Public Sector Unions in the Age of Austerity." In *Public Sector Unions in the Age of Austerity*, ed. S. Ross and L. Savage, 9–17. Winnipeg: Fernwood Publishing.
Rubinstein, Saul, and James McCarthy. 2012. "Public School Reform through Union-Management Collaboration." *Advances in Industrial and Labor Relations* 20:1–50. https://doi.org/10.1108/S0742-6186(2012)0000020004.
Savage, Larry. 2010. "Contemporary Party-Union Relations in Canada." *Labor Studies Journal* 35 (1): 8–26. https://doi.org/10.1177/0160449X09353028.
Savage, Larry, and Charles Smith. 2013. "Public Sector Unions and Electoral Politics in Canada." In *Public Sector Unions in the Age of Austerity*, ed. S. Ross and L. Savage, 46–56. Winnipeg: Fernwood Publishing.
Slinn, Sara. 2012. "Conflict without Compromise: The Case of Public Sector Teacher Bargaining in British Columbia." In Slinn and Sweetman, *Dynamic Negotiations*, 81–124.
Slinn, Sara, and Arthur Sweetman. 2012. "Introduction: Labour Relations in Primary and Secondary Canadian Education." In Slinn and Sweetman, *Dynamic Negotiations*, 1–12.
Slinn, Sara, and Arthur Sweetman, eds. 2012. *Dynamic Negotiations*. Montreal and Kingston: McGill-Queen's University Press
Sweeney, Brendan. 2013. "The Labour Geographies of Education: The Centralization of Governance and Collective Bargaining in Ontario, Canada." *Geoforum* 44 (1): 120–8. https://doi.org/10.1016/j.geoforum.2012.10.006.
– Forthcoming. "Teacher Bargaining in Ontario, 1998–2014." *Towards a Post-Consolidation Stage of Public Sector Collective Bargaining*.
Sweeney, Brendan, Susan McWilliams, and Rob Hickey. 2012. "The Centralization of Collective Bargaining in Ontario's Public Education Sector and the Need to Balance Stakeholder Interests." In Slinn and Sweetman, *Dynamic Negotiations*, 247–64.

Swimmer, Gene, and Mark Thompson. 1995. "Collective Bargaining in the Public Sector." In *Public Sector Collective Bargaining: The Beginning of the End or the End of the Beginning?* ed. G. Swimmer and M. Thompson, 1–19. Kingston: IRC.

Walchuk, Brad. 2010. "Changing Union-Party Relations in Canada: The Rise of the Working Families Coalition." *Labor Studies Journal* 35 (1): 27–50. https://doi.org/10.1177/0160449X09353036.

Williams-Whitt, Kelly. 2012. "Oil and Ideology: The Transformation of K-12 Bargaining in Alberta." In Slinn and Sweetman, *Dynamic Negotiations*, 125–60.

8 Austerity and the Low-Wage Economy: Living and Other Wages

BRYAN M. EVANS, STEPHEN MCBRIDE, AND JACOB MUIRHEAD

Low wages seem endemic to capitalist economic systems, though the size of the low-wage sector and its characteristics can vary over time. Neoclassical economics points to market forces in an increasingly globalized international economy as the basic unalterable force driving inequality and allocating wages that correspond to the productivity or value of what the worker produces. These accounts suggest a relationship between possession of human capital, productivity, and wages. Here, the responsibility for being low-waged lies with the individual who has neglected to acquire the right amount and type of human capital; the result is a worker less productive than his or her peers who endures low wages as a consequence.[1] Other theories emphasize systemic rather than individual factors – Left Keynesians propose that political institutions have the potential to control capitalism's tendency towards inequality, and Marxists understand capitalism's core dynamic as one of unrelenting exploitation of labour in search of ever-expanding profits.

For both Left Keynesians and Marxists, the decline of labour income can be understood as an expression of the amplified political power of capital relative to the working class. Through the past thirty-five years, informed by neoliberalism, states have intervened to constrain or roll back the economic and political gains the working class made in the post-war period. An important part of the neoliberal package, and one pursued with greater intensity since the economic and financial crisis,

---

1 Human capital theory is open to a number of significant objections (see McBride 2000, 172–6) that undermine its value as an explanation of low wages.

has been budgetary austerity. The emphasis has been on achieving balanced budgets through spending restraint, especially in the social sphere. The social role of the state has been diminished and a greater reliance placed on purely market mechanisms for settling wage issues. This has increased the incidence of low-waged work and income inequality (Hermann 2014; Heyes 2013; Heyes and Lewis 2015; Thomas and Tufts 2015).

This situation has led to renewed efforts to deal with low wages through statutory minimum wages and, more recently, through living-wage campaigns that pressure either government or private employers to pay rates enabling basic survival above the poverty line. In the past, other mechanisms to address the issue have been attempted as well, and we briefly allude to two of them. The focus in this chapter is on low wages and poverty and thus the labour market. However, it is important to keep in mind the intersection between wages and the "social wage," as represented by various income or in-kind supports that are available to those with insufficient market-generated income. The low-waged are part of a larger group comprising all who have low incomes, and the diminished state role in social provision has exacerbated conditions among the non-waged. Both are under increased pressure in an age of austerity.

Earlier methods to address low wages included British Wages Councils in low-waged sectors such as retail, hospitality, social and child care, food processing, cleaning, textiles, and clothing and hairdressing. Founded in 1909 (Bayliss 1962), they were abolished in 1993 under the Conservative government's deregulation of the labour market strategy. Once abolished, it seemed that a national minimum wage had some advantages, not least broader coverage, and support rallied around that option (Manning 2009; Cabrelli 2014, 245–6).[2] In Australia, the "awards" system, considerably revised in the neoliberal period (see Bray and Macneil 2011) had considerable impact, in its pre-1990s heyday. It was largely responsible for establishing minimum pay and standards for the Australian workforce (McCallum 2011). Conciliation

---

2 There was also an institutionalized system of consultation in the public service, particularly for lower-waged public servants. It took the form of joint consultative mechanisms, commonly referred to as Whitley Councils after their originator, John Whitley, whose committee on the relations between employers and employees during the First World War recommended a system of regular formal consultative councils involving workers and employers.

was first attempted: if it failed, labour courts could invoke compulsory arbitration, which led to a binding award governing the employers, workers, unions, and employers' associations applicable to the dispute. The awards specified minimum wages and conditions, though bargaining above these minima could occur. The result was that "all employers who employed workers in the relevant industry or craft were obliged to abide by the terms and conditions of employment" (8). Whatever its limitations, the awards system significantly contributed to one of the most equal distributions of income in the Western world, and its erosion coincided with increased inequality (Pusey 2003, 48).

The Decline of Labour Incomes as Neoliberal Policy and Political Strategy

Increasing inequality of worker relative to capitalist incomes is an important but controversial characteristic of neoliberal capitalism. Despite the significance of this lived life reality, and considering the context of the moral standards of democracy, it is surprising that it was not until the publication of Thomas Piketty's *Capital in the 21st Century* (2014a) that income inequality became a politically legitimate subject for mainstream public policy discussions in countries such as Canada and the United States. This is in spite of a chorus of accusation of fomenting "class warfare" among the public from the political Right (Giles 2014).

With respect to Piketty, the empirical analysis of trends in income distribution strongly implies that the mechanism responsible for the pattern of income distribution is the relative power between two major groups – owners of capital and bearers of labour power. This signals a rediscovery of the questions and even approaches of the older tradition of classical political economy, in which income distribution in terms of class, whose outcomes were determined by relative power, was a central concern (Piketty 2015). In this view, capitalists obtain income in the form of profits, and workers earn wages and salaries. For economic theory, Piketty's conclusions contradict a major tenet of the neoclassical theory of worker wages, in which marginal products of labour determine the wage rate they earn in the labour market. Because wage growth has been stagnant since the 1970s, with productivity growth having been substantial in the context of intensified competition on global and national levels, the mainstream explanation proves inadequate.

Figure 8.1. Share of Employees in Low-Paid Work

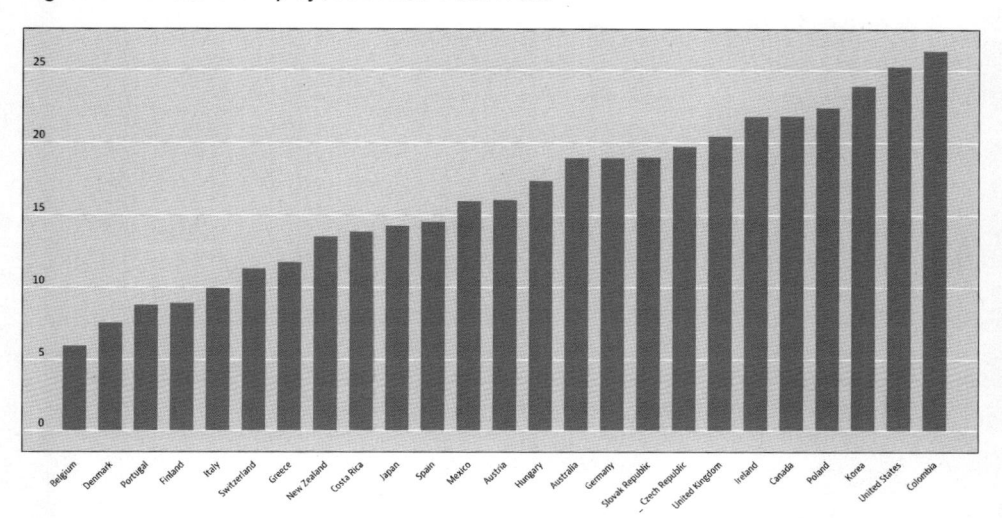

[Bar chart showing share of employees in low-paid work across OECD countries, ranging from Belgium (lowest, ~5%) to Colombia (highest, ~26%). Countries in order: Belgium, Denmark, Portugal, Finland, Italy, Switzerland, Greece, New Zealand, Costa Rica, Japan, Spain, Mexico, Austria, Hungary, Australia, Germany, Slovak Republic, Czech Republic, United Kingdom, Ireland, Canada, Poland, Korea, United States, Colombia.]

Source: OECD Labour Market Statistics, 2009

Income data from the World Wealth and Income Database demonstrates that the top 10 per cent of the population of the Group of Seven countries – Canada, France, Germany, Italy, Japan, the United Kingdom, and the United States – has overall, through the era of neoliberalism, had returned to them an increasing share of the national income. This, of course, means that the bottom 90 per cent of the populations of these countries, most of whom are workers who depend primarily on the labour market for incomes, with the bottom 50 per cent owning no wealth at all, have been paid increasingly less, relative to the value of the total output of the economy.

To provide some indication of the incidence of low-wage work among economies in the Global North, figure 8.1 quantifies the percentage of employees in low-paid work within a sample of OECD countries. In 2009, over 88 million people within the OECD were employed in low-wage work. This number has since increased as a result of the Great Recession, partly resulting from the austerity policies that emerged as the default policy response to the crisis.

The redistributive role of trade unions to enhance both the economic and political power of workers is a key determining factor in the distribution of labour income in a capitalist economy. The union advantage extends beyond direct members by serving to establish employment norms at the sectoral level as well as creating upstream benefits to the larger community by increasing purchasing power (Schmitt and Mitukiewicz 2011). The 1970s crisis of "stagflation" put to an end the "golden age" of capitalism, in which the restructuring required to restore profitability put great emphasis on reforming capital-worker relations by aggressively attacking the political and economic power of workers (Dumenil and Levy 2011; Shaikh 2011; Wahl 2011). On the world stage, this coincided with the national electoral victories of free market advocates Ronald Reagan in the United States and Margaret Thatcher in the United Kingdom. In the United States, Reagan had in 1981 fired the 11,345 striking federal employees who as members of the Professional Air Traffic Controller's Organization were on strike. This event marked a shift in state economic policy thinking from Keynesian to neoliberal in the United States, giving notice to workers and their political and economic organizations, both American and beyond, that the golden age of relative inclusion was over.

The power of capital has become so extreme that forms of labour exploitation thought to be obsolete have been returning since the 1980s (Botwinick 1998). In the face of changes in the nature of employment and the role of the state, trade unions have been less militant, the leadership more conservative, trending towards more collaborative relations with management in a form of neoliberal competitiveness partnership. Globalization and the creation of the dynamics of competitive wage and social austerity is perhaps the best explanation for the larger, structural challenges facing unions (Albo 1994).

Among progressive labour economists, the relationship between union density and the pattern of income distribution is well known and understood (Mishel 2012). Recently, the International Monetary Fund has acknowledged that declining union membership has played a key role in increasing income inequality (Jaumotte and Buitron 2015). For example, in Canada, union density was at 34.9 per cent between 1982 and 1992. This declined to 27.5 per cent for the period 2002–12. In the United Kingdom, the decline was more dramatic. In 1982–92, the UK union density stood at 42.9 per cent. For 2002–12, it had shrunk to 27.6 per cent. And in the United States, where density was already anaemic, the decline from barely 17 per cent in 1982–92 to 11.8 per cent in 2002–12 effectively suggests that private sector unions have all but been eliminated, save for a shrinking presence in core industries such as auto (OECD 2015c). As Richard Freeman argued, the decline of the union movement has been the result of conscious policy by capital (Freeman 2005).

Figure 8.2. Union Density: 1972–2014

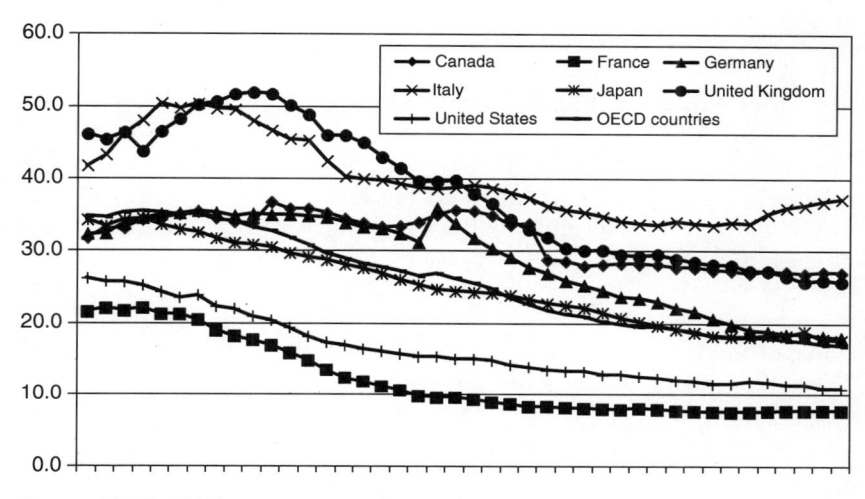

Source: OECD, 2015b

In addition to declining union density, the decline in wages is a function of deindustrialization and the general shrinking of manufacturing in the Global North economies. The role of the expansion of "services" to slower economic and productivity growth rates compared to the "golden age" (Iversen and Wren 1998; Wren 2013a) and to the stagnation in employment and labour-derived income is a considerable factor. Deindustrialization and the expansion of the services characterize the nature of jobs offered in the labour market during neoliberalism. The "New Economy" and financialization allowed for expansion of credit, housing booms, with workers' incomes increasingly involved and dependent on performance of financial markets through housing and pensions. In the varieties of capitalism literature, a "political economy of the services" has emerged to explain the expansion of low-waged work in such sectors as health, educational, and financial services, alongside the more traditional low-wage sectors such as retail and hospitality. In industrial relations, neoliberal hostility to unionization in the growing service (retail, etc.) industries is a matter of managerial policy (Krugman 2015). Wren argues that a combination of employment growth and incomes inequality characterize the era of the service economy (Wren 2013b). This is due to the fact that among many services, the person-to-person quality of, for example, medical services and education frustrates the repetition of a rate of technological dynamism witnessed in other sectors, most commonly in manufacturing.

Strategies Addressing Low-Wage Work: The Minimum Wage

The aforementioned awards system and wages councils have declined or been abolished. In their place there has been renewed interest in minimum wage provisions and, in light of the perceived deficiencies of that model, in the concept of a living wage. The minimum wage has been used by a variety of states to address low-wage work and economic inequality with varying degrees of success.[3] Minimum wage systems now are embedded in over 100 countries (Neumark and Wascher 2008). There is considerable variation in minimum wage policy both historically within countries and comparatively between them. However, the basic function of all minimum wage policy is to legally establish a minimum value which employers cannot go below.

Minimum Wage Systems

There are two distinct approaches to minimum wage regulation. First, and most common, minimum wages can be set universally at the national or, in federal countries, the sub-national level, and are enforced through legislation. These minimum wage systems set a common wage floor, which applies to all employees unless exceptions are specified relating to age, or industry, and historically gender (Schulten 2014). Lower minimums for the young and inexperienced, or workers in industries where tipping is prevalent are example of variations.

Alternatively wage floors can be set through collective bargaining negotiated either bipartite between employer and union representatives, or tripartite between union, employer, and state representatives (Schulten

---

3 Low-wage work has commonly been defined by the Organisation for Economic Co-operation and Development (OECD) as full-time work that pays at or less than two-thirds of median full-time earnings. This definition is not the only one, however, and many countries use their own definitions, which incorporate different thresholds and vary on whether to include part-time, apprenticeship, young workers, and estimates of the informal economy into their measurements. The OECD, for example, does not include part-time work in its estimate and certainly underestimates the size of the low-wage economy in countries. See, for example, Grimshaw (2011).

2014). Minimum wages in bipartite and tripartite agreements generally occur at the sectoral or occupational level. Rather than a common wage floor, there are a number of different minimum wages. Workers in countries using the collective bargaining system for minimum wage determination generally do so because they are well-represented by powerful unions that are highly organized and dense, and provide broad coverage to the majority of workers. Where union density is lower, states using this system often extend agreement coverage from specific negotiations to all workers within a sector, whether unionized or not (Eldring and Alsos 2012). Examples include Finland, Sweden, Denmark, Italy, and Austria.

The two systems are not mutually exclusive. France has a national statutory minimum wage. However, the process by which it is set is heavily influenced through reference to a tripartite committee of government, worker, and employer representatives, which produces a yearly report that helps establish the government's decree on minimum wage levels (Kampelmann, Garnero, and Ryxc 2013, 33). Similarly, Austrian minimum wages are defined primarily through collective bargaining agreements, but there is also a statutory minimum wage that is set for portions of the public sector (31).

A Comparison of Statutory vs Collective Bargaining Minimum Wage Systems

Countries that determine minimum wages collectively appear on average to have both more generous wage floors that provide a decent quality of life and less overall income inequality between top and bottom earners (Kampelmann, Garnero, and Ryxc 2013). Moreover, there is a correlation between high union coverage and a reduction in the size of the low-wage economy more generally, as seen in figure 8.3 (Schmitt 2012, 3).

Statutory, universal minimum wages tend to be lower but all-encompassing, whereas those produced by a collective bargaining system tend to have higher wage floors, less inequality, and are more focused in their coverage. These outcomes are dependent on high rates of bargaining coverage to be effective (Kampelmann, Garnero, and Ryxc 2013). But, as noted earlier, union density and coverage are declining, thus making the second model less effective.

The model of a national statutory minimum has therefore been gaining ground. Ireland, the United Kingdom, and Germany have all introduced a statutory minimum wage in recent years (Bispinck and Schulten 2014; Eldring and Alsos 2012; Schulten 2014). These countries occupy a

Figure 8.3. Low Wage Work and Collective Bargaining

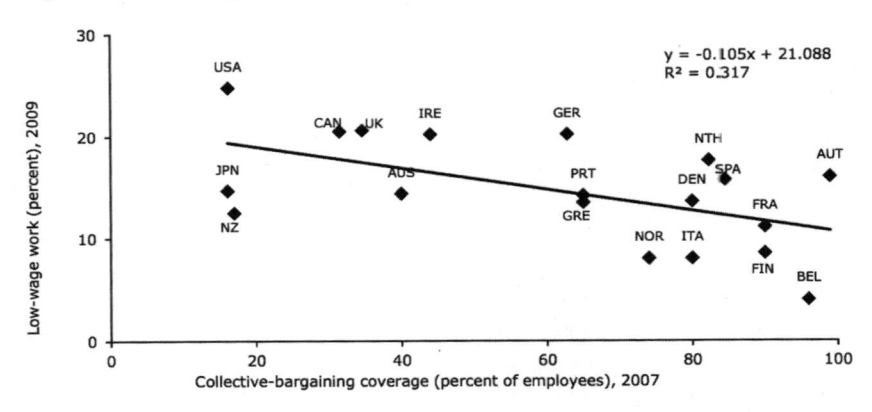

[Scatter plot: x-axis "Collective-bargaining coverage (percent of employees), 2007" from 0 to 100; y-axis "Low-wage work (percent), 2009" from 0 to 30. Data points labeled: USA, CAN, UK, IRE, GER, NTH, AUT, JPN, AUS, PRT, DEN, SPA, NZ, GRE, NOR, ITA, FRA, FIN, BEL. Regression line: $y = -0.105x + 21.088$, $R^2 = 0.317$]

Source: Schmitt (2012)

middle ground in collective-bargaining coverage between unregulated, decentralized labour markets such as the United States, and more regulated centralized labour markets such as Denmark or Finland (see figure 8.3). The result of falling bargaining coverage in all three countries was the growth of a low-wage sector, rising inequality, and the emergence of a dual economy. Work for unionized workers on the "inside" remained well paid and secure, while non-unionized work on the "periphery" became increasingly common, with workers employed in unregulated industries defined by low-pay, insecure, short-term, and flexible employment (Bispinck and Schulten 2014; Milner 1995; Manning 2013; Pothier 2014). One policy response in all three countries was a switch to a statutory universal minimum wage that sets a consistent wage floor at the national level without any gaps in coverage.

Potential of Statutory Minimum Wage Systems

Labour studies literature has identified an interconnected set of sobering themes: precarious work, decline of egalitarian labour market institutions such as unions, stagnant real wages for all but the richest, retrenched welfare states, declining social benefits, and increased social inequality (Appelbaum 2012; Bivens et al. 2014; Branch and Hanley 2011; Brosnan and Wilkinson 1988; Milner 1995; Western and Rosenfeld 2011). Statutory minimum wages have become increasingly impor-

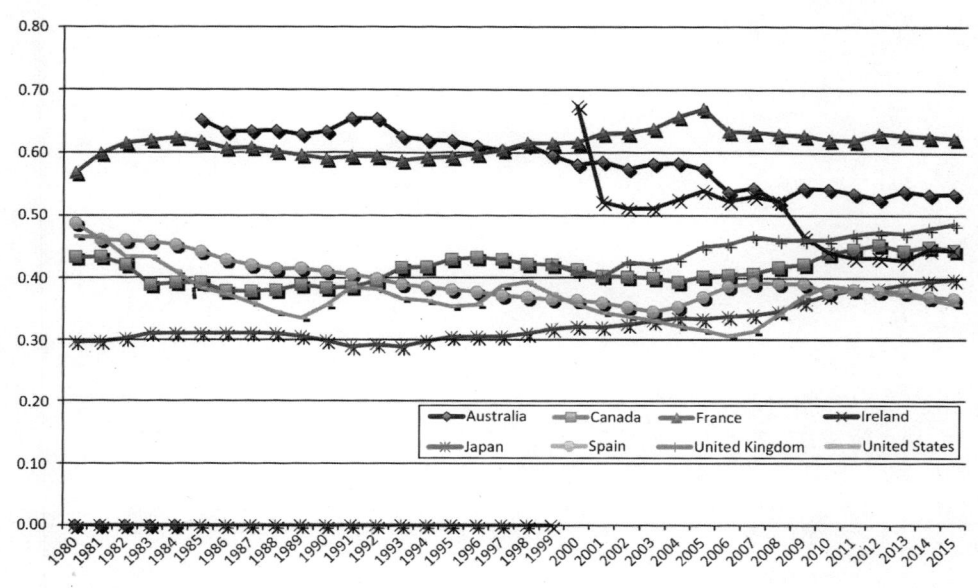

Figure 8.4. Minimum Relative to Median Wage of Full-Time Workers: 1980–2015

Source: OECD (2015a)

tant, not only because of a general rise in low-paying, poor-quality jobs within developed countries, but also because within flexible, deregulated labour markets very few alternative strategies to address low-wage work remain.

However, a cursory analysis of statutory minimum wages reveals their inadequacy in providing a decent standard of living (OECD 2015a). Although there is no commonly accepted definition of what a "fair" minimum wage actually is, both the European Council and the Commission have suggested an equitable minimum wage as 60 per cent of a full-time median salary (Schulten 2014). As figure 8.4 illustrates, most statutory minimum wages are well below this 60 per cent cut-off, ranging between 38 and 48 per cent in 2012.

These meagre wages have remained relatively stagnant in terms of real value since 1975, in spite of consistent growth in labour productivity in the Global North. This relationship can be seen in figure 8.5.

Though becoming more widespread, minimum wages are an inadequate approach to addressing low wage-work. Most statutory

Figure 8.5. Growth in Average Wages vs Growth in Labour Productivity in OECD: 1999–2013

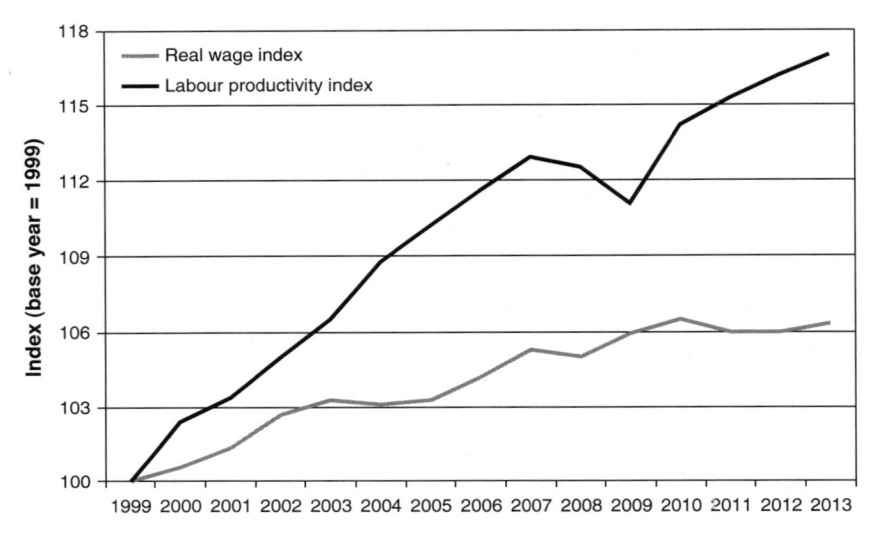

Source: ILO (2014)

Note: Wage growth is calculated as weighted average of year-on-year growth in average monthly real wages for thirty-six developed countries.

minimum wage policies are set too low to meaningfully improve the quality of life for those working in low-wage employment. Systems based on collective bargaining are becoming less feasible in the face of union decline, spotty coverage, and the structural reforms imposed on labour as part of austerity packages.

Minimum Wage Discourses

The discourse around minimum wages has been changing and has become more supportive of the concept. Neoliberal thought, inspired partly by neoclassical economics, dismisses the usefulness of the concept and suggests that a "fair" wage is simply equal to the marginal product of labour (O'Neill 2014). Because wage growth has been stagnant since the 1970s, with productivity growth having been substantial in the context of intensified competition on global and national levels, as noted for the period from 1999 in figure 8.5, this explanation is inadequate. Nevertheless it remains the dominant perspective articulated by economists and politicians. A minimum wage, therefore, is seen as a policy that interferes with the functionality of the market. Opponents of minimum wages argue that they have a negative economic impact. Because minimum wages increase the cost of labour, employers are forced to lay off workers, freeze hiring, increase prices, and reduce hours (Brown, Gilroy, and Kohen 1982; Dolado et al. 1996; Neumark and Wascher 1992; OECD 1994).

Since the 1990s, dissenting economists have shown that minimum wage policies have no or only marginal impact on employment (Betcherman 2014; Card and Krueger 1995; Dolado et al. 1996; Doucouliagos and Stanley 2009; ILO 2014; Manning 2013; Metcalf 1999). In addition, economic research inspired by the recent financial crisis suggests that minimum wage policies do little to hurt employment, but are useful counter-cyclical tools that contribute to stimulating purchasing power and aggregate demand (ILO 2014; IMF 2013a; IMF 2013b; Kampelmann, Garnero, and Ryxc 2013). This should be an attractive feature in times of austerity, especially as other research indicates that austerity policies, predicated on low wages and a low social wage, make little sense (Blyth 2013). Despite the fact that by most accounts the rate of profit – the driver of the rate of capital accumulation and therefore the rate of growth in investment and labour demand – has recovered, and the capitalist class hoards, rather than invests substantial money capital. The disconnect between investment and the rate of profit suggests that policies advocating more austerity for lower workers' incomes do not improve the employment and income problem, though they do diminish the political capacities of workers to resist.

Thomas Piketty (2014a) also suggests that economic inequality is one of the greatest threats to stability in the 21st century. Such analysis has led to some emphasis on interventionist policies, like the minimum wage, which potentially play a role in reducing inequality (Kampelmann, Garnero, and Ryxc 2013; Piketty 2014a). The critical economic argumentation relating to the minimum wage may have helped the adoption of statutory wage floors in the United Kingdom, Ireland, and Germany in 1999, 2000, and 2015 respectively (O'Neill 2014; Pothier 2014). It should be noted, however, that although the wage floors set in these three countries are more generous than in the United States, they are guided by cautious economic reasoning which recommends very gradual and modest increases and stipulates clear "optimal" upper limits to the utility of minimum wages to prevent harm to the labour market. Consequently, although these wage floors hover closer to the 60 per cent of full-time employment metric identified by the EU Commission, they remain below it.

On 1 January 2015, Germany introduced its first national minimum wage level determined largely by the recommendations of a Minimum Wage Commission made up primarily of employer and union representatives. Relative to other advanced countries, the minimum wage level was high (Schulten 2014). At 50 per cent of median full-time income, or €8.50, Germany's minimum wage was sixth-highest in Europe (Schulten 2015). Germany's move to a statutory minimum wage filled a gap left by a collective-bargaining system that had become inadequate in providing coverage and good wages to enough German workers (Eldring and Alsos 2012). For example, increasingly the German labour market featured negotiations at the plant level, and provided irregular coverage between full-time permanent employees and other, less permanent contract and part-time work (Bispinck and Schulten 2014; Hassel 2011). By 2013, less than 60 per cent of workers were covered by collective bargaining agreements in western Germany, and only 48 per cent in eastern Germany (Weinkopf 2015). Both contract and part-time work has been growing in Germany as a percentage of overall employment since the 1980s, with part-time work doubling between 1991 and 2007 (Hassel 2011, 19). The share of low-paid among all workers in Germany increased from 14.5 per cent in 1998 to 21.5 per cent in 2007, or to over nine million workers (20). In addition, the poorest six million of these were earning wages of less than €8.50 per hour, which is a poverty-level wage in Germany (Nowak 2015).

The new wage floor was to raise the income of six million workers and affect 15 per cent of the German workforce (Pothier 2014). Consequently, while it was never intended to eliminate low-waged work, its purpose was to significantly raise the wage floor for a large portion of Germany's working poor. Given the power of austerity discourses in Germany and Europe throughout this period, an important question to answer is how this development came about. The passage of legislation is attributable largely to unions in Germany, which remain relatively powerful actors, despite their declining membership. From 2006 to 2007, the Confederation of German Trade Unions (DGB), the largest association of unions in Germany, began campaigning for a minimum wage and placed the issue at the top of its political agenda. The campaign consisted of rallies and public meetings, in addition to national advertising in mass media on television, radio, the Internet, and in newspapers. Many of these advertisements drew attention to a number of inadequacies in the pay of the working class, such as the going rate of €3.82 per hour for hairdressers, or the €2.82 per hour rate for call centre workers in the Ruhr area (Nowak 2015). The campaign resonated with Germans, and by the time the 2013 national elections began, a statutory minimum wage enjoyed between 70 and 80 per cent public support. This public support in addition to DGB lobbying made the minimum wage a highly salient electoral issue (Bispinck and Schulten 2014; Nowak 2015). The DGB secured political buy-in and support for a minimum wage from the Social Democrats who went on to form a coalition with Angela Merkel's Christian Democrats partly on the condition of minimum wage legislation (Bispinck and Schulten 2014).

The outcome of this protracted union-led campaign for a statutory minimum wage was a wage floor that had the potential to reduce the incidence of low-wage work and income inequality in the country. However, political compromises leading up to and after the statutory wage was enacted into law have ensured that it will have less impact than initially intended (Nowak 2015). The statutory minimum wage was expected to affect up to six million Germans who earned less than €8.50 per hour. Yet political compromises pushed most forcefully by Angela Merkel's lead coalition party, the Christian Democrats, exempted the young, disabled, imprisoned, recently unemployed, and seasonal workers from the legislation. All told, approximately 2.3 million workers earning below €8.50 per hour have now been excluded (ibid.). Despite these shortcomings, the legislation has been viewed as a great accomplishment. It is one of the first major victories for organized labour in Germany in the last two decades. Moreover, despite economic forecasting that predicted the loss of between 200,000 and 1,000,000 jobs as a result of a statutory minimum wage, as of January 2016, Germany had an unemployment rate of less than 6 per cent, which is the lowest rate since the early 1990s and also lower than immediately before the introduction of minimum wage legislation (Amlinger, Bispinck, and Schulten 2016). In addition, a record 43 million Germans were in the labour force, which is the highest level in history (Plociennik 2016). The consensus, then, is no negative effect on the German labour market has resulted from the introduction of the minimum wage (Amlinger, Bispinck, and Schulten 2016).

The British case is also viewed as a success story, although the level of income it provides is less impressive. During the 1980s and 1990s, the number of British workers covered by collective pay-setting institutions such as unions or wage councils fell below 50 per cent (Milner 1995). Within a fiercely free-market neoliberal political climate, successive British governments waged war on organized labour. This led to reduced union strength and coverage, as well as the 1993 abolition of bipartite wage councils, which had set minimum wages for 2.5 million of Britain's poorest (Machin and Manning 1994). Except for the United States, growth in wage inequality in Britain was unmatched in any other industrialized country (Gosling and Lemieux 2004). In 1999 the Labour government introduced a nationwide statutory minimum wage, which was to be monitored by a non-partisan independent expert commission called the British Low Pay Commission (Metcalf 1999). The wage itself is set each year following the commission's recommendation (Kampelmann, Garnero, and Ryxc 2013).

The minimum wage in the United Kingdom did not lead to job losses (Manning 2013), but instead, raised the wages of around 5 per cent of the labour force. It has been credited with reducing income inequality, producing higher than average wage increases, and putting more money into the pockets of the approximately 1.5 million low-wage workers who are directly affected by changes in the minimum wage each year (Low Pay Commission 2015).

Yet a valid criticism of national statutory minimum wages is that they are too modest and conservative to significantly affect low-wage work (Dolton, Rosazza-Bonibene, and Wadsworth 2010). The wage floor leaves workers in poverty, and the low-wage economy continues to grow across the OECD. This brief overview of minimum wage regulation has discussed the potential of these policies to address low wages with mixed conclusions. Collective bargaining systems ensure relatively generous wage floors but rely on strong union membership, which is decreasingly common. Consequently, statutory minimum wages are becoming the dominant approach to minimum wage regulation. These systems are typically ungenerous with low wage floors that leave many full-time workers employed in poverty.

The Living Wage Movement

Increased inequality of worker relative to capitalist incomes has been an important characteristic of neoliberal capitalism (Giles 2014; Piketty 2014a).These pressures have only intensified as a result of the global financial crisis of 2007/8 and subsequent austerity policies. Despite consistent increases in labour productivity, the majority of income growth has gone primarily to the top 1 per cent of earners. Real wages for those in lower-income deciles have remained stagnant or fallen (Western and Rosenfeld 2011). The scope and generosity of social security that welfare states once provided is declining or threatened. Jobs are increasingly temporary, part-time, contract-based, without benefits and low paying (Freeman, Hersch, and Mishel 2005; Muffels 2008).

However, there has been resistance. As well as economics discourse becoming more favourable to minimum wage regulation, popular opinion has become more positive (e.g., Dougan 2013; Pew Research Center 2014; Dahlgreen 2014; Thomas 2014). Moreover, discourses on minimum wages increasingly are influenced by historical and philosophical considerations preoccupied with justice, fairness, human dignity, social decency, and the good society (Brennan 2012; Figart 2004). The contemporary Living Wage campaign has deep historical and philosophical roots (Werner and Lim 2015; Figart 2004; Glickman 1997, 66; Luce 2012).

The Living Wage movement has attracted much attention in recent years (Bennett 2012; Bernstein 2005; Clain 2012; Devinatz 2013; Figart, Mutari, and Power 2002; Figart 2001, 2004; Glickman 1997; Luce 2004, 2012; Pennycook 2012; Pollin et al. 2008; Rossi and Curtis 2013; Adams and Neumark 2005; Wills and Linneker 2013). It has been able to frame the battle over low wages normatively. At its core is a plea to human decency, solidarity, and underlying concepts of "fairness" based on the notion that those who work should not live in poverty.

What constitutes a living wage involves the development of complex calculators to quantify an exact monetary amount in given locations at a particular time[4] (Rossi and Curtis 2013). These are important components of Living Wage campaigns, though the intuitive ideas behind the campaigns are hardly technical. The modern iteration of the Living Wage movement began in Baltimore, Maryland, in 1994. Throughout the early 1990s, soup kitchens run by religious workers operating in the Baltimore area began to notice a rising demand for their services and that many who visited the kitchen or homeless shelter with their families were people who worked (Pollin et al. 2008). The conclusion drawn was that people with families and jobs should not have to work in poverty and bring their families to soup kitchens.

Throughout the next two decades over 140 Living Wage campaigns were won in the United States alone. The movement also expanded

---

4 See, for example, the Living Wage Calculator developed by Glasmeier (2017).

180   Austerity: The Lived Experience

to the United Kingdom (2001), Canada (2010),[5] New Zealand (2014)[6] Ireland (2013–14),[7] and more recently it has also spread to South and Southeast Asia. The campaigns have been a response to mitigate the impact of union jobs lost because of increasing privatization in the public sector. They are also a grassroots response to minimum wages that failed to meet basic living requirements. In addition, they were a response to rising income inequality and wage stagnation in the bottom few income deciles. Finally, they were a means of organizing low-wage workers in a post-union economy (Bernstein 2005; Levin-Waldman 2005; Luce 2004). Living Wage campaigns have often focused on the municipal level, which provides more direct access to the policy process than other levels of government where campaigns have made less headway (Bernstein, 2005; Luce, 2004, 2012).

The specific demands made by Living Wage campaigns differ, depending on geographical location and country, but tend to be modelled on the basic income requirements for a family of three or four that includes the average cost of childcare, food, health care, transportation, clothing, and other basic necessities, while also taking into consideration cost of living and rent in different geographic locations (Brennan 2012; Rossi and Curtis 2013, 122). Using these calculations, campaigns emerge with an income that is generally double the statutory minimum wage, and also includes benefits (Pollin et al. 2008). Advocates argue that these sophisticated models are far more reflective of a basic income than those articulated in relation to state poverty measurements, which are generally simplistic and outdated (Rossi and Curtis 2013; US Department of Health and Human Services 2014; Luce 2012, 13).

The vast majority of Living Wage initiatives fall into three broad models. The first has been operationalized in nearly 150 American cities.[8] It operates through targeted municipal ordinances. They function quite narrowly at the municipal level and affect only those workers whose jobs can be traced to public money (Luce 2004, 45). Specifically, they require any actor who interacts in some financial capacity with the

---

5   See, for example, Brennan (2012).
6   See, for example, Living Wage, New Zealand (2017).
7   See, for example, Living Wage, Republic of Ireland (2017).
8   Outside the United States, it has had much less impact, although notably it is also used by the city of London in the United Kingdom, as well as in the city of New Westminster, Canada (Brennan 2012; Pollin et al. 2008; Wills and Linneker 2013).

municipality to pay its workers a living wage. These ordinances can be targeted towards businesses contracting with the city, businesses that receive economic subsidies from the municipality, subcontractors who work alongside principal contractors on city contracts, businesses that borrow financially from the city, and finally municipal departments themselves (ibid.). Given their narrow parameters, the impact of these ordinances is typically fairly low, directly affecting only 1–2 per cent of a municipality's overall labour force (Bernstein 2005, 117). Although the generosity of these ordinances varies from city to city, generally they require employers to pay wages above the poverty line and to provide benefits for workers. The ordinances are not automatic, and often include minimum requirement conditions to come into effect. For example, many municipal wage ordinances apply only to city contracts valued at $100,000 or more (107).

A second model also is operationalized through municipal ordinances, but instead of targeting businesses involved financially with the municipality, these have much broader coverage and affect all businesses within the municipality. These geographically oriented Living Wage ordinances are functionally equivalent to statutory minimum wage regulation at the state or federal level. They set a wage floor for the entire municipality, and all businesses within it are required to pay their employees the living wage (Pollin et al. 2008). Currently, these Living Wage ordinances are operative only within a small number of cities in the United States. Among larger American cities, they exist in Chicago (2014), Oakland (2014), San Francisco (2003), Santa Fe (2003), Seattle (2014), and Washington, DC (2013), and campaigns with a high probability of success are also underway in Los Angeles, New York, and Portland.[9] Given its broad coverage, this type of Living Wage model has had a greater impact on low-wage work than targeted municipal ordinances, but is less common within the United States, and does not exist outside of it.

A third Living Wage model relies on voluntary adoption by businesses rather than mandated and legally enforceable municipal ordinances. This Living Wage model has been most successful in the United Kingdom, but is also found in Canada, Ireland, New Zealand, and to a lesser extent, the United States. Although initial description of the model as voluntary conjures images of goodwill, corporate social responsibility, and amicable cooperation, successful campaigns are

---

9 For more information, see National Employment Law Project (2017).

also often the result of protracted struggles that rely on public naming, shaming, and blaming (Moore 2015). That said, relationships between businesses and living wage advocates can be less antagonistic, and voluntary cooperation is common (Wills and Linneker 2013). The UK Living Wage movement began in London in 2001 (ibid.). London Citizens, the broad-based community coalition credited with beginning the British iteration of the Living Wage movement, was directly inspired by the success of the American movement and consulted living wage advocates from Baltimore (188).

However, there are key differences between the British and American Living Wage movements. First, Living Wage campaigns in the United Kingdom are much more focused on encouraging voluntary participation by municipalities and businesses to provide a living wage to employees. Far less emphasis is placed on achieving legal ordinances, and much more on developing collaborative partnerships with both employers and municipalities. Second, different strategies to ensure compliance and participation have evolved in the United Kingdom. In particular, an accreditation system developed by London Citizens helps to monitor and ensure company compliance. Perhaps even more important, this accreditation body also gives companies an incentive to participate by turning living wage accreditation into a desirable, club-like good (Jensen and Wills 2013). Finally, the Living Wage movement is far more centralized in the United Kingdom, as a result of London Citizens' clear and continued leadership. They have been involved in every major development in the UK living wage movement, spearheaded the creation of a living wage accreditation body, and they have also controlled the determination of a living wage for London, and nationally. (Wills and Linneker 2013). In the United States, living wages reached through campaigns differ from place to place and are the outcome of individual, isolated contests.

The British Living Wage movement has had some success in securing living wages, but clearly voluntary participation has not been effective enough (Pennycook 2012). Since 2001, the movement has secured a living wage for approximately 14,000 workers out of a low-wage labour force of around six million workers. The main business participants in the movement to this date have been public sector employers and large financial firms in the city of London. A common feature of many private sector participants is that they have very few low-wage workers and therefore benefit disproportionately from accreditation as low-wage employers (ibid.).

In Canada the movement looks quite different from that in the United States and has more in common with the UK movement. There are approximately fifty local Living Wage campaigns in Canada at different levels of organizational sophistication. Most are composed of a number of actors and typically involve anti-poverty, faith-based, and trade union affiliated groups. The provincial office of the Canadian Centre for Policy Alternatives, where there is one, provides capacity to calculate local living wages. This calculated wage becomes the basis for campaigns that, like the British, focus on employer voluntarism and city-level advocacy for a living wage to apply to local government contracting. There is no explicit link to province-wide campaigns for a higher minimum wage. Outside of Ontario, for example, the Fight for $15 campaign is largely notional. Some small groups of activists and some labour unions have taken up the struggle, but so far it has remained marginal. The 2015 electoral victory in Alberta by the New Democratic Party and its position on the minimum wage has boosted the prospects of Canadian activists. The federal NDP's platform of having a federal $15 minimum wage also thrust the issue onto the national stage. Unlike in the United States, there is no workplace aspect to the Fight for $15. In the United States, for instance, the FF$15 is supported by union money and organizers. As a result, the goals of the FF$15 in the United States are multifaceted: increasing the minimum wage at the legislative level, increasing pay and improving working conditions at large corporations, and ultimately trying to achieve union recognition. In Canada no union has offered serious support to the FF$15.

Unions, while supportive, are not using the Fight for $15 as a widescale organizing effort to leverage employers in the service sector. This reflects the differences of labour law, unfair labour practices and economic strikes can be undertaken in the United States with some protections for even non-unionized workers. In Canada this is not the case. Another major difference is the ability to win legislative fights about the minimum wage at the municipal level. In the United States this is possible, while in Canada it is not. This makes building local movements easier in the United States. The Living Wage movement in Canada is largely divorced from the broader North American movement. In the United States, the momentum of the Living Wage movement takes place through efforts to push through state-imposed increases to the minimum wage. In Canada, the non-governmental organizations at the heart of the Living Wage movement have for years been pushing an altogether different approach – the idea of voluntary agreements.

Outside of some municipalities, such as New Westminster near Vancouver, campaigns to pressure local governments to adopt a living wage principle informing their services contracting have been unsuccessful. However, recently in 2015 the cities of Cambridge and Toronto, both in Ontario, have passed motions to implement this principle.

Potential of Living Wage Campaigns

During a time of declining union strength and a neoliberal political climate defined by austere policies and stagnating wages for low-income workers, Living Wage campaigns have enjoyed some campaign victories, and have also provided low-wage workers with improved salaries and benefits (Luce 2004, 2012; Jensen and Wills 2013; Devinatz 2013; Reich et al. 2014). Living Wage campaigns may benefit organized labour (Bernstein 2005; Devinatz 2013; Luce 2004) by providing an effective platform for action, and also help in building a new membership base of affected workers who benefit from union involvement in campaigns (Bernstein 2005; Devinatz 2013; Luce 2004).

A review of the economic literature on the impact of all three Living Wage models outlined above finds only marginal price increases, employment loss, business closure or lost contracts due to a more hostile business environment (Bernstein 2005; Devinatz 2013; Fairris and Reich 2005; Pennycook 2012; Pollin et al. 2008; Pollin and Wicks-Lim 2015). In fact, regardless of the methodology or data set used, the overall aggregated cost of Living Wage ordinances is 1–2 per cent of an employer's total costs (Devinatz 2013). Living wages generally do not have harmful employment effects.[10] They can lead to cost savings for businesses as a result of increased worker retention, decreased absenteeism, improved morale, and improved customer service (Devinatz 2013; Flint, Cummins, and Wills 2013; Pollin et al. 2008).

Perhaps most important, however, is the Living Wage movement's normative appeal. The International Labour Organization identified the potential of the Living Wage movement as a watershed concept capable of uniting the world's labour movement in relation to the shared vision people have with respect to the good life, economic justice, and a living wage (Laliberté 2012, 10). As Wills and Linneker argue, the flexibility of

---

10 However, a few studies have shown significant negative employment effects for low-income earners in some cases (Neumark and Adams 2003; Adams and Neumark 2005).

the Living Wage movement to be "translated across space" and "reconfigured wherever it lands to take root" while still reframing wages as a moral and social justice issue is remarkable (2013, 184).

Despite the potential, there are weaknesses. The proportion of workers covered by living wages is low. Even in the United States, where the campaign is most advanced, the total impact of the living wage involves a few million workers out of a low-wage labour force of 35 or 40 million. In the United Kingdom, the total number of workers affected is below 20,000 low-wage workers out of 6 or 7 million (Jensen and Wills 2013). An additional limitation is the real difficulty in ordinance implementation (Luce 2004). For a variety of reasons, municipalities do not do a good job of implementing, monitoring compliance, and enforcing living wage ordinances (ibid.). And, of course, even to the extent they are successful, living wages address only part of the low-*income* problem, which results from low *wages*. The broader issue of low incomes and the adequacy of the social wage is not addressed by this strategy (Bennett 2014).

Conclusions

A significant sector of low-waged workers seems endemic to capitalist economies. Its existence, and that of an involuntarily unwaged sector outside the labour market, arguably exerts a depressing effect on all wages. Nonetheless, continual efforts have been made to alleviate the conditions of low-waged employees. These attempts include wages councils, the awards system, minimum wages of either statutory or collectively bargained types, and living wages. Each mode has advantages and disadvantages. For example, universal statutory minimum wages provide the most coverage, but typically at rates that hover below the poverty line. Collectively bargained minimum wages have tended to be more adequate than statutory ones, but their coverage is less, and they depend for their success on strong trade unions. But unionization rates and union power have been in decline throughout the neoliberal period, so the preconditions for sustaining, still less expanding such systems may no longer exist.

Living wages have enormous ideological appeal – the idea that someone working full-time should earn enough to live on resonates with basic concepts of fairness. However, coverage is spotty, and in conditions where full-time, full-year work is declining, the hourly rates that express what a living wage is may fall short of an adequate standard of living. As with so much else in the labour market, the low-wage issue could be more easily addressed in conditions of full employment.

All these modes of dealing with low wages have enjoyed some success, at least for a time, yet none have seriously dented the low-waged sector. Precluding any enduring and widespread reduction in the low-wage economy are the deeply embedded structural and systemic features of contemporary labour markets, and the reinforcement of these characteristics through austerity policies. In order to reduce the low-wage economy, potential solutions must overcome the precariousness of work, the highly concentrated power of capital, the high and enduring levels of unemployment that exert downward pressure on wages, and the neoliberal architecture that informs the majority of public policy.

How might this happen? Some have made the argument that the growth of low-waged work is an inevitable, epiphenomenal consequence of economic globalization, and technological innovation, and consequently difficult to control. While these factors have certainly played an important part in shaping labour markets, the role of politics must not be underestimated. The war on organized labour and the dismantling of labour laws over the past few decades was an explicitly political project. These decisions have hindered pro-labour opposition from the Left and contributed significantly to the construction and advancement of a low-wage economy dependent on reserves of cheap labour.

One way to alleviate low-waged conditions lies in a revived trade union movement with the strength to push back against a political and corporate elite interested in maintaining the structural conditions necessary for the mass reproduction of cheap labour. However, the rebirth of organized labour in such impressive fashion seems highly unlikely, at least for the present.

Despite its shortcomings, the Living Wage movement may provide a starting point for an effective pro-labour agenda. It has widespread ideational appeal that resonates across the political spectrum. Moreover, the grassroots nature of the movement makes it less susceptible to co-optation or control by traditional political actors and thus, harder to extinguish.

With that said, it is clear that the Living Wage movement is still in the embryonic stages and that the structural and political conditions required for the widespread adoption of living wages do not exist. The open question yet to be answered, therefore, remains whether the ideological appeal of the living wage can prevail within neoliberal labour markets whose current structural conditions lead to a systematic mass reproduction of cheap labour.

REFERENCES

Adams, S., and D. Neumark. 2005. "Living Wage Effects: New and Improved Evidence." *Economic Development Quarterly* 19 (1): 80–102. https://doi.org/10.1177/0891242404268639.

Albo, G. 1994. "Competitive Austerity and the Impasse of Capitalist Employment Policy." *Socialist Register* 30:144–70.

Amlinger, M., R. Bispinck, and T. Schulten. 2016. "The German Minimum Wage: Experiences and Perspectives after One Year." *Institute of Economic and Social* Research 28 (1): 1–19.

Appelbaum, E. 2012. "Reducing Inequality and Insecurity: Rethinking Labour and Employment Policy for the 21st Century." *Work and Occupations* 39 (4): 311–20. https://doi.org/10.1177/0730888412444883.

Bayliss, F.J. 1962. *British Wages Councils*. Oxford: Basil Blackwell.

Bennett, F. 2014. "The Living Wage, Low Pay and In-Work Poverty: Rethinking the Relationship." *Critical Social Policy* 34 (1): 46–65.

Bernstein, J. 2005. "The Living Wage Movement: What Is It, Why Is It and What's Known about Its Impact?" In *Emerging Labour Market Institutions for the Twenty-First Century*, ed. R. Hersch, J. Lawrence, and M. Lawrence, 99–140. Chicago: University of Chicago Press. https://doi.org/10.7208/chicago/9780226261812.003.0004.

Betcherman, G. 2014. *Labor Market Regulations: What Do We Know about Their Impacts in Developing Countries?* Policy Research Working Paper 6819. Washington, DC: World Bank. https://doi.org/10.1596/1813-9450-6819.

Bispinck, R., and T. Schulten. 2014. "Wages, Collective Bargaining and Economic Development in Germany: Towards a More Expansive and Solidaristic Development?" Diskussionspapier No. 191. Dusseldorf: Institute of Economic and Social Research.

Bivens, J., E. Gould, L. Mishel, and H. Shierholz. 2014. "Raising America's Pay: Why It's Our Central Economic Policy Challenge." Briefing Paper 378. Washington, DC: Economic Policy Institute.

Blyth, M. 2013. *Austerity: The History of a Dangerous Idea*. New York: Oxford University Press.

Botwinick, Howard. 1998. "Labor Must Shed Its Win/Win Illusions: It's Time to Organize and Fight" *New Labor Forum* 2: 92–103.

Branch, E., and C. Hanley. 2011. "Regional Convergence in Low-Wage Work and Earnings, 1970–2000." *Sociological Perspectives* 54 (4): 569–92. https://doi.org/10.1525/sop.2011.54.4.569.

Bray, M., and J. Macneil. 2011. "Individualism, Collectivism, and the Case of Awards in Australia." *Journal of Industrial Relations* 53 (2): 149–67.

Brennan, J. 2012. *Enhancing Democratic Citizenship, Deepening Distributive Justice: The Living Wage Movement*. Toronto: Canadian Centre for Policy Alternatives.

Brosnan, P., and F. Wilkinson. 1988. "A National Statutory Minimum Wage and Economic Efficiency." *Contributions to Political Economy* 7 (1): 1–48. https://doi.org/10.1093/oxfordjournals.cpe.a035722.

Brown, C., C. Gilroy, and A. Kohen. 1982. "The Effect of the Minimum Wage on Employment and Unemployment: A Survey." *Journal of Economic Literature* 20 (2): 487–528.

Cabrelli, D. 2014. *Employment Law in Context: Text and Materials*. Oxford: Oxford University Press. https://doi.org/10.1093/he/9780199644889.001.0001.

Card, D., and A.B. Krueger. 1995. "Time-Series Minimum-Wage Studies: A Meta Analysis." *American Economic Review* 85 (2): 238–43.

Clain, S. 2012. "Explaining the Passage of Living Wage Legislation in the U.S." *Atlantic Economic Journal* 40 (3): 315–27. https://doi.org/10.1007/s11293-012-9328-0.

Dahlgreen, W. 2014. "Cross-Party Support for Raising Minimum Wage." YouGov. https://yougov.co.uk/news/2014/01/12/cross-party-support-raising-minimum-wage/.

Devinatz, V. 2013. "The Significance of the Living Wage for US Workers in the Early Twenty-First Century." *Employ Response Rights Journal* 25 (2): 125–34. https://doi.org/10.1007/s10672-013-9219-9.

Dolado, J., F. Kramarz, S. Machin, A.D. Manning, David Margolis, and C. Teulings. 1996. "The Economic Impact of Minimum Wages in Europe." *Economic Policy* 11 (23): 317–72. https://doi.org/10.2307/1344707.

Dolton, P., C. Rosazza-Bonibene, and J. Wadsworth. 2010. "Employment, Inequality and the UK National Minimum Wage over the Medium-Term." CEP Discussion Paper No. 1007. London: London School of Economics and Political Science.

Doucouliagos, H., and T. Stanley. 2009. "Publication Selection Bias in Minimum-Wage Research? A Meta-Regression Analysis." *British Journal of Industrial Relations* 47 (2): 406–28. https://doi.org/10.1111/j.1467-8543.2009.00723.x.

Dougan, A. 2013. "Most Americans for Raising Minimum Wage." Gallup, 11 November. http://www.gallup.com/poll/165794/americans-raising-minimumwage.aspx?utm_source=minimum%20wage&utm_medium=search&utm_capaign=tiles.

Dumenil, G., and D. Levy. 2011. *The Crisis of Neoliberalism*. Cambridge, MA: Harvard University Press.

Eldring, L., and K. Alsos. 2012. "European Minimum Wage: A Nordic Outlook." Fafo Report No. 16. Oslo: Council of Nordic Trade Unions.

Fairris, D., and M. Reich. 2005. "The Impacts of Living Wage Policies: Introduction to the Special Issue." *Industrial Relations* 44 (1): 1–13. https://doi.org/10.1111/j.0019-8676.2004.00370.x.

Figart, D. 2001. "Ethical Foundations of the Contemporary Living Wage Movement." *International Journal of Social Economics* 28 (10/11/12): 800–14. https://doi.org/10.1108/EUM0000000006125.

— 2004. "Introduction to Living Wages." In *Living Wage Movements: Global Perspectives*, ed. D. Figart, 1–13. New York: Routledge. https://doi.org/10.4324/9780203629451.ch1.

Figart, D., E. Mutari, and M. Power. 2002. *Living Wages, Equal Wages: Gender and Labour Market Policies in the United States*. London: Routledge.

Flint, E., S. Cummins, and J. Wills. 2013. "Investigating the Effect of the London Living Wage on the Psychological Wellbeing of Low-Wage Service Sector Employees: A Feasibility Study." *Journal of Public Health* 36 (2): 187–93. https://doi.org/10.1093/pubmed/fdt093.

Freeman, R. 2005. "What Do Unions Do?" The 2004 M-Brane Strongtwister Edition. National Bureau of Economic Affairs Working Paper No. 11401.

Freeman, R., J. Hersch, and L. Mishel. 2005. *Emerging Labour Market Institutions for the Twenty-First Century*. Chicago: University of Chicago Press. https://doi.org/10.7208/chicago/9780226261812.001.0001.

Giles, C. 2014. "Piketty's Findings Undercut by Errors." *Financial Times*, 23 May. https://www.ft.com/content/e1f343ca-e281-11e3-89fd-00144feabdc0.

Glasmeier, A.K. 2017. "Living Wage Calculator." http://livingwage.mit.edu/pages/about.

Glickman, L. 1997. *A Living Wage: American Workers and the Making of Consumer Society*. Ithaca, NY: Cornell University Press.

Gosling, A., and T. Lemieux. 2004. "Labor Market Reforms and Changes in Wage Inequality in the United Kingdom and the United States." In *Seeking a Premier Economy: The Economic Effects of British Economic Reform*, ed. D. Card, R. Blundell, and R.B. Freeman, 275–312. Chicago: University of Chicago Press. https://doi.org/10.7208/chicago/9780226092904.003.0008.

Grimshaw, D. 2011. "What Do We Know about Low-Wage Work and Low-Wage Workers? Analyzing the Definitions, Patterns, Causes and Consequences in International Perspective." Conditions of Work and Employment Series No. 28. Geneva: International Labour Organization.

Hassel, A. 2011. "The Paradox of Liberalization: Understanding Dualism and the Recovery of the German Political Economy." LSE Europe in Question Discussion Series No. 42. https://doi.org/10.2139/ssrn.1921415.

Hermann, C. 2014. "Structural Adjustment and Neoliberal Convergence in Labour Markets and Welfare: The Impact of the Crisis and Austerity

Measures on European Economic and Social Models." *Competition & Change* 18 (2): 111–30. https://doi.org/10.1179/1024529414Z.00000000051.

Heyes, J. 2013. "Flexicurity in Crisis: European Labour Market Policies in a Time of Austerity." *European Journal of Industrial Relations* 19 (1): 71–86. https://doi.org/10.1177/0959680112474749.

Heyes, J., and P. Lewis. 2015. "Relied Upon for the Heavy Lifting: Can Employment Protection Legislation Reforms Lead the EU out of the Jobs Crisis?" *Industrial Relations Journal* 46 (2): 81–99. https://doi.org/10.1111/irj.12095.

International Labour Organization (ILO). 2014. "Annual Average Economic Growth, 1995–2013." http://www.ilo.org/legacy/english/gwr/2014-final-figures.xlsx.

International Monetary Fund (IMF). 2013a. "Germany: 2013 Article IV Consultation." IMF Country Report No. 13/255. Washington, DC: IMF.

– 2013b. "Japan: 2013 Article IV Consultation." IMF Country Report No. 13/253. Washington, DC: IMF.

Iversen, T., and A. Wren. 1998. "Equality, Employment, and Budgetary Restraint: The Trilemma of the Service Economy." *World Politics* 50 (4): 507–46. https://doi.org/10.1017/S0043887100007358.

Jaumotte, F., and C. Osorio Buitron. 2015. "Power from the People." *Finance and Development* 52 (1): 29–31.

Jensen, N., and J. Wills. 2013. *The Prevalence and Impact of the Living Wage in the UK: A Survey of Organizations*. London: Queen Mary's University of London.

Kampelmann, S., A. Garnero, and F. Ryxc. 2013. "Minimum Wages in Europe: Does the Diversity of Systems Lead to a Diversity of Outcomes?" European Trade Union Institute Report 128.

Krugman, Paul. 2015. "Notes on Walmart and Wages." Opinion piece in the "Conscience of a Liberal" series. *New York Times*, 10 June.

Laliberté, P. 2013. "Editorial." *International Journal of Labour Research* 5 (2): 173–7.

Levin-Waldman, O. 2005. *The Political Economy of the Living Wage: A Study of Four Cities*. Armonk, NY: M.E. Sharpe.

Living Wage, New Zealand. 2017. "About." http://www.livingwage.org.nz/about.

Living Wage, Republic of Ireland. 2017. "About." http://www.livingwage.ie.

Low Pay Commission. 2015. "National Minimum Wage: Low Pay Commission Report 2015." https://www.gov.uk/government/publications/national-minimum-wage-low-pay-commission-report-2015.

Luce, S. 2004. *Fighting for a Living Wage*. Ithaca, NY: Cornell University Press.

– 2012. "Living Wage Policies and Campaigns: Lessons from the United States." *International Journal of Labour Research* 4 (1): 11–26.

Machin, S., and A. Manning. 1994. "The Effects of Minimum Wages on Wage Dispersion and Employment: Evidence from the UK Wages Councils." *Industrial & Labor Relations Review* 47 (2): 319–29. https://doi.org/10.1177/001979399404700210.

Manning, A. 2009. *The UK's National Minimum Wage*. London: London School of Economics Centre for Economic Performance.

– 2013. "Minimum Wages: A View from the UK." *Perspektiven der Wirtschaftspolitik* 14 (1–2): 57–66.

McBride, S. 2000. "Policy from What? Neoliberal and Human Capital Theoretical Foundations of Recent Canadian Labour Market Policy." In *Restructuring and Resistance: Canadian Public Policy in an Age of Global Capitalism*, ed. M. Burke, C. Mooers, and J. Shields, 159–77. Halifax: Fernwood.

McCallum, R. 2011. "Legislated Standards: The Australian Experience." In *Work and Employment Relations: An Era of Change*, ed. M. Baird, K. Hancock, and J. Isaac, 6–18. Sydney: Federation.

Metcalf, D. 1999. "The Low Pay Commission and the National Minimum Wage." *Economic Journal (London)* 109 (453): 46–66. https://doi.org/10.1111/1468-0297.00402.

Milner, S. 1995. "The Coverage of Collective Pay-Setting Institutions in Britain, 1895–1990." *British Journal of Industrial Relations* 33 (1): 69–91. https://doi.org/10.1111/j.1467-8543.1995.tb00422.x.

Mishel, L. 2012. "Unions, Inequality, and Faltering Middle-Class Wages." Economic Policy Institute Wages Income and Wealth Report.

Moore, G. 2015. "Living Wage Campaign: It's Time for Football to Lead the Way and Defeat Negativity." *Independent*, 15 March. http://www.independent.co.uk/sport/football/news-and-comment/living-wage-campaign-its-time-for-football-to-lead-the-way-and-defeat-negativity-10121427.html.

Muffels, R., ed. 2008. *Flexibility and Employment Security in Europe*. Cheltenham: Edward Elgar Publishing. https://doi.org/10.4337/9781781007693.

National Employment Law Project. 2017. "Minimum Wage City Campaigns." http://raisetheminimumwage.com/city-campaigns/.

Neumark, D., and S. Adams. 2003. "Do Living Wage Ordinances Reduce Urban Poverty?" *Journal of Human Resources* 38 (3): 490–521.

Neumark, D., and W. Wascher. 1992. "Employment Effects of Minimum and Subminimum Wages: Panel Data on State Minimum Wage Laws." *Industrial & Labor Relations Review* 46 (1): 55–81. https://doi.org/10.1177/001979399204600105.

- 2008. *Minimum Wages*. Cambridge, MA: MIT Press. https://doi.org/10.7551/mitpress/9780262141024.001.0001.
Nowak, J. 2015. "Union Campaigns in Germany Directed against Inequality: The Minimum Wage Campaign and the Emmely Campaign." *Global Labour Journal* 6 (3): 366–80. https://doi.org/10.15173/glj.v6i3.2323.
O'Neill, D. 2014. "Divided Opinion on the Fair Minimum Wage Act of 2013: Random or Systematic Differences." IZA Discussion Paper No. 8601, Institute for the Study of Labour, Bonn.
Organisation for Economic Co-operation and Development (OECD). 1994. *The Jobs Study: Facts, Analysis, Strategies*. Paris.
- 2015a. "Minimum Relative to Average Full-Time Workers." http://stats.oecd.org/.
- 2015b. "Statistics: Real Minimum Wages." http://stats.oecd.org/.
- 2015c. "Trade Union Density." http://stats.oecd.org/.
Pennycook, M. 2012. *What Price for a Living Wage? Understanding the Impact of a Living Wage on Firm-Level Wage Bills*. London: Resolution Foundation.
Pew Research Center. 2014. "Most See Inequality Growing, but Partisans Differ over Solutions." http://www.people-press.org/2014/01/23/most-see-inequality-growing-but-partisans-differ-over-solutions/.
Piketty, T. 2014a. *Capital in the 21st Century*. Boston: Harvard University Press.
- 2014b. "My Response to the Financial Times." *Huffington Post*, 29 May. http://www.huffingtonpost.com/thomas-piketty/response-to-financial-times_b_5412853.html.
- 2015. "Putting Distribution Back at the Center of Economics: Reflections on *Capital in the Twenty-First Century*." *Journal of Economic Perspectives* 29 (1): 67–88. https://doi.org/10.1257/jep.29.1.67.
Plociennik, S. 2016. "The Bothersome Success of the Minimum Wage: The German Labour Market Faces the Refugee Crisis." *Polish Journal of International Affairs* 2 (852): 1–2.
Pollin, R., M. Brenner, J. Wicks-Lim, and S. Luce, eds. 2008. *A Measure of Fairness: The Economics of Living Wages and Minimum Wages in the United States*. Ithaca, NY: Cornell University Press.
Pollin, R., and J. Wicks-Lim. 2015. "A $15 US Minimum Wage: How the Fast Food Industry Could Adjust without Shedding Jobs." Political Economy Research Institute Working Paper Series No. 373. Political Economy Research Institute, Amherst.
Pothier, D. 2014. *A Minimum Wage for Germany: What Should We Expect?* Roundup No. 7. Berlin: Deutsches Institut für Wirtschaftsforschung.

Pusey, M. 2003. *The Experience of Middle Australia: The Dark Side of Economic Reform*. Cambridge: Cambridge University Press. https://doi.org/10.1017/CBO9780511481628.

Reich, M., K. Jacobs, A. Bernhard, and I. Perry. 2014. *The Mayor of Los Angeles' Proposed City Minimum Wage Policy: A Prospective Study*. Berkeley: Institute for Research on Labor and Employment, University of California Berkeley.

Rossi, M., and K. Curtis. 2013. "Aiming at Half of the Target: An Argument to Replace Poverty Thresholds with Self-Sufficiency, or 'Living Wage' Standards." *Journal of Poverty* 17 (1): 110–30. https://doi.org/10.1080/10875549.2012.747997.

Schmitt, J. 2012. *Low Wage Lessons*. Washington, DC: Center for Economic and Policy Research.

Schmitt, J., and A. Mitukiewicz. 2011. "Politics Matter: Changes in Unionization Rates in Rich Countries, 1960–2010." Center for Economic Policy Research, November.

Schulten, T. 2014. *Contours of a European Minimum Wage Policy*. Berlin: Friedrich Ebert Stiftung Working Paper. http://library.fes.de/pdf-files/id-moe/11008.pdf.

– 2015. "WSI-Mindestlohnbericht 2015 – Ende der Lohnzurückhaltung?" *WSI-Mitteilungen* 68 (2): 133–40.

Shaikh, A. 2011. "The First Great Depression of the 21st Century." In *Socialist Register Fall 2011: The Crisis This Time*, 44–63. London: Merlin.

Standing, G. 1999. *Global Labour Flexibility*. London: Macmillan

Thomas, A. 2014. "German Parliament Approves Minimum Wage from 2015." *Wall Street Journal*, 3 July. https://www.wsj.com/articles/german-parliament-approves-minimum-wage-from-2015-1404386860.

Thomas, M., and S. Tufts. 2015. "Austerity, Right Populism and the Crisis of Labour in Canada." *Antipode* 48 (1): 1–19.

US Department of Health and Human Services. 2014. "Poverty Guidelines." https://aspe.hhs.gov/2014-poverty-guidelines#thresholds.

Wahl, A. 2011. *The Rise and Fall of the Welfare State*. London: Pluto.

Weinkopf, C. 2015. "The Bumpy Road to a National Minimum Wage in Germany: Towards Revitalizing Collective Bargaining." In *Global Wage Debates: Politics or Economics*, ed. G. Randolph and K. Panknin, 97–114. JustJobs Network. http://justjobsnetwork.org/wp-content/pubs/reports/Joint%20Report%202015.pdf#page=181.

Werner, A., and M. Lim. 2015. "The Ethics of the Living Wage: A Review and Research Agenda." *Journal of Business Ethics* 137:433–47.

Western, B., and J. Rosenfeld. 2011. "Unions, Norms, and the Rise in US Wage Inequality." *American Sociological Review* 76 (4): 513–37. https://doi.org/10.1177/0003122411414817.

Wills, J., and B. Linneker. 2013. "In-Work Poverty and the Living Wage in the United Kingdom: A Geographical Perspective." *Royal Geographical Society* 39:182–94.

World Wealth & Income Database. http://topincomes.parisschoolof economics.eu/.

Wren, A., ed. 2013a. *The Political Economy of the Service Transition.* Oxford: Oxford University Press. https://doi.org/10.1093/acprof:oso/9780199657285.001.0001.

– 2013b. "The Political Economy of the Service Transition." *Renewal* 21 (1). http://www.renewal.org.uk/articles/the-political-economy-of-the-service-transition/.

9 Immigration in an Age of Austerity: Morality, the Welfare State, and the Shaping of the Ideal Migrant

SUSAN BARRASS AND JOHN SHIELDS

Introduction

In the current era of austerity precipitated by the financial crisis of 2008, blame for increasing national debt has been shifted away from the workings of the financial sector and the lack of regulation under neoliberal governance to what has been identified as the problem of unrestrained government spending and the burden of the welfare state. As a result, many Western governments are looking for ways to curb welfare state spending and access to social entitlements. This has been accompanied by arguments that call on a discourse of neoliberal "morality" reflected in sentiments of the value of hard work, individual responsibility, and self-reliance, and a strong backlash against those seen as "freeloading" and placing burdens on taxpayers. In the process, notions of broader inclusion and social citizenship have been downgraded.

Immigrants and immigration policy have come to be cast as a burden on state finances and a potential threat to the welfare of the nation. In much of Europe and the United States, immigrants and so-called immigrant-friendly policies like multiculturalism have become the target of political attack, especially by right-wing populist parties/movements. When examined more closely, however, immigration poses a more complex and nuanced response from neoliberal policymakers, because of the reality of aging populations, shifting labour market needs, and global competition for high human capital. Clearly not all immigrants are seen as a negative. The austerity agenda, and neoliberalism more generally, has consequently been compelled to reposition its policies around immigration.

In part, the neoliberal response has been to focus narrowly on the value of the short-term economic benefits of the immigrant to the immigrant-receiving country. Immigration policy in many countries has consequently been "reformed" along these lines. Immigrants have had their access to the welfare state and other benefits curtailed, and many governments are redefining the notion of the "ideal immigrant" along a neoliberal value system, with those who fail to meet such attributes cast as undesirable migrants who should not be granted immigrant status and are often denied access to the country altogether. This chapter seeks to examine the ways in which immigration policy in the age of austerity has changed to alter the pattern of immigration/migration, to curb access to welfare state benefits for many migrants, and the manner in which the perception of migrants is being shaped as a duality between desirable or undesirable, based on their perceived "virtue"/value by neoliberal governments. While we will consider neoliberal shifts in immigration policy more broadly in the OECD, given the centrality of immigration to economic development and the more favourable social and political climate to immigrants in Canada, it is useful to focus on the neoliberal policy response to immigration policy in Canada. The Canadian case enables us to more starkly draw attention to the neoliberalization of immigration policy in contrast to the more open and inclusive policies that existed before.

Crisis, Austerity, and the Neoliberalization of Immigration Policy

The Great Recession of 2008 profoundly affected the economies of the OECD, threatening the very integrity of the financial system and resulting in a prolonged and deep recession from which numerous economies have failed to fully recover. The crisis was unevenly experienced, with countries such as Greece and Spain confronting steep downturns in GDP and mass unemployment, and other nations such as Germany and Canada facing far less severe recessionary impacts (Collett 2011b, 3). The effects of the crisis were also felt unevenly by different segments of the population. While the problem of youth unemployment have been widely reported (United Nations Regional Information Centre for Western Europe 2014), less well acknowledged are the detrimental effects of the crisis on immigrant populations. Recent immigrants bore the brunt of job losses. For example, in Spain, by 2010 immigrant unemployment exceeded 30 per cent, with very high levels also documented in Ireland, Sweden, and the United States (OECD 2012, 100; Collett 2011a, 4–5).

In Canada between October 2008 and October 2009, during the height of the recession, immigrants with five years or less residence in the country "absorbed 21.6 percent of job losses, despite representing only 3.1 percent of the employed, meaning they were approximately 6.9 times as likely to lose employment as the average worker" (Rosher et al. 2012, 45). Immigrants with five to ten years of residence also experienced very high levels of job loss and joblessness. Less-established immigrants also have experienced higher rates of job precariousness, especially for women, which has been accelerated by economic restructuring promoted by the crisis (Kelly, Park, and Lepper 2011, 14; Gottfried et al. 2016; Goldring and Joly 2014; PEPSO 2013; Shields et al. 2010).

Newer immigrants, in particular, share many of the characteristics of other vulnerable workers like youth, in that they are more recent entrants into the labour market and are overrepresented in sections of the economy particularly vulnerable to recession, like manufacturing, construction, and hospitality (Papademetriou and Terrazas 2009, iii). The longer-term economic and psychological scarring effects of disrupted employment for newer immigrants trying to establish themselves in the labour market is quite profound (Kelly, Park, and Lepper 2011, 14).

Even though immigrants were particularly negatively affected by the crisis, such "uncertain times" do "test the capacity and willingness of receiving countries to include new arrivals. Uncertain times also disrupt and can even destroy previous policies and consensus on immigration" (Duncan 2012, 1). In many countries, the crisis brought to the fore anti-immigrant sentiments and right-wing populism, but overall the crisis reinforced pre-existing neoliberal policy trends that had been at work redirecting immigration policy direction (Shpaizman 2010; Root et al. 2014; Shields, Drolet, and Valenzuela 2016). These trends include:

1 the securitization of borders, placing greater restrictions on migrant access to countries;
2 focusing recruitment of immigrants to those with high human capital;
3 tightening the rules on citizenship acquisition by newcomers with reinforced emphasis on division between migrants with permanent residence status and those with temporary status;
4 making immigrants themselves more responsible and accountable for their own settlement and integration;
5 devolving responsibility for settlement and integration services by central governments to sub-national governments, non-profit organizations, businesses, and other societal agents, while concentrating policymaking power over immigration in the hands of executive authorities in national governments; and

6 increased placement of restrictions or exclusion of immigrant newcomers from access to many public services offered through the welfare state in areas such as health care and social services.

Austerity deepened this neoliberal change, with many countries seeing deeper cuts to integration services and welfare support to immigrants at the very time when such needs were greatest (Collett 2011b; Pagliaro and Mahoney 2011). Hence, both the political/policy and socio-economic climate for immigrants has become much more difficult. The warmth of immigrant welcome, as Jeffrey Reitz calls it (1998), has cooled considerably in the climate of neoliberalism, crisis, and austerity.

While immigration policy has come under considerable challenge, immigration has been identified as central to address pressing policy problems. These relate particularly to (1) shrinking labour forces, (2) aging populations, which are increasing age dependency ratios (immigrants through positive tax contributions can help sustain the generational social security contract), and (3) the need to enhance national competitiveness through access to the global pool of human capital assets at both the high and lower skill levels (Fargues et al. 2011). Hence, the recruitment of immigrants and immigration policy remains central to countries in the OECD, but austerity has pushed for a redesign of immigration policy to better match the new reality of a neoliberal world.

Central to the austerity agenda is the need to address state deficits, which are seen as key to restoring market-based economic growth. This agenda requires not just restraint. It is also "predicated on a highly flexible labour force with abundant competitively priced human capital assets" (Root et al. 2014, 15). The need for immigrant labour has become essential for the effective working of advanced capitalism (Hampshire 2013, 11).

Given the centrality of immigration to address austerity and restore prosperity, neoliberalism seeks to direct the more extreme right-wing anti-immigrant sentiment in the direction of a discourse on "good" versus "bad" immigration. The idea of the "good immigrant" in opposition to the "bad immigrant" has come to be constructed around "personality, cultural, and skill-based characteristics." The "good or model immigrant" in the neoliberal view is one who has high human capital, able to fill skills gaps in the economy, and embraces the virtues of "self-sufficiency, hard work, and effective and efficient labour market participation" (Root et al. 2014, 5). Migrants who fail to match these norms are deemed largely as being unsuitable for citizenship and a burden on society.

The Problematization of Migrants in Public Discourse

Public opinion on immigration has always been a contentious issue, as it throws into question the level of immigration that should be pursued, the extent to which immigrants pose a threat to members of the receiving nation, and the challenge to the social cohesiveness they may present to society, whether or not those seeking asylum are in legitimate need of assistance, and the ability of newcomers to adapt to their new country and integrate (Esses, Medianu, and Lawson 2013). In addition, public opinion on immigration can solidify a discourse that draws a distinction between "us" and "them," and the "othering" of migrants (Bradimore and Bauder 2011), defining who belongs and who is unwanted. As Forkert argues, a distinct narrative relies on emotive appeals and "nostalgia for a lost era of social cohesion," which has been disrupted by access to services for those who are deemed "undeserving citizens" (2014, 41). Dauvergne (2005) maintains that migration policy works as the site of national identity formation and articulation, as it sets the parameters for inclusion and exclusion in society. A defining feature of this era of austerity has been a turn to discourses centred on calls for "morality" and "virtue," with increased focus on personal responsibility, individual self-sufficiency, and challenging the "rights discourse," placing greater emphasis on a "duties discourse" by advocates of neoliberalism (Lister 1997). This is clearly articulated through increased reliance on human capital theory as the dominant driver of immigration policy, a key aspect of the neoliberal paradigm, and a critical element of advancing the austerity agenda in relation to migrant selection.

When examining the conceptual ideas surrounding the articulation of austerity and neoliberalism, a number of authors have identified the challenges associated with the transformation of the concept and its uses over time. Austerity has been introduced as a mechanism to battle inflationary pressures, as in the 1980s (Clarke, this volume); as a form of "consumption critique" stretching back to classical philosophy, alluding to claims of the morality of "moderation, selflessness and cathartic cleansing" (Schui, as quoted in Clarke, this volume); and as "collective self-sacrifice," in particular in the years following the Second World War (Kynaston 2007; Zweiniger-Bargielowska, 2000, in Clarke, this volume).

Such a transformation of terms is also apparent in the morality arguments present in discourses of the ideal migrant and the ways in which these concepts have fluctuated to fit the ideological direction of policy.

Within neoliberal discourse, a distinct framing has emerged surrounding the economic value of migrants in industrialized nations, shaping the basis for inclusion and exclusion. In more recent years, the Canadian government led by the "hyper-neoliberal Harper Conservative Government" (2006–15) carefully crafted the narrative of what role immigration should play. Contrary to the historic discourse surrounding immigration dominated by a language of nation-building, the shift in political dialogue became one of building a flexible workforce focused on a "'just-in-time' competitive immigration system" (Flaherty, as quoted in Siemiatycki 2010). Although economic migration has always been a driving force in Canadian policy, it had been associated with permanent settlement, family-based migration addressing long-term economic and social goals and a commitment to citizenship (Alboim and Cohl 2012). Contributions to the country, particularly under the Conservatives, came to be measured not in time spans of a working life, or even second and third generations, but rather by the need to show more immediate dividends (Root et al. 2014, 13). A discourse where the availability of "just-in-time" labour is viewed as the principal driving force behind immigration has lessened the focus on citizenship and defined migration purely in terms of economic utility.

In countries with aging populations and/or low or negative projected population growth, highly skilled migrants are cast as a possible answer to declining population growth, a source of tax revenue, and a necessary component to maintaining global competitiveness (Arat-Koc 1999, 2012). By contrast, low-skilled migrants have been cast as a solution for temporary labour shortages in low-wage, low-skilled industries, by governments and employers alike (Nakache 2013). However, for these workers, access to citizenship is extremely limited; they are positioned as disposable workers to be returned to their home country when they are no longer required.

While other countries have seen a rise in anti-immigrant sentiment, Canadians on a whole continue to support high levels of immigration (Banting and Kymlicka 2010; Reitz 2011). However, within the public discourse, there is a polarization of opinion on the basis of what Bauder (2011, 128) presents as the contrasting discourses of the immigrant as victim and the immigrant as perpetrator. Immigrants are portrayed as victims of exploitative labour market regulations, while simultaneously as perpetrators who threaten the economic well-being of Canadians. The latter discourse is particularly prevalent in the current era of austerity discourse, as media constructs of immigration often paint the problem of collapsing social cohesion, poverty, and unemployment as being exacerbated by immigration (Anderson 2014).

As Guiraudon (2004) argues, during economic downturns, politicians often use immigrants as a scapegoat to appease public anxieties about responsibility for the crisis and as an impediment to recovery. Problematizing immigrants as a key contributor to the economic crisis and a threat to the nation's recovery further embeds divisive concepts of "us" versus "them." In Canada, there have been fewer and perhaps less overt signs of casting the migrant as the cause of social and economic upheaval. Throughout the economic downturn, Canada has maintained its levels of economic-based migration for permanent settlement and in fact increased temporary migrant programs rather than reduce them. This may be due in part to the degree to which the economic crisis affected Canada compared to the United States and Europe (Rosher et al. 2012). Despite the contraction of the primary and manufacturing sectors, Canadians have continued to exhibit high levels of support for sustaining prevailing levels of migration (ibid.). However, although not quite as striking as the discourse emanating from the United States and many parts of Europe, where the need for policy reform and exclusion is often couched in language of "nativist, xenophobic or racial arguments" (Chock 1995) and a focus on the flow of "illegal migrants" (Edsall 2012), Canadian discourse often casts some immigrants as a threat to the welfare state for their perceived low performance in the labour market, characterizing them as dependent on state benefits (Bauder 2011, 130) as well as a source of labour market distortion. The former has led neoliberal policy-makers in Ottawa to justify restrictions to social entitlements in numerous newcomer categories (ibid.), while the latter has been particularly evident within the debates on the temporary foreign worker program, which continued to grow unabated during the economic downturn and resulted in strong public opposition to the program (Worswick 2013), leading to its overhaul in 2014.

Changes to Canadian Immigration Policy

One significant shift to immigration policy has been the adoption of a very short-term and one-dimensional consideration of the value of immigration that is focused on immigrants' narrow economic benefit, their flexible utilization, and minimizing settlement and integration costs to the state under the Harper Conservative government. In this regard Alexandra Dobrowolsky (2012) argues that neoliberal immigration policy in Canada is aimed at several goals: "(a) attract highly skilled immigrants; (b) expand low wage, temporary foreign worker programs; (c) diversify immigration 'entry doors' and make some more flexible; (d) cut admission and settlement costs; (e) encourage settlement in less well-populated areas; (f) tighten border controls and crack down on undocumented migrants; (g) 'change citizenship rules to reduce risks of undesired costs and unrealized benefits to the state'; and (h) 'sell immigration to the Canadian public ... through a policy rhetoric that emphasizes the hoped-for benefits of immigration while downplaying risks and disappointing outcomes'" (197).

Central to this focus has been stronger emphasis on a human capital approach to immigrant recruitment with a preference for highly skilled migrants, who are seen as being able to contribute to the receiving nation's economy and global competitiveness (Hampshire 2013). These are the kinds of newcomers that the state deems suitable for citizenship.

In the Canadian context, this approach has been apparent through the increased preference for the economic class category, which has gone through significant redesign in recent years (Ali 2014). The entry categories through which economic class migrants can gain permanent residency display a distinct preference for permanent settlement of those perceived to have high human capital (Bauder 2011, 118–19), while simultaneously reinforcing a more flexible approach to low-skilled labour. Economic class migrants, in particular highly skilled migrants, are viewed as less reliant on state-funded services to achieve a living wage, and considered to be more adaptable to the norms of their host nation, and consequently face fewer barriers to integration, due to the entry requirements that encourage economic security that accompanies earning a secure income (Alboim and Cohl 2012, 23; Duffy 1999, in Bauder 2011, 130). The introduction of the Canadian Experience Class in 2008, the Federal Skilled Trades Program, the Venture Capital Pilot Program, the Start-up Visa Program, and the expansion of opportunities for those in the live-in caregiver program to work their way into permanent residency have created greater opportunities for permanent settlement among skilled and semi-skilled migrants, while simultaneously reinforcing the one-sided nature of Canadian immigration policy based on market incentives.

At many points in history, immigration policy has been characterized by divisions of whom policymakers view as the desired or ideal migrant, versus the undesired migrant. Canada, as a settler society, has a long history of immigration policy driven by economic development objectives, but also one that was distinctly geared towards maintaining ethnic homogeneity and exclusionary goals (Kelley and Trebilcock 2010, 318; Rajkumar et al. 2012). Prior to the introduction of the points system in 1967, immigrant suitability in Canada was determined primarily on ethnic background, with preference for those migrating from European nations and the United States. Following the shift to the points-based system, however, immigration policy took an increasingly human capital approach, and aimed to remove explicit racial and ethnic discrimination from immigration laws (Duncan 2012; Kelley and Trebilcock 2010, 357), with emphasis on pathways to citizenship based on labour market potential, re-commodifying migrant labour. Increasingly, this has been driven by shortages in skilled labour within Canada, with allowances for non-economic migrants through family class sponsorship and economic class migrants' dependents. In recent years, however, greater restrictions have been placed on the criteria to qualify for family class sponsorship, as well as those eligible to be claimed as dependents of economic class migrants. The perceived burden stemming from economic class dependents and family class sponsorship, often viewed as non-economic contributors, has resulted in the breadth of eligibility within these categories being curtailed (CIC 2014b), with family members no longer cast as an important component to successful settlement, which encourages the continued commitment to nation building, but rather as those responsible for strain on the social safety net. This has also been apparent in the recent changes to regulations surrounding humanitarian class migrants in terms of eligibility criteria for claiming asylum in Canada, benefits accorded to those awaiting approval of their claims, and the selection criteria for government-assisted refugees. Such shaping of migration policy signalled a clear shift towards more restrictive and market-oriented policymaking that moves towards the exclusion of all but the "best and the brightest," as permanent settlers in Canada.

Changes to Family Class Sponsorship

Family class sponsorship – also referred to as "family reunification" – has been a mainstay of Canadian immigration recruitment policy for decades. This has allowed Canadian citizens and permanent residents to sponsor certain family members for permanent residency in Canada, which historically has been seen as a critical element in the successful settlement of new migrants (Wayland 2006). The centrality of older parents to family life, both economically and socially, contributes to the social capital of newcomers as they integrate into Canadian society (McLaren Tigar 2006, 35; Neborak 2013, 7). Moreover, the shift in source countries in Canada signals a need to reconsider the conception of family. Extended family as the mode of familial organization and multigenerational households are common in many source countries, and it has been identified as being an important factor in the economic and social success of immigrants (Neborak 2013). While family class immigrants have not been brought into Canada through an economic stream, the bulk of such newcomers contribute substantially to the labour market and economy. There is ample research evidence that family migrants represent a critical component to supporting economic integration among sponsoring migrants. As Arat-Koc (1999) observes, sponsored parents often play a critical role in supporting the family through childcare, working in family businesses, or finding other employment outside the home. It is striking that in this era of austerity, which includes calls for the reformation of the welfare state and increased self-sufficiency, key contributors to the self-sufficiency of immigrant families are being limited in their access to migration pathways.

Under the Harper Conservatives, eligibility criteria for family members was tightened and significant changes to sponsorship agreements between the federal government and the sponsoring party have signalled a shift to personal responsibility and a move away from state involvement in providing for sponsored family members. Since the mid-1990s, there has been a steady decline in the number of family class migrants coming to Canada, which has accelerated since the 2008 crisis. By 2012, family class represented less than a third of all landed immigrants (Neborak 2013, 3). This became an issue in the 2015 federal election, and the new Liberal government did restore greater balance by increasing the absolute number of family class immigrants let into Canada (although economic class immigrants remained the dominant category) and easing the rules on family reunification (CIC 2016).

The one-sided neoliberal agenda designed to maximize the short-term narrow economic benefits of immigration has contributed to a skewed debate on the role and importance of family sponsorship. As Neborak argues, "Family reunification has been redefined as being important only insofar as it maximizes economic outcomes" (2013, 2). This has been a driving force in how the Harper Conservative government reshaped the family class. Policy changes that affect the eligibility criteria for family class migrants were designed to lessen the number of family sponsored migrants, minimize their potential dependency on the state, and proactively address the crisis of an aging Canadian population (7). The reduction in age for eligible children to be sponsored was reduced from twenty-two to nineteen (CIC 2014b), while a temporary moratorium was placed on the sponsorship of parents and grandparents in 2011, which resulted in a severely scaled-back replacement program under the "supervisa." However, these changes come at a time where both state-funded settlement services for newcomers and welfare state programs are being curtailed, with greater onus placed on the individual and family to ensure integration into Canadian society, both economically and socially. The changes in their implications for immigrant families and a leaned-out welfare state are well articulated by Anna Boucher:

> Immigrant sponsors are increasingly bearing the brunt of financial costs of their parents and partners. Immigration selection policies place enduring contractual obligations upon adult immigrant sponsors to support their grown relatives, sometimes for long periods of time following immigration entry. These new forms of contractual obligations not only illuminate the stringent world of immigrant welfare provision, they also extend our understanding of familialism within welfare studies.
>   Liberal welfare states typically do not place obligations on adult family members to provide for adult children, or parents. Such familial models of welfare are more likely associated with the conservative welfare states of countries like Italy and Germany. However, in recent years, leading immigration receiving nations such as Australia and Canada – also liberal welfare states – have recast their immigration and welfare laws to place heavy contractual burdens upon adult immigrant sponsors to provide for their adult spouses and parents. These obligations extend for many years after the initial point of entry, in some cases, in excess of ten. A central difference between migrants and citizens is, of course, that governments may use immigration in addition to welfare laws, to limit access to social rights by rendering immigration entry conditional upon delayed access to the welfare state. And governments have exploited the dual pincer effect of immigration and welfare policy to considerable effect. (2014)

The recently elected "anti-austerity" Liberal government has moved to reverse some of the more anti-family measures brought in by the Harper government.

Changes to the Refugee Class

Canada has a long tradition of humanitarian assistance. Canadians often pride themselves on it, and it is often used in nationalist sentiments of our collective identity (Bauder 2011, 100). Despite certain historical inaccuracies that this represents, Canada's humanitarian past has been among the strongest in the OECD. Conservative government policy reforms significantly altered this reality, fuelled by neoliberal policy agendas employing the language of morality and illegality. Henry and Tator (2002) identify three key themes that have steered the direction of this discourse surrounding refugees: (1) "bogus refugees," particularly those who arrive by boat, are flooding into Canada and trying to take advantage of our lax refugee policy; (2) the lax refugee policy allows terrorists to enter Canada and obtain refugee status; and (3) immigrants are not appropriately screened at our borders and thus bring in diseases that threaten the health of Canadians. The refugee stream of immigration has in fact seen the largest proportional cuts in the period of austerity. Between 2005 and 2012, for example, the annual number of refugees landed in Canada fell from 35,775 to 23,094, a 12,681 drop (Griffith 2013, 105).

In 2012, the federal government introduced changes to the refugee class through the Balanced Refugee Reform Act (Refugee Reform) and the Protecting Canada's Immigration System Act that impose greater restrictions on asylum claimants, designed to prevent false claims and abuse of the Canadian immigration system (Canadian Council for Refugees 2012) and to ensure that only "legitimate" refugees seek asylum in Canada. The changes under Refugee Reform made it increasingly difficult for many asylum claimants to gain access to a fair hearing and the assurance of personal safety, as the framework for determining the legitimacy of a claim has become increasingly dictated by political whims (ibid.). Also in 2012 the Conservative government significantly curtailed benefits to health care for refugee claimants, using arguments about the excessive cost to taxpayers, refugee abuse, and suggesting that overly generous health benefits could make Canada a refugee health magnet (Jackson 2012).

A turning point in Canada's approach to the refugee class followed the arrivals by boat of Tamil refugees on the West Coast of Canada in

2009 and 2010. The federal government, building on the media's framing of these asylum claimants in a discourse of risk and illegality (Bradimore and Bauder 2011), responded with the passing of the Protection of Canada's Immigration System Act. The changes, sold as an approach to reduce human smuggling and profiteering from these activities, unfairly punishes refugee claimants rather than those running human smuggling activities. Moreover, under the provisions surrounding mass or "irregular" arrivals, it discounts the perceived legitimacy of those who arrive en masse. The act gives the minister of public safety the power to arbitrarily designate arrivals as "irregular," which not only centralizes power in the executive, but also has the potential to discriminate against certain unwanted or undesirable migrants based on country of origin.

Once again the newly elected Liberal government has worked to "liberalize" the stand on refugees, boosting the numbers to be let into the country (CIC 2016) and in particular welcoming over 25,000 new Syrian refugees. The new government brought back a more balanced selection process between economic, family, and humanitarian class immigrants. It is worth remembering, however, that previous Liberal governments had greatly tightened refugee acceptance into Canada through its own securitization policies (Amin-Khan 2015).

Temporary Foreign Workers and the Rise of Precariousness

Among the most significant changes in immigration policy in Canada, and more generally in the OECD, has been the growth in the use of temporary foreign workers (TFWs) to address labour market needs, particularly for low-skilled occupations. In Canada, for instance, between 2005 and 2012 the number of temporary foreign workers nearly doubled, jumping from 122,365 to 213,573 (Griffith 2013, 105). The rate of recruitment of low-skilled temporary workers has surpassed those falling into high-skilled categories. In 2002, 57 per cent of all temporary foreign workers were high-skilled, whereas 26.3 per cent were in low-skilled occupations. By 2008, however, the high-skilled workers represented only 36.8 per cent, whereas low-skilled workers represented 34.2 per cent (Nakache and Kinoshita 2010, 5). In the United States the temporary workforce expanded rapidly, between 2009 and 2010 alone growing from 1.7 to 2.8 million, while US unemployment rates remained very high as a consequence of the Great Recession of 2008 (Massey 2012, 1). In the OECD as a whole, TFWs have been increasing by 4–5 per cent per year since 2000 (Thomas 2010, 3). Consequently, increasingly labour migration in the OECD is being characterized by temporariness, where foreign workers are recruited to fill short-term labour shortages in both skilled and unskilled jobs. In Canada, growth in TFWs has been concentrated in low-skilled employment. With few to no avenues for permanent residency among low-skilled temporary foreign workers, this shift represents a growing stock of temporary migrants living in a continuous state of insecurity, without access to rights associated with permanent residency. This point is made in a recent Statistics Canada report:

> Temporary worker programs are attractive because they enable countries to quickly address labour market needs in an expanding economy [or as has been shown an economy still experiencing the negative employment effects of recession] without the increased costs associated with maintaining unemployed workers during a downturn – the costs associated with social and economic integration are also reduced. (Thomas 2010, 3)

TFWs, especially those recruited for the low-skilled jobs, are a significant part of Guy Standing's precariat, made up of those who do work that is poorly paid, insecure, and unprotected. and who lead lives that are absent of predictability and security (2011). Although the federal government introduced sweeping changes to the temporary foreign worker program in 2014, many of these changes support increased restrictions on usage of the program for employers to ensure they utilize Canadian labour first, while imposing few – if any – changes to better protect temporary foreign workers against employer abuse, precarious living conditions, and their appeal as free, no-cost, self-sufficient migrants.

An emerging and significant body of literature has been devoted to conceptualizing the growing global crisis of precariousness and insecurity for migrants under neoliberal reforms. De Genova (2002), Goldring, Berinstein, and Bernhard (2009), Goldring and Landolt (2013), and Rajkumar et al. (2012) have examined how precarious status has been institutionalized throughout a variety of entry mechanisms and pathways to a loss of status once in the United States and Canada, particularly for low-skilled temporary migrants. Precarious status, they argue, is defined by an absence of several elements: (1) work authorization, (2) the right to remain permanently in the country, (3) not depending on a third party for one's right to be in Canada (such as a sponsor), and (4) social citizenship rights available to permanent residents (Goldring, Berinstein, and Bernhard 2009, 240–2; Goldring and Landolt 2013, 14). Migrants who find themselves at the "temporary-permanent divide" (Rajkumar et al. 2012) often have difficulty in attaining full or even partial rights to the benefits of citizenship and depend on their tenuous attachment to the state to maintain a foothold in Canada. This limits their personal security and reifies the power of the state to limit or withdraw their status within Canada. The degree of personal security for those living with precarious legal status, in particular temporary foreign workers, is reinforced by the move towards increased private sector involvement in migration management.

Marketization of Immigration and Government Realignment

In line with the neoliberal imperative, which seeks to roll back state spending and activity in favour of allowing the free market to direct activity, immigration policymaking has taken a decidedly market-oriented turn. Increasingly employers in private industry are participating in directing the course of immigration policy. This has been influential not only in guiding new forms of permanent migration, as well as the industries prioritized for selecting migrants; they have also shared responsibility for managing and regulating migrant labour (Rheault 2013; Valiani 2013). This is particularly true in the case of the United States and Europe concerning skilled migration (Anwar 2014). Unlike permanent economic class immigrants to Canada, who are not yet required to have an offer of employment prior to admission, the shift of responsibility for skilled labour in the United States and many parts of Europe has fallen to the employer, based on the offer of employment. However, in 2008, the Canadian government introduced the Canadian Experience Class (CEC), which allows international students and skilled temporary foreign workers to apply for permanent residency upon completion of twelve or twenty-four months of work respectively (Valiani 2013). Gaining access to secure employment to fulfil these requirements is entirely dependent upon the employer, which is empowering employers, in essence privatizing the selection of immigrant newcomers, while simultaneously reinforcing the dependency of the migrant on the employer, furthering the precariousness that migrants experience while awaiting permanent residency.

Employer-based management and regulation of migrant labour is particularly prominent in temporary foreign worker programs. Employees are recruited directly by employers, and their security – both economic and individual – is managed directly by employers. These employment schemes have come under fire recently, particularly in Canada, for a number of reasons. The growth in temporary foreign worker recruitment over the past two decades has called into question the legitimacy of the program as truly one of temporariness. As Nakache (2013) argues, many of the labour market vacancies being filled by temporary foreign workers are doing so on an ongoing basis, throwing into question the veracity of the claim that they are, in fact, temporary. Although Canada's economic downturn was much less pronounced than it was in the United States and parts of Europe, the continued growth of the program has brought about public outcry about the extent to which and the growth in the program is being used, casting temporary foreign workers as the enemy and the root of the problem of the growth in unemployment (Cohen 2013).

Federal policy decisions have led to heightened employer control and flexibility within the criteria for selection that have shown mixed results for temporary foreign workers and Canadian workers. In 2006, the federal government reduced the required length of time employers in certain sectors were required to advertise job opportunities in Canada, prior to recruiting temporary workers, from six weeks to one (Valiani 2013), signalling a deeper shift towards flexible labour arrangements that are potentially harmful for national unemployment levels as well as a continued move towards temporary labour and insecurity for migrants. In addition, in 2012, it was announced that employers would be permitted to pay temporary foreign workers 15 per cent less than the average wage paid to Canadians (Curry 2014). Although this decision has since been repealed, the ideological and moral significance behind it is powerful. It reinforces the notion that to relieve the burden on the welfare state and to promote business profitability, it is justifiable to devalue TFWs by denying them access to social benefits (even though they pay taxes) and simultaneously TFWs' basic rights to a living wage are undercut.

In tandem with greater power-sharing with the private sector, there have been changes to the internal legislative and regulatory processes within the Canadian government, promoting an increased centralization of powers, which has allowed greater manipulation of the immigration system overall. In 2008, the Budget Implementation Act amended the Immigration and Refugee Protection Act (IRPA), giving the minister authorization to issue ministerial instructions (MIs) to immigration officers on which applications were eligible for processing, based on the government's immigration priorities (CIC 2011). In contrast to previous eras of policymaking, whereby new legislation would go through parliamentary debate and public consultations, the minister of citizenship and immigration now has sole discretion over limiting the number of applications processed, accelerating applications, and returning applications without processing them to conclusion (Alboim and Cohl 2012). Despite the ideological commitment of neoliberalism, which advocates a smaller state and decreased government intervention, the centralization of power is a critical element in assuring the success of the neoliberal project. According to Lee and McBride (2007, 5), coercive powers of the state have simply been redefined rather than reduced. As Evans argues, the neoliberal shift demonstrated the inability for welfare state leaders to govern, due to "mass democracy and welfare state policies, a politics where subordinate social actors had some influence over policy" (2014, 8). The centralization of decision-making power reinforces the ability to ensure the success of neoliberal policymaking and alignment with the market-driven focus of the state, crowding out spaces for dissent.

The centralization of power (see Evans, this volume) within the minister's office has been critical to the reinforcement of the neoliberal conception of the good/ideal migrant. Griffith (2013) presents us with an in-depth analysis of recent changes to the Canadian Citizenship and Multiculturalism branch within Citizenship and Immigration Canada under the Conservatives. His analysis points to a changing policy environment that had been fuelled less by evidence-based policymaking, and increasingly by framing policy discussions and policymaking around the anecdotal evidence coming out of the minister's office (Griffith 2013, 36–7). Griffith reveals instances where anecdotal evidence, often lacking in empirical data and clearly designed to "crack down" on those taking advantage of the welfare state (the unwanted migrant), were used to direct policy, despite their empirical shortcomings. This is perhaps best exemplified in the powers assigned to the minister regarding implementation of the Designated Country of Origin (DCO) policy within the refugee class. The DCO gives the minister the power to deem a country safe on the basis of the country's *perceived* respect for human rights and the provision of state protection (CIC 2014a). The legislation was put in place to deter those deemed to be "bogus" refugees from applying for refugee status in Canada, and can be based on the minister's opinion (Canadian Council for Refugees n.d.), despite evidence that many asylum claimants coming from DCOs may be subject to persecution. Those coming from DCOs claiming asylum have reduced rights in their refugee claim process, leaving them vulnerable to deportation and continued persecution.

Although the expansion of powers for the minister has affected all classes of migrants, many of the provisions affecting economic class migrants have been short-term and are in response to fluctuations in the labour market as well as the need to clear up administrative backlogs. More sweeping changes to the refugee class and non-economic migrants are more permanent and are likely to have long-lasting effects. These changes have been driven by the narratives of protecting Canada's immigration program from "bogus" refugee claims, lowering the costs associated with maintaining basic protections for refugees and asylum claimants (Jackson 2012), and a high dependency ratio among family class immigrants whose economic contribution to the state is seen as minimal, placing greater pressure on the welfare state (Arat-Koc 1999, 2012; Neborak 2013). In addition, greater powers given to the minister under the Immigration and Refugee Protection Act, which came into effect in 2002, allowed the government greater flexibility to enact new regulations and categories of temporary foreign workers, largely out of the purview of the public eye (Fudge and MacPhail 2009, 11).

Immigrant Integration: From Immigrant Accommodation to the One-way Street

The successful integration of immigrants into society is important, and the means by which it is achieved reveals the orientation of the state and public policy. Canada has long been considered a model to be closely studied and emulated in successful immigrant settlement and integration. By the 1970s Canada had established what was, by international standards, a rather elaborate support system of community-based service provision for immigrant newcomers funded by the state but delivered through non-profit organizations. These programs included such things as language training, employment and affordable housing supports, access to social services, and "orientation to Canada" programming (Richmond and Shields 2005).

The value of these programs were not just the material support they offered to immigrants but also the symbolic message their existence sent to society and newcomer communities that Canadian governments valued immigrants and actively supported their smooth transition into society (Siemiatycki and Triadafilopoulos 2010). The Canadian model of immigrant integration was a two-way street model involving ongoing "mutual adaption, requiring effort on the part of both the receiving society and the newcomer: the newcomer adapting to life in the new society, and the new society adapting to the newcomer in its welcome and responsiveness to new cultural and individual needs and contributions" (Kilbride 2014, 328). This model of immigrant settlement and integration has come to be challenged and undermined by an increasing neoliberal approach to integration and settlement support in Canada.

This reorientation around integration is closely linked to the neoliberal notion of the "ideal immigrant" and the greatly reduced role it holds for the place of the state in society and economy. As identified earlier, ideal immigrants for the neoliberal perspective are thoroughly self-sufficient and take responsibility through their work ethic and resilience for their own and their families' well-being without the need to turn to state support. Individuals are to be held responsible "for their own economic and social 'inclusion'" (Kilbride 2014, 329). Moreover, rather than a two-way street approach to integration, neoliberals embrace a one-way street on which immigrant newcomers are expected to adapt and change to meet the expectations and value systems of the host society (Griffith 2013, 21–33).

Revealingly, in the movement to promote TFWs as a solution to meet the labour market needs of the country, TFWs have become something of an invisible model of the ideal migrant as they epitomize labour flexibility, pose no burdens on the welfare system or settlement support system (as TFWs they have no rights to such services), enjoy no claim to permanent residency, and hence are disposable. Hence, there is little integration concerns around TFWs.

In the Canadian model of settlement support, neoliberal structuring over the last decade or so, and the impact of particularly deep cuts to settlement programming since the imposition of austerity after 2010 in Canada, has been particularly damaging to the level and quality of settlement supports available to immigrants today. Funding to settlement agencies have not only been cut, but the nature of reduced financial support from the state has changed. It has shifted away from stable core funding to precarious short-term and contract-based financing, seriously destabilizing non-profit agencies (Baines et al. 2014). The immigrant settlement sector is compelled to "do more with less" while also being closely controlled through contract financing with stringent vertical accountability to the state (Evans, Richmond, and Shields 2005). Non-profit independence and their links to the community are compromised in the process, as non-profit providers are directed by state funders to reduce their "dependency" by finding alternative sources of funding support, and to restructure and rationalize their operating models along business and market-friendly avenues (Shields 2014; Joy and Shields 2014; see Joy and Shields 2017). In the process, immigrant settlement support for integration, like the welfare state more generally, has come to be hollowed out, leaving immigrants far more vulnerable in a "risk society" (Beck 1992).

Conclusion

This chapter seeks to locate immigration policy more prominently within neoliberal restructuring and the post-financial crisis austerity agenda. Immigration has become an important part of the economies and societies of virtually every OECD nation. To some significant degree, after the "Great Recession," immigrants and immigration policy have become scapegoats for contributing to elevated unemployment, lowering wages, and contributing to welfare burdens and state fiscal crisis, with many calling for harsh immigrant-restricting policies (a closed borders strategy). However, we point to the reality that immigration continues to be vitally important to modern societies and to neoliberalism itself. Hence, neoliberalism has sought to use such anti-immigrant sentiment to deepen a neoliberalization of immigration policy. In doing so, neoliberal policymakers have not rejected immigration but rather sought to recalibrate immigration policy to meet their own goals related to competitiveness, labour flexibility, reduction of state social supports, and promotion of neoliberal values. Using Canada as a focus of analysis, we point to how neoliberal governments have used a politics of "good" vs "bad" immigrants to reconfigure the classes of immigrants recruited and excluded, to diminish immigrant access to social welfare and settlement supports, and to promote narrow, short-term economic benefits over longer-term nation-building goals.

REFERENCES

Alboim, Naomi, and Karen Cohl. 2012. *Shaping the Future: Canada's Rapidly Changing Immigration Policies*. Toronto: Maytree.
Ali, Loft A.J. 2014. "Welcome to Canada? A Critical Review and Assessment of Canada's Fast-Changing Immigration Policies: Literature Review." RCIS

Working Paper 2014/6, October. Toronto: Ryerson Centre for Immigration and Settlement.

Amin-Khan, T. 2015. "Security and Its Impact on Immigrants and Refugees." In *Immigrant Experiences in North America: Understanding Settlement and Integration*, ed. Harald Bauder and John Shields, 118–43. Toronto: Canadian Scholars'.

Anderson, Bridget. 2014. "Exclusion, Failure, and the Politics of Citizenship." RCIS Working Paper 2014/1, January. Toronto: Ryerson Centre for Immigration and Settlement.

Anwar, Arif. 2014. "Canadian Immigration Policy: Micro and Macro Issues with the Points Based Assessment System." *Canadian Ethnic Studies* 46 (1): 169–79. https://doi.org/10.1353/ces.2014.0004.

Arat-Koc, Sedef. 1999. "Neo-liberalism, State Restructuring and Immigration: Changes in Canadian Policies in the 1990s." *Journal of Canadian Studies / Revue d'études canadiennes* 34 (2): 31–56. https://doi.org/10.3138/jcs.34.2.31.

– 2012. "Invisibilized, Individualized and Culturalized: Paradoxical Invisibility and Hyper-Visibility of Gender in Policy Making and Policy Discourse in Neoliberal Canada." *Canadian Women's Studies* 29 (3): 6–17.

Baines, Donna, John Campey, Ian Cunningham, and John Shields. 2014. "Not Profiting from Precarity: The Work of Nonprofit Service Delivery and the Creation of Precariousness." *Just Labour: A Canadian Journal of Work and Society* 22 (Autumn): 74–93.

Banting, Keith, and Will Kymlicka. 2010. "Canadian Multiculturalism: Global Anxieties and Local Debates." *British Journal of Canadian Studies* 23 (1): 43–72. https://doi.org/10.3828/bjcs.2010.3.

Bauder, Harald. 2011. *Immigration Dialectic: Imagining Community, Economy, and Nation*. Toronto: University of Toronto Press. https://doi.org/10.3138/9781442687196.

Beck, U. 1992. *Risk Society: Towards a New Modernity*. London: Sage.

Boucher, Anna. 2014. "Welfare Restrictions Place Financial Pressure on New Immigrant Families." Policy & Politics Journal Blog, 9 July. https://policyandpoliticsblog.com/2014/07/09/welfare-restrictions-place-financial-pressure-on-new-immigrant-families/.

Bradimore, Ashley, and Harald Bauder. 2011. "Mystery Ships and Risky Boat People: Tamil Refugee Migration in the Newsprint Media." *Canadian Journal of Communication* 36 (4): 637–61.

Canadian Council for Refugees. 2012. "Concerns about Changes to the Refugee Determination System." http://ccrweb.ca/en/concerns-changes-refugee-determination-system/.

– n.d. "Refugee Determination System." http://ccrweb.ca/en/refugee-reform.

Chock, Phyllis. 1995. "Ambiguity in Policy Discourse: Congressional Talk about Immigration." *Policy Sciences* 28 (2): 165–84. https://doi.org/10.1007/BF00999674.
Citizenship and Immigration Canada (CIC). 2011. *Evaluation of Ministerial Instructions (Implementation)*. http://www.cic.gc.ca/english/pdf/research-stats/min-instruct.pdf.
– 2014a. "Designated Countries of Origin," 10 October. http://www.cic.gc.ca/english/refugees/reform-safe.asp.
– 2014b. "Family Sponsorship," 15 April. http://www.cic.gc.ca/english/immigrate/sponsor.
– 2016. "Government of Canada Plans on Admitting Record Numbers of New Immigrants in 2016." *CIC News: Canada Immigration Newsletter*, 8 March. http://www.cicnews.com/2016/03/government-canada-plans-admitting-record-numbers-immigrants-2016-037396.html.
Cohen, Tobi. 2013. "Cap Temporary Foreign Workers." *Ottawa Citizen*, 17 October.
Collett, Elizabeth. 2011a. "Immigrant Integration during the Recession: Effects, Policies, and Policies in Europe." In *Looming Shadows: Migration and Integration at a Time of Upheaval: European and American Perspectives*, ed. V. Dzihic and T. Schmidinger, 1–21. Washington, DC: Center for Transatlantic Relations.
– 2011b. *Immigrant Integration in Europe in a Time of Austerity*. Washington, DC: Migration Policy Institute.
Curry, Bill. 2014. "Everything You Need to Know about Temporary Foreign Workers." *Globe and Mail*, 2 May. http://www.theglobeandmail.com/news/politics/temporary-foreign-workers-everything-you-need-to-know/article18363279/.
Dauvergne, Catherine. 2005. *Humanitarianism, Identity, and Nation Migration Laws of Australia and Canada*. Vancouver: UBC Press.
De Genova, Nicholas. 2002. "Migrant 'Illegality' and Deportability in Everyday Life." *Annual Review of Anthropology* 31:419–47.
Dobrowolsky, Alexandra. 2012. "Nuancing Neoliberalism: Lessons Learned from a Failed Immigration Experiment." *International Migration and Integration* 14:197–218.
Duncan, Howard, John Nieuwenhuysen, and Stine Neerup. 2012. "Introduction." In *International Migration in Uncertain Times*, ed. John Nieuwenhuysen, Howard Duncan, and Stine Neerup, 1–6. Montreal and Kingston: McGill-Queen's University Press.
Duncan, Natasha. 2012. *Immigration Policymaking in the Global Era*. New York: Palgrave Macmillan.

Edsall, Thomas Byrne. 2012. *The Age of Austerity: How Scarcity Will Remake American Politics*. New York: Doubleday.

Esses, Victoria M., Stelian Medianu, and Andrea S. Lawson. 2013. "Uncertainty, Threat, and the Role of the Media in Promoting the Dehumanization of Immigrants and Refugees." *Journal of Social Issues* 69 (3): 518–36. https://doi.org/10.1111/josi.12027.

Evans, Bryan. 2014. "The Ideational Foundations of Economic Policy in an Age of Austerity: Ideas, Agents, Institutions and the Neoliberal State." Manufacturing and Framing Austerity Workshop, McMaster University, 30 October.

Evans, Bryan, Ted Richmond, and John Shields. 2005. "Structuring Neoliberal Governance: The Nonprofit Sector, Emerging New Modes of Control and the Marketization of Service Delivery." *Policy and Society* 24 (1): 73–97. https://doi.org/10.1016/S1449-4035(05)70050-3.

Fargues, P., D.G. Papademetriou, G. Salinari, and M. Sumption. 2011. *Shared Challenges and Opportunities for EU and US Immigration Policymakers*. Migration Policy Institute. http://www.migrationpolicy.org/pubs/US-EUimmigrationsystems-finalreport.pdf.

Forkert, Kristen. 2014. "The New Moralism: Austerity, Silencing and Debt Morality." *Soundings* 56 (56): 41–53. https://doi.org/10.3898/136266214811788808.

Fudge, Judy, and Fiona MacPhail. 2009. "The Temporary Foreign Worker Program in Canada: Low-Skilled Workers as an Extreme Form of Flexible Labour." *Comparative Labor Law and Policy Journal* 31:101–39.

Goldring, Luin, Carolina Berinstein, and Judith Bernhard. 2009. "Institutionalizing Precarious Immigration Status in Canada." *Citizenship Studies* 13 (3): 239–65.

Goldring, Luin, and Patricia Landolt. 2013. "The Conditionality of Legal Status and Rights: Conceptualizing Precarious Non-Citizenship in Canada." In *Producing and Negotiating Non-Citizenship: Precarious Legal Status in Canada*, ed. Luin Goldring and Patricia Landolt, 3–27. Toronto: University of Toronto Press.

Goldring, Luin, and Marie-Pier Joly. 2014. "Immigration, Citizenship and Racialization at Work: Unpacking Employment Precarity in Southwest Ontario." *Just Labour: A Canadian Journal of Work and Society* 22 (Autumn): 94–121.

Gottfried, Keren, J. Shields, N. Akter, D. Dyson, S. Topkara-Sarsu, H. Egeh, and S. Guerra. 2016. "Paving Their Way and Earning Their Pay: Economic Survival Experiences of Immigrants in East Toronto." *Precarious Work and the Struggle for Living Wages – Alternate Routes: A Journal of Critical Social Research* 27:137–61.

Griffith, Andrew. 2013. *Policy Arrogance or Innocent Bias: Resetting Citizenship and Multiculturalism.* Toronto: Anar.

Guiraudon, Virginie. 2004. "Immigration Reform in Comparative Perspectives: Sunshine and Shadow Politics in the United States and Europe." In *Transatlantic Policymaking in an Age of Austerity*, ed. Martin Levin and Martin Shapiro, 131–57. Washington, DC: Georgetown University Press.

Hampshire, James. 2013. *The Politics of Immigration.* Cambridge: Polity.

Henry, Frances, and Carol Tator. 2002. *Discourses of Domination Racial Bias in the Canadian English-Language Press.* Toronto: University of Toronto Press. https://doi.org/10.3138/9781442673946.

Jackson, Samantha. 2012. "The New Interim Federal Health Program: How Reduced Coverage Adversely Affects Refugee Claimants' Employment." RCIS Research Brief 2012/1, November. Toronto: Ryerson Centre for Immigration and Settlement.

Joy, Meghan, and John Shields. 2014. "Austerity and the Non-profit Sector: The Case of Social Impact Bonds." Manufacturing and Framing Austerity Workshop, McMaster University, 30 October.

– 2017. "Austerity and the Non-profit Sector: The Case of Social Impact Bonds." In *The Austerity State*, ed. Stephen McBride and Bryan Evans. Toronto: University of Toronto Press.

Kelley, N., and M. Trebilcock. 2010. *The Making of the Mosaic: A History of Canadian Immigration Policy.* 3rd ed. Toronto: University of Toronto Press.

Kelly, Phillip, Stella Park, and Laura Lepper. 2011. *Economic Recession and Immigrant Labour Market Outcomes in Canada, 2006–2011.* TIEDI Analytical Report 22. Toronto: York University. http://www.yorku.ca/tiedi/doc/AnalyticalReport22.pdf.

Kilbride, Kenise Murphy, ed. 2014. *Immigrant Integration: Research Implications for Future Policy.* Toronto: Canadian Scholars'.

Kynaston, D. 2007. *A World to Build: Austerity Britain 1945–48.* London: Bloomsbury.

Lee, Simon, and Stephen McBride. 2007. "Introduction: Neo-Liberalism, State Power and Global Governance in the 21st Century." In *Neo-Liberalism, State Power and Global Governance*, ed. Simon Lee and Stephen McBride, 1–24. Dordrecht: Springer. https://doi.org/10.1007/978-1-4020-6220-9_1.

Lister, Ruth. 1997. "Citizenship: Towards a Feminist Synthesis." *Feminist Review* 57 (Autumn): 28–48.

Massey, Douglas S. 2012. *Immigration and the Great Recession.* Stanford, CA: Stanford Center on Poverty and Inequality.

McLaren Tigar, Arlene. 2006. "Immigration and Parental Sponsorship in Canada: Implications for Elderly Women." *Canadian Issues* (Spring): 34–7.

Nakache, Delphine. 2013. "The Canadian Temporary Foreign Worker Program: Regulations, Practices and Protection Gaps." In *Producing and Negotiating Non-Citizenship Precarious Legal Status in Canada*, ed. Luin Goldring and Patricia Landolt, 71–95. Toronto: University of Toronto Press.

Nakache, Delphine, and Paula Kinoshita. 2010. "The Canadian Temporary Foreign Worker Program: Do Short-term Economic Needs Prevail over Human Rights Concerns?" *IRPP Study*, no. 5.

Neborak, Jacklyn. 2013. "Family Reunification? A Critical Analysis of Citizenship and Immigration: Canada's 2013 Reforms to the Family Class." RCIS Working Paper 2013/8, November. Toronto: Ryerson Centre for Immigration and Settlement.

Organisation for Economic Co-operation and Development (OECD). 2012. "Settling." In *OECD Indicators of Immigrant Integration*. Paris: OECD.

Pagliaro, J., and J. Mahoney. 2011. "Funding Cuts Threaten Immigrant Agencies." *Globe and Mail*, 4 February.

Papademetriou, Demetrios G., and Aaron Terrazas. 2009. *Immigrants and the Current Economic Crisis: Research Evidence, Policy Challenges, and Implications*. Washington, DC: Migration Policy Institute.

PEPSO. 2013. *It's More Than Poverty: Poverty and Employment Precarity in Southern Ontario*. Toronto: McMaster University and United Way of Toronto.

Rajkumar, Deepa, Laurel Berkowitz, Leah F. Vosko, Valerie Preston, and Robert Latham. 2012. "At the Temporary-Permanent Divide: How Canada Produces Temporariness and Makes Citizens through Its Security, Work, and Settlement Policies." *Citizenship Studies* 16 (3–4): 483–510. https://doi.org/10.1080/13621025.2012.683262.

Reitz, Jeffrey G. 1998. *Warmth of the Welcome: The Social Causes of Economic Success for Immigrants in Different Nations and Cities*. Boulder, CO: Westview.

– 2011. *Pro-immigration Canada: Social and Economic Roots of Popular Views*. Montreal: Institute for Research on Public Policy.

Rheault, Ludovic. 2013. "Corporate Lobbying and Immigration Policies in Canada." *Canadian Journal of Political Science* 46 (3): 691–722. https://doi.org/10.1017/S0008423913000644.

Richmond, Ted, and John Shields. 2005. "NGO-Government Relations and Immigrant Services: Contradictions and Challenges." *Journal of International Migration and Integration* 6 (3/4): 513–26. https://doi.org/10.1007/s12134-005-1024-3.

Root, Jesse, Erika Gates-Gases, John Shields, and Harald Bauder. 2014. "Discounting Immigrant Families: Neoliberalism and the Framing of

Canadian Immigration Policy Change." RCIS Working Paper 2014/7, October. Toronto: Ryerson Centre for Immigration and Settlement.
Rosher, Albert, Soojin Yu, Sasha Badr, and Catherine Liu. 2012. "Canada." In *International Migration in Uncertain Times*, ed. John Nieuwenhuysen, Howard Duncan, and Stine Neerup, 35–49. Montreal and Kingston: McGill-Queen's University Press.
Shields, John. 2014. "Constructing and 'Liberating' Temporariness in the Canadian Nonprofit Sector: Neoliberalism and Nonprofit Service Providers." In *Liberating Temporariness? Migration, Work and Citizenship in an Age of Insecurity*, ed. Robert Latham, Valerie Preston, and Leah Vosko, 255–81. Montreal and Kingston: McGill-Queen's University Press.
Shields, John, Julie Drolet, and Karla Valenzuela. 2016. "Immigration Settlement and Integration Services and the Role of Nonprofit Providers: A Cross-National Perspective on Trends, Issues and Evidence." RCIS Working Paper 2016/1, February. http://www.ryerson.ca/content/dam/rcis/documents/RCIS%20WP%202016_01%20Shields%20et%20al%20final.pdf.
Shields, John, Maryse Lemoine, Mai Phan, Philip Kelly, Lucia Lo, Valerie Preston, and Steven Tufts. 2010. *Do Immigrant Class and Gender Affect Labour Market Outcomes for Immigrants?* TIEDI Analytical Report 2, January. Toronto: Toronto Immigrant Employment Data Initiative, York University. http://www.yorku.ca/tiedi/doc/AnalyticalReport2.pdf.
Shpaizman, I. 2010. *The Influence of Neo-Liberal Ideas and Political Conflict on the Privatization Process of Immigrant Policy: A Comparison of Israel, Canada and the Netherlands*. College Park, MD: Center for International Policy Exchanges.
Siemiatycki, Myer. 2010. "Marginalizing Migrants: Canada's Rising Reliance on Temporary Foreign Workers." *Canadian Issues* (Spring): 60–3.
Siemiatycki, M., and T. Triadafilopoulos. 2010. *"International Perspectives on Immigrant Service Provision."* Mowat Centre for Policy Innovation. School of Public Policy and Governance. Toronto: University of Toronto.
Standing, Guy. 2011. *The Precariat: The New Dangerous Class*. London: Bloomsbury.
Thomas, Derrick. 2010. *Foreign Nationals Working Temporarily in Canada*. Ottawa: Statistics Canada.
United Nations Regional Information Centre for Western Europe (UNIRC). 2014. "Youth: The Hardest Hit by the Global Financial Crisis." New York: UNIRC, 24 October. http://www.unric.org/en/youth-unemployment/27414-youth-the-hardest-hit-by-the-global-financial-crisis.
Valiani, Salimah. 2013. "The Shifting Landscape of Contemporary Canadian Immigration Policy: The Rise of Temporary Migration and Employer-Driven Immigration." In *Producing and Negotiating Non-Citizenship Precarious*

Legal Status in Canada, ed. Luin Goldring and Patricia Landolt, 55–70. Toronto: University of Toronto Press.

Wayland, Sarah. 2006. *Unsettled: Legal and Policy Barriers for Newcomers to Canada: Literature Review*. Ottawa: Community Foundations of Canada and the Law Commission of Canada.

Worswick, Chris. 2013. "Economic Implications of Recent Changes to the Temporary Foreign Worker Program." Montreal: Institute for Research on Public Policy.

10 Pension Reforms in the Context of the Global Financial Crisis: A Reincarnation of Pension Privatization through Austerity?

YANQIU RACHEL ZHOU AND SHIH-JIUNN SHI

Introduction

The 2007–8 global financial crisis (GFC) greatly undermined the performance of the pension fund markets in countries of the Organisation for Economic Co-operation and Development (OECD), including both many advanced welfare states (e.g., the United Kingdom and Australia) and some less-affluent ones (such as the Czech Republic and Hungary). While no two countries have been affected by the crisis in exactly the same way, the similar pattern of pension reforms, ostensibly in the cause of austerity, throughout many OECD countries poses the question of the real nature of those reforms. Are they simply, as claimed, crisis responses, or are they, rather, essentially welfare retrenchments under another name? In pursuit of a critical understanding of austerity, this chapter analyses pensions in the context of the GFC. Rather than comparing experiences of OECD countries, the discussion considers relationships among the GFC, post-crisis pension reforms, and the prospects for old age security through a review of the literature. Some secondary empirical data, such as statistics at the nation-state and OECD levels, are also called upon to illustrate the convergent trends in pensions.

The analysis in this chapter consists of three sections. The first, focusing on the direct impacts of the GFC on pensions, explores changes in the relationship between pensions and financial markets ensuing from earlier "pension privatization." Those impacts have been complicated by the increase in the importance of private pensions. This analysis establishes a macro-structural context in which to illustrate the true nature of the disingenuous pension reforms during and after the GFC, which are discussed in the second section. Situating austerity in the historical context of pension retrenchments since long before the GFC, in the third section we reflect on the repercussions of population aging, as a major social problem for old age security and as a political construction, for the politics of pension reforms. Doing so will help us discover the connections between the past (for instance, neoliberalism-oriented pension privatization), the present (including pension reforms under the umbrella of austerity), and the future (e.g., old age security in the context of the accelerated demographic shift of aging populations) of the changing pension landscapes. We argue that the pension reforms under the rubric of austerity during and since the GFC are essentially a continuation of neoliberal welfare retrenchments since the 1980s and pension privatization since the 1990s. Consistent with the spirit of neoliberalism, these policy changes are primarily about cutbacks to public benefits, the extension of private pensions, and further downloading the responsibility of old age security onto individuals. To some extent, the paradigm of pension privatization that was once at risk of extinction or, at least, radical change has now de facto revived; it has evolved, through the GFC and subsequent rationalization of austerity, into a crisis response. Although the supposed need for austerity has been used as a political excuse for the unpopular regressive welfare reforms that continue to ignore the reality of population aging, a real pension crisis has yet to come. For this reason we should be alert to the "new politics" of the welfare state and the neoliberal convergence of welfare policies (including pension policies) – in such forms as fiscal austerity and further privatization – that have been observed in many OECD countries (Peters 2012).

The Impacts of the GFC on Pensions: Endogenous or Exogenous Shock?

Across the OECD, the GFC and economic recession have strained government budgets through loss of revenues and social contributions, and increasing demand for social benefits (e.g., a guaranteed minimum income). In 2009, on average across OECD countries, public social spending to gross domestic product (GDP) ratios increased from around 19 per cent in 2007 to 22 per cent in 2009[1] (OECD 2012c). The same year, public

---

[1] After the adjustment for the changes in prices, this marked increase in *real* social spending continued for most OECD countries, with the sharpest decline (–14 per cent) in Greece, and the largest increase (29 per cent) in Korea (OECD 2012c).

social spending on *the elderly* alone – including cash benefits and public health expenditure – amounted to 11 per cent of GDP, on average, across these same countries (ibid.). In addition, the GFC had some major *direct* impacts on the pension systems in OECD countries, including the low or negative return rate of pension funds, the insolvency or deficit of funded defined benefit (DB) plans, and some less-affluent countries' inability to cover the funding gap in the pay-as-you-go (PAYG) system (Drahokoupil and Domonkos 2012; Lagoutte and Reimat 2013; OECD 2012b). These effects will be discussed in detail later. To better contextualize them, we first look at pension privatization, which has fundamentally changed the composition of pension systems and the relationship between pensions and financial markets.

Since the 1990s, a multi-pillar pension model that combines public and private pensions[2] as a means of "risk diversification" has been promoted around the world by powerful international organizations like the World Bank and the International Monetary Fund (IMF) (Ebbinghaus, Orenstein, and Whiteside 2012, 241; Holzmann 2013, 12; World Bank 2008; Orenstein 2013). This model is referred to as "pension privatization," and through it the pre-existing, publicly funded PAYG systems, where the revenues from the current generation of workers are used to pay the current generation of pensioners, are being partially or fully replaced by ones based on individual private pension savings accounts (Ebbinghaus, Orenstein, and Whiteside 2012). As a result, pension fund markets in the OECD have rapidly expanded: its total pension fund assets increased to US$17.9 trillion in 2005 from US$13 trillion in 2001 (OECD 2006). By 2005 the United States alone had accumulated a quantity of financial pension wealth equivalent to more than 160 per cent of GDP (ibid.). Although the specific allocation of pension investments varies considerably across countries, in the OECD as a whole bonds and shares remain the two most important asset classes. In 2006 bonds and shares accounted for 50 per cent of the total pension fund

---

2 The proposed multi-pillar pension system comprises five basic elements: (1) a non-contributory "zero pillar," to provide minimal protection; (2) a mandatory "first pillar," with contributions linked, to varying degrees, to earnings, typically financed on a PAYG basis; (3) a mandatory "second pillar," typically an individual savings account; (4) a voluntary "third pillar" that takes many forms; and (5) a non-financial "fourth pillar" that includes access to informal support, other formal social programs, and other individual financial and non-financial assets (Holzmann and Hinz 2005; Holzmann 2013; World Bank 2008).

portfolio in most OECD countries, and for over 80 per cent in some: e.g., 89.3 per cent for the Netherlands and 97.5 per cent for Mexico (OECD 2007). The dominance of pension funds in the world's financial markets also suggests the emergence of "pension fund capitalism," in which "pension funds, financial institutions in their own right, increasingly become the source of corporate engagement and the providers of social welfare and public infrastructure in the twenty-first century" (Clark 2000; Dixon 2008, 249).

The heavy blow dealt by the GFC to the pension markets should thus not come as any great surprise. In the OECD from December 2007 to October 2008, pension fund assets declined by about US$3.3 trillion (OECD 2008, 2). From December 2007 to June 2011, most countries' pension funds experienced a negative annual real rate of investment returns. In 2008, a year in which the crisis hit particularly hard, the real return rate of pension funds across the OECD was –10.5 per cent: Ireland had the worst (–35.7 per cent), followed by Australia (–20.93 per cent), Belgium (–19.89 per cent), and the Netherlands (–15.7 per cent) (Natali 2011; OECD 2012b). Despite the slight market recovery thereafter, in the period 2007–11 most countries' pension funds were still in the red in cumulative investment performance (OECD 2012b).

The collapse of the expected returns on private savings has left a deficit of funded DB schemes, in which the plan sponsors (the employers) assume responsibility for keeping a certain level of future benefits for the employees, and thus bear the investment risk. In the United Kingdom (which embraced pension privatization as early as 1986), for instance, in 2009 more than 80 per cent of DB plans recorded a deficit of £122.1 billion (Lagoutte and Reimat 2013; Orenstein 2013). The insolvency of DB plans also makes government intervention to meet solvency rules all the more urgent. Also in the United Kingdom, financial support from the Pension Protection Fund, a statutory fund intended to protect pensioners if their pension fund becomes insolvent, has led to an increase in the public deficit (Lagoutte and Reimat 2013). For the same reason, in 2009 Germany's Pension Security Fund (PSV), a mutual insurance association, reported record payments and was obliged to raise the levy on employers to unprecedented levels (Casey 2012). In other words, in times of crisis, private pension funds still require public financial support, despite the alleged advantage of pension privatization for reducing the government's responsibility. Public interventions in such private pensions also raise questions about their long-term impacts on the boundaries between public and private responsibility for pensions, inasmuch as when "distinctions between public and private dissolve, responsibility diffuses" (Ebbinghaus, Orenstein, and Whiteside 2012, 241).

The enduring shift from DB to defined contribution (DC) plans,[3] in which only employer contributions – not the future benefits – to the private savings account are guaranteed, and the beneficiary (the individual pensioner) bears the investment risk, has also been accelerated in the context of GFC, given employers' lower liabilities for DC pension schemes (Casey 2012; OECD 2012a). By 2012 DB pension plans constituted the smaller part of the pension markets in seven OECD countries (Denmark, Italy, Australia, Mexico, New Zealand, Iceland, and Spain), and did not exist at all in eight (Chile, the Czech Republic, Estonia, France, Greece, Hungary, Poland, and the Slovak Republic) (OECD 2013c). Despite the measures taken by some nations to regulate and monitor private pension investments, this development may mean that pensioners will bear more investment risk themselves, which is especially alarming considering how many are ill-prepared to manage their savings at pension markets.

In Central and Eastern Europe (CEE) the GFC also compromised the ability of states to cover the funding gap in the PAYG system because the resources previously designated to finance this public pension were diverted to fund private pension savings accounts, leaving the PAYG system unavailable to pay current pensioners' benefits during the crisis (Casey 2012; Drahokoupil and Domonkos 2012). Caught between the reduced revenues and the PAYG system's liabilities, and between the fiscal crisis and the pressure of the Maastricht criteria, which require EU member states to keep their public deficits and public debts low (under 3 per cent and 60 per cent of national GDP, respectively), some countries (e.g., Estonia, Poland, and Hungary) resorted to radical reform measures. Pension privatization was, for instance, temporarily, partially, or completely reversed through postponing or reducing contributions to private plans, increasing contributions in the PAYG system, or even nationalizing pension funds from the funded private pension system. In Hungary, as of 2011 all contributions in private pensions – a total of

---

3 In the United States, for example, the transition from DB to DC plans started long before the crisis. Between 1979 and 2004 the share of workers covered by DB plans dropped from 62 to 10 per cent, while that of DC plans rose from 16 to 63 per cent (Employee Benefit Research Institute 2005, cited in Meyer 2013).

around US$14 billion in assets – had reverted to the public PAYG system (Drahokoupil and Domonkos 2012; OECD 2012b; Orenstein 2011). These strategies were possible in part because the withdrawal of the World Bank and the IMF from the pension privatization agenda after 2008 made pension reforms there "essentially a domestic affair" (Drahokoupil and Domonkos 2012, 291; Orenstein 2011).

The multi-pillar pension model was initially conceived of by the World Bank (1994) as a way to meet the aging population challenge with risk diversification. The crisis has, however, severely damaged the performance of the pension fund markets in OECD countries, including many advanced welfare states. It also revealed the weakness of pension privatization as a remedy for population aging and economic crisis (Drahokoupil and Domonkos 2012; Ebbinghaus, Orenstein, and Whiteside 2012). The increasing dependence of old age security on private pensions and the changing private-public ratio in pension funding have not only complicated the issues of government liability in the context of financial crisis; they have also revealed the complexity of the GFC's impacts on pensions.

Is the crisis, then, an endogenous or, rather, an exogenous shock to the pensions? Precisely, is this a crisis *"in* the system" of pensions, or *"of* the system" (McBride and Merolli 2013, 300)? The question is important, given that public policy (including pension policy) responses to the crisis are determined largely by our interpretation of it. Further, the question emphasizes the paradox that although the GFC has exposed the risks of and limits to pension markets, pension fund capitalism itself has grown in significance since the crisis. Amounting to US$32.1 trillion in 2012, private pension systems in the OECD comprised pension funds (67.9 per cent), banks and investment companies (18.5 per cent), insurance companies (12.8 per cent), and employers' book reserves (0.8 per cent); and, strikingly, total pension fund assets grew from $15.4 trillion in 2008 to $21.8 trillion in 2012 (OECD 2013c). Seeing the crisis as inherent in "finance capitalism" – a new phase in capitalism led by financial capital – Peet (2011) pointed out that "the financialization of everything" means the control by finance of all other areas of the economy; debt, speculation, risk, and fear are *structurally* inherent in finance capitalism, which "invents, or intensifies, new methods of exploitation that pass mainly through the sphere of reproduction [such as various financial products] rather than the sphere of production" (393). As pension funds are now increasingly integral to the global financial markets, old age income–security systems are not only subject to financial market risks like the GFC, but also subordinated to the interests of global financial capital when it comes to "crisis responses" like austerity.

Pension Reforms in the Context of the GFC: The Paradox of "Crisis Responses"

Under the rubric of austerity, various pension reforms, as well as reforms of other social policy areas, were carried out in OECD countries during the GFC and thereafter. In some, such as Greece, Hungary, and Ireland, substantial pension reforms were part of the fiscal consolidation required for international bailouts (OECD 2011). The 2010 Greek pension reforms "cut every dimension possible," including by raising pension ages, tightening rules for early retirement, prolonging the contribution period, reducing benefit levels, and changing indexation and taxation of benefits (Casey 2012, 254). The public deficit and the weakened solvency status of pension funds also motivated other countries to contain both short- and long-term pension expenditures in order to reduce budget deficits and keep sovereign debts in check. In Canada, for instance, the debates on pension reforms were sparked by the damage inflicted by the GFC on its pension system, which strongly relied on voluntary private pensions, and by the deterioration of its fiscal situation caused by the high stimulus spending of 2009, which led to large federal deficits for the first time in more than a decade (Béland and Waddan 2011). These conditions paved the way for the welfare retrenchment that occurred soon after the Conservative Party won a majority in 2011.

Targeting current pensioners, some countries (such as Austria, Germany, Italy, Japan, Korea, Portugal, and Turkey) cut benefits across the board (i.e., with equal impacts on low and high earners), while others (e.g., Finland, France, Sweden, and the United Kingdom) either protected low earners from some or all of the benefit reductions or emphasized means-tested benefits for the same purpose. Some countries (such as Finland, Greece, and Slovenia) froze their pensions, and others (for instance, Sweden, Norway, and the United Kingdom) reduced them through less generous indexation policies (Lagoutte and Reimat 2013; OECD 2012b). In the United Kingdom, for instance, the switch from the Retail Price Index (RPI) to the Consumer Prices Index (CPI), which was introduced for the calculation of all benefits (not limited to pension benefits), enabled the state to save about £5.8 billion in 2014–15 (IFS 2010, cited in Heise and Lierse 2011, 509). When widely adopted in the context of austerity, suspending indexation rules or making them less favourable can ease the financial pressure of public schemes, on the one hand, and cause an immediate negative impact on the living conditions of pensioners and workers close to retirement, on the other (Hinrichs 2015).

Most OECD members have also begun to increase their pensionable age, or are planning to do so: sixty-seven – or higher – is the new sixty-five for about thirteen countries (OECD 2012c). Some (such as Italy and Denmark) are trying to link pensionable age with life expectancy, while in others (such as Austria, Estonia, the Slovak Republic, and the United Kingdom) pension age increases exceed the projected growth in life expectancy. Citing longevity as a core rationale, in 2012 Canada's Conservative government also raised the pensionable age from sixty-five to sixty-seven when it introduced a federal budget featuring the biggest cutbacks – a total CDN$5.1 billion in annual federal spending – since the mid-1990s (*Telegraph* 2012). Longer working lives are being encouraged by measures to strengthen the work incentive and discourage early retirement: for example, granting (in Sweden) older workers an in-work tax credit, exempting them (in Portugal) from contributions, tightening (in Greece, Hungary, Italy, and Austria) the conditions for receiving a pension early, and (in Poland) cancelling early-retirement privileges for some (Casey 2012; OECD 2012c). Although greater life expectancy makes later retirement appear "the most natural and best solution" when compared with other options, such as higher contributions and lower benefits, its effects may be very uneven, given that life expectancy varies greatly with geography, class, and gender (Holzmann 2013, 6; OECD 2012a).

To prevent a significant drop in living standard for future retirees that would otherwise be caused by cutbacks to public benefits, the OECD, like other international organizations (IOs), advocates private pensions as "essential" to fill the huge "pension gaps," the income difference between pre- and post-retirement (World Bank 2009; OECD 2011). In about a third of OECD countries the coverage of both mandatory and voluntary private pensions since the crisis has consistently been extended, for example, mandating occupational private pensions (e.g., in Israel and Norway), bringing the self-employed into mandatory private pensions (e.g., in Chile), or adopting the mechanism of automatic enrolment of individuals into private pensions (e.g., in New Zealand, Italy, and the United Kingdom) (OECD 2012b). While automatic enrolment in private pensions does allow people – with various degrees of difficulty – to opt out, in practice lower-income workers are more likely to do so for other reasons, such as to pay for education, health expenses, or family obligations, leaving them less economically secure in old age (Meyer 2013). Some countries (e.g., Chile, Poland, Germany, the United Kingdom, and the United States) also use regressive tax incentives to promote private pensions, but the tax relief mainly helps the highest earners, and low-income workers benefit little from it (Ginn and MacIntyre 2013; OECD 2012b). These trends indicate that while public transfer remains the primary source of old age income for most OECD countries, its redistributive role has increasingly diminished (OECD 2011).

In addition to longer working lives and individual savings, the OECD (2011) also explicitly recommended another way of achieving both adequacy (of pension income) and financial sustainability (of pension systems): "concentrate the efforts of public retirement provision on the most vulnerable" (10). Accordingly, some OECD members introduced measures to prevent and alleviate old age poverty, such as protecting low-earners from the full force of benefit cuts and offering more generous minimum-income benefits (OECD 2011). To promote the role of minimum pensions in protecting the most vulnerable, Canada, along with the Netherlands and New Zealand, was cited by the OECD (2011) as a shining example of having both lower public pension spending and a lower elderly poverty rate. Yet a more recent OECD report (2013a) shows that Canada was one of the few countries to have witnessed rising poverty among older people in the three years to 2010, proving the inadequacy of such a residualism-oriented safety net. Taken as a whole, such measures are not sufficient to address the structural issues of elderly poverty and pension inequalities. The broader role of the public pension system (not limited to a minimal level of protection) in wealth redistribution and poverty aversion among different pensioner groups remains very important. Despite the increase in the number of atypical (e.g., part-time) and unemployed workers – primarily temporary, young, female, and older ones – during and since the crisis, France's PAYG-based pension insurance system, for instance, remained focused on preserving a high level of protection for its core and standard workers in order to maintain corporate competitiveness (Lagoutte and Reimat 2013). A polarization is thus expected between those who qualify for full pensions and those who are entitled only to a means-tested solidarity allowance (ibid.).

Situating the pension reforms in the evolving history of pension privatization, these policy changes can be understood as a resilient, yet less visible alternative used by privatization advocates to pursue flexibility that remains within the paradigm. From 2005 to 2010 pension privatization, as a new pensions paradigm or orthodoxy, was interrupted by such economic and ideational shocks as the fiscal crisis relating to transition costs, a shift in the World Bank's perspective, and strenuous anti-privatization efforts outside the World Bank (Orenstein 2013; Borzutzky 2012). To survive the shocks, changes within the paradigm were advocated, including the "first-order" changes to the *parameters* or *settings* of the existing pension policies (e.g., changes in eligibility criteria, retirement age, and benefits calculation) and the "second-order" changes to the *instruments* of the policies (such as switching from mandatory to automatic enrolment with opt-outs) (Orenstein 2013). Although strengthening the role of minimum pensions in the post-GFC context can also be viewed as progress resulting from shifts within the leadership of pension reforms at a global level (in other words, the withdrawal of the World Bank and the increasing influence of the International Labour Organization), its paradoxical politics and implications, especially in the affluent welfare democracies, should also be critically considered. When commenting on the "social" regulation of private pensions in the United Kingdom and Germany, for instance, Leisering (2012) viewed social assistance or a minimum income scheme for pensioners as a new instrument of the state's economic intervention in private pensions. "If private provision fails, only the state may be available as a security net of last resort. We therefore conceive of financial safeguards as ways of regulating the pension markets" (ibid., 142).

The sovereign debt crisis that started in 2009 has produced a new setting in which IOs can effectively influence or coerce national pension reforms. In particular, the Troika (the EU, the IMF, and the European Central Bank) played a crucial role in facilitating and, in some cases, enforcing the implications of austerity measures (O'Brien and Zhang 2014). The austerity package, a central component of which has been substantial pension reform, was imposed on those most indebted countries, such as Greece, Portugal, Spain, and Ireland, to meet the loan conditions of the Troika (Stepan and Anderson 2014). The austerity agenda also pressured most governments to define such reforms as "an irrefutable necessity" in their national contexts (Hinrichs 2015, 26; van Kersbergen, Vis, and Hemerijck 2014). In his study of the post-2008 pension reforms in eight crisis-stricken European countries (including five OECD members), Hinrichs (2015) argued that the post-GFC pension reforms in these countries are not very different from those before

2008, apart from the magnitude of the former and the swift implementation of legislation due to increased pressure from the IOs.

It is also important to note the various degrees of diminution of the role of public pensions across the OECD. In 2012, for instance, in ten members – Australia, Iceland, Canada, Chile, Denmark, Korea, the Netherlands, Switzerland, the United Kingdom, and the United States – private pension arrangements already accounted for one-third of benefits provision to current retirees (OECD 2013b). Not surprisingly, most of these countries' pension systems have developed historically on the Beveridge model, in which the state provides a minimum benefit to prevent poverty among pensioners, while responsibility for old age security rests with individuals through private pension planning (Myles and Pierson 2001). Against the background of the GFC, however, the policy convergence across pension systems, as well as in other contexts (e.g., domestic politics, fiscal situations, and the economy), appears clear. A study of welfare state reforms between 2010 and 2012 in four welfare state regimes (liberal, United Kingdom; conservative, Germany; social democratic, Denmark; and hybrid, the Netherlands) revealed that pension retrenchment is prominent in their agendas, despite the variety of their specific reform measures (van Kersbergen, Vis, and Hemerijck 2014). Similarly, reducing public pension expenditures in the short and long run was found to be common throughout the reforms in eight European countries, each of which represents one of three types of pensions systems: Ireland with the Beveridge model; four southern European countries (including Greece) with social insurance schemes on the Bismarck model; and three CEE countries (including Hungary) that have adopted the multi-pillar pensions system promoted by the World Bank (Hinrichs 2015).

Population Aging, Austerity, and Pension Retrenchments: The Prospects for Old Age Security

In the OECD, the average proportion of the population aged over sixty-five years increased from less than 9 per cent in 1960 to 15 per cent in 2010, and it is expected to nearly double in the next four decades, reaching 27 per cent in 2050. In Japan, Korea, and Spain by that year it is expected to be nearly 40 per cent (OECD 2013b). Despite the GFC and the subsequent fiscal consolidation efforts that have put pressure on social protection systems, pension spending in most OECD countries is projected to increase in a way consistent with an aging population. As shown by figure 10.1, however, the growth of the population aged sixty-five and over is expected to outpace growth of public pension spending as a percentage of GDP from 2009 to 2025[4] in all OECD countries except Korea (OECD 2012c). The number of elderly in the OECD is expected to increase by 43 per cent during this period, but public pension expenditure is expected to increase by only 14 per cent of GDP (ibid.).

Long before the GFC, Pierson (1998) argued that the welfare states among affluent democracies face permanent austerity because of three major post-industrial transitions: the transition to massive, yet relatively stagnant service employment; the maturation of welfare states and the institutionalization of government commitments, including pensions; and rapidly aging populations, along with the shrinking working age (fifteen to sixty four years) population. These changes have instigated deep conflicts between slow economic growth and the increasing costs of the welfare system, and between budgetary strain and high public expectations of (and demand for) social protection. Despite these pressures, and given the strong electorate desire for social protection, Pierson (2002) ruled out the possibility of the collapse of welfare states and the rise of pension privatization as a form of radical retrenchment. Instead, path-dependent reforms are likely to be enacted through incremental cutbacks and adjustments. Witnessing the intense pressures on social programs caused by acute financial crises, combined with the steep decline of unions and the proliferation of centre-right governments, however, he suspects that "the real era of retrenchment begins now," after the almost four decades–long "era of austerity" (Pierson 2011, 22).

Despite the predominant econometric discourses on the expanding impacts of population aging on pension spending, the actual demographic trend was not well incorporated into the reform agenda of OECD governments (Fernandez 2010). Based on his study of sixty-two pension policy retrenchments in fourteen affluent democracies from 1981 to 2005, Fernandez (2010) concluded that under these circumstances, it is also important to understand population aging as a socio-political construction. On the one hand, economic crises and high public spending bring the pension issue back into the reform agenda. On the other, these unpopular reforms are ultimately enforced because policymakers are able to minimize the political costs by timing them strategically. Given that "population aging" has unanimously been

---

4 The projections do not account for reforms introduced after December 2011 (OECD 2012b).

Figure 10.1. Pension Spending Will Grow, but Not as Fast as Elderly Populations

- Expected change in the number of elderly (%) 2009-2025
- Expected change in the percentage of public pension expenditure in GDP (%) 2009-2025

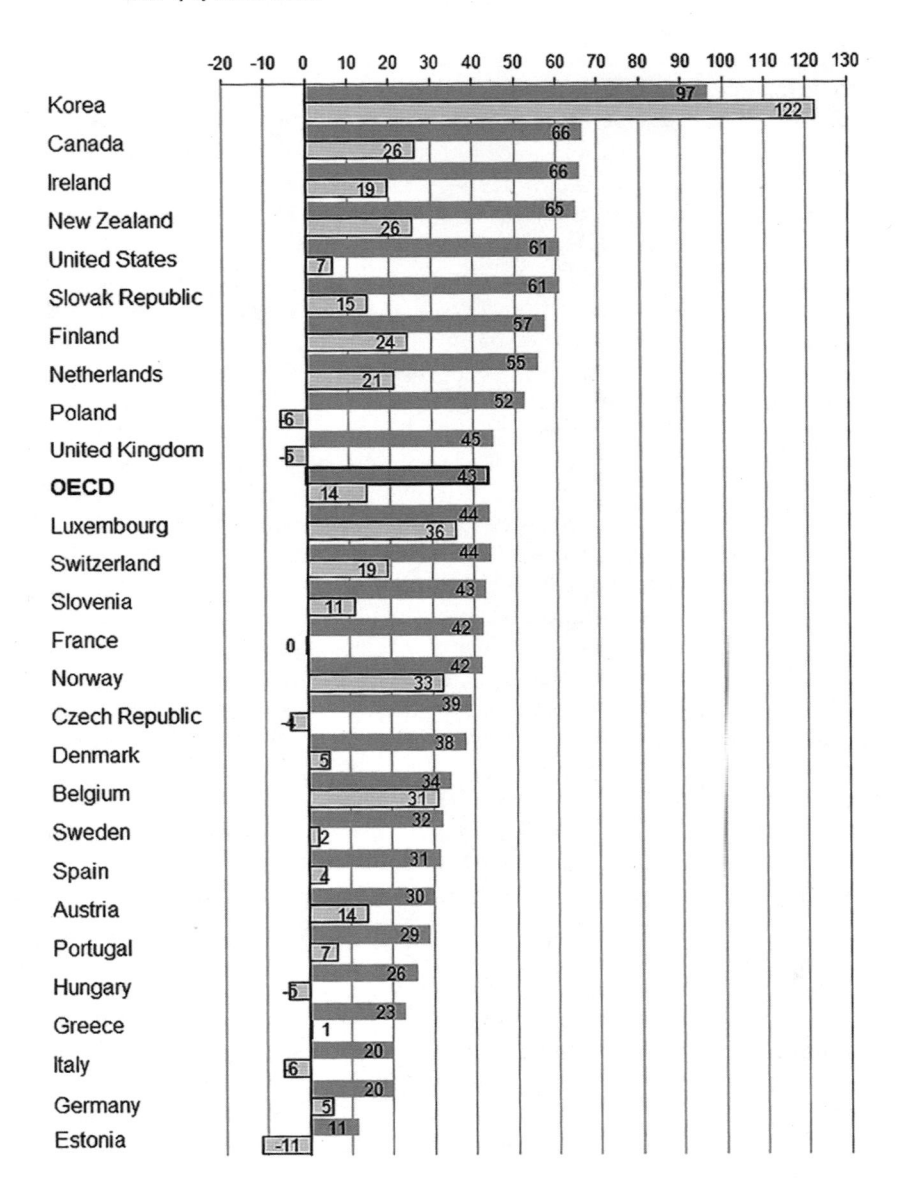

Country	Change in elderly (%)	Change in pension expenditure (%)
Korea	97	122
Canada	66	26
Ireland	66	19
New Zealand	65	26
United States	61	7
Slovak Republic	61	15
Finland	57	24
Netherlands	55	21
Poland	52	-6
United Kingdom	45	-5
OECD	43	14
Luxembourg	44	36
Switzerland	44	19
Slovenia	43	11
France	42	0
Norway	42	33
Czech Republic	39	-1
Denmark	38	-5
Belgium	34	31
Sweden	32	2
Spain	31	-4
Austria	30	14
Portugal	29	-7
Hungary	26	-5
Greece	23	1
Italy	20	-6
Germany	20	5
Estonia	11	-11

Source: OECD (2012a, 7), (note original)

Note: Public pensions refer to old-age and survivors cash benefits. Calculations are based on SOCX data and public pension projections from OECD Pensions Outlook 2012.

used to justify retrenchment by policymakers in countries with very different demographic situations, it becomes the way "to elude political blame for welfare retrenchment projects" (Fernandez 2010, 34). That is to say, post-GFC pension reforms are not simply the collateral damage, but a major target, of austerity policies, given that pensions – because of their high costs – have long been at the top of the reform agenda in all affluent democracies (Pierson 1998; Fernandez 2010). According to the OECD (2011), public pensions alone are often the largest single item among government expenditures, accounting for 17 per cent of total government spending on average.

In other words, the GFC and the subsequent economic crisis have indeed provided policymakers with both the motives for "radical retrenchments" and the ideal timing to achieve the impossible "harmony" between welfare retrenchment and enduring political popularity. Across the OECD countries, the grand narratives of austerity as an urgent necessity, and as "shared sacrifice and common purpose," have been institutionally generated and circulated to secure consent from the public (Clarke and Newman 2012; White House 2010, 6). Parallel to the unprecedented spending cuts (including cuts in the state pension), for example, the UK government has tried to present austerity as a moral necessity, as well as a nation-building project, by emphasizing the importance of maintaining solidarity in order to endure it (Cameron 2010; Clarke and Newman 2012). In the United States, similarly, austerity is reframed by the government as a noble duty that responsible citizens must fulfil for "a better future for *all* our fellow citizens" (White House 2010, 5–6; original emphasis). The moralizing austerity discourses have transformed a disaster into a triumph, and a crisis rooted in structural problems – such as the high-risk strategies of banks, regressive taxation, and the government's ongoing bailout of private sectors and the financial system – into one of the unwieldy and expensive welfare state (Clarke and Newman 2012; Peet 2011). In the name of austerity, the governments were able to mobilize "political resources sufficient to overcome organized opponents and other barriers to change" (Pierson 2002, 370).

Regardless of how questionable they are at balancing the short-term government budget, pension reforms in the OECD countries since the crisis have, to varying degrees, reconstructed both pension systems and old age income sources. In the mid-2000s in the OCED, public transfers (such as earnings-related and means-tested benefits), capital (mostly private pensions), and work, respectively accounted for, on average, about 60 per cent, 20%, and 20% of retirement income (OECD 2011). These recent pension reforms will, however, lead to 20–25 per cent smaller (on average) public pensions for future generations of retirees than under the old rules (OECD 2012b). Despite its "essential" role in filling the huge pension gaps, however, access to private pensions has long been unequal, based as it is on occupation, income, gender, "race," and so on; and it continues to disadvantage workers in low-paid and insecure employment (Lagoutte and Reimat 2013; Meyer 2013). By their nature, private pensions exacerbate the investment risks borne by the poor and their cumulative disadvantage (Frericks 2012). Furthermore, as a source of retirement income, work is becoming more important for older people, who have to stay in it longer to ensure adequate pension income. Making people work longer before they have enough to retire also overlooks the fact that some simply are unable to continue working (Biggs and Kimberley 2013).

Some OECD countries practise "asset-based" welfare (home ownership functioning as a pension) and acknowledge other income sources that "are not formally defined as pensions," including interfamily transfers (Elsinga, Quilgars, and Doling 2012; Doling and Ronald 2010; Holzmann and Hinz 2005, 83). Yet the experiences of Japan and Australia, two countries with high levels of home ownership, suggest that this approach is unsustainable if public support for a minimum pension is fragile, and that older households without access to home ownership are multiply disadvantaged (Hirayama 2010; Yates and Bradbury 2010). Even in Confucianism-influenced East Asia, where the intergenerational family used to undertake essential welfare functions, the family is no longer a pillar of old age security. Welfare systems there are gradually dropping family-based old-age support, and embracing state-led welfarism (Kwon and Holliday 2007; Kwon 2009). Public pensions in Korea and Taiwan were extended to cover the wider population during the democratization of the 1990s, but the unprecedented speed of population aging has made the financial sustainability of their old-age security systems increasingly problematic. The existing public schemes were therefore retrenched, and more options in private pensions to supplement pension income were developed (Shi and Mok 2012; Choi and Kim 2010).

Despite the World Bank's recent prudent approach to global pension policy, the OECD has largely carried on with both the former's conception of aging as a welfare burden and its approaches to pension privatization by promoting recalibration of the public-private pension mix in favour of the latter (OECD 2011, 2012b). Long before the GFC, as well, the EU advocated restructuring public pensions in response to aging populations and labour market changes, and recommended expanding private pensions (second and third pillars) to supplement public ones (Natali 2008; Stepan and Anderson 2014; Tholoniat 2010). While the 2010 Green Paper of the European Commission on pensions emphasized superior regulation of financial institutions to ensure the adequacy and security of funded pensions, the "sustainability" theme – with a focus on labour market participation – dominated its 2012 White Paper on pensions (EC 2010, 2012; Casey 2012). In Europe, the countries most afflicted by the economic crisis – such as Italy, Spain, Greece, and Portugal – are those with the lowest fertility rates and the most expensive pension systems (Hansen and Gordon 2014). Its demographic configuration has long been known, but the EU and its member states were still ill-prepared for the crisis. Although it is extremely challenging to further raise retirement ages, increase women's labour participation, or encourage a higher birth rate, migration as a solution to demographic decline has been neglected. Migrants are already "Europe's outsiders," but they are even more vulnerable in the context of austerity, because the pursuit of "low-cost" flexibility and competitiveness means further exploitation of the non-unionized, immigrant, and illegal labour market (1216). Given the overlapping and mutually reinforcing nature of economic, democratic, and demographic crises, the EU's demographics and official positions on migration are crucially relevant to its ability to address its fiscal and political challenges. At the level of member states, the capacity of a "demographically impoverished" country like Germany to continue to act as the core of the European economy is also questionable (1214).

Old age security in the OECD will continue to be shaped by demographic changes, pension arrangements, and politics at both national and supranational levels. Although pension outcomes do not depend solely on the relative proportions of public and private pensions in the pension mix, but rather on the overall arrangements of old age security (Leisering 2012), the general trend to cut public in favour of private pensions has aroused serious concerns about compromising public pensions' significance for social protection and poverty prevention among older people (Lagoutte and Reimat 2013; OECD 2013a). While population aging is a very complex, long-term social issue, austerity as the justification and, indeed, basis for the rationale for short-term "crisis responses" against the backdrop of finance capitalism has, to varying degrees, damaged welfare states' capacity to prepare for the impending demographic crisis.

Conclusion

We argue that under the rubric of post-GFC austerity, pension reforms in the context of the GFC are essentially a continuation of the pension retrenchments that emerged in individual countries in the 1980s, and of the pension privatization that has spread globally since the 1990s. These reforms – primarily about cutbacks to public benefits, the extension of private pensions, and further downloading the responsibility of old age security onto individuals – are "within-paradigm" changes that aim at "achieving a similar policy result by different means" (Orenstein 2013, 264). Through the GFC and subsequent rationalization of austerity measures, the paradigm of pension privatization, which abruptly paused in 2005 and until 2010, has now actually been revived, or reincarnated, through austerity. Premature as it may appear to maintain that austerity advocates have smuggled pension privatization in as an instrument to further their agenda, in 2011 two countries – the Czech Republic, an OECD country in Central Europe, and Malawi, a non-OECD country in Africa – adopted private pension systems (Orenstein 2013). In other words, the reinvention, rather than death of pension privatization is closer to reality now; and the public pension cuts have indeed left a big space for further expansion of private pensions at some point in the future.

With a further eroded role of public pensions in social redistribution among older people and across generations, pension reforms will intensify, and perpetuate the individual's cumulative advantage or disadvantage into old age: those with atypical employment are more vulnerable to old-age poverty than those with formal employment, given the former's limited access to all major retirement income sources (public benefits, capital, and work). Manipulating the discourses on "austerity" to canvass citizens' compliance with welfare retrenchment that directly hurts the lower-income groups undermines the political legitimacy of the democratic state; it also shifts the question of "the social" to "the realm of economics and the economic contribution of citizens" (Clarke and Newman 2012; Taylor-Gooby 2013; Zinn 2013, 320). The uneven distribution among social groups of the pain produced by pension reforms and the further disadvantage of the poor suggest that the austerity doctrine is just an attempt to humanize and socialize neoliberalism (Clarke and Newman 2012; OECD 2013a). Viewing it as relevant to class relations, Robinson (2013) diagnosed it as part of the recent stage of global capitalism, and thus to be included among capital's transfer mechanisms. While "[the] bailouts of transnational capital represent in themselves a transfer of devaluation of capital onto labor," austerity allows global capitalism and its political agents to claim the future wages of workers through public debt (664). In this light, austerity can be understood as an act of class warfare, through which income and wealth are redistributed from the poor to the rich (Levitas 2012).

The analysis in this chapter also uncovers the paradoxical relationships between Keynesian-like state interventions (such as stimulus spending and bailouts) and neoliberal-like welfare retrenchments, and between the significant vulnerability of private pensions during the crisis and IOs' advocacy of the further extension of private pensions as a "crisis response." It has become clear that from the perspectives of the policymakers who favour this paradigm, austerity (including in the area of pensions) also serves to stabilize, both financially and politically, the system, and to save it "from itself and from more radical responses from below" (Robinson 2013, 665), rather than to challenge global financial capital or prepare for major socio-economic risks (such as population aging). Collaborating with or being "hijacked" by finance capitalism, nation states, individually or collectively, "have to support financial institutions and the integrity of the financial system, for that is what keeps their economies going" (Peet 2011, 385). As a result, as illustrated by the pension reforms in the context of the GFC, we are witnessing the transformation of the "welfare state" (the state as the provider of old age security) into a regulatory state in social welfare (the "social" regulation of private pensions), and of "social citizens" (e.g., older citizens with access to social rights) into "consumer citizens" (such as older citizens divided by their access to private pensions) (Leisering 2011, 2012).

Austerity policies will also have broader and long-term socio-political impacts beyond the context of the GFC. The recent political demonstrations, strikes, and riots provoked by austerity measures not only undermine social stability and the legitimacy of the democratic state; they also signal increasing division among social groups (between, for example, public sector workers with good pensions and those with private or no pensions) and the erosion of social solidarity across classes and generations (Clarke and Newman 2012; Taylor-Gooby 2013). Both pension privatization and pension inequalities among older people are expected to advance in the years ahead, because the public pension systems continue to shrink, and citizens' reliance on private pensions and other non-state sources of retirement income keeps growing (Ebbinghaus, Orenstein, and Whiteside 2012; Orenstein 2011; Zhou 2014). Although historically a crisis is often a turning point, and a time of major welfare reforms, the OECD states' unanimous adoption of austerity as a standard policy response is an expression of their failure to challenge the status quo of global capitalism. It is also important to note that the pension system is interwoven with other systems (such as the economy, ideology, and political culture) in a society; therefore the pension reforms under discussion are not solely an unavoidable response to the crisis, but the result of politics (Clarke and Newman 2012; Lagoutte and Reimat 2013). The ability of further pension privatization to create old age security will be tested by economic turbulence and demographic challenges, as well as by the crisis of democracy: "The true struggle – the one analysts need to keep their eyes on, even as the locations of those struggles shift over time – is over how societies that combine democratic politics and market economies distribute economic and social risks and rewards" (Pierson 2011, 27).

REFERENCES

Béland, Daniel, and Alex Waddan. 2011. "Social Policy and the Recent Economic Crisis in Canada and the United States." In *Social Policy in Challenging Times: Economic Crisis and Welfare Systems*, ed. Kevin Farnsworth and Zoë Irving, 231–49. Bristol: Policy.

Biggs, Simon, and Helen Kimberley. 2013. "Adult Ageing and Social Policy: New Risks to Identity." *Social Policy and Society* 12 (2): 287–97. https://doi.org/10.1017/S1474746412000656.

Borzutzky, Silvia. 2012. "Pension Market Failure in Chile: Foundations, Analysis and Policy Reforms." *Journal of Comparative Social Welfare* 28 (2): 103–12. https://doi.org/10.1080/17486831.2012.655980.

Cameron, David. 2010. "We Must Tackle Britain's Massive Deficit and Growing Debt." SayIt. http://conservative-speeches.sayit.mysociety.org/speech/601466.

Casey, Bernard H. 2012. "The Implications of the Economic Crisis for Pensions and Pension Policy in Europe." *Global Social Policy* 12 (3): 246–65. https://doi.org/10.1177/1468018112455633.

Choi, Young-Jun, and Jin Wook Kim. 2010. "Contrasting Approaches to Old-Age Income Protection in Korea and Taiwan." *Ageing and Society* 30 (7): 1135–52. https://doi.org/10.1017/S0144686X10000413.

Clark, Gordon. 2000. *Pension Fund Capitalism*. New York: Oxford University Press.
Clarke, John, and Janet Newman. 2012. "The Alchemy of Austerity." *Critical Social Policy* 32 (3): 299–319. https://doi.org/10.1177/0261018312444405.
Dixon, Adam D. 2008. "The Rise of Pension Fund Capitalism in Europe: An Unseen Revolution?" *New Political Economy* 13 (3): 249–70. https://doi.org/10.1080/13563460802302560.
Doling, John, and Richard Ronald. 2010. "Home Ownership and Asset-Based Welfare." *Journal of Housing and the Built Environment* 25 (2): 165–73. https://doi.org/10.1007/s10901-009-9177-6.
Drahokoupil, Jan, and Stefan Domonkos. 2012. "Averting the Funding-Gap Crisis: East European Pension Reforms since 2008." *Global Social Policy* 12 (3): 283–99. https://doi.org/10.1177/1468018112455653.
Ebbinghaus, Bernhard, Mitchell A. Orenstein, and Norman Whiteside. 2012. "Governing Pension Fund Capitalism in Times of Uncertainty." *Global Social Policy* 12 (3): 241–5. https://doi.org/10.1177/1468018112456765.
Elsinga, Marji, Deborah Quilgars, and John Doling. 2012. "Where Housing and Pensions Meet." *International Journal of Housing Policy* 12 (1): 1–12. https://doi.org/10.1080/14616718.2012.651296.
European Commission (EC). 2010. *Green Paper: Towards Adequate, Sustainable and Safe European Pension Systems*. Brussels: Sustainable and Safe European Pension Systems.
– 2012. *White Paper: An Agenda for Adequate, Safe, and Sustainable Pensions*. Brussels.
Fernandez, Juan J. 2010. "Economic Crises, High Public Pension Spending and Blame-Avoidance Strategies: Pension Policy Retrenchments in 14 Social-Insurance Countries, 1981–2005." MPIfG Discussion Paper 10/9. http://www.mpifg.de/pu/mpifg_dp/dp10-9.pdf.
Frericks, Patricia. 2012. "Funded Pensions and Their Implications for Women and Migrant Workers." *Global Social Policy* 12 (3): 342–4. https://doi.org/10.1177/1468018112456766d.
Ginn, Jay, and Kate MacIntyre. 2013. "UK Pension Reforms: Is Gender Still an Issue?" *Social Policy and Society* 12 (1): 91–103. https://doi.org/10.1017/S1474746412000504.
Hansen, Randall, and Joshua C. Gordon. 2014. "Deficits, Democracy, and Demographics: Europe's Three Crises." *West European Politics* 37 (6): 1199–222. https://doi.org/10.1080/01402382.2014.929336.
Heise, Arne, and Hanna Lierse. 2011. "The Effects of European Austerity Programmes on Social Security Systems." *Modern Economy* 2 (4): 498–513. https://doi.org/10.4236/me.2011.24055.

Hinrichs, Karl. 2015. "In the Wake of the Crisis: Pension Reforms in Eight European Countries." ZeS-Arbeitspapier 01/2015. https://www.econstor.eu/bitstream/10419/106399/1/815227388.pdf.

Hirayama, Yosuke. 2010. "The Role of Home Ownership in Japan's Aged Society." *Journal of Housing and the Built Environment* 25 (2): 175–91. https://doi.org/10.1007/s10901-010-9183-8.

Holzmann, Robert. 2013. "Global Pension Systems and Their Reform: Worldwide Drivers, Trends and Challenges." *International Social Security Review* 66 (2): 1–29. https://doi.org/10.1111/issr.12007.

Holzmann, Robert, and Richard P. Hinz. 2005. *Old-Age Income Support in the Twenty-First Century: An International Perspective on Pension Systems and Reform.* Washington, DC: World Bank. https://doi.org/10.1596/0-8213-6040-X.

Kwon, Huck-Ju. 2009. "The Reform of the Developmental Welfare State in East Asia." *International Journal of Social Welfare* 18 (1): S12–S21. https://doi.org/10.1111/j.1468-2397.2009.00655.x.

Kwon, Soonman, and Ian Holliday. 2007. "The Korean Welfare State: A Paradox of Expansion in an Era of Globalisation and Economic Crisis." *International Journal of Social Welfare* 16 (3): 242–8. https://doi.org/10.1111/j.1468-2397.2006.00457.x.

Lagoutte, Christine, and Anne Reimat. 2013. "Public or Private Orientation of Pension Systems in the Light of the Recent Financial Crisis." *Review of Social Economy* 71 (3): 306–38. https://doi.org/10.1080/00346764.2012.761755.

Leisering, Lutz. 2011. *The New Regulatory State: Regulating Pensions in Germany and the UK.* Basingstoke, UK: Palgrave Macmillan.

Leisering, Lutz. 2012. "Pension Privatization in a Welfare State Environment: Socializing Private Pensions in Germany and the United Kingdom." *Journal of Comparative Social Welfare* 28 (2): 139–51. https://doi.org/10.1080/17486831.2012.655984.

Levitas, Ruth. 2012. "The Just's Umbrella: Austerity and the Big Society in Coalition Policy and Beyond." *Critical Social Policy* 32 (3): 320–42. https://doi.org/10.1177/0261018312444408.

McBride, Stephen, and Jessica Merolli. 2013. "Alternatives to Austerity? Post-Crisis Policy Advice from Global Institutions." *Global Social Policy* 13 (3): 299–320. https://doi.org/10.1177/1468018113499980.

Meyer, Madonna Harrington. 2013. "Changing Social Security in the US: Rising Insecurity?" *Social Policy and Society* 12 (1): 135–46. https://doi.org/10.1017/S1474746412000486.

Myles, John, and Paul Pierson. 2001. "The Comparative Political Economy of Pension Reform." In *The New Politics of the Welfare State*, ed. P. Pierson,

305–33. New York: Oxford University Press. https://doi.org/10.1093/01982 97564.003.0011.
Natali, David. 2008. *Pensions in Europe, European Pensions: The Evolution of Pension Policy at National and Supranational Level*. Brussels: Peter Lang S.A.
– 2011. "Pensions after the Financial and Economic Crisis: A Comparative Analysis of Recent Reforms in Europe." ETUI Working Paper 2011.07. https://doi.org/10.2139/ssrn.2221827.
O'Brien, Robert, and Falin Zhang. 2014. "Structural Adjustment for the North." In *Orchestrating Austerity*, ed. Donna Baines and Stephen McBride, 21–33. Halifax: Fernwood Publishing.
Orenstein, Mitchell A. 2011. "Pension Privatization in Crisis: Death or Rebirth of a Global Policy Trend?" *International Social Security Review* 64 (3): 65–80. https://doi.org/10.1111/j.1468-246X.2011.01403.x.
– 2013. "Pension Privatization: Evolution of a Paradigm." *Governance: An International Journal of Policy, Administration and Institutions* 26 (2): 259–81. https://doi.org/10.1111/gove.12024.
Organisation for Economic Co-operation and Development (OECD). 2006. *Pension Markets in Focus*. OECD Publishing. http://www.oecd.org/finance/private-pensions/37528620.pdf.
– 2007. *Pension Markets in Focus*. OECD Publishing. http://www.oecd.org/finance/private-pensions/39509002.pdf.
– 2008. *Pension Market in Focus*. OECD Publishing. http://www.oecd.org/finance/private-pensions/41770561.pdf.
– 2011. "Pensions at a Glance 2011: Retirement-Income Systems in OECD and G20 Countries." http://www.oecd.org/pensions/pensionsataglance.htm.
– 2012a. "Health at a Glance: Europe 2012." OECD Publishing. http://www.oecd-ilibrary.org/social-issues-migration-health/health-at-a-glance-europe-2012/life-expectancy-and-healthy-life-expectancy-at-age-65_9789264183896-5-en.
– 2012b. "Pensions Outlook 2012." OECD Publishing. http://www.oecd-ilibrary.org/finance-and-investment/oecd-pensions-outlook-2012_9789264169401-en.
– 2012c. *Social Spending during the Crisis: Social Expenditure (SOCX) Data Update 2012*. OECD Publishing. http://www.oecd.org/els/soc/OECD2012SocialSpendingDuringTheCrisis8pages.pdf.
– 2013a. "Crisis Squeezes Income and Puts Pressure on Inequality and Poverty: New Results from the OECD Income Distribution Database." OECD Publishing. http://www.oecd.org/els/soc/OECD2013-Inequality-and-Poverty-8p.pdf.

- 2013b. *Pensions at a Glance 2013: OECD and G20 Indicators*. OECD Publishing. http://www.oecd.org/pensions/public-pensions/OECDPensionsAtAGlance2013.pdf.
- 2013c. *Pension Markets in Focus: 2013*. OECD Publishing. http://www.oecd.org/pensions/PensionMarketsInFocus2013.pdf.

Peet, Richard. 2011. "Inequality, Crisis and Austerity in Finance Capitalism." *Cambridge Journal of Regions, Economy and Society* 4 (3): 383–99. https://doi.org/10.1093/cjres/rsr025.

Peters, John. 2012. "Neoliberal Convergence in North America and Western Europe: Fiscal Austerity, Privatization, and Public Sector Reform." *Review of International Political Economy* 19 (2): 208–35. https://doi.org/10.1080/09692290.2011.552783.

Pierson, Paul. 1998. "Irresistible Forces, Immovable Objects: Post-Industrial Welfare States Confront Permanent Austerity." *Journal of European Public Policy* 5 (4): 539–60. https://doi.org/10.1080/13501769880000011.

- 2002. "Coping with Permanent Austerity: Welfare State Restructuring in Affluent Democracies." *Revue française de sociologie* 43 (2): 369–406. https://doi.org/10.2307/3322510.
- 2011. "The Welfare State over the Very Long Run." ZeS-Arbeitspapier 02/201. https://www.econstor.eu/dspace/handle/10419/46215.

Robinson, William I. 2013. "Global Capitalism and Its Anti-'Human Face': Organic Intellectuals and Interpretations of the Crisis." *Globalizations* 10 (5): 659–71. https://doi.org/10.1080/14747731.2013.828966.

Shi, Shih-Jiunn, and Ka-Ho Mok. 2012. "Pension Privatisation in Greater China: Institutional Patterns and Policy Outcomes." *International Journal of Social Welfare* 21:S30–S45. https://doi.org/10.1111/j.1468-2397.2012.00875.x.

Stepan, Matthias, and Karen M. Anderson. 2014. "Pension Reform in the European Periphery: The Role of EU Reform Advocacy." *Public Administration and Development* 34 (4): 320–31. https://doi.org/10.1002/pad.1690.

Taylor-Gooby, Peter. 2013. "Riots, Demonstrations, Strikes and the Coalition Programme." *Social Policy and Society* 12 (1): 1–15. https://doi.org/10.1017/S1474746412000401.

Telegraph. 2012. "Canada Raises Retirement Age to 67." 30 March. http://www.telegraph.co.uk/news/worldnews/northamerica/canada/9175139/Canada-raises-retirement-age-to-67.html.

Tholoniat, Luc. 2010. "The Career of the Open Method of Coordination: Lessons from a 'Soft' EU Instrument." *West European Politics* 33 (1): 93–117. https://doi.org/10.1080/01402380903354122.

van Kersbergen, Kees, Barbara Vis, and Anton Hemerijck. 2014. "The Great Recession and Welfare State Reform: Is Retrenchment Really the Only Game

Left in Town?" *Social Policy and Administration* 48 (7): 883–904. https://doi.org/10.1111/spol.12063.
White House. 2010. *The Moment of Truth*. Washington, DC: National Commission on Fiscal Responsibility and Reform.
World Bank. 1994. *Averting the Old Age Crisis: Policies to Protect the Old and Promote Growth*. Oxford: Oxford University Press.
– 2008. *The World Bank Pensions Conceptual Framework*. Washington, DC: World Bank. https://openknowledge.worldbank.org/handle/10986/11139.
– 2009. *Pensions in Crisis: Europe and Central Asia Regional Policy Note*. http://documents.worldbank.org/curated/en/651741468302962293/pdf/584600ESW0ENGL1Box353801B01PUBLIC1l.pdf.
Yates, Judy, and Batcheldern Bradbury. 2010. "Home Ownership as a (Crumbling) Fourth Pillar of Social Insurance in Australia." *Journal of Housing and the Built Environment* 25 (2): 193–211. https://doi.org/10.1007/s10901-010-9187-4.
Zhou, Yanqiu Rachel. 2014. "Austerity Now, Poverty Later?: Pensions." In *Orchestrating Austerity*, ed. Donna Baines and Stephen McBride, 120–33. Halifax: Fernwood Publishing.
Zinn, Jens O. 2013. "Risk, Social Inclusion and the Life Course: Review of Developments in Policy and Research." *Social Policy and Society* 12 (2): 319–33. https://doi.org/10.1017/S1474746412000711.

PART THREE

Class, Resistance, Alternatives

Introduction: The Old Strategies Don't Work, so What's Possible?

BRYAN M. EVANS AND STEPHEN MCBRIDE

The third and final section of this volume, as the subtitle suggests, is concerned with the class dimensions of austerity, and specifically the intersections of class politics and forms of resistance with the construction of alternatives to austerity and neoliberalism itself. The four chapters presented here address key questions of political strategy and public policy in an effort to assess the possibilities beyond the dictum that "There Is No Alternative." What is striking throughout this section, and the cohering theme, is the role of political agency in constructing political reality. That agency may be that of the ruling elite or of the working class, but it is the ideational and structured terrain of conflict that gives rise to neoliberalism or its alternatives. The contributions here canvass a rich and varied range of cases, including the defeat of the social dimension of the European Union's integration project, the challenges of sustaining and transforming resistance into a viable political and economic alternative, the role of social democracy as an enabler of austerity through social pacts and multi-class competitiveness alliances, and, given the de-politicization of class politics, the stresses liberal democracy faces as centrifugal forces push those most affected by globalization to the radical Left and, more importantly, the Far Right nationalist parties, which express an increasingly uncomfortable new authoritarianism in Europe.

Hermann's lead chapter reminds us that the crisis that arrived in Europe in 2007–8 was an American-born banking crisis and spread to Europe through the purchase of toxic debt by European banks. Magically, deftly, the gamble of mortgage loan entrepreneurs was, from 2010 forward, transformed into a crisis of public finance as states moved to socialize these massive bad debts and provide relief to the financial system. What ensued would, if we were talking about less-developed countries, be termed structural adjustment, but this time it was Europe that would impose austerity on itself, including public sector wage and pension cuts, job losses, and privatization of public assets, thus bringing about the demise of the European social model. Not only was the decades-old ambition to extend social democracy through the apparatus of the European Union destroyed, but the EU's central purpose as a relay to fortify the neoliberal project became firmly embedded and apparent. In no small way, this exercise of agency by the machinery of the EU, as witnessed most clearly in the case of Greece, embedded and set in motion a competitive austerity logic. Faced with a conflict between the imposition of neoliberal certainties like austerity, and the expression of democratic objection to it at the national level, there seemed little doubt that European elites were prepared to jettison democracy. Similarly, the EU contributed to the refashioning of European social democracy as an important ally in neoliberalization. This process was not confined to the European Union. Graefe and Rioux, as well as Evans, examine the limits of social democracy and the challenges presented to a social democratic project in the context of a reanimated neoliberalism. The case of the Canadian province of Quebec, whose broadly social democratic and nationalist party, the Parti Québécois, has been in and out of government, is studied by Graefe and Rioux. In their critique of the Quebec Left project, resisting austerity is alone insufficient. To be sustained, resistance must be accompanied by a vision, a program for an alternative political and economic framework. The inherent tension that Graefe and Rioux trace is one where the political struggle is fought on two fronts – the immediate political necessity of resisting neoliberalism and austerity here and now, while in parallel building the ideological capacity to imagine what is to be built in its place. As the chapters by Evans and Burron point out, this tension is not new to the Left, but the failure to develop real alternatives has certainly been apparent in the current crisis. Paralleling the difficulties of the political Left, there has been a rise in authoritarian populism on the Right nationalist parties, which now participate in governments or are posing a serious electoral threat in a number of European countries. Although the radical Left has enjoyed a resurgence in some countries, it has not been the primary beneficiary of anti-globalization, anti-austerity sentiment, and electoral mobilization.

Thus we live in the denouement of the golden age of democratic capitalism. The post-war class compromises no longer align to political and structural reality. The centre of liberal democracy wobbles and perhaps is yet to fall. The old is dying, as Gramsci wrote and is now so often cited, and the new cannot yet be born. Indeed.

11 From Austerity to Structural Reform: The Erosion of the European Social Model(s)

CHRISTOPH HERMANN

Introduction

The Great Recession began as an American crisis, or more precisely as a crisis of the American housing market and related collateralized debt. As a result of the interconnectedness of the global financial system, the economic problems quickly spread to Europe. Here the crisis arrived as a banking crisis, as several European banks had purchased "toxic" American debt obligations. In a number of European countries, the tightening of financial markets and the "credit squeeze" caused by the banking crisis revealed homemade problems in European housing markets and led to the bursting of national real estate bubbles. This put even more strain on the banking sector and demanded even larger bank rescue packages to stabilize the financial sector. The rescue packages put additional pressure on public budgets, which were already stretched because of falling tax income and rising social expenditure. Some countries, including most notably Greece, were ill-prepared for such a situation, as they had failed to reduce public debt in the boom years that preceded the crisis. From 2010 onwards, the crisis mainly became a European fiscal one with public deficits in some countries approaching unsustainable levels. The response to the budgetary crisis was the largest austerity program in European post-war history. However, in several cases, including the economic adjustment programs imposed on those countries that received emergency funding from the other euro countries and from the International Monetary Fund, austerity was coupled with structural reforms. Structural reforms differ from regular austerity measures inasmuch as their main purpose is not the consolidation of public budgets; instead their main focus is the elimination of rigidities, obstructing the free play of market forces (Hermann 2014, 112). Since structural rigidities were seen as a major cause of the crisis and as an obstacle to renewed growth, the European Commission subsequently increased efforts to enforce structural reforms across the European Union through the newly established economic governance framework.

This chapter argues that in the European Union austerity was closely linked to the promotion of structural reforms and that the adoption of structural reforms led to an erosion of the European social model(s). The chapter also shows that the consequences of the changes include growing poverty and inequality. The first section describes the shift from economic stimulation to austerity, followed by an overview of structural reforms in labour markets and social systems introduced in the crisis countries as part of the economic adjustment programs. The next section presents the main components of the new EU economic governance framework and points to the similarities between the structural reforms adopted in the crisis countries and the country-specific reforms proposed as part of the European semester. The following sections discuss the impact of austerity and structural reforms on the European social model(s) as well as on poverty and inequality in the crisis countries. The chapter ends with some concluding remarks.

From Economic Stimulation to Austerity

Apart from saving failing banks, European governments initially responded to the crisis with Keynesian-inspired deficit spending. The European Commission initiated an economic stimulus plan (officially called the European Economic Recovery Plan) in November 2008 with a total volume of €200 billion, 85 per cent coming from national budgets, or an equivalent of 1.5 per cent of EU-wide GDP (EC 2008; Cameron 2012). The goal was to provide "a major injection of purchasing power into the economy, to boost demand and stimulate confidence" (EC 2008, 2). Economic injections, together with automatic stabilizers (e.g., increases in spending for unemployment benefits) resulted in substantial fiscal stimuli in 2008–9 accounting for 14.4 per cent of GDP in Ireland, 13.0 per cent in Spain, 9 per cent in Greece, and 8.7 per cent in the United Kingdom (ibid., 10). The total expansionary effect of the changes in revenues and expenditures in the EU reached 5.9 per cent of GDP in those two years. As such it was significantly higher than the expansionary effect in Japan (3.9 per cent) but also substantially lower than the US stimuli (8.4 per cent) (ibid.).

Table 11.1. Social Protection Spending

	Cuts in unemployment benefits	Reduced duration of unemployment benefits	Reduced access to unemployment benefits
Greece	X	X	
Hungary	X	X	X
Ireland	X	X	
Italy			X
Latvia			X
Portugal	X	X	X
Romania	X		
Spain	X		X

Source: Compiled from various resources.

However, from 2009 onwards, deficit spending gave way to austerity policies (Theodoropoulou and Watt 2011; Bieling 2012). With the exception of Sweden, all member states adopted austerity packages, and in some cases several packages in a row. The largest fiscal effort was made by Greece (23 per cent of GDP), followed by Latvia (16 per cent), Ireland (14 per cent), Romania (13 per cent), Cyprus (13 per cent), and Spain (11 per cent). Until 2013, average fiscal consolidation across the EU amounted to 4.7 per cent of GDP (Darvas et al. 2014, 11).

Welfare programs became a major target of budget consolidation (Heise and Lierse 2011; Hermann 2015a). While in 2009 social protection expenditure increased by 7 per cent in the EU-27, expenses essentially stagnated in 2010 and then declined in 2011 and 2012 – in spite of continuously high and partly rising unemployment (Bontout and Lokajickova 2013, 14–17). The cuts were particularly severe in countries that were hit hardest by the crisis (and had comparably less-developed welfare states before the crisis). A major target of cuts was unemployment benefits (see table 11.1). Greece, for example, cut unemployment benefits by 22 per cent. In Portugal, a reduction in unemployment benefits was coupled with a shortening of the period for which unemployment benefits can be obtained. Hungary reduced entitlement to unemployment benefit to three months while introducing the obligation to perform community work (Hermann 2015b, 3–4).

Cuts affected not only cash benefits but even more so the provision of public services. Between 2009 and 2012, expenses for in-kind-benefits fell by 29 per cent in Greece, 19 per cent in Portugal, 16 per cent in Ireland, and 12 per cent in Spain (EC 2012a, 38). In Greece, Portugal,

Ireland, and Latvia, cuts in health-care spending led to hospital closures (Tzannatos and Monogios 2013, 278; Rato 2013, 436; Masso and Espenberg 2013, 116), while Spanish hospitals responded to the budget fallout with downsizing and temporary shutdowns (de Bastillo Munoz and Anton 2013, 536).

In addition to welfare cuts, austerity also affected the public sector and here especially the public sector workforce. The Greek government released plans to cut the public workforce by 25 per cent, mainly by not replacing workers who retire or otherwise leave the public sector (Tzannatos and Monogios 2013, 268). As of mid-2013, the actual reduction amounted 10 per cent (Darvas et al. 2014, 119). After an initial ban on all new hiring, only every tenth public sector employee is to be replaced in Greece. In Romania this applies to every seventh and in Italy to every fifth worker (Hermann 2014, 113–14). While the job cuts were justified by the need to shrink "inflated" state bureaucracies, many of the cutbacks actually took place in health care, education, and social services (Vaughan-Whitehead 2013).

Public sector job cuts were complemented by wage cuts and pay freezes. In Greece, the public sector workforce is not only destined to shrink by a third; those who keep their jobs will on average also receive about a third less pay. Substantial public sector wage cuts were also introduced in Portugal, Romania, Latvia, and Hungary (Hermann 2014, 114). Rather than cutting pensions, the Irish and Cypriot governments increased the pension contributions of its public sector workers.

From Austerity to Structural Adjustment

Austerity early on was coupled with structural reforms. In countries that were dependent on external support to remain solvent, structural reforms were a condition for emergency funding and as such agreed upon in the so-called memoranda of understanding signed by the crisis countries and the representatives of the European Commission, the European Central Bank, and the International Monetary Fund (also known as the Troika). Greece, Ireland, Portugal, and Cyprus borrowed money from the other euro partners through a newly established emergency funding scheme, while Latvia, Hungary, and Romania applied for regular IMF loans to cope with payment difficulties. Spain avoided state funding but applied for emergency funding for its banking system and subsequently also agreed to introduce structural reforms. Formally Italy did not apply for emergency funds, but informally accepted a series of conditions demanded by the ECB in exchange for the support of the struggling Italian banking system.[1] The promotion of structural reforms also became a major goal of the new economic governance framework established in response to the crisis (see below). And while the new president of the European Commission, Jean-Claude Juncker, acknowledged the need for investments to kick-start growth in Europe, he and his administration continues to emphasize the obligation to introduce structural reforms to make growth sustainable.[2]

The demand for structural reforms is not entirely new. In Europe it goes back to the establishment of the common market. In the 1993 White Paper on growth, competitiveness, and employment, the European Commission (1993, 48–9) already emphasized the "need to accompany and accelerate structural change instead of trying to slow it down." The authorities in the member states should therefore identify and remove "remaining barriers and obstacles to the successful implementation of strategies for change" (ibid.). Chang (2003, 45–6) has summarized the rationale behind structural reforms: "This view sees all rules, regulations and institutions other than the ones necessary for market exchange to occur (e.g., property rights, contract laws) as rigidities which prevent the smooth operation of market forces." The sluggish industrial adjustments of certain European countries in the 1980s are therefore understood as the result of institutional rigidities, preventing the movement of factors of production into more profitable activities. Accordingly, in this perspective, "countries with less state intervention and other institutional rigidities are likely to have better records of growth and structural change" (ibid.).

The adoption of structural reforms subsequently was also an important element in the Lisbon Strategy, adopted in 2000 with the objective to make the European Union the most competitive economic area in the world

---

1 The Italian newspaper *Corriere della Sera* revealed a letter sent by the ECB president to the Italian prime minister laying out which measures the ECB expects Italy to adopt in the face of the crisis (*Financial Times* 2011).
2 The so-called Juncker Plan proposed by the new president of the commission in fall 2014 includes investments in the range of €315 billion in areas such as infrastructure, renewable energy, and research and development. However, only €21 billion is supposed to come from public sources. The public money should be used mainly to allocate an additional €294 billion from private investors.

by 2010.[3] With the Lisbon process the focus of structural reforms increasingly shifted from the liberalization of product and service markets to the deregulation of employment and social systems. "Structural policies that foster the smooth adjustment of prices and wages are essential to ensure that euro area Member States have the capacity to rapidly adjust to shocks ... Policies that increase the responsiveness of labour markets ... are particularly important in this respect" (EC 2005, 16).

While the demand for structural reforms is not new, it has become increasingly popular during the crisis as several commentators, and especially the representatives of the Troika, have branded structural rigidities as the major cause of the growth problems in Southern Europe. Greece, for example, is criticized for having "rigid product and labour markets" which "unless tackled in earnest ... may undermine the Greek economy's capacity to adjust to the current situation" (EC 2010, 6). In this view the lack of structural reforms in Southern European countries has resulted in mounting current-account deficits, built up since the introduction of the euro in 2002 (which had rendered the traditional method of maintaining competitiveness by depreciating Southern European currencies obsolete). According to this narrative, unreasonably high wage increases pushed up unit labour costs in the years before the crisis, which, in turn, made Southern European industries increasingly uncompetitive. Structural reforms are presented as a solution to this problem, because they facilitate a downward adjustment of wages and other social expenses to market rates. While there are other interpretations of the crisis and other proposals to solve the problems of the common currency area, the Troika insisted on internal devaluation enforced through economic adjustment programs (Armingeon and Baccaro 2012).[4] The following section gives an overview of structural reforms in labour markets and welfare systems introduced in the nine EU member states subjected to formal or informal adjustment.

Pensions

Public pensions are part of the welfare system, and given the fact that they account for a major part of social spending in European countries,

---

3 The Lisbon Strategy failed bitterly and was replaced in 2010 by the "Europe 2020" plan.
4 As the problem was not only excessively high wages in Southern Europe but also excessively low wages in Germany; some commentators have suggested EU-wide wage coordination to avoid economic imbalances.

Table 11.2. Pension Reforms

Pensions	Adjustment programs	Country-specific recommendations
Increase of retirement age	Greece, Italy, Spain, Ireland, Hungary, Romania, Latvia	Austria (women), Bulgaria, Czech Republic, Spain, Croatia, Malta, Netherlands, Romania (women), Slovenia (women)
Reduction of pension payments	Greece, Portugal, Hungary	
Limitation of access to early retirement and invalidity pensions	Italy, Portugal, Hungary	Austria, Belgium, Bulgaria, Finland, Croatia, Lithuania, Luxembourg, Slovenia
Extension of contribution periods	Greece, Spain, Italy, Romania	Cyprus
Extension of calculation periods	Greece, Spain	
Automatic adjustment of life expectancy	Greece, Spain, Italy	Austria, Belgium, Cyprus, Czech Republic, Spain, Finland, Lithuania, Luxembourg, Malta, Netherlands, Poland, Slovenia, Slovakia

Source: Hermann (2015c).

they were also a major target of budget consolidations (see table 11.2; for the connection between austerity and pension reform, see Zhou and Shi in this volume). However, while some measures have an immediate effect on public spending and result in short-term savings, other elements of the reform need time to become effective. Among the short-term measures introduced in the crisis countries were pension cuts and pension freezes. In Portugal and Greece, pension reforms included an elimination of parts of the thirteenth and fourteenth pension payments, while Hungary cancelled the thirteenth payment (Hermann 2015b, 4–5). In contrast, long-term measures include the increase of the retirement age, extension of contribution periods, and new calculation methods. These measures not only save costs in the coming years or decades; they also amount to a greater individualization and hence differentiation of pension entitlements. Except for Portugal, all countries covered in this analysis have increased the retirement age during the crisis (ibid.). Usually the changes are introduced gradually over several years. In Italy, however, the retirement age of women employed in the public sector was raised from sixty-one to sixty-five between 2010 and 2011 and then to sixty-six in the following year (ibid.). In addition, three countries have introduced "automatic stabilizers," which assess the life expectancy every three or five years and adjust the retirement age to changes in life expectancies (ibid.).

While the regular retirement age is increasing, access to early retirement and disability pensions has been restricted. Five countries have also extended the contribution period that makes retirees eligible for a minimum or full pension (Hermann 2015b). In Latvia the minimum period of contributions has been increased from ten to twenty years (ibid.). Greece and Spain have also extended the contribution periods upon which the pension payments are calculated. In Greece, calculations are now based on the entire employment career instead of the best five of the last ten years. The expected result of such changes is lower pension payments (ibid.).

Labour Markets

As mentioned before, labour markets play an essential role in structural adjustment programs (see table 11.3). Perceived labour market rigidities are reduced through the promotion of non-standard employment and the weakening of employment security (Hermann 2014, 115–16). Greece, Romania, and Portugal have relaxed regulations of fixed-term employment. In Portugal the maximum length of fixed-term contracts has been increased from six to thirty-six months (ibid.). In Spain temporary jobs already accounted for 35 per cent of all jobs before the crisis. The government initially responded to the crisis and growing unemployment by adopting legislation according to which temporary jobs would automatically be transformed into permanent jobs after two years of uninterrupted employment. However, this regulation was later abandoned and any restrictions on temporary employment lifted (124). Spain has also introduced a new employment contract that lasts for two years and pays 75–80 per cent of the national minimum wage. However, workers under these contracts not only earn less, they can also be laid off at any time. Other countries achieved a similar situation by extending probation periods. In Greece, the probation period now lasts for twelve instead of two months (115–16).

Changes have also made it easier to lay off workers. In Greece, workers have to be given notice in three instead of five months; in Spain the period has been reduced from thirty to fifteen days. Layoffs have become not only easier, but also cheaper. In Greece, Spain, and Portugal severance pay has been halved (Hermann 2014, 116–17). In the

Table 11.3. Labour Market Reforms

Labour markets	Adjustment programs	Country-specific recommendations
Promotion of non-standard (flexible) employment (fixed-term employment, part-time employment, new contracts, etc.)	Greece, Spain, Romania, Portugal	Czech Republic, Poland, Malta, Lithuania
Reform of employment security (reduction of severance pay, shortening of notice periods, changes in the definition of fair and unfair dismissals)/reduction of labour market rigidities	Greece, Spain, Italy, Hungary, Romania, Portugal	France, Italy, Lithuania, Netherlands, Slovenia

Source: Hermann (2015c).

European Union there are specific regulations for mass layoffs (including, for example, special consultation rights), which tend to make them more expensive than individual dismissals. In order to reduce costs for companies, the Greek government has increased the minimum number of workers that need to be made redundant simultaneously to qualify for a mass lay off (ibid., 117).

While redundancy rules have been relaxed, it has become more difficult for employees to fight unfair dismissals. In Spain, the definition of fair dismissals has been expanded. It is now sufficient for companies to refer to technological or economic reasons to justify a fair dismissal. Even if an employee can prove an unfair dismissal, the right to be reinstated has been restricted. In Italy, a planned labour market reform will continue to grant victims of an unfair dismissal financial compensation. However, they will no longer be able to return to their former job. The Hungarian government refrained from altering the definition of unfair dismissals, but reduced the maximum fine from thirty-six to twelve months' wages (Hermann 2014).

Collective Bargaining

Another major target of structural reforms is collective bargaining, and the major goal is decentralization (see table 11.4). In the EU crisis countries, decentralization has been imposed in three different ways: First, countries have abandoned national or sector-wide collective

Table 11.4. Collective Bargaining Reforms

Collective bargaining	Adjustment programs	Country-specific recommendations
Decentralization of bargaining systems (suspension of national agreements, suspension of favourability principle, approval of exceptions and divergences)	Greece, Spain, Ireland, Italy, Romania	Belgium, Italy, Portugal
Weakening of collective bargaining (suspension or reduction of extension procedures, limitation of "after effect")	Greece, Spain, Hungary, Portugal, Romania	
Reform of wage indexation	Cyprus	Belgium, Cyprus, Luxembourg, Malta
Minimum wage cuts/reform of minimum wage setting	Greece, Ireland	Bulgaria, France, Romania, Slovenia
Wage moderation/nominal wage increases equal or below real productivity gains		Belgium, Bulgaria, Croatia, Finland, Spain, Italy, Slovenia

Source: Hermann (2015c).

agreements. While in Romania the government suspended the national collective agreement through legislative reform, in Ireland the social partnership on which the national agreement was based collapsed after the government opened an existing agreement and unilaterally cut public sector wages (Hermann 2014, 117–18). Second, countries have eradicated the favourability principle. The favourability principle is a cornerstone of many bargaining systems and stipulates that, in the case of multiple collective agreements, those regulations prevail that grant the most favourable conditions for workers. As a result, company agreements have an effect only when they contain better conditions than multi-employer agreements. In Greece and Spain this is no longer the case. Since the crisis, company agreements apply even if they provide for poorer employment conditions than sector or regional agreements (ibid.). Third, countries have promoted decentralization by granting exceptions and accepting deviation from sector-wide standards. Italy adopted a reform that allows for a wide range of derogations in essential bargaining matters (ibid.). As a result, the number of collective agreements in Spain has decreased by 60 per cent and the number of workers covered by collective agreements by 40 per cent (Schulten and Müller 2015, 348–9).

Decentralization and flexibilization of bargaining were complemented by a weakening of bargaining institutions and trade union representation. In the past, collective bargaining systems in the Southern European countries greatly relied on so-called extension procedures. With these procedures governments extended the scope of an agreement negotiated between a trade union and an employer organization to cover an entire sector, even though only a minority of the workers in the sector belonged to the trade union. While Greece has suspended all extension procedures, Portugal introduced a reform according to which signing parties must at least 50 per cent of the workforce in the sector (Hermann 2014, 118). In Portugal, subsequently, the number of workers covered by collective agreements declined by almost 90 per cent between 2008 and 2013 (Schulten and Müller 2015, 348–9).

Bargaining systems were also weakened through the elimination or shortening of the "after effect," in which regulations continue to apply after an agreement has expired. By doing so, they encourage employers to negotiate a new contract. In Greece, the "after effect" was halved from six to three months (ibid.). In some countries trade union power has been curbed by the changes. In Greece, company agreements can now be signed by staff representatives without trade union affiliation. In smaller companies they can do so despite the presence of designated trade unionists (Voskeritsian and Kornelakis 2011, 18–19). The combination of company bargaining and non-union bodies signing the agreements has resulted in an average 22 per cent decrease in collective wages (Georgiadou 2012). Romania has introduced tougher criteria for trade unions to qualify as representative organizations that have the right to sign collective agreements, while Hungary abolished the tripartite national forum for the discussion of wage developments (Schulten and Müller 2015, 348).

In some countries, changes in collective bargaining was linked to changes in wage-setting systems. In Greece and Ireland, the governments reduced minimum wages during the crisis – in the case of Greece by ignoring a social partner agreement on a moderate wage increase. Several countries introduced temporary freezes on minimum wages, while Cyprus suspended wage indexation – a mechanism with which wages are automatically adjusted to inflation (Hermann 2014, 114–15).

Economic Governance of Austerity and Structural Adjustment

The Troika played a pivotal role in imposing austerity and structural adjustment in the European crisis countries. However, the European

Union as such also responded to the crisis by introducing an institutional reform that gives the European Commission greater powers to pressure and in some cases even police member states to continue exercising austerity and to adopt structural reforms (Degryse 2012; Oberndorfer 2012). The new economic governance framework contains three major components: First, a yearly cycle of analysing member states' budgetary and (macro)economic performances as well as commenting on national reform efforts – in the form of country-specific recommendations. Second, a procedure for countries violating the fiscal rules set out in a tightened Growth and Stability Pact.[5] Third, a new procedure for countries whose economies are believed to be out of proportion, because some national indicators lay outside the range allowed by a specifically designed macroeconomic scoreboard.[6] The different components of the governance framework are integrated in the European semester, which establishes a specific sequence of the different but complementing procedures. Furthermore, while the first component has also been described as a pre-emptive arm – member states are monitored and urged to introduce reforms – the latter two present the commission's corrective arm. In both cases, member states can ultimately be fined if they repeatedly violate the rules and ignore the commission's proposals to correct the insufficiencies.[7]

The country-specific recommendations show strong similarities with the structural reforms implemented in the crisis countries under the supervision of the Troika. Pension reforms, for example, were not only top on the list of the economic adjustment programs introduced during the crisis; they also figure prominently in the European semester. For nine member states the commission recommends an increase in the legal retirement age, in three countries an equalization of the existing

---

5 The Growth and Stability Pact limits yearly deficits of EU member states to a maximum of 3 per cent of GDP and the accumulated debt to a maximum of 60 per cent of GDP. Especially since the crisis, a large number of countries exceed the limit for accumulated debt.
6 The scoreboard include indicators such as current account balance; net international investment position; real effective exchange rate; export market shares; labour unit costs; house prices; private sector credit flow; private sector debt; general government debt; unemployment rate; and total financial sector liabilities.
7 In the case of the excessive deficit procedure, member states can be ordered to make a deposit of between 0.2 and 0.5 per cent of national GDP, which after two years can be turned into a fine; in the case of the macroeconomic imbalance procedure, the fines for euro zone members can amount to 0.1 per cent of GDP.

retirement ages of men and women. Fourteen countries are advised to introduce an automatic mechanism that adjusts the retirement age to the growing life expectancy, while ten are urged to limit access to early retirement and disability pensions and to adjust the effective retirement age to the legal threshold (Hermann 2015c).

The flexibilization of labour markets is also a recurrent theme in the crisis programs and in the country-specific recommendations. However, the recommendations are usually less specific than the measures listed in the economic adjustment programs. Exceptions include Lithuania, where the commission recommends adaptation of legislation to promote temporary work; Poland, where the government is advised to extend the probation period; and the Czech Republic, Finland, and France, which are urged to create conditions for a greater use of part-time work. In addition to promoting atypical forms of employment, commission staff also urge member states to reduce labour market rigidities by reforming employment protection regulation and by reviewing dismissal rules and procedures (ibid.). In the case of France, the commission recommends a review of "selected aspects of employment protection legislation ... in particular related to the administrative procedure for individual dismissals" (EC 2012b, 7).

Member states are also urged to reform their collective bargaining systems to allow for greater decentralization of wage setting (Hermann 2015c). In the case of Belgium, commission staff advise the government to introduce opt-out clauses from sector-wide bargaining. In Portugal, where the limitation of extension clauses has already resulted in a 90 per cent drop in bargaining coverage, the commission recommends a "firm-level temporary suspension of collective agreements" (EC 2014, 7). In Italy, where the government has already adopted new legislation that allows for opt-out clauses in essential bargaining matters such as wages and working hours, the commission still sees more room for flexibilization: "Wages in Italy are still not sufficiently responsive to productivity developments. In this area, further progress in promoting the shift to wage bargaining towards the company level would play an important role" (EC 2013a, 35).

Commission staff are particularly troubled with the practice of wage indexation (Hermann 2015b). As mentioned before, wage indexation mechanisms automatically adjust wages to inflation and thereby protect the real value of wages (European Foundation 2010). Essentially all member states that have wage indexation systems are advised to suspend or substantially modify them, with the aim that wages can decrease in real terms. In the case of Belgium, there is the following recommendation: "Reform the wage setting system including wage indexation in particular by taking structural measures … to ensure that wage setting is responsive to productivity developments, reflects local differences in productivity and labour market conditions, and provides automatic corrections when wage evolution undermines cost-competitiveness" (EC 2013b, 7).

The promotion of productivity-oriented wage settlements is also a popular demand in the European semester (Hermann 2015c). However, the commission does not support a productivity-oriented wage policy in the traditional sense – i.e., wage increases that cover inflation and account for the progress in productivity. Instead the commission suggests that nominal wage increases should not exceed real productivity gains (Schulten and Müller 2015, 339). According to this formula, productivity-oriented wages can actually result in real wage losses. In addition, recommendations frequently urge governments to support wage moderation and to set minimum wages at a level where they do not endanger the competitiveness of national industries. Even though the analysis did not result in a recommendation, commission staff have noted that the Swedish practice of solidaristic wage policy – in which lower wages are increased more than higher wages – results in relatively high wage levels at the lower end of the wage scale, which, in turn, distorts labour markets and results in structural unemployment (EC 2011).

In sum, *structural reform* as introduced in the EU crisis countries and as recommended in the European semester is a code word for neoliberal restructuring. As such, it nicely complements the dogma of austerity, which limits economic choices to supply-side growth strategies. Structural reforms are also an attack on many of the achievements of labour movements during the post-war period. In labour markets and social systems, the removal of market rigidities means less employment security, lower wages, and more years to be worked before retirement – which then has to be spent with less retirement income.

The Erosion of the European Social Model(s)

Structural reforms as adopted during the crisis and as proposed in the European semester have a profound impact on the European social model(s). The invention of the term *European social model* is commonly attributed to Jacques Delors. As president of the European Commission, the social democrat Delors introduced the idea of a European social model in the early 1980s to distinguish Europe from the United States (Hermann and Hofbauer 2007, 126). As such, the European social model initially was a political intervention, a fiction launched to strengthen the rather fragile European identity and to propose an alternative to the ultraliberal capitalisms of American and, from the late 1970s onwards, British imprinting. However, it was not long before an academic debate emerged on the usefulness of the concept. Analytically, the term raises a number of difficulties. According to quantitative indicators such as (per capita) GDP, inequality, or unemployment, differences within the EU-27 are actually larger than differences within the United States. Institutionally, Europe combines different varieties of capitalism as well as different welfare state models (Schmidt 2009).

While acknowledging national diversity in Europe, Hyman (2005, 11) argues that the common features in continental Western Europe are strong enough to distinguish a European social model from an American model of largely deregulated labour markets, and a Japanese model of management-dominated company employment relations. According to Hyman (ibid.), Europe is unique, inasmuch as there are "substantial limits to the ways in which labour (power) can be bought and sold." These limits constrain the autonomy of employers to "a degree unknown elsewhere in the world" (ibid., 11). The limits are set primarily through comprehensive employment protection legislation, as well as encompassing and centralized collective bargaining structures. Schiek (2013, 4) makes a similar argument when she notes, "Despite all these differences, European national social and economic models converge on a common core." More specifically, European social models "share the idea that there is a responsibility of societies for the individuals' well-being, which in particular inform policies of transfer payments for periods of loss incomes and correcting labour markets through legislation and collective bargaining" (ibid.).

For Hermann and Mahnkopf (2010, 318), the "essence of the European Social Model ... is the comparatively high level of de-commodification provided by the institutionally and politically highly disparate European social systems." De-commodification is understood as *relative* independence from markets (315–16). De-commodification is achieved primarily through extensive employment regulation, constraining labour market transactions, and access to non-market income, allowing workers to exist at least for some time without selling their labour power. The exceptional degree of de-commodification in core European countries is mirrored in a relatively low proportion of poverty and a high degree of equality. By promoting market forces and by weakening employment and social security, the structural reforms introduced during the crisis precisely undo the de-commodifying features of the European social model(s). Schmitter (2012, 5) is therefore entirely right to state that "the vision of Europe as the site of an alternative form of 'social capitalism' has been seriously tarnished by the current crisis."

The Effects of Austerity and Structural Reform

Contrary to the logic of austerity and structural reforms, budget consolidations and the elimination of market rigidities have so far failed to stimulate a phase of stable economic growth in the European crisis countries. As of 2016, three of the nine European countries subjected to conditional reforms has made up for the loss of GDP incurred since the start of the crisis. Greece has experienced six consecutive years of economic contraction and lost 29 per cent of its GDP between 2008 and 2016. In addition Italy, Cyprus, and Portugal will also likely face a "lost decade" following the start of the crisis.

Shrinking GDP was accompanied by growing unemployment. In Greece and Spain, the unemployment rates exceeded 25 per cent during the crisis and the youth unemployment rates reached 50 per cent. In 2016, the unemployment rate was still 23.6 per cent in Greece and 19.6 per cent in Spain. Even in Ireland, which recorded the fastest recovery among the crisis countries, it was still higher in 2016 than in 2008. Only in Hungary and Romania unemployment declined to the pre-crisis level.

Growing unemployment numbers also pushed up poverty rates. Poverty in the EU is usually measured as the share of the population that lives with 60 per cent or less of the country's median income. Between 2008 and 2013 the proportion grew in six out of the nine reform countries, in Greece as much as 3 per cent. However, relative poverty is not an adequate measure, since median incomes have also fallen during the crisis, which means that individuals may earn less than before the crisis but no longer qualify as poor (Hermann 2015b, 10–11). Eurostat measures absolute poverty as the share of population that experiences severe material deprivation. Here a different picture emerges: except for Romania, the proportion of deprived citizens increased in all nine countries, and it almost doubled in Greece, Spain, Italy, and Ireland.

In addition, austerity and structural adjustment have also fuelled inequality. The Gini coefficient and the share of the top 20 per cent of the income scale (as proportion of total income) has increased (between 2008 and 2013) in six of the nine countries under observation – the latter by as much as 17 per cent in Hungary, 14 per cent in Cyprus, and 12 per cent in Greece and Italy. In Ireland, Greece, Spain, and Italy, furthermore, the bottom income decile lost more between 2007 and 2010 than the top income decile. In the case of Spain, the top 10 per cent lost only 1 per cent of their income, while the bottom 10 per cent lost 14 per cent (OECD 2013). Hence as the OECD (2014, 22–3) notes, in Europe "lower income households have lost greater proportions of their income than the better-off ... particularly in the hardest hit countries like ... Greece, Ireland, Italy and Spain."

Conclusion

In sum, the crisis has resulted in a fortification of neoliberalism in the European Union and in a weakening of the European social model(s) (Hermann 2007; Hermann and Mahnkopf 2010). While initially there were signs of a moderate shift to a more Keynesian-inspired economic policy, the neoliberal forces quickly gained momentum and enforced austerity and structural adjustment as the adequate response to the crisis. In this framework it was not financial capital, causing the crisis, which had to pay for the costs of the economic downturn, but workers and poor families. As van Apeldoorn (2013, 197) notes, "The crisis is perceived by the European ruling class and much of its political elite as an opportunity to accelerate so-called structural reforms and thus deepen neoliberal discipline. Here the 'fiscal myth' serves as a stick to beat the welfare state with and to entrench and deepen the so-called reforms, that is, the neoliberal restructuring which the EU institutions, implementing an agenda set by Europe's capitalist class elite, have been pursuing since the early 1990s."

How can we explain the deepening of neoliberalism in Europe, in spite of the link between neoliberal deregulation and the financial roots of the crisis? One reason is the lack of democratic accountability. Several of the crisis measures were introduced by emergency decrees, avoiding the need to gain approval by the national parliaments, or by so-called technocratic governments installed because the elected leaders declined to take responsibility for the adjustment programs (Contiades and Fotiadou 2013). In addition the introduction of the new economic governance framework has further strengthened the role of the European Commission in developing and imposing European policy guidelines

(Oberndorfer 2012). The European Commission is not the result of democratic elections, but of a complicated and opaque power-sharing process. As such it cannot be voted out by frustrated voters.[8] Because of the lack of accountability and of political control, the commission staff, filled with neoliberal ideology from Europe's leading business and law schools, can continue to propose the same neoliberal remedies against a wall of empirical evidence that shows that the remedies are not working. Given the persistence of neoliberal ideas in Europe, the EU, indeed, looks more and more like Hayek's vision of an economic union (Hayek 1939; Streeck 2014). The chief character of this interstate federation, however, is not the reduced scope of state interventions, as has Hayek predicted. As shown in the previous pages, the Troika had no problems in enforcing austerity and structural adjustment in the crisis countries, and the commission wants to impose similar reforms as part of the European semester. The chief character is rather the freedom of politicians and bureaucrats to ignore popular demands and the consequences of one's policies in a system that is formally based on free and universal elections.

REFERENCES

Armingeon, Klaus, and Lucio Baccaro. 2012. "Political Economy of Sovereign Debt Crisis: The Limits of Internal Devaluation." *Industrial Law Journal* 41 (3): 254–75. https://doi.org/10.1093/indlaw/dws029.
Bieling, Hans-Jürgen. 2012. "EU Facing the Crisis: Social and Employment Policies in Times of Tight Budgets." *Transfer: European Review of Labour and Research* 18 (3): 255–71. https://doi.org/10.1177/1024258912448591.
Bontout, Olivier, and Terezie Lokajickova. 2013. "Social Protection Budget in the Crisis in the EU." European Commission Working Paper 1/2013, Brussels.
Cameron, David. 2012. "European Fiscal Responses to Great Recession." In *Coping with the Crisis: Government Reactions to the Great Recession*, ed. Nancy Bermeo and Jonas Pontusson, 91–129. New York: Russell Sage Foundation.

---

8 Since the 2014 elections to the European Parliament there is an informal agreement that the largest party in the parliament nominates the president of the Commission. However, the nominee has still to be confirmed by the heads of states and in the elections voters still vote for national parties which form European political associations but do not take the responsibility for European policies.

Chang, Ha-Joon. 2003. *Globalisation, Economic Development and the Role of the State*. London: Zed Books.

Contiades, Xenophon, and Alkmene Fotiadou. 2013. "How Constitutions Reacted to the Financial Crisis." In *Constitutions in the Global Financial Crisis: A Comparative Analysis*, ed. Xenophon Contiades, 9–62. Farnham: Ashgate.

Darvas, Zslot, Huettls Pia, Carlos De Sousa, Alessio Terzi, and Olga Tschekassin. 2014. "Austerity and Poverty in the European Union." Report prepared for the European Parliament.

de Bastillo Munoz, Rafael, and Jose-Ignacio Anton. 2013. "Those Were the Days My Friend: The Public Sector and Economic Crisis in Spain." In *Public Sector Shock: The Impact of Policy Retrenchment in Europe*, ed. Daniel Vaughan-Whitehead, 511–44. Cheltenham: Edward Elgar.

Degryse, Christophe. 2012. "The New European Economic Governance." Working Paper ETUI Brussels. https://doi.org/10.2139/ssrn.2202702.

European Commission. 1993. "Growth, Competitiveness, Employment: The Challenges and Ways Forward into the 21st Century." White Paper, COM (93) 700, 5 December, Brussels.

– 2005. "Integrated Guidelines for Growth and Jobs (2005–2008)." 141 final, 4 December, Brussels.

– 2008. "A European Economic Recovery Plan." COM 800 final, 26 November, Brussels.

– 2010. "The Economic Adjustment Programme for Greece." *European Economy Occasional Papers* 61.

– 2011. "Commission Staff Working Paper. Assessment of the 2011 National Reform Programme and Convergence Programme for Sweden." SEC 735 final, 6 July, Brussels.

– 2012a. "Brussels: Employment and Social Developments in Europe."

– 2012b. "Recommendation for a Council Recommendation on France's 2012 National Reform Programme." COM 313, 30 May, Brussels.

– 2013a. "Macroeconomic Imbalances Italy 2013." *European Economy Occasional Papers* 138, April.

– 2013b. "Recommendation for a Council Recommendation on Belgium's 2013 National Reform Programme." COM 251 final, 5 May, Brussels.

– 2014. "Recommendation for a Council Recommendation on Portugal's 2014 National Reform Programme." COM 423 final, 2 June, Brussels.

European Foundation for the Improvement of Living and Working Conditions. 2010. "Wage Indexation in Europe." Background paper. Dublin.

Financial Times. 2011. "ECB Letter Shows Pressure on Berlusconi." 29 September.

Georgiadou, Penny. 2012. "Company-Level Employment Contracts Trigger Wages Drop." Eurofound. https://www.eurofound.europa.eu/eiro/2012/06/articles/gr1206019i.htm.

Hayek, Friedrich. 1939. "The Economic Conditions of Interstate Federalism." *New Commonwealth Quarterly* 5:131–49.

Heise, Arne, and Anna Lierse. 2011. *Budget Consolidation and the European Social Model: The Effects of European Austerity Programmes on Social Security Systems.* Berlin: Friedrich Ebert Foundation.

Hermann, Christoph. 2007. "Neoliberalism in the European Union." *Studies in Political Economy* 79 (1): 61–90. https://doi.org/10.1080/19187033.2007.11675092.

– 2014. "Structural Adjustment and Neoliberal Convergence in Labour Markets and Welfare: The Impact of the Crisis and Austerity Measures on European Economic and Social Models." *Competition & Change* 18 (2): 111–30. https://doi.org/10.1179/1024529414Z.00000000051.

– 2015a. "Crisis and Social Policy in Europe." *Global Social Policy* 15 (1): 82–5. http://journals.sagepub.com/doi/abs/10.1177/1468018114566360a.

– 2015b. "Crisis, Structural Reform and the Dismantling of the European Social Model(s)." *Economic and Industrial Democracy* 38 (1): 51–68. https://doi.org/10.1177/0143831X14555708.

– 2015c. "Vergangenheit, Gegenwart und Zukunft struktureller Reformen in Europa." Research report. Vienna: Chamber of Labour.

Hermann, Christoph, and Ines Hofbauer. 2007. "The European Social Model: Between Competitive Modernisation and Neoliberal Resistance." *Capital and Class* 93:125–39.

Hermann, Christoph, and Birgit Mahnkopf. 2010. "Still a Future for the European Social Model?" *Global Labour Journal* 1 (3): 314–30.

Hyman, Richard. 2005. "Trade Unions and the Politics of the European Social Model." *Economic and Industrial Democracy* 26 (1): 9–40. https://doi.org/10.1177/0143831X05049401.

Masso, Jann, and Kerly Espenberg. 2013. "Early Application of Fiscal Austerity Measures in the Baltic States." In *Public Sector Shock: The Impact of Policy Retrenchment in Europe*, ed. Daniel Vaughan-Whitehead, 84–133. Cheltenham: Edward Elgar.

Oberndorfer, Lukas. 2012. "Hegemoniekrise in Europa – Auf dem Weg zu einem autoritären Wettbewerbsetatism." In *Zwischen autoritärem Etatismus und europäischem Frühling*, ed. Forschungsgruppe Staatsprojekt Europa, 50–72. Münster: Westfälisches Dampfboot.

OECD. 2013. *Crisis Squeezes Income and Puts Pressure on Inequality and Poverty.* Paris: OECD.

– 2014. "Society at a Glance 2014." Paris: OECD.
Rato, Helena. 2013. "Portugal: Structural Reforms Interrupted by Austerity." In *Public Sector Shock: The Impact of Policy Retrenchment in Europe*, ed. Daniel Vaughan-Whitehead, 411–48. Cheltenham: Edward Elgar.
Schiek, Dagmar. 2013. "The EU's Socio-economic Model(s) and the Crisi(e)s: Any Perspectives?" In *The EU Economic and Social Model in the Global Crisis: Interdisciplinary Perspectives*, ed. Dagmar Schiek, 1–22. Farnham: Ashgate. https://doi.org/10.2139/ssrn.2386217.
Schmidt, Ingo. 2009. "New Institutions, Old Ideas: The Passing Moment of the European Social Model." *Studies in Political Economy* 84 (1): 7–28. https://doi.org/10.1080/19187033.2009.11675044.
Schmitter, Phillipe. 2012. "Classifying and Anomaly." *New Left Review* 73:19–27.
Schulten, Thorsten, and Torsten Müller. 2015. "European Economic Governance and Its Intervention in National Wage Development and Collective Bargaining." In *Divisive Integration: The Triumph of Failed Ideas in Europe Revisited*, ed. Steffen Lehndorff, 331–64. Brussels: ETUI.
Streeck, Wolfgang. 2014. *Buying Time: The Delayed Crisis of Democratic Capitalism*. London: Verso Books.
Theodoropoulou, Sotiria, and Andrew Watt. 2011. "Withdrawal Symptoms: An Assessment of the Austerity Package in Europe." Working Paper ETUI, Brussels. https://doi.org/10.2139/ssrn.2221838.
Tzannatos, Zafiris, and Yannis Monogios. 2013. "Public Sector Adjustment Admits Structural Adjustment in Greece: Subordinate, Spasmodic and Sporadic." In *Public Sector Shock: The Impact of Policy Retrenchment in Europe*, ed. Daniel Vaughan-Whitehead, 259–99. Cheltenham: Edward Elgar.
van Apeldoorn, Baastian. 2013. "The European Capitalist Class and the Crisis of Its Hegemonic Project." In *Socialist Register 2014*, ed. Leo Panitch, Greg Albo, and Vivek Chibber, 189–206. London: Merlin.
Vaughan-Whitehead, Daniel. 2013. "Public Sector Shock in Europe: Between Structural Reforms and Quantitative Adjustment." In *Public Sector Shock: The Impact of Policy Retrenchment in Europe*, ed. Daniel Vaughan-Whitehead, 1–42. Cheltenham: Edward Elgar.
Voskeritsian, Horen, and Andreas Kornelakis. 2011. "Institutional Change in Greek Industrial Relations in an Era of Fiscal Srisis." Hellenic Observatory Papers on Greece and Southeast Europe 52. http://www2.lse.ac.uk/europeanInstitute/research/hellenicObservatory/pdf/GreeSE/GreeSE52.pdf.

12 Austerity of Imagination: Quebec's Struggles in Translating Resistance into Alternatives

PETER GRAEFE AND X.H. RIOUX

Introduction

For austerity to be "manufactured," resistance to austerity needs to be contained and alternatives neutralized. Work on responses to austerity has, for all its quality, tended to have three shortcomings: First, it focuses on the post-2008 period, and so tends to accentuate particular policy decisions (and defensive reactions thereto) over longer-term political exchanges. Second and relatedly, it tends to emphasize resistance, downplaying the distinction between resistance and alternatives, and by extension whether those responses simply slow the implementation of austerity, or instead lay some grounds for superseding it. Finally, it may capture themes such as street protest, the strategies of social democratic parties, or the limitations of corporatist management of crisis, but more rarely does it consider all of them in their interactions.

In an attempt to overcome these shortcomings, we apply Dufour's (2009, 2013) Political Action Diamond, which is a heuristic tool for mapping the strategies of actors as they fit around various poles of political activity, to Quebec. While we pay particular attention to the past ten years, our timescale reaches back to the mid-1990s, recognizing that the theme of the unsustainable nature of Quebec's debt situation, while present in the 1970s and 1980s, came to the fore in the context of the mid-1990s' Quebec deficit and declining federal transfers. In considering the various attempts to counter or resist austerity at each point of the Diamond, we capture some elements of alternatives, although generally an argument could be made that politics has grown more defensive and less efficient recently. Taken as a whole, an enduring question has been the translation of resistance into alternative policies through partisan politics, and here again, recent developments suggest a narrowing strategic imagination.

Austerity, Resistance, Alternatives

In this chapter, we take a particular view of resistance and alternatives to austerity. Our understanding of resistance is simple: it involves opposing attempts to curtail state activity, particularly in social and economic domains, in the name of strict standards of budgetary rigour. Resistance seemingly takes on a particular relevance when this need for rigour is advanced in a language of crisis and urgency: cuts need to be made, or else the state will be bankrupt or unable to borrow at less than usurious rates. Yet austerity seems to have become a "normal," resilient, and recurrent part of neoliberal statecraft, beyond moments of crisis and recession (McBride and Whiteside 2011).

Indeed, less radical understandings of austerity also point to its "normality." For instance, Schäfer and Streeck's *Politics of Austerity* (2013) points to a prolonged period where the maturation of universalist welfare state programs, coupled with demographic change, puts constant pressure on budgetary balances and constrains the capacity of contemporary political actors to free up resources for new initiatives. This argument shares the pessimistic tone of earlier work on post-industrial trilemmas, where demographic change and the shift to a service economy meant that welfare states maintaining budgetary balance could at best achieve *either* full employment *or* increased equality, but not both (Iversen and Wren 1998).

Without necessarily endorsing the determinism of this argument, it does suggest that a politics of resistance to austerity is one of managing state retrenchment, to the extent that the pressure of austerity is continuous. As a result, the question of alternatives becomes crucial. Despite persistent budgetary pressures, there can be innovations at the margins of every budget. The capacity to affect the form those innovations take, or to reform policies to help sustain alternatives to austerity, becomes a crucial attribute for those seeking to transform resistance into alternatives. Or, to look at this from the opposite angle, the process of manufacturing austerity necessarily runs up against resistance. Even where austerity prevails, this confrontation may leave a sedimentation of compromises that might be used to construct alternate paths (Crouch 2001). It may also change the shape austerity takes, as it may have to work with and around projects built on different logics (Newman 2013).

In other words, we take seriously Clarke's (this volume) reflections on Raymond Williams's concepts of the *residual* and the *emergent*. In any conjuncture, there will be issues from the past that persist and cannot be resolved by the dominant approach, just as there will be emergent resistances and challenges to the dominant paradigm. This means that actors can work "creatively with institutional materials" from various institutional legacies, including ones that may be relatively submerged at the moment, in order to craft new practices and institutions (Crouch and Keune 2005, 84–5). This opens the door to consider a broader range of strategic agency, recognizing that dominant projects are themselves contingent, contradictory, and based on alliances that can be disaggregated and delegitimized (Cox and Nilsen 2014, 181).

In this light, developing resistance and especially alternatives to austerity requires some sort of larger vision of a different political economy (be it a light reform to the existing one or a more dramatic departure), the pragmatic ability to break the achievement of that vision into a series of more incremental stages, and perhaps most importantly the strategic willingness to build political alliances with the capability to gain state power and implement these incremental changes.

In thinking this way, we adopt an analytical posture with a sense of time and politics that is different from those that focus on specific moments of contested budgetary consolidation. In taking a longer view, we can get a better sense of whether resistance in fact provided openings for alternatives. Small things that might escape notice in the sound and fury of protests, or as side deals in corporatist bargaining, can be better incorporated, providing a greater sense of nuance and possibilities. Taking a longer-term timescale, we are also pushed to consider how resistance and alternatives to austerity are developed in a variety of political forums, as well as in the capacity of actors to build political leverage for their projects across a variety of domains. At particular moments of crisis, the streets, the parties, the Parliament, or meetings of social partners may be key choice points for the adoption or rejection of specific austerity measures. In the longer run, the contestation of austerity will occur in a variety of environments, but alternatives are still likely to emerge from state power.

This applies especially well to a case like Quebec, where the push to austerity is prolonged but never based on a dire situation, such as the inability to borrow or needing to head off a default. While austerity dates from the Parti Québécois' (PQ) attempts to fight the deficit by rewriting public sector contracts and legislating public sector strikers back to work in 1982–3, but also from periodic business cycle pressures (early and late 1990s, post-2008), these austerity drives were always based on a proximate threat of crisis rather than a present crisis. The late 1990s and early 2000s present a slightly more complex case, as calls for budgetary consolidation focused not on crisis, but on the need to reduce taxes to ensure longer-term economic competitiveness. Another wrinkle in the Quebec case is that the call for public sector reform has not been based solely on economic claims that it diverts resources from economic growth, but also that it has created a sclerotic corporatism that stifles innovation and adaptability (Rouillard et al. 2006). Nevertheless, the general point that austerity has been a slow-moving process, where "crises" have always been a bit artificial and instrumentalized, suggests the value in the type of analysis we provide below.

Spaces of Resistance and Alternatives

In order to understand how resistance to austerity has affected Quebec's landscape, Dufour's Political Action Diamond offers a useful typology, making sense of the variety of arenas through which oppositional politics is organized. Dufour considers four poles of participation, distinguished by whether or not they involve representation, whether they are located in the arena of electoral politics or are outside the state in the "social conflicts arena," and whether the forms of interactions are more cooperative/collaborative or conflict-based. On this basis, she distinguishes an *electoral democracy pole*, based in the electoral arena and on a logic of representation; a *social democracy pole*, based on organizations in the social conflicts arena that engage the state on the basis of delegated representation (such as unions and interest groups); and a *protest democracy pole*, again in the social conflicts arena, but based on direct participation.[1]

To get a better grasp of how resistance succeeds or fails to translate into alternatives, one needs to analyse how actors who are opposed to austerity, or are seeking to affect how it is manufactured, engage in politics at the social democracy, protest democracy, and electoral democracy poles. In looking in a variety of places, and in the interaction between

---

1 A fourth pole of *participative democracy* will interest us less here, being based on accepting the rules of the electoral arena, but seeking to act on it through direct participation.

them, we hope to better capture the nuance and texture of resistance to austerity, and the manner in which resistance affects the manufacturing of austerity and opens avenues for alternatives or fails to do so.

Social Democracy Pole

In studying the politics of austerity, particular attention has been given to the role of social partnership institutions in managing crises. The entanglement of labour in these institutions, however, can sometimes mean that it ends up ratifying cuts to public sector employment and programs. In the process, rather than organizing opposition to austerity, they end up selling it (Evans 2014).

Quebec stands out on the Canadian scene in the periodic use of concertation. Haddow (2015) considers collaborative interest mediation and higher unionization as important causes for Quebec having a larger and more redistributive state than the other provinces. The usual image is of big summits, such as socio-economic summits held in 1996, which we will discuss below. But to this we must add periodic sector-specific summits (such as on agriculture, post-secondary education, or technology), ongoing partnership institutions on specific issues like occupational health and safety or labour force training, as well as regional health and social services boards.

Consistent with the literature on social partnerships and austerity, observers of the labour unions' support for forms of partnership have suggested that these can lead to labour agreeing to a series of one-sided deals, thereby losing their ability to define a longer-term strategic vision (Piotte 1998; Graefe 2005). They often point to the 1996 Social and Economic Summits, which intended to find a societal consensus on deficit reduction on the one hand, and respond to high rates of unemployment on the other. In the critical literature, the unions' lack of a clear vision and bargaining position led them astray: they signed on to the goal of balancing the budget, which necessitated the largest public sector layoffs in Quebec's history, in return for weak employer commitments to increase employment. Lacking an alternative strategy on taxes and public services, they could only end up bargaining at the margins of the state's project (Piotte 1998; Graefe 2005).

This analysis has some limitations, however. While it captures the weakness of the unions' ability to put forward alternatives, the summits themselves can be seen as the seedbed of alternatives. While union acceptance of balanced budgets had no solid quid pro quo in employment, the PQ government did offer significant openings to social actors – unions, women's groups, community groups, anti-poverty groups – at the summit (Arsenault 2016). Most important among those was the commitment to launch a new family policy, which included three significant departures. The most well-known is the universal, low-cost childcare program, which represented a significant new outlay of public funds, and provided a common target (the state) for early childcare workers to bargain with in order to improve wages and working conditions. In addition, there was the new parental leave scheme – which prompted the federal government to improve the EI parental leave program in 2000, in an attempt to head it off – as well as a new set of income-tested child benefits. The latter have proven to be workhorses of redistribution, pushing money into Quebec's families at two to three times the levels seen elsewhere in Canada.

The summits also garnered consensus on a fund to support anti-poverty initiatives. This can be seen as a first re-awakening to poverty, helping open the state to subsequent mobilizations for the adoption of an anti-poverty policy in 2002. There were also state commitments to go further in developing the social economy or third sector. While some of the emphasis on the social economy was rhetoric to distinguish a "social democratic" Quebec from a "neoliberal" Canada (Salée 2003), actors involved in social entrepreneurship and community economic development did receive resources and a fuller hearing in the years preceding and following the summit, as evidenced notably by the establishment of the tax-advantaged Fond*Action* in 1995–6 and of the Chantier de l'économie sociale in 1999 (its investment fund, the Fiducie du Chantier de l'économie sociale, was launched in 2006).

As such, while the dominant thrust of budgetary austerity won out, social democratic mobilization forced accommodations with other projects that expanded social rights in domains like family policy and provided policy footholds for alternative development strategies such as those of the women's movement on social infrastructures or the community sector's on the social economy. Therefore, when explaining Quebec's persisting divergence from Canadian social policy in general, or from the Canadian pattern of increased income inequality in particular, many insist on the social democratic pressures of the mid-1990s as a central explanator (Noël 2002, 2013; Vaillancourt and Thériault 2008).

Perhaps as a result of this experience, this form of peak-level social concertation has not been experimented with since by successive Liberal governments. The Conseil du Patronat du Québec, the main employers' federation, was not pleased with the development of a new tax to fund anti-poverty initiatives, and the political Right more generally developed a critique of "corporatism" as a brake on innovation. The Charest Liberals took this view from 1998 onward and acted on it following their election in 2003. While some concertational institutions (health and safety, labour market training) continued to function relatively unchanged, the steam was out of the program of partnership. Indeed, the PQ government itself was already less interested in social partnerships by the end of the 1990s, and more enthusiastic about European policy designs for the knowledge economy and entrepreneurial state, aligning economic liberalism with strategic interventionism (Investissement Québec, Capital régional et coopératif Desjardins) and compensating social investments (McGrane 2014).

The unions also had their role in the closure of this form of social democracy. In the late 1980s, they could embrace social partnerships as part of a "progressive competitiveness" strategy, but by the late 1990s it was a harder sell: the power of business was such that the promised "positive sum" compromises they intended to create increasingly looked like a way to manage stagnation in levels of employment, salaries, and work conditions. In a period where capital in Quebec could continue to reproduce itself despite slow growth and budget restraint, there was no longer an obvious partner for "win-win" strategies (Pineault 2013). By the 2000s, union responses to austerity became a defence of the post-war social state against cutbacks, in the well-worn form of community coalitions defending health and social services. In 2014–15, for instance, this took the form of the Refusons l'austérité collective, building against the 2015 budget and around May Day 2015.

These coalitions stood and stand somewhere between the social democracy and protest democracy poles. While an important part of their power comes from the ability to mobilize members and citizens to protest, they also engage in traditional practices of representation such as presenting briefs to pre-budget consultations or to special commissions on user fees and health-care financing. But if we expand the social democracy pole to embrace the engagement of other social interests, we should also look at the strategies of women's and community organizations to obtain representation on regional development or other multi-stakeholder institutions (Masson 2006), and in policy networks more generally.

In the 1990s, the women's movement developed a counter-vision of development based on taking action to invest in meeting human needs, to end poverty and violence. This included raising state revenues in order to invest in "social infrastructures" that supported caring work and community development. The community movement, meanwhile, emphasized measures to reduce poverty, leading to the anti-poverty Bill 102 under the PQ government in 2002. More entrepreneurial elements also stressed the importance of social entrepreneurship and community-based initiatives ("the social economy") as a key to democratizing economic development. The advent of the Réseau d'investissement social du Québec in the late 1990s, and that of the Conseils locaux des partenaires, later rebranded as the Centres locaux de développement, are cases in point.

However, the vision of the women's movement was already beginning to lose some steam in the late 1990s: the weak response to the World March of Women in 2000 (a ten-cent raise in the minimum wage) led to frustration or burnout for some, and a turn to electoral considerations (building an alternative to the PQ) for others. While the women's movement remains an important political actor, its response to austerity has shared similarities with those of the unions, namely criticizing retrenchment or user fees, but showing less originality in how alternatives might be built. The community movement likewise maintained the anti-poverty policy despite political will to wrap it up, much like the social economy supporters have substantially weathered state retrenchment. Although actors from these networks have been important nodes in the development of the Coalition Main Rouge, a more grassroots and protest-based alternative to the Refusons l'austérité collective, it remains harder to see them as movements with the potential to push these projects to a stage where they would prove more transformative than palliative.

Protest Democracy Pole

The past two decades have also seen large protests to move the state away from austerity policies. Much like the labour-community coalitions, they have been hybrid mobilizations. While they were about trying to push the government to step back from particular policy decisions, they were also about strengthening the hand of union or student organizations at the social democracy pole.

The recourse to mass protest against austerity is a feature of the last decade, although the 1990s included some large movements such as the 1995 Bread and Roses March against Poverty in Quebec, big rallies against the Axworthy federal social security review, protests against the 1996–8 reform of social assistance, and May Day marches that expressed disquiet with the social cuts made to balance federal and provincial budgets. This was a disparate set of events, however. The Bread and Roses March did protest cuts to the state, but had a more proactive stance in proposing alternatives based on the priorities of reducing poverty and violence. The social assistance demonstrations, in turn, while recognizing that the reform was about trying to save money, were much more about contesting the workfarist spirit of the reform than about austerity.

The first major cycle of protests against austerity arguably date from the fall of 2003, when the union federations rallied against the Charest government's changes to the labour code and its unilateral redrawing of accreditations in the public sector. This cycle included a Day of Disruption in December 2003, notable for many workers withdrawing their labour as well as for some acts like road blockages. It is not clear how directly this can be tied to austerity, however, as these changes were sold less on budgetary grounds than on trying to reform the Quebec model of governance, to make it less concertational and more market based (Rouillard et al. 2006; Boismenu, Dufour, and Saint-Martin 2004).

While the Day of Disruption seemed more about blowing off steam than taking a step towards a more general social strike, it fed into student organizing in opposition to cuts in student aid. The students could surf on the anti-Liberal public sentiment in April and November 2004 marches, right into a successful student strike in February and March 2005, pushing the government to retreat from its cuts. The more radical student associations were disappointed, nonetheless, that the strike was settled before it could spill over into a broader debate about tuition fees and the modern university. Relations with the unions, and particularly the Fédération des travailleurs et travailleuses du Québec, were also poisonous, given the latter's lukewarm support for the students.

The Maple Spring of 2012 replayed this pattern of more general organizing spurring a successful student mobilization. Left student organizations had been active in a community-labour coalition against user fees, which was an inheritor of early 2000s' coalitions to safeguard health and social services but focused more directly on attacking the Charest government's interest in adopting user fees (Québec, Ministère des Finances 2009). These fees were seen by many not only as an austerity tool, but also as a de-solidarizing instrument, in that they individualized and (partially) marketized state services (Nadeau-Dubois 2013; Collombat 2014;

Pineault 2016). When the Charest government chose to let tuition fees creep upwards, on the grounds that users (students) should assume a greater share of the cost of their studies, this organizing spilled into a widespread student strike in the spring of 2012.

Unlike 2005, the originally narrow conflict over fees expanded into a broader debate over the role and value of public services, and the vocation of the modern university. While this was given some form when the lead student organization, the CLASSE, released a manifesto (2012), it happened relatively late. Its anti-neoliberal and anti-oppressive vision, however, while enriching public debate, had limited reach in the absence of influential organizations to embrace it. Other protest surges in the spring of 2012, such as the "casserole movement" to denounce and ridicule the circumventing of civil rights to protest, likewise lacked the organization necessary to elaborate a counter-imaginary to austerity. Nevertheless, the networks formed, and the framing developed in this period bootstrapped protest actions against the Liberal government's budget strategies both before and after 2014, particularly through the Coalition Main Rouge.

The point here is not to belittle these events at the protest democracy pole, but to underline that they have been largely reactive and reliant on organizations at the social democracy pole (unions and student organizations) to fashion alternative imaginaries, and strategies for reaching them. In some ways, this almost goes by definition, as the emphasis on direct action and the non-delegation of authority to institutional representatives that characterizes such mass actions makes the aggregation of participants' meanings into concrete political strategies difficult to accomplish. Therefore, as with the social democracy pole, it inevitably raises the question of how such resistances become translated into institutional politics, at the electoral pole. Can they translate into alternatives to austerity? Do programs of austerity start to look different as they must work around these resistances? A look at the 2012–14 PQ interim will serve as an illustration.

Electoral Democracy Pole

"Austerity of imagination," in the arena of electoral politics, points to an under-appreciation that incremental departures from budget austerity and state retrenchment, first, can constitute stepping stones towards alternatives. Small alterations to the big picture of cutbacks, in turn, can safeguard gains for public sector and civil society organizations.

Finally, too many, in Quebec and elsewhere, tend to perceive austerity mainly as a budgetary phenomenon, relating to counterproductive limits on government revenues and spending. But austerity is also and perhaps most importantly about subordinating all forms of social, cultural, and political progress to budget balance, low inflation, and fiscal conservatism. Therefore, even when implemented within a context of budget restraint, innovative measures that address issues not generally associated with austerity should be regarded as slowly removing the blinders it places on legislators.[2] It is based in part on such premises that the illustrative example of the 2012–14 PQ interim can be read.

On the one hand, as an opposition to successive Liberal administrations between 2003 and 2012, the PQ often criticized the government for running deficits, including after 2008 and with surprising disregard for both the necessity of public spending for economic recovery and the fact that the Liberals were already engaged on an austerity path (Dutrisac 2008). This soured relations between the union movement and the newly elected PQ leader, Pauline Marois, after 2007. On the other hand, the PQ also rejected the Liberals' strategy to pursue budget balance through increased resort to user fees (Ouellet 2009), as set out in the 2009 "Policy for the Funding of Public Services" (Québec, Ministère des Finances 2009). It opposed the hike in electricity prices, the imposition of an annual $200 "health contribution" across the board, and the two successive 1 per cent increases of the Quebec Sales Tax, in 2009 and 2010 (Salvet 2010). In the opposition, the PQ thus played an ambivalent game, trying to position itself as an alternative rooted in compromise.

This became clear during and after the Maple Spring of 2012. When, in part to curb recurrent deficits but mainly to implement a user-based funding system, the Liberal government announced the $1650 hike in university tuition fees from 2012 to 2017, the PQ opposed this measure, despite its relative popularity. As this hike triggered what would become, as mentioned above, one of the most important student and popular mobilizations in Quebec's history, all Left-leaning sovereigntist parties – the PQ, QS, and the young Option Nationale (ON) – tried to gain electoral points by taking sides with the protestors and suggesting

---

2 For this reason, while Haddow (2015) may be correct in noting the Quebec party system's (historically) lower degree of polarization over economic/distributive issues, the differences between the PQ and PLQ programs remain crucial in the range of options they open and foreclose.

progressive substitutes to the tuition hike. This actually contributed, as is now clear and in contrast with Haddow's (2015) arguments for the 1990–2010 period, to a significant widening of the party system's polarization over economic/distributive issues in Quebec.

In this context of crisis, and with the Liberal administration nearing the end of its 2008–12 mandate, the most strategic approach would have been for these three parties to offer a united electoral front and alternative. Looking at the results of the September 2012 elections by electoral riding, such a coalition might have reached a majority. The clearest example of this lost opportunity was Montreal's Laurier-Dorion riding, where PQ, QS, and ON candidates reaped over 53 per cent of the popular vote but allowed the Liberal contender to be elected with only 34 per cent. Of course, citizens might have voted differently if such a united front had been offered, and there is no assurance these seats would have been won. Still, with hindsight, it can be said this would have been a risk worth taking.[3] Responsibility for this missed opportunity lay with the three parties that, despite serious talks and converging interests, lacked the imagination necessary to reach common ground.

Among the reasons an alliance with the PQ was rejected by QS and ON was the fact that the former favoured, as an alternative to the Liberal hike, indexing tuition fees over introduction of free higher education. Yet if indexing tuition fees based on available household income never was a consensual policy, it always was (1) an option largely preferred to a drastic increase, and (2) the closest thing to Quebec's traditional tuition freeze policy, which would have been electorally tenable at the time (Léger 360 2013). Even a Left-leaning PQ-QS-ON coalition advocating free education or a tuition freeze would arguably have hit an electoral wall, considering the marginal backing of this alternative and the 58 per cent of the popular vote the only two parties favouring tuition hikes were able to gather in 2012.[4]

Although this could not and probably should not have been the basis of an alliance, however, other elements of the PQ platform clearly could have been, such as Quebec's sovereignty, reforming the mining royalties system, electrifying transportation infrastructures, establishing a

---

[3] A majority could have been won, for instance, even if only 50 per cent of the QS votes had been carried over to the PQ in the context of an electoral alliance (Le Directeur général des élections du Québec 2012).
[4] Ibid.

national development bank, promoting the social economy, halting the exploitation of nuclear energy and shale gas, eliminating the $200 health contribution, increasing taxes for top earners, introducing an "autonomy insurance" to help seniors age in place, legalizing euthanasia, requesting jurisdiction over employment insurance, improving social housing, and broadening access to legal aid (Parti Québécois 2012). That no common ground was found among them arguably reveals the extent of the lack of longer-term vision and strategic imagination among the Left.

Moreover, the election of a minority government limited opportunities to implement such policies. Not only did this precarious position weaken the PQ's legislative capacity, it also undermined its political legitimacy.[5] That explains in part why the PQ backed up on some of its electoral pledges while reducing the scope of others. On the basis of what was probably an ill-advised political calculus, the PQ government decided not to increase taxes on capital gains and dividends as had been announced, and to make the health contribution more progressive, instead of eliminating it altogether. The upside story, however, is that the health contribution was completely abolished or significantly reduced for 65 per cent of the population while increased to $1000 for citizens with net incomes over $150,000, and that a fourth income tax bracket was introduced that represented a 1.75 per cent increase of the marginal rate for revenues exceeding $100,000.

Over the course of eighteen months in power, the PQ played some bad anti-austerity cards. Such was the decision to aim for budget balance within a year, in 2013–14. To reach that goal, the growth of operating expenses had to be limited to 1.8 per cent for 2013–14, perpetuating the downward budgetary trend initiated by the Liberals. Yet, in reality, the PQ actually presided over a 4.2 per cent increase in operating expenses (including debt servicing) between April 2013 and March 2014, including a 3.9 per cent increase for health and social services, as well as a 4.1 per cent increase for education and culture (Québec, Ministère des Finances 2014). That represented, respectively, $1.2 billion and $682 million in additional spending for these portfolios. Following the April 2014

---

5 In his recollection of the PQ interim (2014), MNA Jean-François Lisée alleges that, in the weeks following the election, Pauline Marois rejected the idea of a coalition government with the CAQ's François Legault and Jacques Duchesneau as well as QS's Françoise David as Cabinet members. Such a government could have claimed to represent, indirectly, 65 per cent of the electorate.

elections, a report was ordered that, on the basis of numbers provided by the Treasury Board, even pointed to a possible 6.1 per cent increase in operating expenses after carrying out the PQ's 2014–15 budget plan (Godbout and Montmarquette 2014). If the PQ advocated budget austerity, it hasn't been sufficiently recognized that it did not put its money where its mouth was.

Furthermore, from a social-democratic perspective, the PQ also played good cards over these eighteen months. In addition to the legislative work that led to Bill 52 on end-of-life care, a groundbreaking policy that moved Quebec – and now Canada as a whole – closer to European social-democracies, at least three other bills could have been stepping stones towards progressive alternatives. The Social Economy Act (Québec, Assemblée Nationale 2013) adopted in late 2013 is one, and will promote the multiplication of social economy initiatives by stating that "all ministers must, in their actions and with respect to any agency for which they are responsible, recognize the social economy as an integral part of the socioeconomic structure of Quebec by taking it into consideration in measures and programs ... and in developing new tools for enterprises" (art. VII). Although it might be too early to assess the real impact of this Act, promoting the growth of the third sector does constitutes a real, if limited, departure from the low road to economic competitiveness, and one that builds upon efforts dating back to the 1990s.

The two other bills did not get through the legislative process but revealed an intention to widen the scope of provincial health insurance and to address poverty and housing seriously. In the first case, the Autonomy Insurance Act (Québec, Assemblée Nationale 2013) would have established a new, public insurance plan dedicated to providing professional care and services directly in people's living environments. In the second case, the "Act to promote the inclusion of social housing or affordable housing in new construction projects" did not raise media interest but could have constituted an important headway. This bill would have given "local municipalities the power, by by-law, to make the issue of a building permit for the construction of housing units subject to the signing of an agreement between the applicant and the municipality to increase the supply of social housing or affordable housing in the territory of the municipality" (Québec, Assemblée Nationale 2014).

All of this suggests that the September 2012 election probably was a missed opportunity. It was then that the political stars aligned for the formation of a social-democratic coalition and the offering of a strong alternative to parties embracing state retrenchment. After the disastrous PQ campaign in April 2014, the Liberals won back a majority of seats (70 out of 125) with only 41.5 per cent of the vote. With a turnout of 71 per cent, this should have reminded everyone that, notwithstanding complexities based, inter alia, on the linguistic composition of particular ridings in Greater Montreal, support from around 30 per cent of the eligible population is sufficient, under the current first-past-the-post system, for a party to command extensive legislative power. The last time a "social-democratic" formation reached that threshold in Quebec was in 1998, under virtual bipartism. Only if we take the PQ, QS, and ON together in 2012 can we say a partisan alternative to austerity reached it since then.

After fifteen years of failure extending over five general elections, strategic imagination is certainly required. The inconvenient truth might be that under the current system, and given the additional division of the nationalist opposition to the Liberals between the PQ and CAQ, there is not much room for three centre-Left parties. Whether or not the new PQ leadership can get the party to a majority in 2018 will only illustrate the point: if it can, it will certainly be at the expense of the other two; if it can't, it will most probably be the result, in part, of the redistribution of its support among QS, ON, and the CAQ. In both cases, a tripartite alternative to austerity is unsustainable. Quebec's sovereigntist Left thus seems to be caught up in a classic "coordination game": the three parties can reach their "lowest common denominator" objective – replacing the Liberals – only if they take mutually compatible strategic paths. An electoral coalition of some sort,[6] the dissolution of the PQ or QS, or the merger of the two seem to be the only paths available.

More generally, however, strategic alliances within and across poles of resistance will prove harder to construct as the Liberals continue to unfold a full-fledged and multi-sectoral reconfiguration of the state by relying on politicized "expert committees"[7] rather than on the collaborative interest mediation mechanisms identified by Haddow (2015) and others. Over the last three years, for instance, both

---

6 A first move of the new PQ leadership, it should be noted, was to launch an initiative, headed by MNA Véronique Hivon, aiming at a "convergence" with QS and ON.
7 On this issue in particular, see Graefe and Rioux (forthcoming).

the Commission de révision permanente des programmes (Québec, Conseil du Trésor 2014) and the Commission d'examen de la fiscalité québécoise (Québec, Ministère des Finances 2015) have made, on behalf of the Liberal government, recommendations on a very long list of sectors. As sectoral reforms – focusing mostly on state retrenchment and fiscal reorganization – multiply, so will sectoral oppositions, which do not always have converging interests. In other words, the more the effects of austerity are scattered across different fields of state intervention, the more coordination between poles of resistance could be challenging. That is precisely why, from an anti-austerity viewpoint, a long-term vision will be key and a return to strategic electoral thinking unavoidable.

Conclusion

This discussion of the PQ interim and the dilemmas with which it left Quebec brings us full circle. As with the social democracy and the protest democracy poles, there has been resistance to austerity, as well as moves to implant alternatives. As with these other poles, however, one can ask whether these alternatives are connected to bigger imaginaries, and whether this would be necessary or even useful. While at one time the PQ engaged with big ideas of "progressive competitiveness," by 2012 its alternatives to austerity seemed rooted in compromise and attempts to reach specific voting constituencies. Yet its Left challenger, less inclined to beat the drum of sound finance and thus a more vocal defender of the social state, was not much more coherent in enunciating an alternative political economy, let alone means to achieve it. The contribution of this chapter, in this context, is to initiate a discussion on the respective merits of compromise, incrementalism, and strategy over short-term, transformative, and radical thinking.

If the point is to find a way to move beyond austerity, our discussion of Quebec suggests several lessons. First, while austerity politics can be very fast, in the sense of using a sense of crisis to impose losses on public sector workers or citizens reliant on state programs, it can also be very slow. Indeed, if we take the more Weberian view of Schäfer and Streeck, it will be the natural condition of politics for over a generation. As such, "resisting" the manufacture of austerity depends on the imaginary of an alternative, but most importantly on the strategic capacity to build elements of those alternatives through trade-offs and compromises. The difficulty is in sustaining that imaginary when its achievement is far in the future, and the trade-offs and compromises are treated as betrayals in the here-and-now. This certainly is how the women's movement looked back at its implication in the mid-1990s debates about the social economy, poverty, and violence, and yet, they were arguably the most successful in introducing state action that departed from the general narrative of austerity (e.g., family policy, social economy initiatives).

A second lesson is that the interaction between poles of political engagement is difficult, but crucial. The Quebec Left has contested austerity and proposed alternatives, but this has been largely through efforts in the domains of protest democracy and social democracy. A real stumbling block has been in finding relays in the electoral realm that might open greater spaces to pursue alternatives. Since 1970, the most likely relay for progressive movements has been the PQ, and whether we are talking about developments flowing from the 1996 summits or the departures of the Marois government, it continues to be the electoral vehicle that opens spaces for change at the margins. At the same time, the spaces opened in the late 1990s were not wide enough for the women's movement to embed their social infrastructures, just as the openings of the Marois interim failed to translate the passion for an alternative found in the Maple Spring.

Reflecting soon after the election of the PQ, student leader and now QS MNA Gabriel Nadeau-Dubois (2013) noted that the Maple Spring highlighted the necessity for students to face the question of state power. While one could rehearse the story about the bankruptcy of social democratic politics, Dufour's Diamond leads us to look at this slightly differently. Rather than painting the PQ as the wrecker, it may be more useful to ask why the forces opposed to austerity have been unable to create electoral space, either for a more radical PQ, or for a more successful Left challenger to the PQ. The idea that austerity will remain with us for at least another generation (McBride and Whiteside 2011) and seems endemic to mature and aging welfare states (Schäfer and Streeck 2013) is disempowering. It helps to manufacture austerity by suggesting an inescapable epochal force (Clarke 2014). However, the flipside is that it invites those seeking to manufacture an alternative to also consider possibilities and strategies that can be built over a longer time horizon. It may push the Left to move beyond the defensiveness of protecting public services and assets, and to imagine instead how those might be used to produce a different economic and social model (Pineault 2014).

REFERENCES

Arsenault, Gabriel. 2016. "The Social Investment State and the Social Economy: The Politics of Quebec's Social Economy Turn, 1996–2015." PhD diss., University of Toronto.

Boismenu, Gérard, Pascale Dufour, and Denis Saint-Martin. 2004. *Ambitions libérales et écueils politiques: Réalisations et promesses du Gouvernement Charest*. Outremont, QC: Athéna Éditions.

CLASSE. 2012. "Share Our Future: The CLASSE Manifesto." http://www.stopthehike.ca/2012/07/share-our-future-the-classe-manifesto/.

Collombat, Thomas. 2014. "Labour and Austerity in Québec: Lessons from the Maple Spring." *Labor Studies Journal* 39 (2): 140–59. https://doi.org/10.1177/0160449X14531680.

Cox, Laurence, and Alf Gunvald Nilsen. 2014. *We Make Our Own History: Marxism and Social Movements in the Twilight of Neoliberalism*. London: Pluto.

Crouch, Colin. 2001. "Welfare State Regimes and Industrial Relations Systems." In *Comparing Welfare Capitalism: Social Policy and Political Economy in Europe, Japan and the USA*, ed. Bernhard Ebbinghaus and Philip Manow, 105–24. London: Routledge.

Crouch, Colin, and Maarten Keune. 2005. "Changing Dominant Practice: Making Use of Institutional Diversity in Hungary and the United Kingdom." In *Beyond Continuity: Institutional Change in Advanced Political Economies*, ed. Wolfgang Streeck and Kathleen Thelen, 83–102. Oxford: Oxford University Press.

Dufour, Pascale. 2009. "From Protest to Partisan Politics: When and How Collective Actors Cross the Line? Sociological Perspective on Québec Solidaire." *Canadian Journal of Sociology* 34:55–81.

– 2013. *Trois espaces de protestation particuliers: la France, le Canada et le Québec*. Montreal: Presses de l'Université de Montréal.

Dutrisac, Robert. 2008. "Déficit zéro – Le PQ songe à défier le gouvernement Charest." *Devoir*, 18 June. http://www.ledevoir.com/politique/quebec/194509/deficit-zero-le-pq-songe-a-defier-le-gouvernement-charest.

Evans, Bryan. 2014. "Social Democracy in the New Age of Austerity." In *Orchestrating Austerity: Impacts & Resistance*, ed. Donna Baines and Stephen McBride, 79–90. Halifax: Fernwood.

Godbout, Luc, and Claude Montmarquette. 2014. *Rapport d'experts sur l'état des finances publiques du Québec*. Quebec: Conseil exécutif. http://www.mce.gouv.qc.ca/publications/rapport-experts-etat-finances.pdf.

Graefe, Peter. 2005. "State Restructuring and the Failure of Competitive Nationalism: Trying Times for Quebec Labour." In *Canada: The State of the*

Federation 2005 – Quebec and Canada in the New Century, ed. Michael Murphy, 153–76. Kingston: Institute of Intergovernmental Relations.

Graefe, Peter, and X.H. Rioux. Forthcoming. "From the Bailiffs at Our Doors to the Greek Peril: Twenty Years of Fiscal 'Urgency' and Quebec Politics." In *Canadian Provincial and Territorial Paradoxes: Public Finances, Services and Employment in an Era of Austerity*, ed. Bryan Evans and Carlo Fanelli, 187–218. Montreal and Kingston: McGill-Queen's University Press.

Haddow, Rodney. 2015. *Comparing Quebec and Ontario: Political Economy and Public Policy at the Turn of the Millennium*. Toronto: University of Toronto Press.

Iversen, Torben, and Anne Wren. 1998. "Equality, Employment, and Budgetary Restraint: The Trilemma of the Service Economy." *World Politics* 50 (4): 507–46. https://doi.org/10.1017/S0043887100007358.

Le directeur general des élections du Québec. 2012. "Élections générales 4 septembre 2012." http://www.electionsquebec.qc.ca/francais/provincial/resultats-electoraux/elections-generales.php?e=72&urlamp;s=1&urlamp;c=tous#s.

Léger 360. 2013. "Les frais de scolarité pour l'enseignement supérieur et la Commission Charbonneau." *Le Devoir*, 11 February. http://www.ledevoir.com/documents/pdf/sondage11fevrierecole.pdf.

Lisée, Jean-François. 2014. *Le Journal de Lisée: 18 mois de pouvoir, mes combats, mes passions*. Montreal: Rogers Publishing.

Masson, Dominique. 2006. "Engaging with the Politics of Downward Rescaling: Representing Women in Regional Development Policymaking in Québec (Canada)." *GeoJournal* 65 (4): 301–13. https://doi.org/10.1007/s10708-006-0025-x.

McBride, Stephen, and Heather Whiteside. 2011. *Private Affluence, Public Austerity*. Halifax: Fernwood.

McGrane, David. 2014. *Remaining Loyal: Social Democracy in Quebec and Saskatchewan*. Montreal and Kingston: McGill-Queen's University Press.

Nadeau-Dubois, Gabriel. 2013. "Enseignements printaniers. Quelques éléments à retenir de la grève étudiante de 2012." *Nouveaux cahiers du socialisme* 9:188–97.

Newman, Janet. 2013. "Spaces of Power: Feminism, Neoliberalism and Gendered Labor." *Social Politics* 20 (2): 200–21. https://doi.org/10.1093/sp/jxt008.

Noël, Alain. 2002. "Une loi contre la pauvreté: la nouvelle approche québécoise de lutte contre la pauvreté et l'exclusion sociale." *Lien social et Politiques* 48 (48): 103–14. https://doi.org/10.7202/007895ar.

- 2013. "Quebec's New Politics of Redistribution." In *Inequality and the Fading of Redistributive Politics*, ed. Keith Banting and John Myles, 256–82. Vancouver: UBC Press.
Ouellet, Martin. 2009. "Le PQ promet une bataille en règle contre les hausses de tarifs." *La Presse*, 28 September. http://www.lapresse.ca/actualites/politique/politique-quebecoise/200909/28/01-906321-le-pq-promet-une-bataille-en-regle-contre-les-hausses-de-tarifs.php.
Parti Québécois. 2012. "Agir honnêtement, s'affirmer, s'enrichir, s'entraider." Montreal. http://mon.pq.org/documents/monpq_516f6a49d4ec3.pdf.
Pineault, Eric. 2014. "Neoliberalism and Austerity as Class Struggle." In *Orchestrating Austerity: Impacts and Resistance*, ed. Donna Baines and Stephen McBride, 91–104. Halifax: Fernwood.
- 2013. "Quebec's Red Spring: An Essay on Ideology and Social Conflict at the End of Neoliberalism." *Studies in Political Economy* 90 (1): 29–56. https://doi.org/10.1080/19187033.2012.11674990.
Piotte, Jean-Marc. 1998. *Du Combat au Partenariat*. Montreal: Nota Bene.
Québec, Assemblée Nationale. 2013. "Bill n° 67: Autonomy Insurance Act." http://goo.gl/qSjgLc.
- 2014. "Bill n° 194: An Act to Promote the Inclusion of Social Housing or Affordable Housing in New Construction Projects." http://www.assnat.qc.ca/en/travaux-parlementaires/projets-loi/projet-loi-194-41-1.html.
Québec, Conseil du Trésor. 2014. "Rapport de la Commission de révision permanente des programmes." https://www.tresor.gouv.qc.ca/fileadmin/PDF/revision_programmes/rapport_2014.pdf.
Québec, Ministère des Finances. 2009. *Politique de financement des services publics*. Quebec: Ministère des Finances. http://www.finances.gouv.qc.ca/documents/Ministere/Fr/MINFR_PolitiqueFSP.pdf.
- 2014. *Rapport mensuel des opérations financières* 8 (11). Quebec: Ministère des Finances. http://www.finances.gouv.qc.ca/documents/mensuel/fr/MENFR_rmof_8_11.pdf.
- 2015. *Final Report of the Québec Taxation Reform Committee*. http://www.examenfiscalite.gouv.qc.ca/uploads/media/Volume1CEFQ_ReportENG.pdf.
Rouillard, Christian, Éric Montpetit, Isabelle Fortier, and Alain-G. Gagnon. 2006. *Reengineering the State: Toward an Impoverishment of Quebec Governance*. Ottawa: University of Ottawa Press.
Salée, Daniel. 2003. "Transformative Politics, the State, and the Politics of Social Change in Quebec." In *Changing Canada: Political Economy as Transformation*, ed. Wallace Clement and Leah Vosko, 25–50. Montreal and Kingston: McGill-Queen's University Press.

Salvet, Jean-Marc. 2010. "Québec hausse la TVQ, les tarifs d'Hydro et impose une nouvelle taxe santé." *Le Soleil*, 3 March. http://www.lapresse.ca/le-soleil/affaires/actualite-economique/201003/30/01-4265838-quebec-hausse-la-tvq-les-tarifs-dhydro-et-impose-une-nouvelle-taxe-sante.php.

Schäfer, Armin, and Wolfgang Streeck. 2013. "Introduction: Politics in the Age of Austerity." In *Politics in the Age of Austerity*, ed. Wolfgang Streeck and Armin Schäfer, 1–25. Cambridge: Polity.

Vaillancourt, Yves, and Luc Thériault. 2008. "Social Economy, Social Policy and Federalism in Canada." *Canadian Social Economy Research Partnerships*, Occasional Paper Series 4.

13 Social Democracy and Social Pacts: Austerity Alliances and Their Consequences

BRYAN M. EVANS

In 2003, a full five years before the world realized it was on the precipice of an economic catastrophe, Giorgio Ruffolo, a minister in the centre-Left government of Italy at the time, wrote, "Through globalization, capitalism has won a historical battle: it has defeated the reform-minded left [read social democracy] both in Europe and America" (Bertinotti 2003). Admittedly the globalization of capitalism is a significant structural force reshaping the limits of social democracy. What is perhaps more problematic is social democracy's adaptation to the various components of neoliberal restructuring rather than proposing an alternative. Social democracy's embrace of austerity through the 2007 financial crisis is a case in point, and the political consequences have marked what may be an irreversible turning point in the history of what was the greatest mass political movement in modern Europe. Social democracy's embrace of neoliberalism prior to the crisis was followed by an equally enthusiastic embrace of fiscal consolidation through public sector austerity once it appeared as though economic stability was achieved. Rather than challenge neoliberalism, social democracy demonstrated both an unwillingness and incapacity to consider alternatives. The result has proven devastating, as austerian social democratic parties have either been subject to "Pasokification," that is political disintegration, or a dramatic shrinking of their electoral base, rendering such parties a much diminished stature compared to their former parliamentary significance. Neil Burron's contribution to this volume examines the consequences of austerity and the resulting political polarization. Everywhere one turns, the story of social democracy is a variation on a theme where the once solid foundations are being "eaten" by a newish radical Left of various compositions, a nationalist Right, and, as in some cases, a civic republican and Left nationalism as expressed by the Scottish National Party, Sinn Fein, and various Basque and Catalan parties. The case of social democracy in the twenty-first century gives a lived historical meaning to Gramsci's observation that at "a certain point in their historical lives, social classes become detached from their traditional parties. In other words, the traditional parties in that particular organizational form, with the particular men who constitute, represent, and lead them, are no longer recognized by their class as its expression" (Gramsci 1971, 210).

Social democracy, through the post-1945 golden age of capitalism, was identified with and characterized by policy and political interventions contributing to greater equality and participation of working-class organizations, particularly trade unions, in state policy processes through various corporatist social partnership arrangements. Of course, the unravelling of the Keynesian model through the 1970s and 1980s destroyed the material foundations, and consequently the political arrangements and structures upon which the post-war social democratic project had been built were transformed. Through the 1990s, ever protean social democracy became increasingly neoliberalized. So much so that when the 2008 crisis emerged, social democracy was incapable of responding with an alternative program seeking to roll back the policies and institutions created through four decades of neoliberal ascent and eventual hegemony. Greek Finance Minister Yanis Varoufakis observed that even prior to the 2008 crisis, social democracy had been thoroughly "co-opted into the neoliberal cabal that designed and implemented the faulty Eurozone architecture." And with the 2008 crisis, "once the neoliberal design began to crumble, the parties carrying the torch of the social democratic tradition did not recoil from playing an enthusiastic role as enforcers of ruthlessly reactionary economic policies" (Varoufakis 2014).

This chapter explores the role of social democracy and neo-corporatist social partnerships in forging austerity in the post-crisis period. And a political consequence of social democracy's neoliberal turn, which predates the 2008 crisis, has been the fracturing of its traditional social base, which has, in part, contributed to the emergence of new radical Left parties. Social democracy transformed profoundly as neoliberalism became hegemonic, and this metamorphosis has continued through the period following the 2008 crisis. Thus, rather than presenting itself as an alternative to neoliberal capitalism, post-crisis social democracy has been a key force in forging multi-class austerity alliances. Participation in "grand coalitions" with conservative parties and resort to neo-corporatist social dialogue to negotiate the terms of austerity are all hallmarks of this practice. In some cases the result has been a "Pasokification" or implosion of the social democratic party.

The Consequences of Social Democracy's Historic Conformism

Understanding contemporary social democracy as the end of an alternative requires referencing the political and economic structures that enabled post-war social democracy and how the destruction of these foundations has informed a transformation of social democracy itself. Particularly since 1945, social democracy has been normed into the power structures of the capitalist state and economy to such a degree that its political practice was not to challenge capitalism but to manage it in the interests of its electorate. It is contestable to say that from the 1970s forward, social democracy actually did manage capitalism to the benefit of its working-class electorate, and this would vary by country and indeed specific policy. The central point is that within the context of neoliberalism – and it must be remembered that in the 1970s neoliberalism was only just surfacing as an alternative orthodoxy to Keynesianism – any substantive effort to engage in redistributional policy and worker protection is rendered impossible. Neoliberalized social democracy can be understood as presenting not an alternative to neoliberalism but a variant of neoliberalism whose slogan could well be "Without Us It Would Be Worse." This current impasse is "deeply embedded" in the history of social democracy (Guinan 2013, 12). The interwar years of 1918 to 1939 starkly illustrate the economic vacuity of social democracy where German Social Democrat and British Labour finance ministers pursued nothing more than sound money budget orthodoxy (48). Such conformism "has been part and parcel of Social Democracy from the beginning" (Benjamin 1969, 258).

In the post-1945 period, this ideological and theoretical conservatism was jettisoned in a turn to the "primacy of politics," in which political power was exercised to "reshape society and the economy." And such a project required broad, multi-class "people's parties" to replace narrowly working-class-based organizations. The state played an active role in securing full employment and protecting the public interest by intervening in the economy to ensure social needs took priority over market imperatives. The result was a democratically run capitalist economy characterized by social stability (Berman 2006, 16–17). The ideas of Keynes on economic management provided social democracy with the theoretical tools to sustain its welfare state project. It became explicitly understood that the program of social democracy could be achieved within the democratic political shell of capitalism. Capitalism itself was no longer the object of contestation.

What is of central importance here is the ideological shift noted above leads to a rather different understanding of state power. It is no longer a bourgeois state but rather a field for electoral struggle where the state can easily serve working-class interests as well as bourgeois. It was, in effect, a neutral machine that required only the right sort of driver to enact the program. Of course, this was a misreading of state power. What the revisionists failed to recognize was that a parliamentary majority allowing social democrats to hold ministerial roles was not the same as holding state power. This reframing ensured that the class nature of the state was left unaddressed by official social democracy.

The major interpretations of "traditional" social democracy variously identify its main characteristics as including re-distributional welfare policies delivered through a centralized state; a commitment to achieving government power through electoral means; de-emphasizing the aim of abolishing private ownership of the means of production; a comprehensive commitment to Keynesianism and the regulation of capitalism; an electoral link to the working class but also extending beyond this; and a commitment to the state and a well-functioning market (Bailey 2009, 30). These key characteristics of social democracy from 1945 through to the 1990s accept the capitalist economy and state. The class nature of that state and economy is not acknowledged. The ideological devaluation of ownership is critical in shifting social democracy away from a class-based movement and towards a managerial/technocratic understanding of the state.

The result is a fundamental contradiction at the core of social democracy expressed as where the political objective is "to regulate and contain the demands for de-commodification" made by its electoral constituencies, both working class and others, "in order that those demands might be both a) 'representable' within the institutions of the representative-democratic state, and b) compatible with attempts to achieve the successful reproduction of the capital–labour relationship that constitutes the national capitalist economy" (Bailey 2009, 39–40). In other words, social democracy is embedded within the class contradiction of its own project. Class-based demands for redistributional public policies, protections for workers, trade union rights, and regulation of markets eroded the capacity of the capitalist economy to accumulate profits. Indeed, the very success of social democracy was its ability to redistribute wealth, but this in turn limited wealth creation as the post-war growth model entered into crisis. A noteworthy expression of this is found in various corporatist arrangements characteristic of post-war social democracy in such countries as Britain, Sweden, the Netherlands, Germany, and Austria, where social democracy's ability to reconcile full employment with price stability by exerting its trade union allies to moderate wage demands was a source of its ability to manage capitalism but also resulted in loss of legitimacy by its working-class constituents at different points in time (Notermans 2000).

The historic goal of abolishing the private ownership of the means of production was firmly abandoned and capitalism embraced. Following from the acceptance of capitalist ownership was the recasting of nationalization as a tool to be employed sparingly and only for strategic or practical ends, such as provision of an essential service or supply, to protect jobs, or other development purposes. The new goals of growth, full employment, redistribution, economic stability, and increasing productivity had become the desired end state. The goal of transforming society and economy into something profoundly different was lost. And finally, the de-proletarianization of social democracy came to be understood as key to electoral success. The industrial working class was too narrow an electoral base, therefore it was necessary to appeal to other occupational and class constituencies (Sassoon 1997, 251).

With these developments, socialist and non-socialist approaches became very nearly indistinguishable. In effect, social democracy relinquished socialism for pragmatism (Sassoon 1997, 242, 249). The central question of ownership was replaced by that of control. The new theoretical axiom was that "the de facto management of the instruments of production has ... got out of the hands of the capitalists" (Burnham 1941, 68) and into the hands of technocratic managers. The class struggle had been replaced by rational planning. The key question for social democracy was now what to do to ensure capitalist growth and profitability to generate the state revenue necessary for public expenditure on social programs.

The post-war capitalism of social democracy came to understand that the capitalist ruling class no longer "ruled" in any direct manner. Instead rational state managers ensured the exuberances of the capitalist economy were constrained and checked by fiscal stabilizers, regulation, and if need be, public ownership. Full employment gave workers unprecedented bargaining power (Sassoon 1997, 146). Continuous expansion of working-class incomes and consumption were tied to a robust capitalism where "socialists must logically applaud the accumulation of private profit" (Crosland 1956, 378, 415).

Social democracy was sustainable as long as productivity gains and rates of profit, together with redistributional public policies and effective collective bargaining, enabled the reproduction of the labour–capital relationship on the one hand and the cohesion of the social democratic party's multi-class electoral base. But as that economic paradigm unravelled, so too would that historically specific form of social democracy. With the ascent of neoliberalism through the 1980s, characterized as the "most successful ideology in world history" (Anderson 2000, 17), social democracy, ever adaptable and protean, has transformed to accommodate itself to these new conditions. From the 1980s and into the 1990s, social democracy had undergone "more change than in any decade since World War II" (Kitschelt 1994, 3).

The transformative effect on social democracy was evident where a clear shift in policy objectives and instruments took place. In this decade social democratic parties abandoned Keynesian policies (the British Labour Party explicitly did so in the mid-1970s) and replaced this with supply-side policies centred on skills acquisition at the individual level, retreated from progressive taxation, and cut public expenditures (Merkel et al. 2008, 6, 25). The revisionism of the late 1980s was as significant a reconciliation with capitalism as was the turn to Keynesianism in representing a "compromise on the terms set by neoliberalism" (Sassoon 1997, 733). This ideological victory has been so totalizing that by the mid-1990s the parties of the social democratic Left responded by "accepting many of the tenets of neoliberalism while trying to sustain certain classic left-of-centre goals" (Crouch 2011, 162).

How would social democracy distinguish itself from explicitly neoliberal parties? Or could it? The "new social democracy has definitely not sprung up like some jack-in-the-box ... in a sense, the 'third way' was already present as well, prior to its adoption by New Labour and theoretical formulation by Giddens. The new social democracy of the 1990s is the worthy, direct heir of 1980s social democracy. The continuity between them is manifest, and manifestly strong" (Moschonas 2002, 229). Indeed social democracy was not what it used to be. As a result of the efforts of the "progressive modernizers," this meant deregulation and privatization, an embrace of global capitalism, abandonment of equality, and a purposeful weakening of the state to the advantage of capital (Taylor 2008). Social democratic parties everywhere have accepted "the necessity of adapting to international markets and the austerity policies capital has demanded, arguing mainly their own superior technical capacity to develop and administer the neoliberal policies that will match market imperatives" (Piven 1992, 18).

The financial crisis exposed social democracy for what it actually was, a thoroughly de-classed, professionalized electoral party apparatus completely integrated into the power structures of the capitalist state. The paradox for social democracy is that its electoral base still views it as a better alternative, sometimes, to the excesses of the Right. Social democracy officialdom understood these contradictions and tensions early on. The Amsterdam Process was launched in 2009 by Policy Network, an international progressive think tank, and the Wiardi Beckman Stichting, the Dutch social democratic think tank, in response to the clear need for ideological renewal or, as they put it, "a new revisionism for the 21st century." The problematic was described as one where "social democracy is suspended between embarrassment and complacency. The financial crisis of 2008 has not served as the definitive clarion call for centre-left governance, but rather exposed an ideological vacuum in social democratic thinking" (Policy Network, The Amsterdam Process, n.d.).

The result of this effort to re-launch a post-crisis social democracy has been astonishing. The newest revisionism attacks the legacies of its former self, the remnants of golden age social democracy. Working more and longer is necessary, the welfare state cannot be revived, twenty-first century social democracy must be for business and not against it, and, as electoral majorities become more elusive, social democrats must become comfortable with working in coalition with centrist parties to round up their parliamentary majorities (Cramme et al. 2012, 17–25). We observe in actually existing social democracy an enthusiastic embrace of neoliberalism and, in the wake of the Great Recession, an uncompromising fidelity to austerity, even though such has amounted to electoral suicide. The most significant opening for social democracy since the 1930s to mount a counteroffensive came and went. The problem here was that economic crises alone do not cause an ideological transformation. What is required are political actors, organic intellectuals in Gramscian terms, to advocate for an alternative set of economic ideas that contest the prevailing institutional and distributional settlements (Blyth 1997). Instead, social democrats chose not to play that role. Rather than move to widen the cracks in the edifice of neoliberalism the 2008 crisis and its aftermath created, where social democrats found themselves in government, Britain, Germany, Spain, Portugal, Greece, the Netherlands, Denmark, and Ireland have instead actively pursued austerity (Policy Network 2013).

The social democratic response post-2008 consists of two elements: Third Way Economics + Populist Rhetoric (i.e., abandoning working-class material interests while adopting a populist rhetoric that draws from right-wing competitors for working-class votes). While social democratic parties continue to see their vote share shrink, or at best stabilize at record low levels, it is likely that further instances of "Pasokification," resembling the experience of Greece's social democratic party, will be observed. However, a more general definition of Pasokification has application to virtually all European social democratic parties: "i) the absorption of social democracy into neoliberalism, with the resulting form known as 'social liberalism'; ii) the resulting secular breakdown of the party–base relationship, the loss of party identity and the fragmentation of the class base; iii) the incorporation of 'social liberalism' into an austerity consensus, with the dramatic acceleration of these trends, culminating in a decisive breakdown of the party–base relationship and the effective end of the party as a party of government" (Doran 2015a).

Unable to break the ideological grasp of third way political economy, social democratic parties continue to embrace austerity policy responses to the crisis, thus continuing the now two-decades-long abandonment of the concerns of their traditional working-class constituencies. Instead, they continue to devote much attention to "lifestyle" politics issues that appeal more to educated middle-class constituencies and combine it with neoliberal economics. Though they eagerly embraced the emergency "Keynesianism" of the immediate crisis period as evidence of the intellectual crisis of their centre-Right competitors, most social democratic parties did not and still do not question the fundamental precepts of neoliberal political economy – balanced budget fiscal policy, strict welfare/unemployment eligibility criteria, debt reduction, privatization when deemed necessary, and means-testing, to identify a few key policy directions (Angier 2015). Clever commentators have thus described twenty-first-century social democrats as "surfers without waves" (Lawson 2014) and social democracy as a "religion without preachers" (Mudde 2013). Neal Lawson, a former advisor to Gordon Brown and a supporter of David Miliband in the leadership contest, provocatively captures the ideological and theoretical impasse of social democracy as one where "social democrats seem unable to do anything more than shrug and go back to the same orthodoxies. They push at the edges of fiscal and regulatory boundaries but never really break with the constraints of neo-liberalism ... They vie for office, to pull levers that have long since rusted and seized up. The baggage of the past just seems too heavy to let go" (Lawson 2014). In the absence of their own distinctive ideology and political practice, social democracy adjusts to the requirements of financial capitalism and has no purpose other than to commit fully to an electoralism without any purpose beyond achieving government power simply for the sake of doing so.

In several countries, the loss of any distinctive social democratic politics and, flowing from that, a policy agenda to achieve deeper solidarity and broader equality, has been largely lost and subsumed into "grand coalitions" with mainstream conservative parties, as has been the case in Germany, Austria, the Netherlands, and, of course, the fateful experience of Greece. In Germany, since 2013, the SPD governs together with the conservative Christian Democrats. In this role they have critically supported Merkel's approach to enforcing austerity on Southern Europe and share her basic assumptions that the German approach to dealing with the crisis is correct. As a whole, the party has not retreated from Schroeder's labour market flexibilization reforms, introduced in 2003 and 2005, which alienated a large swathe of the SPD's trade union base and laid the basis for a rift with the left wing of the SPD and helped establish the Left party as a permanent fixture, if not a contender for government power. A similar position seems to characterize the Austrian social democrats under Chancellor Faymann, who has led a grand coalition since the end of 2008. The press often gives him credit for being opposed to Merkel's brand of austerity, but again, like the SPD, the conflict between the two chancellors is more one of degree than of type. He has pressed Greece to live up to its debt obligations. And in the Netherlands, the social democrats have governed together with the explicitly neoliberal Peoples Party for Freedom and Democracy since 2012. Having won nearly 25 per cent of the popular vote then, their share has consistently polled at half that number since. Indeed the 2014 local elections resulted in the social democrats' first defeat in Amsterdam, a city they had governed since 1946 (de Jong 2014).

Indistinguishable from the centre-Right, social democratic parties are feeling the electoral threat. But it is important to note that in many places the threat is not coming from the radical Left per se. Indeed, the electoral squeeze also comes from the radical Right and from Left nationalist parties, as in the case of Sinn Fein in Ireland and the Scottish

National Party (SNP). The SNP in particular has woven its civic nationalism together with an anti-austerity discourse, which was central to the independence referendum of 2014 and the Westminster elections of May 2015, where it decimated the commanding dominance of Scottish Labour. Labour failed to acknowledge that what really drives the success of the SNP is that it has taken on questions of economic inequality (Laxer 2014) and attacked austerity, while Labour has been found complicit.

In the rest of the United Kingdom, Labour faces the small but growing significance of the Greens, and the encroachments of the anti-immigrant, Eurosceptic UKIP on Labour's strongholds in the working-class heartlands of "Middle England." Consequently, Labour in 2015 campaigned on disciplining the unemployed, doing a better job in achieving fiscal balance than the Conservative-led coalition (McDaniel 2014, 299). The results of the May 2015 general election saw the Conservatives, against all opinion, win a narrow but clear majority while Labour lost all but one seat in its previously reliable Scotland. The consequence of Labour's stunning loss may be an acceleration of its own Pasokification (Doran 2015b). And the lesson seems lost on Labour's luminaries, where Tony Blair's post-mortem concluded that Labour could be salvaged if "it reoccupies the centre ground ... proudly championing a pro-business agenda and bold new ideas to reform public services" (Helm 2015). Blair's diagnosis is evidently based on a conclusion that Miliband's "One Nation" platform was too radical and returned Labour to its class politics roots. Yet Labour's proposals such as those concerned with welfare and unemployment emphasized individual responsibility and expressed a fidelity to fiscal conservatism in rejecting debt financing (McDaniel 2014, 299–300). It is difficult to discern how this is radical or in any way a substantive departure from Blair's Third Way. The same dynamic of social democratic drift and consequent electoral fracturing to its Left and Right can be seen in France, the Netherlands, Finland, Sweden, Denmark, Germany, and Belgium. The populist radical Right has certainly siphoned votes from working-class voters who may well have traditionally cast ballots for the centre-Left. Such parties have supplemented their anti-immigration positions by adopting policies that support social security and solidarity and critique globalization, albeit to preserve specific ethno-cultural identities (Bale 2003). But parties to the left of social democracy have also benefited from social democracy's drift.

Spain's social democrats see the threat of "Pasokification" as a real possibility with the significant rise of Podemos, a party created out of the financial crisis and the subsequent austerity policies pursued by both social democrats and conservatives. Spain's social democrats are now polling their lowest numbers since democracy was restored. In several countries, specifically Denmark, Germany, the Netherlands, and to some lesser extent Portugal, social democracy may not be pulverized by the radical Left, but it has certainly lost a significant part of its electorate to them and now wins the lowest share of votes since the end of the Second World War.

Social pacts and specifically their operationalization through neo-corporatist mechanisms is a distinguishing political and policy instrument of classical social democracy. The transition to neoliberalism has transformed these mechanisms for social dialogue from a means to bargain for a more egalitarian redistribution of resources to a means through which austerity is constructed, imposed, and legitimized.

Neo-Corporatism for a Neoliberal Era: From Power Sharing to Austerity Alliances

The lineage of austerity alliances through and after the 2008 crisis originates with the social dialogue mechanisms that so distinctively characterized the high-water mark of classical social democracy. At both levels of ideology and political practice, social democracy's purpose was to mediate class conflict by integrating the working class and its organizations (unions, parties) into the processes of the state apparatus. Best expressing this are the tripartite neo-corporatist arrangements that brought state, labour, and capital together in determining how to distribute the benefits without destroying the economic foundation that enabled the virtuous cycle of increasing productivity, rates of accumulation, and consumption. Of course, the political and economic landscape has transformed dramatically since the end of the post-war boom, and with this the very purpose of neo-corporatist arrangements. Indeed, in the post-2008 crisis period, neo-corporatism has shifted towards "negotiated flexibility" as a means to contain job loss but has also been the site for the manufacturing of austerity policies (Anxo 2015, 263). The result has been one characterization of trade union participation in neoliberal corporatist structures as a "policy of powerless social dialogue" (Wahl 2004, 46).

The genius of social democracy was that by establishing political mechanisms to simultaneously redistribute wealth through the expansion of public services as well as through the creation of mechanisms for social dialogue and partnership, the economic dynamic responsible for wealth creation was enhanced rather than damaged. In this manner social democracy provided the institutional arrangements that ensured economic expansion would lift all boats, or more narrowly, those of the organized and represented working class as well as sustaining capital accumulation.

The history of neo-corporatism corresponds to the golden age of both Keynesian managed capitalism and social democracy. Shonfield (1965) situated the corporatist phenomenon as a characteristic of the modern post-war Keynesian welfare state. His interest was centred upon corporatism as an instrument for state economic management. As the state's role in the economy grew, this would imply greater coordination of various interest groups and economic actors. Schmitter advanced this coordination function by placing the representation of societal interests at the centre of the mechanism "as a system of interest and/or attitude representation, a particular modal or ideal-typical institutional arrangement for linking the associationally organized interests of civil society with the decisional structures of the state" (1974, 86). In other words, these mechanisms served to intermediate sectional interests. He distinguished between *state corporatism* of the fascist and authoritarian type and *societal corporatism* of the modern democratic Keynesian variety, represented most strongly in Scandinavia but present in many other countries (104). Lehmbruch observed that what was distinctly important was the "high degree of collaboration among the groups themselves in the shaping of economic policy" (1977, 94). In this respect, what was of central importance was the *concertation* of multi-actor goals and objectives orchestrated through corporatist mechanisms not only between collective actors but also within them – and as such corporatism was a distinct method of policymaking.

Others, most notably Panitch (1980), signalled a departure in assessing the concept and practice of corporatism and further interrogated the nature of the "interests" such arrangements supposedly mediated. Marxist concerns with class and the management of a capitalist economy were of key importance in this respect. Panitch criticized the pluralism inherent to perspectives reflecting a "group-theoretical" rather than a "class-theoretical" framing (169). Panitch defined corporatism as "a political structure within advanced capitalism which integrates organized socioeconomic producer groups through a system of representation and cooperative mutual interaction at the leadership level and mobilization and social control at the mass level. Seen in this way, corporatism is understood as an actual political structure, not an ideology" (173). In this respect, Panitch identifies the political role of corporatist structures as the containment of the political and economic capacities of the working class in the post–Second World War period. Specifically, corporatist structures provided a space within the state apparatus giving voice to trade union perspectives on economic planning and incomes policy. In exchange, trade unions were required to integrate "capitalist growth criteria in union wage policy and their administration of wage restraint to their members" (174). In this respect, this state-led collaboration is concerned principally with integrating the working class into the capitalist state (175).

As the post-war Keynesian model wobbled through the 1970s and 1980s, so too did the ideological and political foundations of neo-corporatism. As many conceptualizations of corporatism's operation had tied it so closely to the economic management strategies of Keynesianism and the industrial economy of Fordism, when these two were undermined through the 1980s and into the 1990s it was felt that neo-corporatism and the notion of concertation would be rendered useless or impossible. The globalization of capitalism and the political impasse of the working class informed a deepening pessimism. No less a proponent than Schmitter concluded neo-corporatism could not address the new realities: "Negotiations aimed at establishing standard national macro-economic parameters are of decreasing relevance, and at times may even be counterproductive, when what is demanded are policies tailored to improve the productivity and international competitiveness of specific sectors, discrete branches of production and even individual enterprises" (1989, 70). The erosion of the two supporting structures of corporatism – Keynesian policymaking and Fordist industrial organization – was consequential for corporatist governance, as this too, as a policy process derivation, would also fade. Looser labour markets empowered employers, while European integration placed constraints on national-level discretion in the formulation of economic policy. For labour, there were now few remaining incentives to deliver wage restraint in return for improvements to the social wage and employment security, as both state and employer partners held fewer bargaining chips as well as their own diminished incentives to compromise with labour (Streeck and Schmitter 1991). This particular model of social dialogue and bargaining was superseded by market forces that were now singularly capable of imposing discipline on labour (Gobeyn 1993, 20). Financialization and, particularly in the European

Union, economic and political integration required governments to dismantle or restructure institutions and political arrangements that were unacceptable to capital (Kurzer 1993, 244–5). And the transformation of employment relations more generally and the marked decline in working-class political capacities spelled the end of neo-corporatism (Grahl and Teague 1997). But of course, this was but the end of one neo-corporatist form, which had been constructed through the post-war Keynesian period. As neoliberalism ascended, it would not disappear but rather transform to achieve objectives reflecting the profound shift in class power and economic structure.

The 1990s witnessed a "corporatist revival," but the context was one where neoliberalism was consolidating its hegemonic hold. During the post-war period corporatism had been centred on tripartite bargaining for negotiating wages, production, social programs, and labour protections. In the 1980s, this form of corporatism declined and was "modified or recast rather than abandoned" (Rhodes 2001, 167) as a new form of neo-corporatism, no longer oriented towards negotiated incomes policies that traded wage restraint in exchange for an increased social wage (i.e., welfare state growth and job benefits), but instead wage restraint was traded in exchange for a state and employer commitment to employment security (Fajertag and Pochet 1997; Wiarda 1997). The weakening of organized labour in this context also saw policy concerns shift towards public expenditure restraint, and an increased role for monetary policy and central banks in concertation efforts. A key shift was that the tripartite arrangements between state, business, and labour came to include central banks, as these institutions, strengthened by varying degrees of independence, held sway over monetary policy and prioritized inflation containment rather than distribution (Iversen 1999). Thus a new competitive corporatism built on productivity and competitiveness alliances displaced the social corporatism of the Keynesian era. The general focus of public policy shifted towards a pre-eminent concern with inflation, and controlling state debt and deficits (Rhodes 2001). Given this trajectory, neo-corporatism is updated for the neoliberal era, transformed from a mechanism seeking to balance redistribution with the sustainability of capitalism to become an instrument of economic restructuring and fiscal discipline (Crouch 1999). Thus the defining issues requiring concertation in the 1990s were wage discipline, labour market flexibility, and welfare state restructuring (Molina and Rhodes 2002, 317).

Through and following the 2008 financial crisis, a third period in the history of neo-corporatism is discernible. Crisis corporatism turned to social partnerships and social pacts as important mechanisms in negotiating the terms of austerity, as aggressive fiscal consolidation followed the short-lived pragmatic Keynesian revival. Social dialogue in several European countries enabled a negotiated response to the crisis, where trade unions often agreed to "cuts in working time, wage moderation measures and flexibilisation of remuneration contracts" (Urban 2015, 269–70). This defensive "dented shield" strategy of some trade unions participating in social partnerships expressed the weakening of working-class organizations to resist the profound shift in power relations that had taken place since the 1980s. Outside of the PIGS countries (Portugal, Ireland, Greece, and Spain), European trade unions, through their participation in social pacts, demonstrated a willingness "to acquiesce to wage moderation, more flexible working conditions or privatised social services in exchange for maintaining employment" (Bieling and Lux 2014, 154). In other countries where deep fiscal retrenchment and labour market disciplinary policies were constructed through social partnership arrangements, such structures dissolved. The austerity social partnerships were mechanisms for "concession bargaining in the form of wage restraint, longer and more flexible working hours, and welfare reforms in exchange for certain tax cuts and employment promises … the pacts were further backed up by the overall aim to fulfill the requirements of the European Monetary Union (EMU), since the mentioned reform packages contributed to lowering inflation rates and budget deficits" (156). The consequence of austerity corporatism has been to reinforce the declining share of wages as a proportion of GDP, "despite the formal commitment of European unions to a wage policy intended to reverse or at least halt this decline" (Hyman 2010, 8).

The participation of trade unions in competitive and austerity corporatist mechanisms has been characterized as a "yes, but" response to further restructuring (Dølvik 1999), which has not led to significant changes in the deepening of neoliberalism (Bieler 2007, 113). Unions participate in discussions without making much impact. More than defensive bargaining, the "social partnership" approach of the European labour movement "amounts to a strategy that not only further abandons the autonomy of the labour movement but confirms the logic of neoliberalism" (ibid.). In 2008, Italian workers declared, "We are not paying for the crisis," and workers across the EU soon took up the slogan. The renewed militancy across Europe was marked by large mobilizations in several capitals. Even the relatively conservative German unions organized a "Capitalism Congress" to initiate an ideological shift that contested the ideology of the social market economy, which glossed over the fact that capitalism was premised on the basic inequality between labour and capital. The similarly benign Irish Confederation of Trade Unions, which had eagerly participated in a social pact with business and government for twenty years, called for a campaign of "sustained opposition to the government" (Hyman 2010, 4). But such militancy was for the most part short-lived, as unions returned to allocating priority to social dialogue over militancy (European Trade Union Confederation 2012).

The lived experience of neo-corporatism before and after the 2008 crisis is one where "the institutions of social partnership ... by integrating labour's interest representatives in policy-making ... also turned out to be conducive to implementing austerity measures after the crisis" (Hermann and Flecker 2012, 134). In the German case, the contribution of the trade unions to the tripartite negotiations was one where they "proved themselves as crisis managers" (Dörre 2011, 268, as cited in Urban 2015, 273). That these mechanisms have proven so effective in implementing austerity speaks to the weakness of the organized working class, as this bargaining requires concessions (273). Austerity corporatism is significantly different from either social or competitive variants. The power resources of each actor have changed: the class compromises have moved from symmetrical during the height of social corporatism to an alliance of the weak (labour, state, and industrial capital) facing the demands of financial capital. The role of trade unions in this context was to stabilize the economy and thus protect employers in the "real" economy from disaster (278). And in Ireland since the mid-1980s, when the government established a social partnership with the trade unions, the basic model was one of wage restraint in exchange for tax cuts (Baccaro and Simoni 2008, 1331–2; Wickham 2015, 135–7), leading critics to contend that rather than improving working-class social and economic conditions, it instead contributed to and legitimized relative wage and income inequality, comparatively high levels of poverty, and comparatively low expenditure on public services (Dobbins 2011). The Croke Park agreement, brokered as part of Ireland's consolidation strategy in the wake of the 2008 crisis, afforded no substantive protections; there was no guarantee that pay cuts would be reversed; an "escape" clause allowed the government to further cut pay if economic circumstances warranted; strikes and industrial action of any type aimed against any aspect of the agreement were prohibited; overtime pay was prohibited; and a two-tier labour force marked by lower wages, pensions, and working conditions for all new hires was created. At the centre of this capitulation is the "social partnership" process, where in the course of its twenty-three years of existence the ICTU's leadership became integrated, albeit in a junior and supplicant role, with the Irish state. The trade union leadership viewed themselves as responsible partners in the management of austerity (Boyd 2010).

The reconstruction of social pacts as a mechanism for negotiated austerity expresses the profound shift in class power relations that have taken place. Social democratic parties, giving voice and representation to workers' interests, are, if not at an end, clearly much weaker than they were in the 1970s. Through the 1990s, as redistributive social democracy morphed into Third Wayism, the hold of social democracy on its traditional working-class voters began to fracture.

The Crisis, Twenty-First Century Social Democracy, and the Radical Left Alternative

Finding the space and strategy for successful resistance and the construction of achievable alternatives to austerity, a theme dealt with by Graefe and Rioux in this volume, is proving difficult, especially where the anti-austerity forces are uneven in strength, organizational capacity, and ability to analyse the problem. The case of Greece is instructive.

The Greek general election of 25 January 2015 was supposed to be a watershed, a historic rupture with austerity, which would start in Greece and then expand to other states within the European Union. It was furthermore historic, as the election of Syriza, the party of the radical Left, to government, albeit a minority, marked the first instance in Europe at least where a party to the left of social democracy and programmatically committed to a break with neoliberalism, if not capitalism, was elected to lead a government. Not since the late 1970s when the French Left (socialist, communist, and radical), united under the "Common Program," and the Italian Communist Party, threateningly (for some) contended for governmental power, had the possibility of a parliamentary road to socialism been seriously considered. But in January 2015 such a possibility appeared viable once again. However, rather than a Greek-led rupture with austerity, a rapid succession of events raised not the spectre of socialism but rather a return to the despondency of "There Is No Alternative." Negotiations between Greece and the "Troika" (the European Central Bank, International Monetary Fund, and European Commission) over the European Stability Mechanism bailout – the regime of "fiscal waterboarding" as Finance Minister Varoufakis termed it – led to anything but a rupture with austerity. Seeking a popular democratic mandate to compel the Troika to negotiate terms to end the vicious cycle of bailouts paid with austerity measures, Syriza pushed forward with a national plebiscite on 4 July 2015 and won a resounding 61 per cent "No" vote – a "no" to the continuation of fiscal waterboarding. But within hours that mandate translated into total capitulation of the Syriza government to the demands of the creditors. The result was a long way from Syriza's 2014 "Thessaloniki Program," which sought a moratorium on debt servicing, expanded public investment, a Europe-wide New Deal of public investment, the gradual restoration of employment wages and pensions, and rebuilding of the welfare state.

Syriza's experience may contain important lessons for the other new parties of the radical Left in Europe that constitute what may be termed a fourth wave in the history of the Left. This New Left is composed of political parties that reject the practices and politics of the old Lefts of social democracy and Stalinist communism, have a generally weaker relationship to and within trade unions compared to social democracy and even the Communists, and, from the perspective of their own internal party culture, are open to accommodating a plurality of ideological tendencies and encouraging a more heterodox politics of ideas and practice. All are explicitly anti-neoliberal and alter-globalization but also express varying degrees of anti-capitalism. According to Philippe Marlière, the contemporary radical Left in Europe come from one of a few strands: communist parties that remained orthodox Marxist-Leninist; that transitioned/merged into Red/Green eco-socialist-type parties; or emerged from splits and reconfigurations among the Eurocommunist or left social democratic trends (Marlière 2013).

But the advances of the radical Left, while real, are uneven throughout Europe. In Finland, the ex-communists have in fact declined. In the United Kingdom, there is no national radical Left of any significance, though the Greens may be filling that void. In Germany, Belgium, Luxembourg, the Netherlands, and Austria, where social democracy has been in decline since the 1980s, Green parties as well as radical Right parties have taken votes from the centre-Left, but the German Left party has consolidated at approximately 8 per cent of the popular vote, while the Dutch Socialist Party, which stands to the left of social democracy, now routinely poll 10–15 per cent. And in Belgium and Luxembourg, radical Left parties have re-entered the national parliament after a long absence, though with modest total vote shares. In France, the initial excitement for the prospects of the Left Front, especially the 2012 presidential campaign of Jean-Luc Mélenchon, has withered as that project floundered (Marlière 2013). The Communist Party has returned to the politics of the "plural Left," in an effort to unite the broad French Left, while Mélenchon and the Left Party have shifted strategy with the formation of the Movement for a Sixth Republic. This new movement, modelled on Spain's Podemos and Latin American movements, does not seek to bring the organized Left forces together but rather to unite "the people" around a political program for reconstruction of the French state and society (Flenady 2014).

Thus, the experience of Syriza remains exceptional. Some smaller radical Left parties elsewhere have at times joined coalition governments and have proven, like social democrats, willing managers of austerity. Like social democrats, they "have been made hostage to neoliberal policies, including support for privatization and the U.S. war machine, such as its invasion and occupation of Afghanistan. They have not been able to be consistent critics of the system, let alone offer a credible alternative" (Wahl 2014). Thus while social democracy atrophies, the radical Left has been only a partial beneficiary. And the failure of Syriza may have rather dark implications for the electoral fortunes of other Left parties. The radical Right and nationalist parties, progressive and reactionary, continue to siphon off formerly centre-Left support and are doing so with considerable effect in Germany, Sweden, France, Austria, and the Netherlands in particular.

Conclusion

Despite the mainstream celebrity of Thomas Piketty's *Capital in the 21st Century*, which political vehicle will ultimately mobilize the politics for equality and economic democracy is unclear. Social democracy has proven itself unable to serve this role as it did in the decades following 1945. Syriza's efforts to reclaim an authentic social democracy, let alone a democratic socialism, may flounder. And its sister parties, the Danish Red-Green Alliance, Germany's Left Party, the Dutch Socialist Party, Spain's Podemos, and Portugal's Left Bloc, among others, are themselves either stabilizing with serious but modest levels of support or are in fact declining. Other forces, whether nationalist or radical Right, are having a certain success in mobilizing against social and economic insecurity. The political crisis of social democracy, and the real limits of the radical Left, despite the most significant opening for a political and ideological challenge to capitalism since the 1930s, is more importantly an expression of the very deep crisis in working-class politics. If class is not the driving force behind the struggles in the second decade of the twenty-first century, can it ever be?

REFERENCES

Anderson, Perry. 2000. "Renewals." *New Left Review* 1 (January–February): 5–24.

Angier, Tom. 2015. "Why European Social Democracy Is in Danger of Terminal Decline." *Social Europe*, 2 February. https://www.socialeurope.eu/2015/02/european-social-democracy-danger-terminal-decline/.

Anxo, Dominique. 2015. "The Swedish Model in Times of Crisis: Decline or Resilience?" In *Divisive Integration: The Triumph of Failed Ideas in Europe – Revisited*, ed. S. Lehndorff, 253–68. Brussels: European Trade Union Institute.

Baccaro, Lucio, and Marco Simoni. 2008. "Policy Concertation in Europe: Understanding Government Choice." *Comparative Political Studies* 41 (10): 1323–48. https://doi.org/10.1177/0010414008315861.

Bailey, David. 2009. *The Political Economy of European Social Democracy*. Abingdon: Routledge.

Bale, Tim. 2003. "Cinderella and Her Ugly Sisters: The Mainstream and Extreme Right in Europe's Bipolarising Party Systems." *West European Politics* 26 (3): 67–90. https://doi.org/10.1080/01402380312331280598.

Benjamin, Walter. 1969. *Illuminations: Essays and Reflections*. Edited by Hannah Arendt. New York: Schocken.

Berman, Sheri. 2006. *The Primacy of Politics*. New York: Cambridge University Press. https://doi.org/10.1017/CBO9780511791109.

Bertinotti, Fausto. 2003. "Reformist Social Democracy Is No Longer on the Agenda." *Guardian*, 11 August. https://www.theguardian.com/politics/2003/aug/11/globalisation.world.

Bieler, Andreas. 2007. "Co-option or Resistance? Trade Unions and Neoliberal Restructuring in Europe." *Capital and Class* 31 (3): 111–24. https://doi.org/10.1177/030981680709300107.

Bieling, Hans-Juergen, and Julia Lux. 2014. "Crisis-Induced Social Conflicts in the European Union – Trade Union Perspectives: The Emergence of 'Crisis Corporatism' or the Failure of Corporatist Arrangements?" *Global Labour Journal* 5 (2): 153–75. https://doi.org/10.15173/glj.v5i2.1156.

Blyth, Mark. 1997. "Review: 'Any More Bright Ideas': The Ideational Turn in Comparative Political Economy." *Comparative Politics* 29 (2): 229–50. https://doi.org/10.2307/422082.
Boyd, Stephen. 2010. "Union Leaders Have Nothing to Offer but a Sell Out." *Socialist Party*, 14 May.
Burnham, James. 1941. *The Managerial Revolution*. London: Penguin Books.
Cramme, Olaf, Patrick Diamond, Roger Liddle, Michael McTernan, Frans Becker, and Rene Cuperus. 2012. *A Centre Left Project for New Times*. London: Policy Network.
Crosland, Anthony. 1956. *The Future of Socialism*. London: Jonathan Cape.
Crouch, Colin. 1999. "National Wage Determination and European Monetary Union." In *After the Euro: Shaping Institutions for Governance in the Wake of European Monetary Union*, ed. C. Crouch, 203–26. Oxford: Clarendon.
– 2011. *The Strange Non-Death of Neoliberalism*. Cambridge: Policy.
de Jong, Alex. 2014. "Dutch Socialist Party from Sect to Mass Party." *International Viewpoint*, 8 October. http://www.internationalviewpoint.org/spip.php?article3653.
Dobbins, Tony. 2011. *Industrial Relations Profile*. Eurofound. https://www.eurofound.europa.eu/eiro/country/ireland.pdf.
Dølvik, Jon Erik. 1999. *An Emerging Island? ETUC, Social Dialogue and the Europeanisation of the Trade Unions in the 1990s*. Brussels: European Trade Union Institute.
Doran, James. 2015a. "Warning of Pasokification, Not Yearning for It." In The Hands of the Many Blog. http://hands-of-the-many.blogspot.ca/.
– 2015b. "5 Reasons Labour's Pasokification Has Accelerated." *Counterfire*, 8 May. http://www.counterfire.org/articles/opinion/17807-5-reasons-labour-s-pasokification-has-accelerated.
European Trade Union Confederation. 2012. *A Social Compact for Europe*. Brussels: ETUC.
Fajertag, Guiseppe, and Phillipe Pochet, eds. 1997. *Social Pacts in Europe*. Brussels: European Trade Union Institute.
Flenady, Liam. 2014. "France: Left Front Debates 'Uniting the People' vs 'Uniting the Left.'" *Green Left Weekly*, 14 September. https://www.greenleft.org.au/node/57369.
Gobeyn, Mark J. 1993. "Explaining the Decline of Macro-Corporatist Political Bargaining Structures in Advanced Capitalist Societies." *Governance: An International Journal of Policy, Administration and Institutions* 6 (1): 3–22. https://doi.org/10.1111/j.1468-0491.1993.tb00134.x.
Grahl, John, and Paul Teague. 1997. "Is the European Social Model Fragmenting?" *New Political Economy* 2 (3): 405–26. https://doi.org/10.1080/13563469708406315.

Gramsci, A. 1971. *Selections from the Prison Notebooks*. London: Lawrence and Wisehart.

Guinan, Joe. 2013. "Returns to Capital: Austerity and the Crisis of European Social Democracy." *Good Society* 22 (1): 44–60. https://doi.org/10.1353/gso.2013.0006.

Helm, Toby. 2015. "Blair Tells Labour: Return to the Centre Ground to Win Again." *Guardian*, 10 May. https://www.theguardian.com/politics/2015/may/09/tony-blair-labour-return-centre-ground-general-election-defeat.

Hermann, Christoph, and Jörg Flecker. 2012. *Privatization of Public Services: Impacts for Employment, Working Conditions, and Service Quality in Europe*. New York: Routledge. https://www.routledge.com/products/search?author=Christoph%20Hermann.

Hyman, Richard. 2010. "Social Dialogue and Industrial Relations during the Economic Crisis: Innovative Practices or Business as Usual?" ILO Industrial and Employment Relations Department Working Paper 11. Geneva: International Labour Office.

Iversen, Torben. 1999. *Contested Economic Institutions: The Politics of Macroeconomics and Wage Bargaining*. Cambridge: Cambridge University Press.

Kitschelt, Herbert. 1994. *The Transformation of European Social Democracy*. Cambridge: Cambridge University Press. https://doi.org/10.1017/CBO9780511622014.

Kurzer, Paulette. 1993. *Business and Banking: Political Change and Economic Integration in Western Europe*. Ithaca, NY: Cornell University Press.

Lawson, Neal. 2014. "Social Democrats Face Irrelevance at Best, Extinction at Worse." *New Statesman*, 8 December. http://www.newstatesman.com/politics/2014/12/social-democrats-face-irrelevance-best-extinction-worse.

Laxer, James. 2014. "Scottish Referendum: World's First Vote on Economic Inequality." *Globe and Mail*, 8 September. http://www.theglobeandmail.com/opinion/scottish-referendum-the-worlds-first-vote-on-economic-inequality/article20489038/.

Lehmbruch, Gerhard. 1977. "Liberal Corporatism and Party Government." *Comparative Political Studies* 10 (1): 91–126. https://doi.org/10.1177/001041407701000105.

Marlière, Philippe. 2013. "The Radical Left in Europe: An Outline." *Transform!* 13. http://www.transform-network.net/journal/issue-132013/news/detail/Journal/the-radical-left-in-europe-an-outline.html.

McDaniel, Sean. 2014. "Post-Crisis Social Democratic Policy Capacity in France and the United Kingdom: A Lesson from the Globalisation and the Social Democracy Debate." *French Politics* 12 (4): 283–309. https://doi.org/10.1057/fp.2014.23.

Merkel, Wolfgang, Alexander Petring, Christian Henkes, and Christoph Egle. 2008. *Social Democracy in Power: The Capacity to Reform*. London: Routledge.

Molina, Oscar, and Martin Rhodes. 2002. "Corporatism: The Past, Present, and Future of a Concept." *Annual Review of Political Science* 5 (1): 305–31. https://doi.org/10.1146/annurev.polisci.5.112701.184858.

Moschonas, Gerassimos. 2002. *In the Name of Social Democracy – The Great Transformation: 1945 to the Present*. London: Verso.

Mudde, Cas. 2013. "Nothing Left? In Search of (a New) Social Democracy." *Open Democracy*, 21 November. https://www.opendemocracy.net/can-europe-make-it/cas-mudde/nothing-left-in-search-of-new-social-democracy.

Notermans, Ton. 2000. *Money, Markets and the State: Social Democratic Economic Policies since 1918*. Cambridge: Cambridge University Press. https://doi.org/10.1017/CBO9780511521607.

Panitch, Leo. 1980. "Recent Theorizations of Corporatism: Reflections on a Growth Industry." *British Journal of Sociology* 31 (2): 159–87. https://doi.org/10.2307/589686.

Piven, Frances Fox, ed. 1992. *Labor Parties in Postindustrial Societies*. New York: Oxford University Press.

Policy Network. 2013. "State of the Left." www.policy-network.net/content/392/State-of-the-Left.

Rhodes, Martin. 2001. "The Political Economy of Social Pacts: 'Competitive Corporatism' and European Welfare Reform." In *The New Politics of the Welfare State*, ed. Paul Pierson, 165–94. Oxford: Oxford University Press. https://doi.org/10.1093/0198297564.003.0007.

Sassoon, Donald. 1997. *One Hundred Years of Socialism*. London: Fontana.

Schmitter, Phillipe. 1974. "Still the Century of Corporatism?" *Review of Politics* 36 (1): 85–131. https://doi.org/10.1017/S0034670500022178.

– 1989. "Corporatism Is Dead! Long Live Corporatism!" *Government and Opposition* 24 (1): 54–73.

Shonfield, Andrew. 1965. *Modern Capitalism*. London: Oxford University Press.

Streeck, W., and P.C. Schmitter. 1991. "From National Corporatism to Transnational Pluralism: Organized Interests in the Single European Market." *Politics & Society* 19 (2): 133–64. https://doi.org/10.1177/003232929101900202.

Taylor, Robert. 2008. "Does European Social Democracy Have a Future?" *Dissent* (Summer). https://www.dissentmagazine.org/article/does-european-social-democracy-have-a-future.

Urban, Hans-Jurgen. 2015. "Between Crisis Corporatism and Revitalization: Trade Union Policy in the Era of European Financial Market Capitalism."

In *Divisive Integration: The Triumph of Failed Ideas in Europe – Revisited*, ed. S. Lehndorff, 269–94. Brussels: European Trade Union Institute.

Varoufakis, Yanis. 2014. "Europe's Crisis and the Rise of the Ultra-Right Is the Left's Fault." http://www.yanisvaroufakis.eu/2014/06/09/europes-crisis-and-the-rise-of-the-ultra-right-is-the-lefts-fault/.

Wahl, Asbjørn. 2004. "European Labor: The Ideological Legacy of the Social Pact." *Monthly Review (New York, N.Y.)* 55 (8): 37–49. https://doi.org/10.14452/MR-055-08-2004-01_4.

— 2014. "Political and Ideological Crisis in an Increasingly More Authoritarian European Union." *Monthly Review (New York, N.Y.)* 65 (8): 35. https://doi.org/10.14452/MR-065-08-2014-01_3. https://monthlyreview.org/2014/01/european-labor/.

Wiarda, Howard J. 1997. *Corporatism and Comparative Politics: The Other Great "Ism."* Armonk, NY: M.E. Sharpe.

Wickham, James. 2015. "Irish Paradoxes: The Bursting of the Bubbles and the Curious Survival of Social Cohesion." In *Divisive Integration: The Triumph of Failed Ideas in Europe – Revisited*, ed. Steffen Lehndorff, 127–47. Brussels: European Trade Union Institute.

14 Austerity and Political Crisis: The Radical Left, the Far Right, and Europe's New Authoritarian Order

NEIL A. BURRON

Nearly eight years after the onset of the financial crisis, the European economy remains stagnant and the people of Europe worse off than they were before. With sluggish growth rates – averaging 1.6 per cent in early 2016 – and mounting debt (the euro area's debt-to-GDP level reached a record-high 93 per cent in 2016, compared to 79.3 per cent at the end of 2009), austerity policies have failed, even by their own narrow economic objectives. Various countries have consistently experienced near-zero or even negative growth (Fazi 2016). Most worrisome, nearly one-quarter of EU citizens (24.6 per cent) are now regarded as being at-risk-of-poverty or social exclusion, and Oxfam (2015) reports that, between 2009 and 2013, the number of Europeans living in severe material deprivation (i.e., without enough money to heat their homes or cope with unforeseen expenses), rose by 7.5 million to 50 million people. At the same time, the richest have seen their share of income increase, and austerity has been associated with a more unequal distribution of income across Europe (Schneider, Kinsella, and Godin 2015).

The social consequences of austerity have been significant, and citizens have contested the mass public-sector layoffs, social cuts, and privatizations that have further eroded the welfare state. Indeed, austerity has produced a growing crisis of legitimacy in Europe that, according to one scholar, "threatens to derail the neoliberal project that has been spearheaded by the European capitalist class over the past three decades" (van Apeldoorn 2014, 190). In the early years of the crisis, students, unemployed youth, workers, and activists occupied city squares across Europe, trade unions went on mass strike, and governments fell in disgrace as citizens rejected the generous bailout packages for the banks and the cuts foisted upon the public. In the southern periphery, where the imposition of austerity by Germany and the Troika[1] has been harshest, the traditional parties were discredited, and new Left parties such as Syriza in Greece, and Podemos in Spain, have gained considerable popular support. In Greece, where austerity has produced permanent economic and political crisis, the radical Left was elected to form government, though it has been notably unable to exercise state power to break from austerity. Mass strikes and mobilizations also occurred in Britain, France, Belgium, and Iceland, and the explosion of unrest in the ex-communist countries of the eastern periphery was short but unprecedented in the post-communist era. While the nadir of the crisis has long since passed, the European public remains largely opposed to austerity, and a record number of citizens reject the institutions of the European Union (Gallup 2013; Eurobarometer 2014). With growing Euroscepticism, Far Right parties in Greece, Hungary, France, and several other countries have also pitted themselves against the traditional political elite. Europe's political malaise persists.

Yet despite the political crises that unfolded across Europe, beginning in 2008 and continuing, in some places, to the present, the European capitalist classes and political elite have weathered the storm. The crisis of legitimacy did not translate into a crisis of state, even if several governments were forced to resign or were decimated at the polls. Indeed, austerity has become, if anything, even more entrenched. The recent example of Greece, where Syriza, the one anti-austerity party to come to power, is now administering an austerity program imposed by the Troika more draconian than those pursued by its predecessors from the traditional parties, underscores the commitment of the European capitalist class to ensure that there truly is, in the famous dictum of Margaret Thatcher, no alternative. Through a series of new measures, the institutions of the European Union have further embedded the power of finance capital to dictate

---

[1] The three main creditors in Europe: the European Central Bank, the European Commission, and the International Monetary Fund. The term has gained notoriety in several countries, prompting the the Eurogroup, the finance ministers of the Eurozone, to rebrand the trio "the institutions" during the negotiations with Greece for a third memorandum in early 2015. The rebranding exercise did little to quell the wrath of the public.

the fiscal and monetary policies of member states, and the European elite has become increasingly hostile to basic norms of liberal democracy. Threats to the austerity program have been dispatched through illiberal and undemocratic means – including through the suspension of parliamentary democracy – and through campaigns of financial destabilization. Class domination – especially in the European periphery – is losing its hegemonic character, and coercion is increasingly substituting for consent as the European capitalist class deepens the neoliberal project under austerity.

This chapter draws upon the critical literature in European politics and international political economy to provide an overview of the political crises that swept Europe in the wake of the financial crisis, the emergence of counter-hegemonic movements on the Left and Right, and the authoritarian response of the European capitalist class. While the diversity of experiences with austerity and political crisis caution against overgeneralizations – political crises have no doubt followed different paths, time-horizons, and political-economic dynamics across regions and states – the intent of the analysis in the pages that follow is to provide a general survey of the political experience of austerity in Europe from the vantage point of class struggle. The first part of the chapter situates the origin of the crisis in the long unravelling of Europe's post-war class compromise. With the triumph of neoliberal Europe, the shift towards austerity marked a more aggressive phase of class conflict. The second part looks at the political crises that began in 2008, which gave rise to new mass politics and parties on the Left, as well as the resurgence of the reactionary Right. The reasons for defeat and the lessons for the Left from this initial period of resistance are briefly assessed. The final section examines how European states and the EU are responding to the crisis of hegemony through the development of an increasingly authoritarian order.

The Roots of the Political Crisis

The Long Decline of the Post-war Class Compromise

Perhaps the most remarkable feature of the political crisis has been the persistent implementation of austerity measures in the face of widespread opposition. The resolve with which austerity has been pursued suggests that Europe's political elites and dominant classes are no longer committed to maintaining the remnants of the post-war class compromise that helped stabilize social relations in the golden era of capitalism. Yet this hardening of class position comes at the end of a lengthy attrition against the gains made by the working and middle class over the last three decades. The most recent measures favouring deeper social cuts, privatization, and undermining of the employment-generating function of governments signifies a deepening of the neoliberal state. In this sense – and insofar as massive cuts shifted the burden of responsibility of the financial crisis from the bankers to the public, thus generating the sovereign debt crisis leading to the justification for cuts in the first place – austerity is an intensification of class struggle by the European capitalist classes and political elite to further advance a long-standing political and economic project. Understanding the historical process in which austerity need be situated thus requires some general observations on the erosion of class compromise and its effects on European politics in the past few decades.

Gramsci's theory of hegemony provides a useful starting point for exploring the historical roots of the current political crisis. As a participant in the revolutionary events and political turmoil that followed the First World War, Gramsci concluded that, when ruling social blocs fail to create a genuine hegemonic order based on some degree of class compromise and moral-political leadership, prolonged periods of crisis can disrupt the coherence of ruling class ideas. Such crises were particularly apparent in the industrially backward Eastern countries of Europe when Gramsci was writing. In the West, however, where Gramsci witnessed the failed revolutions of Germany after the war, revolution seemed to have been forestalled by the development of hegemonic societies where the ruling classes were being forced to make important concessions, and where the high level of economic development allowed for a higher standard of living (exemplified by American Fordism). Gramsci came to develop a complex theory of hegemony that showed how ruling classes can dispose of different material, ideological, and cultural resources to rule primarily by the consent of the dominated, though the coercion of the state is never far behind. But Gramsci knew that social compromises are always conditional upon the balance of class forces, and that economic and political crises could lead to a general crisis of hegemony where the power and legitimacy of the state, and class rule itself, are called into question. In such circumstances, solutions to the crisis could take radical counter-hegemonic forms or reactionary ones like those that took root in Germany and Italy.[2]

Gramsci's theory provided a prescient conceptual framework for analysing the forms of hegemony that took root in the post-war era. With the end of the political crisis that marked the interwar period, advanced capitalist states enacted considerable social and economic reforms that preserved the property relations of capitalism while accepting the mixed-economy, progressive taxation, and social policies intended to ensure a certain level of social harmony and class conciliation. This was the period of democratic capitalism, when governments had little appetite to return to the labour militancy of the 1930s before the war-economy had solved the problem of mass unemployment. In the Southern European countries, the welfare state was never as fully entrenched, but parties and institutions for mass participation were still present, and the defeat of the dictatorships in Greece, Spain, and Portugal in the 1970s opened the way for social democratic parties to install their own clientelist versions of the class compromises that prevailed in the north. In Central and Eastern Europe, mass politics were certainly not a feature of communist life, but a version of the welfare state did help reduce class tensions (which, of course, did not officially exist).

Yet as Streeck (2013) reminds us, *la trente glorieuse*, the golden era of post-war democratic capitalism, was in fact a short-lived historic exception to the long-standing structural contradictions between capitalism and democracy. Since the 1970s, multinational corporations and finance capital have brought tremendous pressure to bear on the range of policy options that governments can pursue. The welfare state has long been in decline, and even the parties of the Left have implemented neoliberal reforms deregulating the financial sector, privatizing state assets, cutting the public sector, and retrenching social policies. This has often occurred in opposition to their own electoral campaign promises (the Socialist government of François Mitterrand in the early

---

2 Gramsci's theory of hegemony was developed specifically to explain the rise of the Italian fascists in the early 1920s and the support they received from parts of the working class during times of austerity. The relationship between fascism and austerity was not incidental. As Blyth (2013) reminds us, the Nazi Party broadened its appeal by campaigning against the straitjacket of the gold standard and the austerity decrees of the Brüning government, which received tacit support from the Social Democratic Party. Japanese fascism was also closely linked to the unpopularity of austerity measures adopted by the government in the early 1930s.

1980s was the first to undertake a political about-face with its austerity measures. By the time Tony Blair's New Labour came to power in the mid-1990s, social democracy had already accepted large parts of the neoliberal program). The weakening of the traditional manufacturing sectors of the economy and the corresponding decline in the strength of labour unions undoubtedly facilitated this process.

As van Apeldoorn (2014, 190) and others have argued, neoliberalism in Europe must be understood as a hegemonic class project undertaken by class-conscious, transnationally oriented sections of capital to create a "transnational space for capital in which the latter's rule is established precisely by preserving the formal sovereignty of the member states while subordinating their democratic governance to the dictates of the single market." Thus, as national governments everywhere implemented neoliberal reforms, class-conscious collective actors such as the European Round Table of Industrialists pushed for the completion of the internal market through monetary union as part of a larger strategy of globalized accumulation. Attempts to create a "social Europe" in the 1980s were decisively defeated with the Economic Monetary Union, the deregulation of financial markets, and the establishment of the single currency under the authority of the European Central Bank (ECB), designed to uphold an anti-inflationary monetary policy akin to the ordoliberal regime maintained by the Bundesbank in Germany. The ECB was endowed with one mission – price stability – thus making it even more responsive to the interests of bondholders than the US Federal Reserve, which is also expected to maintain employment (Greer 2013). As Stephen Gill observed some time ago, the Economic Monetary Union can be viewed as an intergovernmental framework where economic policy and political accountability are separated so as to "make governments more responsive to the discipline of market forces and correspondingly less responsive to popular democratic forces and processes" (Gill 1998, 5).

The political hegemony of neoliberalism has led to a profound depoliticization of economic questions. In Western Europe, the embrace of neoliberalism by Left parties throughout the 1990s has been a key factor behind the emergence of "partyless" democracies, where parties in power are more concerned with governing than representing, and the ideological space between them diminishes (Mair 2000). In the east, the implementation of neoliberal policies through Shock Therapy in the early 1990s and the conversion of ex-communist parties to neoliberalism played a similar role. Even in the European Parliament, mainstream parties that are in the opposition rarely differentiate themselves from the governing ones on the main political and economic issues (and European politics has institutionalized cross-party and cross-national consensus through the standard practice of package deals) (Gropas 2011). This "post-parliamentary" and "post-democratic" phase of politics[3] has undermined the political arrangements that in part stabilized class compromise. As Crouch (2004) argues, politics has been reduced to a spectacle managed by rival teams of professional experts in the techniques of persuasion with a focus on a small range of issues selected by those teams. Citizens, for their part, are reduced to the role of manipulated, passive, rare participants, and mass parties are demobilized and professionalized.[4]

Austerity as the Intensification of Class Struggle

The long decline of the post-war class compromise was exacerbated by the financial crisis and the austerity measures that followed. Although the peripheral countries of the EU were hit hardest, the negative social and economic effects of austerity were universally felt as austerity became a program to further push ahead the aggressive agenda of Europe's dominant classes and political elites in the face of massive opposition. A few words on the financial crisis are briefly in order.

With the collapse of Lehman Brothers in September 2008, Central and Eastern Europe, with its deep integration into highly deregulated, risk-enhancing global financial markets, was the first to catch the global contagion. Prior to the crisis, the ex-communist states that had acceded to the European Union in 2004 were already pursuing austerity to meet "convergence criteria" designed to reduce government spending, though trade deficits remained substantial. Capital inflows from West European banks helped cover the trade deficit that most of the "EU 10" countries were running with their richer Western neighbours (having lost their own productive capacity through the deindustrialization of the 1990s). At the time of the crisis, over 80 per cent of banking assets in the new EU states were owned by foreign banks (Rae 2011). Within the

---

3 See Gauthier (2012) and Castellina (2012).
4 Early signs of protest against this process included both the rise of the Far Right in Europe in the 1990s and the growth of the anti-globalization movement, both of which were highly critical of European integration.

EU, therefore, there were deep structural imbalances between countries with huge surpluses in their current accounts, particularly Germany, and others with huge deficits that relied upon capital inflows to finance them (Altvater 2012).[5]

Thus, when international financial markets froze up, and governments faced skyrocketing borrowing costs to finance budgetary and balance of payments deficits, the EU 10 countries were quickly exposed, beginning with Latvia and Hungary (Toporowski 2012).[6] Soon after, the crisis spread to the weaker economies in the eurozone – Portugal, Ireland, Italy, Greece, and Spain – which shared the dangerous combination of financialization and large structural deficits. Greece, with its chronic fiscal and current account deficits, came first when the government was forced to acknowledge its deficit was much larger than reported. As investors panicked and bond yields skyrocketed, the financial crisis morphed into a sovereign debt one. Affected countries turned to the ECB, the IMF, and the European Financial Stability Fund to stabilize their financial markets in exchange for massive cuts. Meanwhile, German, French, Dutch, Belgian, UK, and Spanish banks were rescued at public expense. Between 2008 and 2011, while austerity was being implemented across the Continent (notwithstanding a short Keynesian moment at the outset of the crisis), the European Commission approved €4.5 trillion in aid to the financial sector (equivalent to 36.7 per cent of EU GDP).[7] This was on top of the bailout money that came directly from multiple governments (including several hundred billion in Germany and Britain).

The austerity measures only compounded the debt as shrinking economies reduced their tax bases (Blyth 2013). In Greece, for example, the debt-to-GDP ratio went from around 105 per cent at the onset of the crisis to 165 per cent in late 2011. Eastern Europe and Southern

---

5 Rae (2011) provides a useful account of the uneven development of the EU and the effects of the economic crisis on Central and Eastern Europe.
6 Of the ten countries that acceded to the European Union in 2004 (Bulgaria, the Czech Republic, Estonia, Hungary, Latvia, Lithuania, Poland, Romania, Slovakia, and Slovenia), only Slovenia was part of the eurozone when the crisis began in 2008. Slovakia joined in 2009 and Estonia in 2011.
7 On the scope of the short-lived Keynesian policies that some countries pursued in the immediate wake of the financial crisis, Oxfam (2013) notes that the combined wealth of Europe's ten richest people exceeds the total cost of stimulus measures that were implemented across the EU in 2008–10 (€217 billion versus €200 billion).

Europe would pay a particularly high price in massive unemployment, exploding debt traps, and vicious cuts to social spending. The eurozone countries faced the additional burden of not being able to export their way back into growth through currency devaluation; deflating their economies by lowering their labour costs provided the only alternative short of the extremely disruptive process of exiting the euro. Although the richer countries were not forced to swallow the bitter pill of aid conditionality, they too implemented austerity measures to pay for the costs of bailing out the financial sector.

The social and economic effects were devastating. Mass unemployment re-emerged for the first time since the 1930s. In 2013, 26 million people in the EU were unemployed, 11 million of whom had been out of work for longer than a year – almost double the level five years before. Youth unemployment ranged from 33 per cent to more than 60 per cent, and 120 million Europeans were living in or at risk of poverty. The Red Cross reported that the number of people depending upon food distributions increased by 75 per cent between 2009 and 2012. In the Baltic states and Hungary, up to 13 per cent of the populations have left in recent years as the result of economic hardship. But the effects were not confined to the periphery. In France, for example, 350,000 people fell below the poverty line between 2008 and 2011. In Germany, almost all new jobs since 2008 have been low-paid, flexible, and part-time with little security and social benefits (International Federation of Red Cross and Red Crescent Societies 2013). Austerity has thus been a disaster for many Europeans. At the same time, inequality has increased, with the richest having seen their share of total income grow since the onset of austerity, and the poorest having seen theirs fall (Oxfam 2013). Austerity has also included an opportunistic expansion of private wealth, as austerity programs such as the memoranda forced upon Greece have included extensive privatization measures of public assets such as airports, port facilities, and company shares, some of the proceeds of which have gone into recapitalizing banks (the process has been managed by the Hellenic Republic Asset Development Fund).

Austerity as a class-based project and as the intensification of class struggle in Europe has thus included multiple dimensions. Four key features stand out in particular: (1) a broad socialization of financial risk and further privatization of market rewards as the burden of adjusting to the financial crisis has been shifted from the bankers onto the public; (2) an opportunistic attack on the remnants of the welfare state; (3) a new wave of accumulation by dispossession linked to privatization and the financial monopolization of tax revenues; and (4) the deepening of core domination over the periphery through the institutions of the European Union, which have reinforced the structural imbalances between rich and poor countries.

Political Crisis and Class Confrontation

The Return of Mass Politics and the New Parties of the Left

With the intensification of class struggle, mass popular forces re-emerged for the first time in decades. This phenomenon – which occurred, in different degrees, across Europe – signalled a generalized crisis of neoliberal hegemony, one ultimately linked to the growing weakness of the neoliberal project and its shrinking social base (Durand and Keucheyan 2012). But while popular movements temporarily took to the offensive in civil society – and in a few cases even forced the resignation of governments – the traditional parties remained in power. Both the Left and the Far Right – increasingly active in a number of places – have failed to block the austerity agenda.

In the early wake of the crisis, as Europe's leaders turned towards austerity, protests, demonstrations, strikes, and occupations swept the core and periphery. The largest and most sustained strikes occurred in Southern Europe. Between the onset of the crisis and early 2012, Greece experienced twenty-nine general strikes and hundreds of protests against the bailout packages and austerity measures of the social-democratic government (known by its acronym, PASOK) and then the right-wing New Democracy that later replaced it; Spain was shut down by a general strike in September 2010 and March 2012 in response to austerity measures adopted by the Socialist government, and Portugal experienced its first coordinated general strike by two major union federations in twenty-two years in November 2010. Additional general strikes took place in November 2011 and in March 2012 (one week before the Spanish one). In Spain alone, the strikes involved some eight million workers. In November 2012, coordinated general strikes occurred across both Spain and Portugal for the first time since the end of their dictatorships; the day of mass action also included strikes in Italy, Greece, France, and Belgium (Choonara 2013). While these strikes were important – and temporarily reversed the long-term decline of strike action – they were mostly symbolic, limited to one day, and did very little to pose a threat to social cohesion or capital accumulation (Nowak and Gallas 2014).

In France, seven national strikes involving up to 3.5 million people, with public servants at the head, were called in the fall of 2010 to defend pensions against Sarkozy's austerity plans. In Britain, where the immediate years following the crisis were relatively calm, industrial action reached its highest peak in two decades, mostly as a result of one-day public sector strikes triggered by the austerity measures of the Conservative–Liberal Democrat coalition that came to power in the May 2010 election. In November 2011, one such strike included 2.5 million workers in twenty-three unions, the largest strike in Britain since 1926, which coincided with demonstrations across the country (Choonara 2013).

The ex-communist countries witnessed some of the biggest demonstrations the region had seen since the fall of the Berlin Wall, including tens of thousands in the streets of Prague in April 2012 carrying banners screaming "Stop the Thieves." In Latvia, protesters in January 2009 tried to storm Parliament, instigating the worst riots since the country split from Soviet Union in 1991. Most of these actions, however, were short-lived, and there were few instances of popular discontent taking on a more sustained and organized basis. Industrial actions remained low in comparison to other regions, and the Left continued to suffer the legacy of state repression, the post-communist discrediting of notions of social justice, and limited repertoires and experiences of protest and organization (Tamás 2008; Dale and Hardy 2011). On the whole, the nationalism and chauvinism of the Right have received much more support than the Left (discussed below).

Workers were not the only ones to contest austerity in many places. Indeed, in Greece, Italy, Spain, Portugal, France, Britain, and several other countries, students and unemployed youth played a primary role in the opposition to austerity.[8] In May 2011, the well-known *Indignados* movement occupied the Puerta del Sol Square in Madrid at almost the same time as the movement of the *Aganaktismeni* (the outraged) took over Syntagma Square in Athens. As opposition built momentum in the wake of the crisis, over 125 occupations occurred throughout Europe in 2010–11 (Kaldor et al. 2012). Drawing inspiration

---

[8] Socialist parties have fared well in Denmark and Iceland, though they are still more social democratic than they are radical Left.

from the Arab Spring, the mass gatherings included hundreds of thousands of protestors from all sectors of society. The occupations, strikes, and protests united working people from both the private and public sectors in a broad-based class politics that also included sections of the middle class, the unemployed, and the precariat. Misleadingly depicted by the media as opponents of liberal democracy, the social movements leading the occupations called for participatory and deliberative democracy while denouncing the corruption of the traditional parties (Della Porta 2012). With significant social bases, the messages of the social movements enjoyed broad "resonance" with the public (Kaldor et al. 2012), which is largely against austerity. A European-wide Gallup (2013) poll, for example, found that 51 per cent of Europeans felt that austerity was not working, 10 per cent were unsure, and only 39 per cent felt that it was working (or would work with time). This coincides with widespread mistrust of the European Union. In 2014, the Eurobarometer standard (2014) registered the lowest level of popularity in the institutions of the EU ever recorded. For the first time, fewer than one-third of Europeans indicated that they had confidence in the commission, the ECB, and the European Parliament.

The social movements have been an important element in the constitution of new socialist parties, which have broken from Social Democracy and have formed Red-Green coalitions with ties to social movements and the old parties of the far Left (Marlière 2013). Their support base comes from the unemployed and the working class (see Visser et al. 2013). The new Left parties in Western Europe have registered some modest gains but still remain, mostly, small parties of the socialist faithful. In France, the leader of *La Gauche* (The Left), Jean-Luc Mélenchon, took 11 per cent of the vote in the first round of the 2012 presidential election behind Marine Le Pen (left-wing voters closed ranks behind the centre-Left under François Hollande to prevent the Far Right from coming to power in the second round of voting). Mélenchon's party is noteworthy for having gone beyond the standard critique of "inequality" that is popular among today's Left to rehabilitate the existence of social classes in public discourse, their struggles and consciousness (Gauthier 2012). Other Western European countries have developed important post–social democratic left-wing parties, such as *Die Linke* (The Left) led by Oskar Lafontaine in Germany, though it lost seats in recent elections (as have the Dutch socialists). Both France's *La Gauche* and Germany's *Die Linke* are split-offs of the left wings of social democratic parties.[8] New Left parties are virtually non-existent in Central and Eastern Europe, with the exception of Slovenia.

The new Left parties have received the most support in Greece and Spain. Syriza, a coalition of Left groups led by Alexis Tsipras founded in 2004, formed a government in January 2015, when it won 36 per cent of the vote in the legislative election. Syriza was once described as a "mass connective party" that flexibly coordinates multiple movements and initiatives and translates their struggles into effective political action (Spourdalakis 2013). As such, the party moved beyond the sectarianism of much of the twentieth-century Left and the anarchism of the anti-globalization movements (though there were still Left groupings that remained outside the party). No radical Left party has performed better in Europe since the 1970s, and the party managed to cement a new social alliance of working people in the public and private sector, part-timers, full-timers, independent professionals, shopkeepers, youth, and the precariat. Yet since forming government, Syriza has been ruthlessly squeezed by Germany and the Troika to prevent them from setting an example to other upstarts in the eurozone. As the president of the European Council, Donald Tusk, candidly noted in the summer of 2015, "I am really afraid of this ideological or political contagion, not financial contagion, of this Greek crisis" (Spiegel 2015), conflating the politics of the radical Left with those of the Far Right.[9] Even before coming to power, the party underwent centralization and considerably moderated its program (e.g., the originally autonomous groups in the party were dissolved, and the commitment to nationalize the banks contained in the 2012 40-Point Program was removed from the 2014 Thessaloniki Program).

One year into its mandate, the experience of Syriza has been disastrous. The new Greek government immediately faced the

---

9 This is standard fare among the European political elite, as well as among academics and journalists, who lump the two together as "anti-systemic" populism (e.g., Grabow and Hartleb 2014; Pappas 2013). Overlooking obvious ideological distinctions, such readings ignore the fact that the biggest threat to liberal democracy has come, not from the Left nor the Right, but from the traditional governing parties, under whose watch European states have undergone considerable "democratic backsliding," to use the language of liberal political science. As Stavrakakis (2014) argues, the accusation of populism is made to discredit any political force resisting austerity measures and defending democratic and social rights.

hostility of its creditors, who insisted on the conditions imposed by the previous memorandum, despite the social crisis in Greece, and demanded even greater concessions to keep the economy afloat (going so far as to cause a massive liquidity crisis – discussed below). As Kouvelakis (2016) and other figures formerly associated with the Left platform of Syriza argue, the party also adopted a disastrous strategy based entirely on the idea that the Troika and the Eurogroup (led by German Finance Minister Wolfgang Schäuble) would eventually agree to an "honourable compromise" that would spare the Greeks the worst of the austerity measures. Consequently, no preparations were made to leave the eurozone should the strategy fail (so-called Grexit). When Tsipras called a referendum in July 2015 to put the proposed third bailout agreement to a vote, presumably to frighten the Europeans, Syriza seemed entirely unprepared for the popular rejection that the referendum garnered (61.3 per cent voted against the agreement). Not prepared to leave the eurozone, Syriza had no option but to undertake a massive about-face and sign the agreement. Tspiras then moved to consolidate a more centrist version of the party, calling a snap election for September 2015 in which Syriza captured 36 per cent of the vote, falling just short of an absolute majority (Syriza's Left platform, meanwhile, left the party and formed a coalition with several other groups called Popular Unity, which did not manage to build a significant support base in time for the election).

In Spain, the Communist-led United Left won 10 per cent of votes in the 2014 European parliamentary election, while a new radical party associated with the *Indignados*, Podemos (We Can), earned 8 per cent. Most impressively, Podemos received 21 per cent of the vote in the Spanish parliamentary election of December 2015, becoming the third-largest party in the Parliament and ending the reign of the two-party system. Unlike Syriza, Podemos did not emerge from a reconstitution of the Left, but rather from a top-down project of organization galvanized by a small group of radical intellectuals. While the leadership has had considerable success expanding the support base of the party through the establishment of "circles" (*círculos*) grouping together activists from the anti-austerity movements at the local level (the party currently boasts nearly 400,000 members), it remains surprisingly centralized under the leadership of its secretary general, Pablo Iglesias, and its tactics remain focused primarily on discursive confrontation with the "establishment" at the expense of mass mobilization against the state.[10] With a keen eye on developments in Greece, no doubt, the party has refused to enter into a coalition government with any of the traditional parties, which would require it to implement austerity. For the time being, it remains to be seen whether Podemos will succeed, where Syriza has failed, in building mass support for a concrete alternative to the eurozone.[11]

Despite these important experiences of Left resurgence, the traditional parties have largely held on. This is not to say that governments that implemented austerity did not pay the price. Incumbent governments were defeated in sixteen of twenty-seven elections held in EU member states between 2008 and the end of 2011, with several austerity governments suffering crushing defeats (Greece, Italy, Spain, Czech Republic, Latvia, and Hungary) (LeDuc and Pammett 2013). In two countries (Italy and Greece), the traditional party system collapsed altogether (we can now add Spain to the list). But nearly everywhere the machinery of government switched hands from the traditional centre-Left parties to traditional centre-Right ones or vice versa, and austerity remained the order of the day. The crisis spelled disaster for parties of the Left in particular, with social democratic or socialist-led governments going down to defeat in Bulgaria, Hungary, Lithuania, the United Kingdom, and Spain (ibid.).[12] In each of those countries with the exception of Hungary, however, austerity continued, as it did in countries where the centre-Left defeated the Right, including in France, where it took the socialist government of François Hollande less than

---

10 See Hassan (2016) for a critique of the limitations of Podemos's top-down strategy of mobilization and rejection of Left-coalition building in favour of a discursive strategy of counter-hegemony.

11 Italy has also witnessed the emergence of a new mass party, the Five Star Movement (M5S), led by Beppe Grillo, a millionaire popular activist, comedian, and blogger. Launched in 2009, the party advances an amalgam of political ideologies that draws heavily on the Left but embraces aspects of conservatism (for example, Grillo rejects unions and opposes citizenship rights for the children of immigrants born in Italy). M5S's program is perhaps better described as one of anti-politics than of a genuine left-wing alternative, and its hierarchical structure ensures that the party is basically the personal property of Grillo and his partner, web marketing guru Gianroberto Casaleggio (Phillips 2013).

12 Left-nationalist parties of the centre, however, have done well in Scotland and modestly in Ireland. Sinn Féin obtained 10 per cent of the vote in 2011, and the Scottish Nationalist Party (SNP) obtained 45 per cent of the vote in the same year. The SNP forms the national government of the Scottish Parliament.

a year to abandon its anti-austerity commitments after being elected in May 2012.[13] The inside of the state thus remained impervious to the social opposition to austerity of the most active sectors of civil society.

There are many reasons why widespread opposition to austerity and the rejection of austerity parties has not led to a viable confrontation with the neoliberal state beyond the political disengagement of large sectors of society. When the crisis began, the Left was still victim of its past accommodations to neoliberal post-democracy and the abandonment of a popular ideological alternative by political parties and organized labour. The popular opposition that emerged in the early stages of the mobilizations was organized loosely and without effective political structures or leadership to challenge state power. Some of the movements were anti-political and consciously wary of entering into the political arena. Post-democracy thus proved capable of weathering the political storm. Union mobilization also had its limitations, and the lack of a more sustained effort by organized labour led many social movement activists to feel betrayed when the unions capitulated to austerity governments.[14] In Greece, Syriza's confrontation with austerity was cut short by its own failed strategy of negotiation and its unwillingness to build support for an alternative strategy that would include exit from the eurozone (a strategy that was predicated on undermining party democracy; see Kouvelakis 2016).

Of course, not all of the reasons were internal to the Left. The coercive turn of the state and the institutions of the European Union also played a decisive role, as we shall see shortly. But before turning to that, we

---

13 Outside the European Union, popular mobilizations in Iceland forced the government to switch course. In the lead up to the financial crisis, the hyper-leveraging of bank assets reached such an absurd point that the bank asset-to-GDP ratio was nearly 1,000 per cent. When the bubble burst and the state was expected to step in and save the banks, thousands took to the streets in the so-called Kitchen Implement Revolution, eventually forcing the resignation of the right-wing Independence Party. Under a Left-coalition, Iceland organized a series of referenda to determine the fate of Icesave Icelandic and its foreign creditors, who were forced to bear the costs of adjustment (Blyth 2013).

14 "Taken in isolation," Choonara (2013) argues, "these struggles could perhaps be regarded as bureaucratic mass strikes designed to allow rank and file workers to 'let off steam' – ineffective and ultimately leading nowhere. Taken together, and viewed with sensitivity to the tensions running through them, we can begin to see them for what they are: part of a developing cycle of struggle with the potential to challenge those presiding over European capitalism."

assess how the other major ideological challenger to neoliberal austerity has fared: the Far Right.

The Reactionary Right

The political parties of the Far Right have also denounced the EU and the imposition of austerity but remain resolutely pro-capitalist. Instead of neoliberalism, they call for a state that provides social rights to members of the ethnically defined nation and in which the economically strong are still encouraged to thrive. As populations have become more socially insecure, social scapegoating has worked, and the Far Right has managed to pick up support from parts of the working class (notably in France), as well as in its traditional base among artisans, storekeepers, and other sectors of the middle class (Gauthier 2012). Muslims, of course, are a favoured target of the Far Right. While many of the Far Right parties are reminiscent in their nationalist discourses of the fascist movements of the 1930s, few have an organized mass following; they are, for the most part, organizationally weak and centred largely on the charisma of an authoritarian leader (with the exception, again, being Greece).[15]

In Western Europe, some Far Right parties have done well since the onset of austerity. In Finland, for example, the Finns Party (previously known as the True Finns) formed the opposition following the 2011 legislative election; in Denmark, the Danish People's Party performs well electorally; and in Austria, the Far Right received one-fifth of all votes in the parliamentary election of 2013. In France, support for Marine Le Pen's National Front (FN) has been on the rise (she received 17.9 per cent of the vote in the first round of the 2012 presidential election compared to 11 per cent in 2007), though the right-wing leader has also come up against the limitations of the majority-electoral system (she did not make it to the run-off election in 2012, which was contested by Sarkozy and Hollande). Still, at the time of writing, she is expected to emerge as a major contender in the presidential election in April 2017. FN won eleven municipalities in the 2015 elections, and the party scored a first-place finish in the European parliamentary election in May 2014 with 25 per cent of the vote. Le Pen's strategy of combining nationalism and xenophobia with a more bread-and-butter approach to economic issues

---

15 See Panitch and Albo (2015) for a recent overview of right-wing resurgence in Europe.

(referred to as *gauchisation*) has paid off significantly (McDonnell 2016), and could find even broader resonance in the wake of large-scale terrorist attacks.

With Europeans expressing record low levels of confidence in European institutions (see above), the Far Right is finding fertile ground for resurgence. The results of the last European parliamentary election are again instructive. The Danish People's Party topped the poll in Denmark, the New Flemish Alliance won the most votes in Belgium (16.4 per cent), and both the Austria Freedom Party (19.7 per cent) and the Dutch Party for Freedom (13.2 per cent) came third in their respective countries. Most alarmingly, the FN took 26 per cent of French votes, and the United Kingdom Independence Party 26.8 per cent in Britain. Even in Germany, the neo-Nazi NPD managed to obtain three seats in the European Parliament. All of these parties have benefited from widespread anti-EU sentiment. At the same time, the electoral gains of the Far Right must be put into perspective. As Mudde (2014) notes, "populist radical right" parties have lost ground nationally; in the early 2000s, seven majority governments and three minority ones included "populist radical right parties"; by 2014, only Switzerland's majority government included the participation of one such party.

On the European periphery, the Far Right has fared much better. In the ex-communist countries, nationalism, xenophobia, and extreme social conservatism have achieved mainstream status. In Hungary, the Far Right Viktor Orbán and his Fidesz Party have ruled with a majority or supra-majority since 2010. Orbán, highly critical of the austerity program passed by the previous socialist-liberal coalition, cut spending in some areas but combined this with unorthodox measures such as "crisis taxes" on banks and financial institutions and other large sectors that garnered him widespread support (Fabry 2012). Anti-Muslim, anti-immigrant, and anti-Roma, Fidesz has aligned with the even more extremist and thug-controlled Jobbik, which won 20.5 per cent of votes in the April 2014 parliamentary election, making them the third-largest party in the National Assembly (see Fabry 2012). In Latvia, the Far Right has done well in recent years, with the National Alliance entering a centre-Right coalition following the September 2011 general election.[16] In Poland, the Far Right Law and Justice party was returned to power

---

16 Further east, the neo-Nazi Svoboda in the Ukraine has dramatically increased its support in recent years and was part of a centre-Right governing coalition in 2014.

in October 2015, and in Slovakia, the People's Party recently received 200,000 votes in the March 2016 parliamentary election, going from zero to 14 seats (of a total of 150).

In Greece, Golden Dawn, the Far Right party in Europe that most calls forth the spectre of the 1930s, has combined a mass base with organized violence. Draped in Nazi-inspired symbols and iconography, assembling at mass rallies and protests, and actively seeking to inspire public terror, Golden Dawn's mercenaries have gained notoriety for their physical attacks on immigrants and leftists. With its consistent opposition to austerity, Golden Dawn has done well in both national parliamentary elections (winning 7 per cent of the vote in the September 2015 election) and European parliamentary elections (where it won 10 per cent of Greek votes in the 2014 election).[17] For the time being, its level of support has stabilized, though the collapse of Syriza's resistance to austerity may draw more Greeks into its ranks.

If the Far Right is still largely on the fringes of political power in most places, its impact has been greater than this would suggest. As Berezin (2013) argues, the authoritarian and xenophobic attitudes of the Far Right have entered into the mainstream right-wing discourse through figures such as Nicolas Sarkozy in France, or David Cameron in the United Kingdom. In this sense, even if the Far Right is far from taking political power in most places, it has become a convenient rampart for European leaders who are all too willing to find an authoritarian solution to social dislocation to safeguard the unravelling of the neoliberal hegemonic project. This is perhaps the greatest political significance of Europe's Far Right, a significance that could grow in the context of the terrorist attacks in Paris and Brussels and Europe's largest refugee crisis in the post-war era.

Securing Austerity

The Coercive Politics of the Neoliberal State

The European political elite and dominant classes have reacted to the groundswell in popular opposition by further insulating political

---

17 See Toloudis (2014) for a useful description and analysis of the party. Although Toloudis acknowledges that the party's rise is linked to its rejection of austerity, he is careful to note that its long-term development must also be situated within the historical context of Greek right-wing populism.

power from popular democratic control. This process has included two notable aspects: (1) the further fusion of financial and political power within the juridical order of the European Union; and (2) political interference and financial destabilization by core governments and EU officials against governments that are insufficiently committed or opposed to austerity. This has occurred in conjunction with a further banalization of liberal democracy as parties running on anti-austerity platforms have simply abandoned them once coming to power (a bait-and-switch strategy pioneered in Latin America in the 1980s and 1990s recently adopted by François Hollande in France).

The fusion of financial and political power has occurred through a further concentration of fiscal decision-making in the institutions of the European Union and the ECB, along with the enhanced surveillance powers of these institutions over member states. While several directives and policies have been put into place to extend coercive control over national budgetary procedures, the adoption of the European Fiscal Compact (the Treaty on Stability, Coordination, and Governance) in March 2012 – a stricter version of Stability and Growth Pact – marked a turning point. The compact requires that countries with a debt-to-GDP ratio exceeding 60 per cent enact an implementation law to limit budget deficits to no more than 0.5 per cent under the surveillance of independent fiscal advisory councils. If a state legally bound by this provision is found to be non-compliant, the European Court of Justice can impose a penalty. "For all practical purposes," Greer argues, "the new Treaty makes Keynesian aggregate demand management unconstitutional in Europe" (2013, 16). The new rules also imply more sanctions on recalcitrant countries, an explicit orientation in favour of pension reforms and the liberalization of labour markets, and a new monitoring cycle of economic policies through an examination of national budgetary programs before discussion by national parliaments. These procedures reinforce the disciplinary and structural power of finance capital over national governments, further contributing to the long-term trend of post-democracy and the depoliticization of economic questions. Drawing upon Gramsci, Durand and Keucheyan (2012) argue that the enhanced power of the EU bureaucracy has led to a new form of "bureaucratic Caesarism" that responds to the overall crisis of hegemony by centralizing power in institutions away from democratic control.

In parallel to this process of changing the rules of the game to ensure more favourable outcomes, European leaders have suspended democracy altogether when outcomes appear uncertain. Indeed, political interference and financial destabilization – the traditional tools of imperial control in Latin America and other peripheral regions – have become standard practice in the European Union since the financial crisis. In the early years of the crisis, Draghi repeatedly stated that the Bank would not protect bond markets, in effect disciplining and punishing elected officials insufficiently committed to the new austerity. More direct actions were forthcoming. Thus, early in the crisis, in October 2011, Greek Prime Minister George Papandreou was publicly denounced by Merkel and Sarkozy for announcing that he would hold a referendum before signing a second bailout in October 2011. Breaking the convention of non-interference in the politics of a member state, the leaders of the Frankfurt Group triggered a crisis of confidence in Papandreou's leadership, soon to be replaced by unelected technocrat Lucas Papademos by the Greek parliament, a former governor of the Bank of Greece, vice president of the ECB, and negotiator of Greece's first bailout (Phillips 2013; Verney and Bosco 2014).

At around the same time, the ECB engineered the toppling of the Berlusconi government in Italy (leading many to quip that the only thing more harmful to Italian democracy than Berlusconi was the unaccountable Bank). With Berlusconi wavering on austerity reforms, the ECB limited its bond-buying operations to signal its lack of confidence, forcing the resignation of the prime minister, who was promptly replaced by Mario Monti, a former European commissioner and president of the private Bocconi University (the home of modern-day austerity economics). Monti then led a government of unelected technocrats that implemented austerity by decree over the course of the next year (Phillips 2013; Verney and Bosco 2014). In Portugal, the intervention occurred behind the scenes. When Prime Minister José Sócrates promised to avoid an austerity agreement, Portuguese banks indicated that they would no longer purchase bonds if a bailout was not requested. A few days after Sócrates reversed course and announced a bailout to avoid insolvency, the head of the country's banking association revealed that he had been under "clear instructions" from the ECB and the Bank of Portugal to turn off the liquidity tap (Phillips 2013).

But the recent example of Syriza indicates that such interference was not confined to the exceptional circumstances of the post-financial crisis. Even prior to the Greek election in January 2015, European leaders publicly sought to prevent a Syriza victory, suggesting that an openly undemocratic ideology was increasingly becoming an acceptable part of the European political discourse.[18] Upon taking office, Syriza began negotiation with the Eurogroup over the next several months on the extension of the second agreement and the terms for a third. The campaign of financial destabilization began with the ECB's refusal to accept Greek collateral in exchange for emergency assistance within days of Syriza's electoral victory (leading to massive capital flight in the banking system), the refusal to release €7.2 billion held back in loan money until all conditions were met (despite the obvious economic disaster the Greeks were enduring), and the refusal to disburse €1.9 billion in profits made on Greek debt bonds to which the government was legally entitled. The strategy was twofold: create a liquidity crisis and force the government into insolvency. The Greek experience indicates that the recourse to financial destabilization and political interference have become accepted means of maintaining neoliberal control to forestall leftist alternatives.

Taken together, these developments constitute a startling erosion of liberal democracy and a hardening of the neoliberal regional order around an increasingly narrow set of class interests and a more pronounced domination of the periphery by the core. In this new integument, a more explicitly authoritarian (if impersonal) political order seems to be the flipside of the undemocratic economy. Democratic capitalism, in short, seems to be running out of steam.

Conclusions: The Implications of Post-Hegemonic Neoliberalism

With the further unravelling of the post-war class compromise through the imposition of austerity, ideological alternatives from both the Far Right and radical Left are being posed for the first time in decades. While the cycle of protest that erupted in 2009 has largely dissipated,

---

18 To take two examples, in the lead up to the January 2015 parliamentary election in Greece, Commission President Jean-Claude Juncker warned Greek voters on Austrian television, "I think that the Greeks – who have a very different life – know very well what a wrong election result would mean for Greece and the Eurozone." Schäuble, for his part, noted "We want to give Greece further support on its path of reform, helping it to help itself. If Greece chooses another way, it will be difficult. New elections will not change any of the agreements made with the Greek government. Any new government must keep to the contractual agreements of its predecessor" (quoted in Ryan 2015). Such remarks have become so commonplace as to no longer elicit much reaction.

the contradictions of the neoliberal project, rooted in a shrinking social base, continue to grow. Yet the increased reliance upon coercive strategies to maintain these contradictions within a quasi-democratic framework – however hollowed out – may be politically unviable in the long term. Indeed, three possible scenarios seem to present themselves.

The first scenario is a continued repudiation of the social function of the state and a further drift towards authoritarianism. Maintaining austerity, the clear preference of Europe's political elite and capitalist classes, will necessitate the ongoing concentration of executive power in the institutions of the European Union and those parts of the state most insulated from popular control. While parts of the middle class may precariously hang on to their class status under the new austerity capitalism, and richer states will retain zones of privilege, the offensives against civil servants and public services will further narrow the scope of the ruling social bloc. Increased security measures and the criminalization of dissent are likely corollaries. In such a scenario, control over the popular classes of Europe will be increasingly exercised through direct class domination as the ruling class itself becomes increasingly decadent (a strategy of rule that Gramsci referred to as "minimalist" hegemony or class supremacy). Regional variations will of course continue to persist, with post-democratic solutions still preferred in the core and more direct forms of control exercised in the periphery. A second scenario would largely mirror the first one, with more states moving towards a far-right populist solution. In this scenario, neoliberalism would likely remain the dominant ideology both nationally and regionally, but a more aggressive xenophobic solution to social instability, coupled with an exclusivist welfare state, would help paper over the contradictions. In both scenarios, resistance would continue against growing odds.

The third scenario is the emergence of a Left alternative based on the reactivation of class conflict from below on a more organized, coordinated, and regional basis. To be effective, however, this would require not only the fusion of mass social movements and radical political parties, but also a popular mandate and the political will to break from the eurozone. As we have seen in Greece, within the confines of the eurozone, capturing state power to create an alternative to austerity is not enough: Keynesianism in one country – let alone socialism – is no longer even a possibility. Left parties and governments will be forced to articulate concrete alternative economic strategies and to defend themselves against campaigns of destabilization that were once reserved for the

Global South. This will require both a massive shift in consciousness – including countering the considerable attachment of the populations of many peripheral countries to the idea that the European Union signifies progress and modernity – and the ongoing mass mobilization and self-organization of the popular classes. Without constant pressure from below, Left governments – even those with the best of intentions – will invariably succumb to the pressures of neoliberal Europe. This is a tall order by any standard, but the recent experience of Syriza suggests that breaking from the eurozone (if not the EU as a whole) is a necessary precondition for regaining fiscal and monetary sovereignty. The perennial questions of socialist strategy – how to build the democratic movement for socialist transformation, and how to maintain the impetus for transformation once in power – will haunt the European Left with a renewed sense of urgency in Europe's new austerity capitalism.

REFERENCES

Altvater, Elmar. 2012. "From Subprime Farce to Greek Tragedy: The Crisis Dynamics of Financially Driven Capitalism." *Socialist Register* 47:271–87.
Berezin, Mabel. 2013. "The Normalization of the Right in Post-Security Europe." In *Politics in the Age of Austerity*, ed. Armin Schafer and Wolfgang Streeck, 239–61. Cambridge: Polity.
Blyth, Mark. 2013. *Austerity: The History of a Dangerous Idea.* New York: Oxford University Press.
Castellina, Luciana. 2012. "Conclusions." Paper presented at workshop, "New Populisms and the European Right and Far Right Parties: The Challenge and the Perspectives for the Left," organized by Transform! Europe, Punto Rosso, and Rosa Luxemburg Foundation, Milan, 9–10 March.
Choonara, Joseph. 2013. "The Class Struggles in Europe." *International Socialism* 138 (Spring).
Crouch, Colin. 2004. *Post-Democracy.* Malden: Polity.
Dale, Gareth, and Jane Hardy. 2011. "Conclusion: The 'Crash' in Central and Eastern Europe." In *First the Transition, then the Crash*, ed. Gareth Dale, 251–64. London: Pluto.
Della Porta, Donatella. 2012. "Critical Trust: Social Movements and Democracy in Times of Crisis." *Cambio* 2 (4): 33–44.
Durand, Cédric, and Razmig Keucheyan. 2012. "Bureaucratic Caesarism: A Gramscian Outlook on the Crisis of Europe." *Centre d'économie de l'Université Paris Nord CNRS*, Working document 2012–13.

Eurobarometer. 2014. *Standard Eurobarometer* 81. http://ec.europa.eu/public_opinion/archives/eb/eb81/eb81_en.htm.

Fabry, Adam. 2012. "Nach Rechts! Demystifying the Rise of Populist and the Far Right in Post-Transition Hungary." Paper presented at the workshop, "New Populisms and the European Right and Far Right Parties: The Challenge and the Perspectives for the Left," organized by Transform! Europe, Punto Rosso, and Rosa Luxemburg Foundation, Milan, 9–10 March.

Fazi, Thomas. 2016. "How Austerity Has Crippled the European Economy – In Numbers." *Social Europe*, 31 March. https://www.socialeurope.eu/2016/03/austerity-crippled-european-economy-numbers/.

Gallup. 2013. *Debating Europe: Austerity Policies – Key Results of an Opinion Survey*. September.

Gauthier, Elisabeth. 2012. "Confronting the Extreme Right: A Challenge for the Left Lessons Learned from the 2012 Elections in France." Paper presented at the workshop, "New Populisms and the European Right and Far Right Parties: the Challenge and the Perspectives for the Left," organized by Transform! Europe, Punto Rosso, and Rosa Luxemburg Foundation, Milan, 9–10 March.

Gill, Stephen. 1998. "European Governance and New Constitutionalism: Economic and Monetary Union and Alternatives to Disciplinary Neoliberalism in Europe." *New Political Economy* 3 (1): 5–26. https://doi.org/10.1080/13563469808406330.

Grabow, Karsten, and Florian Hartleb. 2014. *"Europe – No, Thanks?" Study on the Rise of Right-Wing and National Populist Parties in Europe*. Konrad Adenauer Stiftung.

Greer, Scott. 2013. "European Citizenship in Crisis: Citizenship Rights and Austerity Politics." Social Science Research Network, February. https://papers.ssrn.com/sol3/papers.cfm?abstract_id=2214868.

Gropas, Ruby. 2011. "Resisting Europe: Protest and Opposition in the EU." CDDRL Working Papers 123, May.

Hassan, Omar. 2016. "Podemos and Left Populism." *Marxist Left Review* 11.

International Federation of Red Cross and Red Crescent Societies. 2013. *Think Differently: Humanitarian Impacts of the Economic Crisis in Europe*. Geneva.

Kaldor, Mary, Sabine Selchow, Sean Deel, and Tamsin Murray-Leach. 2012. *The "Bubbling Up" of Subterranean Politics in Europe*. London: Civil Society and Human Security Research Unit, London School of Economics and Political Science.

Kouvelakis, Stathis. 2016. "Syriza's Rise and Fall." *New Left Review* 97 (January–February): 45–70.

LeDuc, Lawrence, and Jon Pammett. 2013. "The Fate of Governing Parties in Times of Economic Crisis." *Electoral Studies* 32 (3): 494–9. https://doi.org/10.1016/j.electstud.2013.05.022.

Mair, Peter. 2000. "Partyless Democracy and the Paradox of New Labour." *New Left Review* 2 (March/April): 21–35.
Marlière, Philippe. 2013. "The Radical Left in Europe: An Outline." *Transform* 13.
McDonnell, Hugh. 2016. "How the National Front Changed France." *Jacobin* 11:23.
Mudde, Cas. 2014. "Fighting the System? Populist Radical Right Parties and Party System Change." *Party Politics* 20 (2): 217–26. https://doi.org/10.1177/1354068813519968.
Nowak, Jörg, and Alexander Gallas. 2014. "Mass Strikes against Austerity in Western Europe: A Strategic Assessment." *Global Labour Journal* 5 (3): 306–21. https://doi.org/10.15173/glj.v5i3.2278.
Oxfam. 2013. "A Cautionary Tale: The True Cost of Austerity and Inequality in Europe." Briefing Report 174 (September).
– 2015. "A Europe for the Many, Not the Few." Oxfam Briefing Paper (September). Accessed on 8 April 2016. https://www.oxfam.org/sites/www.oxfam.org/files/file_attachments/bp206-europe-for-many-not-few-090915-summ-en.pdf.
Panitch, Leo, and Greg Albo, eds. 2015. "Socialist Register 2016: The Politics of the Right." *Socialist Register* 52.
Pappas, Takis. 2013. "Embattled Democracy: Legitimation Crisis and the Rise of Political Extremism in Greece." Paper presented at the conference, "More Europe? Thinking beyond the Crisis in Transnational Dialogue. University of Bremen, 8 November.
Phillips, Leigh. 2013. "Kick 'em all out? Anti-Politics and Post-Democracy in the European Union." *Statewatch* 23 (1): 9–19.
Rae, Gavin. 2011. "On the Periphery: The Uneven Development of the European Union and the Effects of the Economic Crisis on Central-Eastern Europe." *Global Society* 25 (2): 249–66. https://doi.org/10.1080/13600826.2010.548057.
Ryan, John. 2015. "The Eurozone Should Be Flexible with Greece." *Blog*, 8 June. https://www.europeanspring.org/node/6.
Schneider, Markus P.A., Stephen Kinsella, and Antoine Godin. 2015. "Redistribution in the Age of Austerity." Levy Economics Institute, Working Paper 856 (December). Accessed on 8 April 2016. http://www.levyinstitute.org/publications/redistribution-in-the-age-of-austerity-evidence-from-europe-2006-13.
Spiegel, Peter. 2015. "Greece: Donald Tusk Warns of Extremist Political Contagion." *Financial Times*, 16 July.
Spourdalakis, Michalis. 2013. "Left Strategy in the Greek Cauldron: Explaining Syriza's Success." *Socialist Register* 49: 98–119.

Stavrakakis, Yannis. 2014. "The European Populist Challenge." *Annals of the Croatian Political Science Association* 10 (1): 25–39.

Streeck, Wolfgang. 2013. "The Crisis in Context: Democratic Capitalism and Its Contradictions." In *Politics in the Age of Austerity*, ed. Armin Schafer and Wolfgang Streeck, 262–86. Cambridge: Polity.

Tamás, G.M. 2008. "Counter Revolution after a Counter Revolution: Eastern Europe Today." *Socialist Register* 44: 284–94.

Toloudis, Nicholas. 2014. "The Golden Dawn: The Financial Crisis and Greek Fascism's New Day." *New Labor Forum* 23 (1): 38–43. https://doi.org/10.1177/1095796013513566.

Toporowski, Jan. 2012. "Eastern Europe: Post-Communist Assets in Crisis." *Socialist Register* 47: 235–48.

van Apeldoorn, Bastiaan. 2014. "The European Capitalist Class and the Crisis of Its Hegemonic Project." *Socialist Register* 50: 189–206.

Verney, Susannah, and Anna Bosco. 2014. "Living Parallel Lives: Italy and Greece in an Age of Austerity." *South European Society & Politics* 18 (4): 397–426. https://doi.org/10.1080/13608746.2014.883192.

Visser, Mark, Marcel Lubbers, Gerbert Kraaykamp, and Eva Jaspers. 2013. "Support for Radical Left Ideologies in Europe." *European Journal of Political Research* 53 (3): 541–58. https://doi.org/10.1111/1475-6765.12048.

15 Conclusion

STEPHEN MCBRIDE AND BRYAN M. EVANS

The financial and economic crisis of 2007–8 led to major dislocations and costs for societies and people. They included economic costs – unemployment and lost incomes, social damage – to physical and mental health and foregone futures as employment opportunities for the young dried up; and political costs – coercion against states and individuals that opposed the received wisdom and an erosion of democracy.

In this context, many harboured hopes for change in the neoliberal system of globalization that seemed responsible for the crisis and that has been dominant in most Western societies since the 1970s. Judging by enthusiastic support for Left politicians like Bernie Sanders in the United States, Jeremy Corbyn in the United Kingdom, and Pablo Iglesias in Spain, and right-wing populist leaders such as Marine Le Pen in France or Heinz-Christian Strache in Austria, alternative visions are diverse, yet many still want change. Whether on the small and immediate scale of the workplace – as shown, for example, in Donna Baines's chapter on the techniques used by care-workers to retain some sense of dignity and provide service to those they serve in the face of austerity and neoliberal managerialism – or at the more elevated level of organized politics (see the chapter by Neil Burron), there has been resistance to the austerity response to the crisis.

The diversity of the discontent, and its internal divisions, was laid bare in the so-called Brexit referendum, 23 June 2016, in which 52 per cent of the UK electorate voted to leave the European Union. One narrative of the campaign depicts it as a battle between supporters of racism and other forms of social bigotry, and those who were older and poorly educated, and therefore unable to understand the benefits of the prevailing policies and institutions like the European Union. Certainly the prominence of the United Kingdom Independence Party (UKIP) and its leader, Nigel Farage, in the Leave campaign lent substance to charges of racism. In contrast the young, the better educated, socially liberal, and residents of cosmopolitan London – together with, though perhaps for different reasons, Scotland and Northern Ireland – supported the Remain option. But the geography and class basis of the voting results, as least in England, tells another story. Outside London and a few other large cities that have done well out of the new global economy, the Leave option had strong support. In these areas people consider themselves to have lost as a result of economic changes, to have been left behind, and indeed betrayed by the political system. Crucial components of the Remain campaign included a cosmopolitan affluent elite; among Leave supporters, an alienated and angry working class. Torsten Bell, director of the Resolution Foundation, commented after the result, "The legacy of increased national inequality in the 1980s, the heavy concentration of those costs in certain areas, and our collective failure to address it has more to say about what happened last night than shorter term considerations from the financial crisis or changed migration flows" (cited in Cassidy 2016).

The mood between the two camps is captured by Owen Jones: "Many of the nearly half of the British people who voted remain now feel scared and angry, ready to lash out at their fellow citizens ... Many of the leavers already felt marginalised, ignored and hated. The contempt – and sometimes snobbery – now being shown about leavers on social media was already felt by these communities, and contributed to this verdict. Millions of Britons feel that a metropolitan elite rules the roost which not only doesn't understand their values and lives, but actively hates them" (Jones 2016; see also Jack 2016).

It is possible, though much too soon to say at the time of writing, that this referendum will mark a turning point in which some of the edifices of neoliberal globalization will start to collapse. The immediate effects in the United Kingdom include a crisis within the political parties and possible disintegration of the polity itself as Scotland voted heavily for Remain and is resistant to being ejected from the EU because of what is seen as an English decision. Within the EU, there seemed differences between those who wish reform to create a more human and just community, as the Italian prime minister expressed it, and those who want tough terms of exit for Britain to deter potential backsliders, coupled with intensification of the EU model and the austerity that goes with it.

Our concern in this volume has been with austerity after the financial and economic crisis. The overarching elite narrative in that period has been one of post-crisis continuity rather than change. Continuity involves restoration, and even intensification of the very policies that gave rise to the crisis. That is to say, neoliberal globalization remains firmly in place and remains backed by the states, international organizations, and social forces that have promoted it for four decades. And austerity is a central component of the orthodox response to the crisis. That said, there were already some signs of elite divisions between those who support intensification of the package and those who see a need for moderation.

States, backed by advice or coercion from international organizations, have typically pursued policies of austerity that comprise fiscal consolidation (in the name of balanced budgets, lowering the public debt to GDP ratio, and slimming the state, especially in its social dimensions), restructuring the public sector (through downsizing, marketizing, contracting out, or privatizing its functions), and labour market restructuring (aimed at enhancing the flexibility of employers by diminishing the security of employees).

As will be apparent from the list, there is little that is really new. Fiscal consolidation and structural reforms of the public sector and labour market have been long-standing ingredients of neoliberalism. The persistence and intensification of this approach in the years after the crisis raised the political profile of austerity measures, and there has been considerable public protest and intellectual controversy. However, these factors have failed to deflect the implementation of austerity policies. Nor is it clear that the impact of the Brexit vote will alter this situation, at least in the short term. So an essential question in the analysis of austerity is, Why has its lived experience failed to generate more widespread and effective opposition and the development of real alternatives?

Looked at from the point of view of elite proponents of austerity, it has been necessary to manage and contain the anger and discontent the policies have aroused. In part this has been accomplished through the familiar couplet of coercion and persuasion. In part it rests on the dull compulsion of deteriorating material conditions that make vulnerable populations passive rather than active in their opposition. They may already have lost much in the way of security and living standards, but the perception that they may lose yet more constrains their thinking and actions. They may be disaffected but their passivity constitutes consent of a sort. Moreover, populations are bombarded with ideological messages – some taking the form of rational economic theories about the positive effects of implementing austerity, at least in the long run. Others connect to a deeper individualist sense of how to react to hard times, using the imagery of belt-tightening, shared sacrifice, and a reconstituted form of fairness. In addition, political vehicles, like socialist or social democratic parties that might traditionally have led the fight against austerity, have been so thoroughly incorporated into neoliberalism that they offer no alternative, thus reinforcing the orthodox position and fuelling the popular belief that there is none. Even so, surges in favour of new Left and Right parties or movements, not to mention the results of the Brexit vote against continued EU membership (the EU serving here as a proxy for a wide variety of discontents, many – though not all – of which could be laid at Brussels' door), indicate the fragility of the managed consensus.

In the remainder of this conclusion, we highlight some of the insights of our contributors that bear on these issues: Why has the lived experience of austerity so far not led to change? And how has it been possible for elites to institute continuity in a context where the prevailing neoliberal ideas and policies have been or should have been discredited?

Austerity, as the chapters by John Clarke and Sorin Mitrea remind us, is more than a set of policies. It is an idea, a shorthand for a moral economy, a discourse, a set of principles to live by, and it has proved capable of adaptation to circumstances in different time periods and settings. There is a common sense quality to it that generates an air of inevitability when applied at the individual level. The injunction to cut back and practise thrift when times are hard, and perhaps loosen the purse strings in times of prosperity, resonates as an individual call to action. Of course, this recipe is nonsensical when applied to collectivities – if all cut back at the same time, times will become harder still. Nonetheless, considered at the individual level it is intuitive, and its alternative – to practise countercyclical spending, for example – seems counter-intuitive.

Austerity connects to certain ideals of the disciplined and restrained individual practising self-reliance and responsibility, however remote that ideal type is from the consumerist and often wasteful practices that characterize life under contemporary capitalism. The gap between ideal and reality could provide a rationale for imposing austerity. If humankind is too feeble to do what is necessary, perhaps the state should oblige its citizens to adopt austere ways in crises. Accompanied by a rhetoric of "we are all in this together," such measures might even be depicted as fair, in that conceptually at least they demand equal sacrifice from all. Acceptance of such messaging, whether passive or active, provides the basis for "disaffected consent."

Eric Pineault's analysis of the condition of the middle class under austerity is suggestive of some of the dilemmas. However middle class is defined (and this is a notoriously difficult exercise), the impact of austerity, inequality, and declining opportunities for social mobility and intergenerational transfer of advantage has a serious impact on its members. The whole sense of being middle class in Western societies has been one of "betterment" – for the individuals themselves and for their children. The fear of middle-class parents that their children will be worse off than themselves is palpable. In many countries, expectations of social mobility and even of secure professional jobs for the next generation have been dashed as a result of neoliberal austerity. But it remains unlikely that the amorphous category of the middle class has the capacity to mobilize and launch effective resistance.

In this context, expert arguments that "all will be well" as a result of austerity may have a comforting effect. Such messaging is contained in rationally based economic arguments, or at least arguments that appear to have a rational basis. Economic research that can be used to justify austerity policies falls into this category. The influence of such research, produced by "experts," frequently economists, may lie as much in its ability to provided assurances about the future and deflect consideration of alternatives, as in its empirical validity. Ellen Russell makes this argument about one body of such research, which posits expansionary fiscal contraction (EFC). Indeed, that particular thesis and others such as Reinhardt and Rogoff's (Reinhart and Rogoff 2010a; 2010b) account of how certain levels of public debt produce dramatic reductions in economic growth rates have been subject to detailed critique and are scientifically discredited (Blyth 2013; Herndon, Ash, and Pollin 2013). Even researchers working for organizations like the IMF that have long promoted neoliberalism and austerity have come to question many of their postulates. Thus, in a revisionist and somewhat self-critical report on neoliberalism, IMF researchers concluded, "No fixed agenda delivers good outcomes for all countries for all times. Policymakers and institutions like the IMF that advise them must be guided not by faith, but by evidence of what has worked" (Ostry, Loungani, and Furceri 2016, 5). Correctly described as "a remarkable breach of the neoliberal consensus by the IMF," the report nevertheless has its limits and, again so far, does not appear to have changed how the IMF acts, as opposed to what its researchers think (Chakrabortty 2016).[1] Without diminishing the significance and future potential of such a rethink, it can be noted that such acknowledgments have come long after the austerity horse has left the stable. Furthermore, elite positions have not changed appreciably as a result of this self-criticism, nor did the discrediting of the Reinhart and Rogoff or the EFC theses provoke any sign of a rethink among practitioners. It is for this reason that Russell points to their utility as flanking arguments, helpful in creating an initial aura of legitimacy for political leaders and the economic elites supporting them when deploying the case for austerity.

On the receiving end of austerity, the higher-level theoretical arguments and empirical controversies may seem less important. Structural reforms are imposed on and condition the behaviour, and perhaps the thinking of the "clients" of the welfare state and those who work in the public sector.

The implementation of New Public Management techniques in the long-term care sector that impose work practices and reporting and accountability mechanisms, as Donna Baines shows, impede workers' ability to provide care in a humane and supportive fashion. The techniques control their time and the nature of the assistance they can provide, and serve to reduce costs and establish metrics by which service to recipients can be recorded and measured. But the metrics do not include the quality of care as represented in human interaction and kindness, and it can be presumed that the recipients are the losers as a result of these transactions. Those dependent on the care system have even less voice or influence on the way their care is provided than do the workers in these facilities. Workers find ways to resist the imposition of practices they deem harmful, but their efforts to escape the controls established by the system are limited and hardly represent a major challenge to the new mode of providing care.

---

1 One sign of disaffection may be found in the rejection of expertise by many people. One Conservative Leave campaigner in the Brexit referendum, Michael Gove, seems to have captured this sentiment quite well: "People in this country have had enough of experts" (cited in McSmith 2016). The context of his remark was the mobilization of an astonishing array of individuals and organizations giving, as their expert opinion, the inadvisability of Britain leaving the EU.

Much the same is true of other public sector workers, like teachers. In some countries they have experienced vilification and frontal attacks on incomes and rights. In Canada, this may have been more muted compared, say, to the United States. In this context, Ontario teachers adopted a pragmatic strategy and tried to adapt to the political economy of austerity (Sweeney and Hickey, this volume). This involved collaboration with governments imposing austerity in the education sector in an attempt to mitigate its impact. The strategy was not entirely successful, however, as collective bargaining and the right to strike were diminished, and teachers' unions continue to bemoan the effect of austerity measures on teachers' ability to deliver quality education.

Rising inequality has been a feature of the whole neoliberal period and has certainly not lessened as a result of post-crisis austerity. For unorganized workers (the majority of the labour force in most OECD countries where union decline has been apparent) two main strategies have developed to address the plight of those living on low wages. These strategies are the minimum-wage and the living-wage approaches to dealing with inadequate wage levels. Neither has proven particularly effective, though mobilization around them is a sign of resistance to austerity (Evans, McBride, and Muirhead, this volume).

The recasting of immigration as a problem to be managed, rather than as a building block of an improved society, is a feature of the age of austerity. Migration has become a hot-button item in many post-crisis societies as the range of economic opportunities has narrowed and immigrants are seen as competitors. Even in countries like Canada, where hostility to immigration is less intense than in many parts of Europe, instrumental, short-term evaluations of immigration, and immigrants, has displaced more open and welcoming approaches. Susan Barrass and John Shields depict the "ideal" immigrant as increasingly viewed instrumentally in cost-benefit terms and needing to be an instant contributor.

The transfer of responsibility to the individual can be observed also in provision for the aged (Zhou and Shi, this volume). Social solidarity has eroded, and risk and responsibility for one's old age has been transferred from society to the individual. These trends have a longer history than the immediate post-crisis period but have continued apace as austerity has been implemented. Evidence is found in the shift from public to private pensions and, within the latter, increased prominence for defined contribution plans in which the individual bears the risk of investment performance of pension funds, rather than receiving a guaranteed pension, as was the case under the previously more widespread defined benefit plans. Similarly, envy and resentment is directed against those with (adequate) public sector pensions, and the demand for downward levelling (in the name of fairness) has entered public discourse.

It is clear that austerity has adversely affected the lived experience of those who work in the public sector and those who have depended on it, but it has a broader impact, too, as seen in the chapter on the middle class. The sociological erosion of the middle class is paralleled by and partly created by the erosion of state supports and public sector employment that had been a feature of many countries and an important ideological-political component of the European Union through such concepts as the European social model. There, as Christoph Hermann explains, structural reforms embedded in austerity policies have meant the erosion of that model through cuts to cash benefits, social programs, and public sector employment, as well as the replacement of those made redundant.

Where is resistance to be found? The final chapters in the book explore three possible centres of resistance. None provide major grounds for optimism. One arises where minority nationalism provides a social glue that, together with social democratic principles, could create enough social solidarity to enable effective action in the face of global demands for austerity. The Quebec case study, presented by Peter Graefe and Hubert Rioux, shows that these factors have facilitated contestation but that translating such opposition into effective and electorally successful alternatives to austerity has proven more difficult. The situation seems even more dire in social democratic parties that might traditionally have been seen as bearers of alternative solutions to crisis. Our view of social democracy is that it has come to the end of the road in developing or even articulating alternatives. Bryan Evans's chapter argues that ideological integration with neoliberalism is so complete that the best it can offer is to manage austerity more effectively and, perhaps, more humanely. Even if social democratic parties could deliver on these promises, and there is little evidence to suggest they can, this hardly provides an inspirational stance to trouble elite orthodoxy.

Finally, Neil Burron's survey of political resistance to austerity draws similar conclusions. The long decline of the post-war compromise is largely complete. Capital is no longer interested in or needs to engage in class compromise. The contradiction between democracy and capitalism is increasingly apparent and seems to be resolved through diminished democracy. Islands of residual attachment to the old order remain and can stimulate resistance. But emergent resistance that could lead to an alternative remains inchoate. It is certainly visible in the rejection of elite platitudes indicated by support for Left and Right populist movements and candidates but has yet to cohere. Where it came closest, in the victory of Syriza in Greece, it was confronted with brutalism by Europe's political and economic elites. The Greek attempt to renegotiate the imposition of austerity ended in an abject capitulation by the party that had won elections and a referendum on an anti-austerity platform. To date, therefore, such developments show no way out of the impasse and dead end that austerity represents.

And yet, while political and economic elites may have weathered the storm, they face multiple challenges. The growth in non-social democratic Left parties is one; right-wing populist parties with contempt for liberal political values another; and there is increased questioning of trade and investment agreements that lock in neoliberal economic policies, and scepticism about and possible rejection of the European Union itself. A Pew poll across Europe noted a rise in Euroscepticism and significant bodies of public opinion in favour of returning some powers from Brussels to nation states (Pew Research Center 2016; see also Elliott 2016). The lived experience of austerity in many ways triggers disaffected consent. But there is a possibility that disaffection will outgrow consent and, as the Brexit result shows, lead to unpredictable challenges to the political and economic order that austerity is designed to protect.

REFERENCES

Blyth, M. 2013. *Austerity: The History of a Dangerous Idea*. Oxford: Oxford University Press.

Cassidy, John. 2016. "Why the Remain Campaign Lost the Brexit Vote." *New Yorker*, 24 June. http://www.newyorker.com/news/john-cassidy/why-the-remain-campaign-lost-the-brexit-vote?mbid=nl_160625_Daily&CNDID=36506022&spMailingID=9111072&spUserID=MTA5MjQwODg4ODYwS0&spJobID=942410256&spReportId=OTQyNDEwMjU2S0.

Chakrabortty, Aditya. 2016. "You're Witnessing the Death of Neoliberalism." *Guardian*, 31 May. https://www.theguardian.com/commentisfree/2016/may/31/witnessing-death-neoliberalism-imf-economists.

Elliott, Larry. 2016. "Brexit Is a Rejection of Globalisation." *Guardian*, 26 June. https://www.theguardian.com/business/2016/jun/26/brexit-is-the-rejection-of-globalisation.

Herndon, Thomas, Michael Ash, and Robert Pollin. 2013. "Does High Public Debt Consistently Stifle Economic Growth: A Critique of Reinhart and Rogoff." Working Paper 322. Amherst: University of Massachusetts, Political Economy Research Institute.

Jack, Ian. 2016. "In This Brexit Vote the Poor Turned on an Elite Who Ignored Them." *Guardian*, 25 June. https://www.theguardian.com/commentisfree/2016/jun/25/brexit-vote-poor-elite.

Jones, Owen. 2016. "Grieve Now if You Must – but Prepare for the Great Challenges Ahead." *Guardian*, 23 June. https://www.theguardian.com/commentisfree/2016/jun/24/eu-referendum-working-class-revolt-grieve.

McSmith, Andy. 2016. "Brexit Project Fear Had Reason on Its Side but Anti-Experts Caught Public Mood." *Independent*, 24 June. http://www.independent.co.uk/news/uk/politics/brexit-project-fear-had-reason-on-its-side-but-anti-experts-caught-public-mood-a7101841.html.

Ostry, Jonathan D., Prakash Loungani, and Davide Furceri. 2016. "Neoliberalism: Oversold?" *Finance and Development* 53 (2).

Pew Research Center. 2016. "European Views of the EU and Potential Brexit," 6 June. http://www.pewglobal.org/2016/06/07/euroskepticism-beyond-brexit/brexit-lede-graphic-web-version/.

Reinhart, C.M., and K.S. Rogoff. 2010a. "Growth in a Time of Debt." *American Economic Review* 100 (2): 573–78.

– 2010b. "Growth in a Time of Debt." Working Paper 15639. National Bureau of Economic Research. http://www.nber.org/papers/w15639.

Contributors

Donna Baines is chair of Social Work and Policy Studies, University of Sydney (Australia). She teaches anti-oppressive theory and practice, social policy, and social research. Baines has published recently in *Critical Social Policy, Economic and Industrial Democracy,* and *British Journal of Social Work.*

Susan Barrass is a PhD candidate in policy studies at Ryerson University. Her research engages with critical narrative analysis to explore the neoliberal conceptualization of the "ideal migrant" under Canada's former Conservative government of Stephen Harper. Her recent publications include *Issues of Cultural Diversity in Long-term Care for Immigrant Seniors* (co-authored with Doug Durst).

Neil A. Burron completed a PhD in political science at Carleton University. He is the author of *The New Democracy Wars: The Politics of North American Democracy Promotion in the Americas* (Ashgate, 2012). Neil resides in the Ottawa region, where he is a labour activist in the struggle against austerity.

John Clarke is an emeritus professor of social policy at the United Kingdom's Open University and a recurrent visiting professor at Central European University in Budapest. His most recent book is *Making Policy Move: Towards a Politics of Translation and Assemblage* (with Dave Bainton, Noémi Lendvai, and Paul Stubbs; Policy Press, 2015).

Bryan M. Evans is a professor in the Department of Politics and Public Administration at Ryerson University. His research interests focus on the political and public administrative impact of neoliberalization and the political economy of Canada's provinces. Recent publications include "Alternatives to the Low-Waged Economy: Living Wage Movements in Canada and the United States," *Austerity, Urbanism, and the Social Economy – Alternate Routes: A Journal of Critical Social Research* 28 (2017); and "Policy Dialogue and Engagement between Non-Government Organizations and Government: A Survey of Processes and Instruments of Canadian Policy Workers" (with Adam Wellstead), in *Policy Work in Canada*, edited by Michael Howlett, Adam Wellstead, and Jonathan Craft (University of Toronto Press, 2017).

Peter Graefe is an associate professor of political science at McMaster University. He is a co-editor of *Overpromising and Underperforming: Understanding and Evaluating New Intergovernmental Accountability Regimes* (University of Toronto Press, 2013).

Christoph Hermann is a lecturer in the Sociology Department, University of California Berkeley. He specializes in the political economy of work, employment, commodification, and European integration.

Robert S. Hickey is an associate professor of industrial relations at Queen's University, where he teaches courses on labour relations, negotiations, and dispute resolution. Robert worked as a union organizer and representative for ten years in the Teamsters Union. He earned his PhD from the School of Industrial and Labor Relations at Cornell University. His research examines the impact of economic restructuring and technological change on union strategies and labour-management relations. His work has been published in a variety of academic journals, including the *British Journal of Industrial Relations*, *Relations Industrielles/Industrial Relations*, and *Labour/Le Travail*.

Stephen McBride is professor of political science and Canada Research Chair in Public Policy and Globalization at McMaster University, where he is also a member of the Institute of Globalization and the Human Condition and an associate member of the School of Labour Studies. Recent publications include *After '08: Social Policy and the Global Financial Crisis* (co-edited with R. Mahon and G. Boychuk).

Sorin Mitrea is a comparative public policy PhD candidate at McMaster University. His research explores how the cognitive elements of policy interact with their material effects to shape the behaviour and subjectivity of workers. He approaches cognition at the intersection of political economy and labour market policy in Canada. His most recent publication is *ASEAN at 50: The Global Political Economy's Contribution to Durability* (2017), with Richard Stubbs.

Jacob Muirhead is a doctoral candidate at McMaster University. His work focuses on the intersection between globalization, and its impacts on the transnational regulation of labour and the environment, with a particular focus on the agricultural sector. Recent publications include "Challenging the Low Wage Economy: Living and Other Wages," *Alternate Routes: A Journal of Critical Research* 27 (with S. McBride).

Eric Pineault teaches at the Department of Sociology and the Institute of Environmental Sciences at the University of Quebec in Montreal and has recently published *Le Piège Énergie Est, Sortir de l'impasse des sables bitumineux* (The Energy East Trap) with Écosociété.

X.H. Rioux holds a master's degree in sociology and is finishing a PhD in comparative public policy at McMaster University. He has developed an expertise in the analysis of economic and fiscal policymaking, having published on these topics in other edited books and peer-reviewed periodicals such as the *Canadian Journal of Political Science* and *Regional & Federal Studies*.

Ellen D. Russell is an associate professor in digital media and journalism and social and environmental studies programs at Wilfrid Laurier University. Her recent publications include *New Deal Banking Reform and Keynesian Welfare State Capitalism* and "Why the Rising Tide Doesn't Lift All Boats: Wages and Bargaining Power in Neoliberal Canada," *Studies in Political Economy*. She received her PhD in economics from the University of Massachusetts Amherst, and has degrees from Queen's University and University of Toronto. She was formerly senior economist at the Canadian Centre for Policy Alternatives, and is an occasional columnist on economic affairs for rabble.ca.

Shih-Jiunn Shi is a professor in the Graduate Institute of National Development, National Taiwan University, Taiwan. His research focuses on comparative social policy in East Asia and Greater China.

His recent publications include papers in *Journal of Asian Public Policy* and *Public Management Review*.

John Shields is a professor in the Department of Politics and Public Administration at Ryerson University. His recent publications include *Immigrant Experiences in North America: Understanding Settlement and Integration* (edited with Harald Bauder, Canadian Scholars' Press, 2015) and he is a core researcher and one of the authors of *The Precarity Penalty: The Impact of Employment Precarity on Individuals, Households and Communities – and What to Do about It* (United Way of Greater Toronto, 2015).

Brendan A. Sweeney is the project manager of the Automotive Policy Research Centre. He also teaches labour studies at McMaster University. He holds a PhD in geography from Queen's University. His research is published in several journals, including *Labour/Le Travail*, *Antipode*, *Canadian Public Policy*, and *Gender, Place and Culture*.

Yanqiu Rachel Zhou is a professor at the Institute on Globalization and the Human Condition and the School of Social Work, McMaster University. She has published over thirty scholarly articles and also co-edited a special issue on time and globalization in *Globalizations* and a book titled *Time, Globalization, and Human Experience: Interdisciplinary Explorations* (Routledge, 2016).